Twin Star Exorcists

ONMYOJI

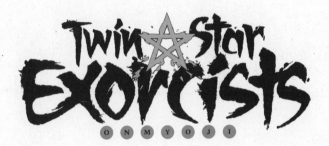

Twin Star Exorcists

ONMYOJI

13

STORY & ART
YOSHIAKI SUKENO

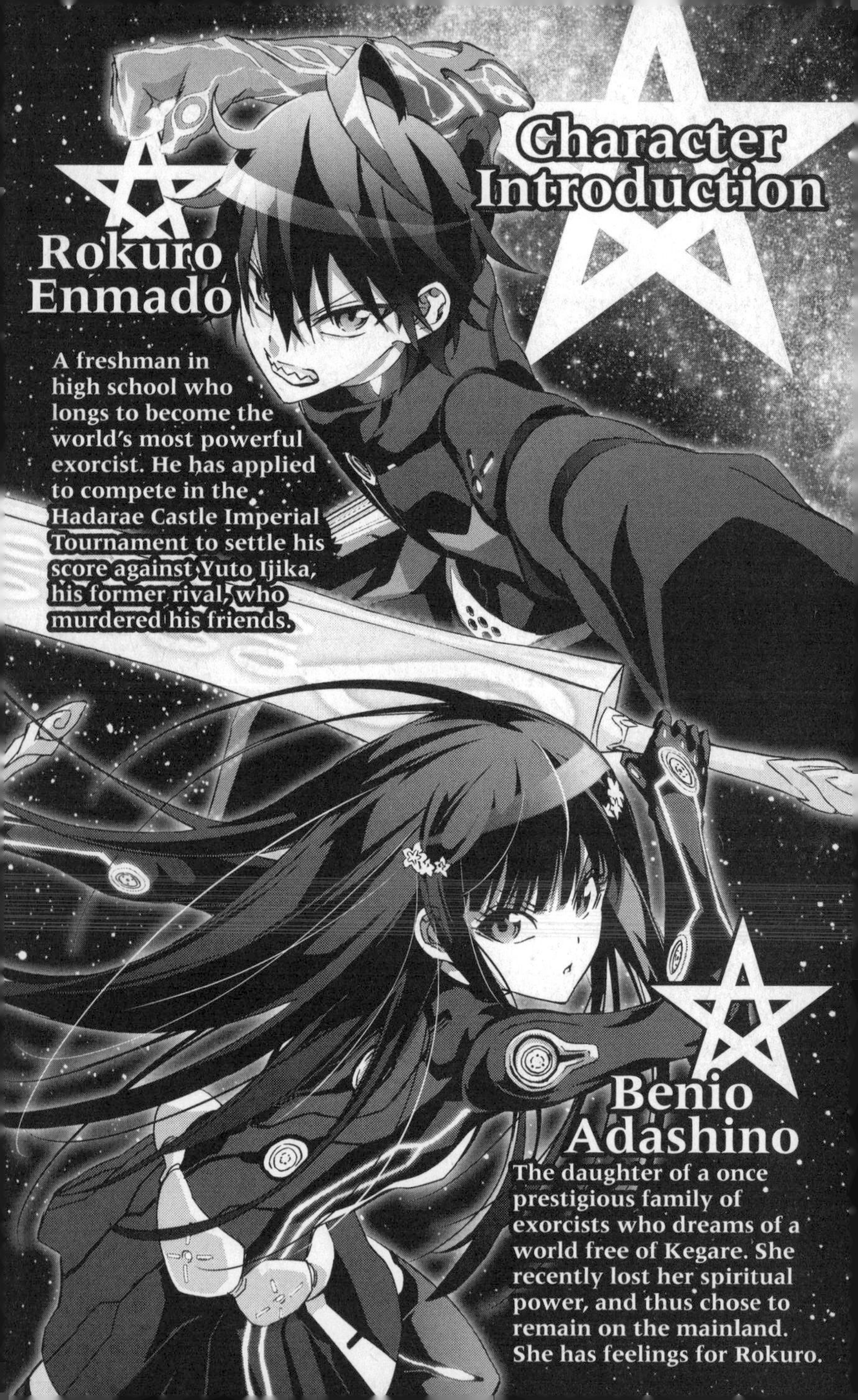

Character Introduction

Rokuro Enmado

A freshman in high school who longs to become the world's most powerful exorcist. He has applied to compete in the Hadarae Castle Imperial Tournament to settle his score against Yuto Ijika, his former rival, who murdered his friends.

Benio Adashino

The daughter of a once prestigious family of exorcists who dreams of a world free of Kegare. She recently lost her spiritual power, and thus chose to remain on the mainland. She has feelings for Rokuro.

Kankuro Mitosaka

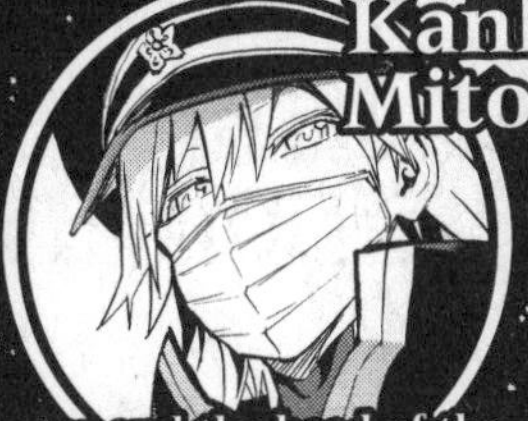

A doctor and the head of the Mitosaka Family. He is the Azure Dragon, one of the strongest of the Twelve Guardians.

Kengo Uji

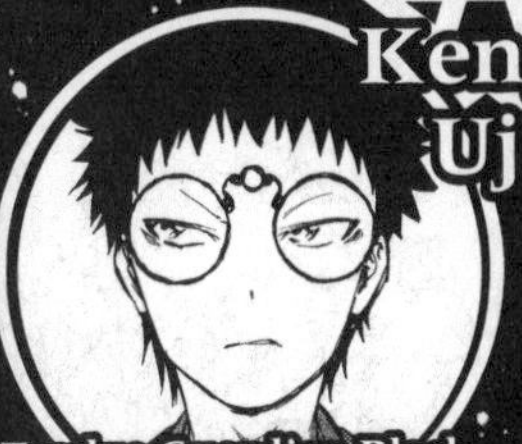

Twelve Guardian Black Tortoise and the head of the Uji Family. Often teams up with Kankuro.

Arata Inanaki

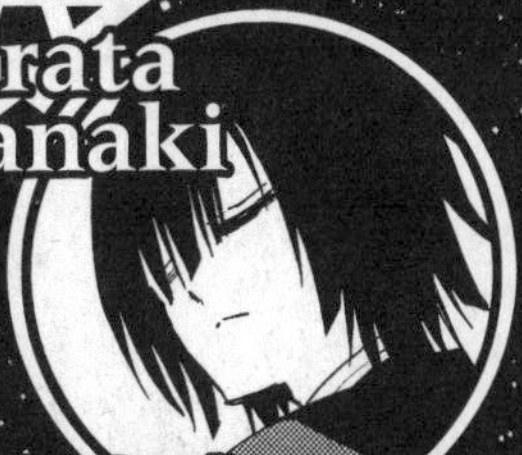

Twelve Guardian member Scholarly Scribe. In charge of the academic institutions on the island and also actually a serious otaku.

Narumi Ioroi

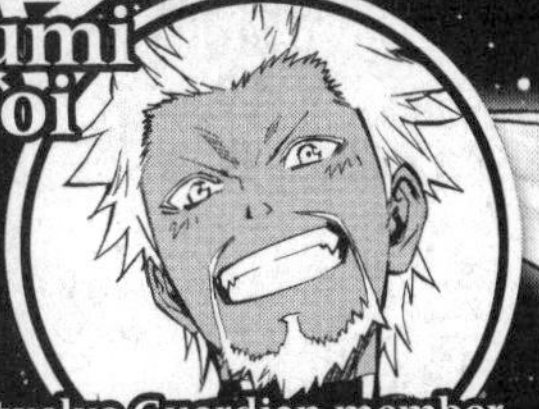

Twelve Guardian member Golden Snake. A bright, dynamic man who is devoted to his wife and nine children.

Shimon Ikaruga

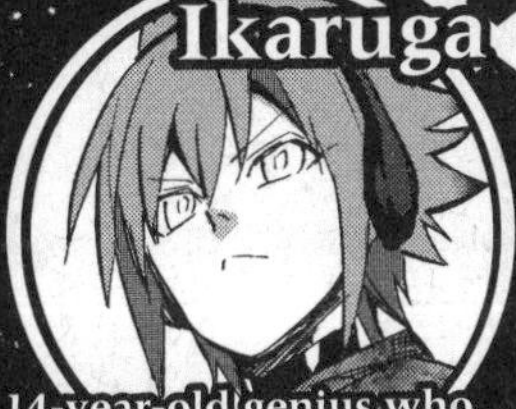

A 14-year-old genius who succeeded as Vermillion Bird of the Twelve Guardians. He has deep respect for his mentor, Seigen.

Tenma Unomiya

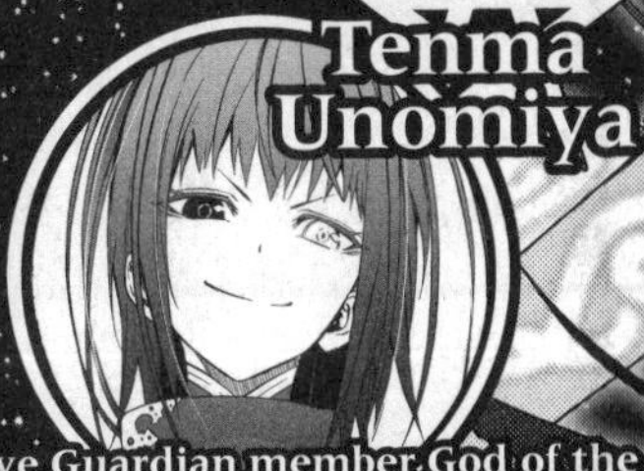

Twelve Guardian member God of the In-Between. Head of the Unomiya Family and said to be the most powerful exorcist. He habitually gives people weird nicknames.

Story Thus Far...

Kegare are creatures from Magano, the underworld, and it is the duty of an exorcist to hunt, exorcise and purify them. Rokuro and Benio are the Twin Star Exorcists, fated to bear the Prophesied Child who will defeat the Kegare. Their goal is to go to Tsuchimikado Island to get revenge on Yuto, Benio's brother and the mastermind behind the Hinatsuki Tragedy.

After two years, Rokuro qualifies to go to the island, but Benio loses her spiritual power in battle. Leaving her behind, Rokuro instead moves to the island with his childhood friend and newbie exorcist Mayura. In order to compete in the Hadarae Castle Imperial Tournament to earn the right to join the hunt for Yuto Ijika, Rokuro founds a new clan in his name, the Enmado Family. Rokuro's opponent is Dr. Kankuro Mitosaka, a much stronger exorcist. Before the match, Rokuro receives a tip from Kengo Uji to help him defeat Kankuro. Will it work...?

Twin Star Exorcists

ONMYOJI

EXORCISMS

13

ONMYOJI have worked for the Imperial Court since the Heian era. In addition to exorcising evil spirits, as civil servants they performed a variety of roles, including advising nobles by foretelling the future, creating the calendar, observing the movements of the stars, measuring time...

#45: Welcome Back, Dr. Kanny

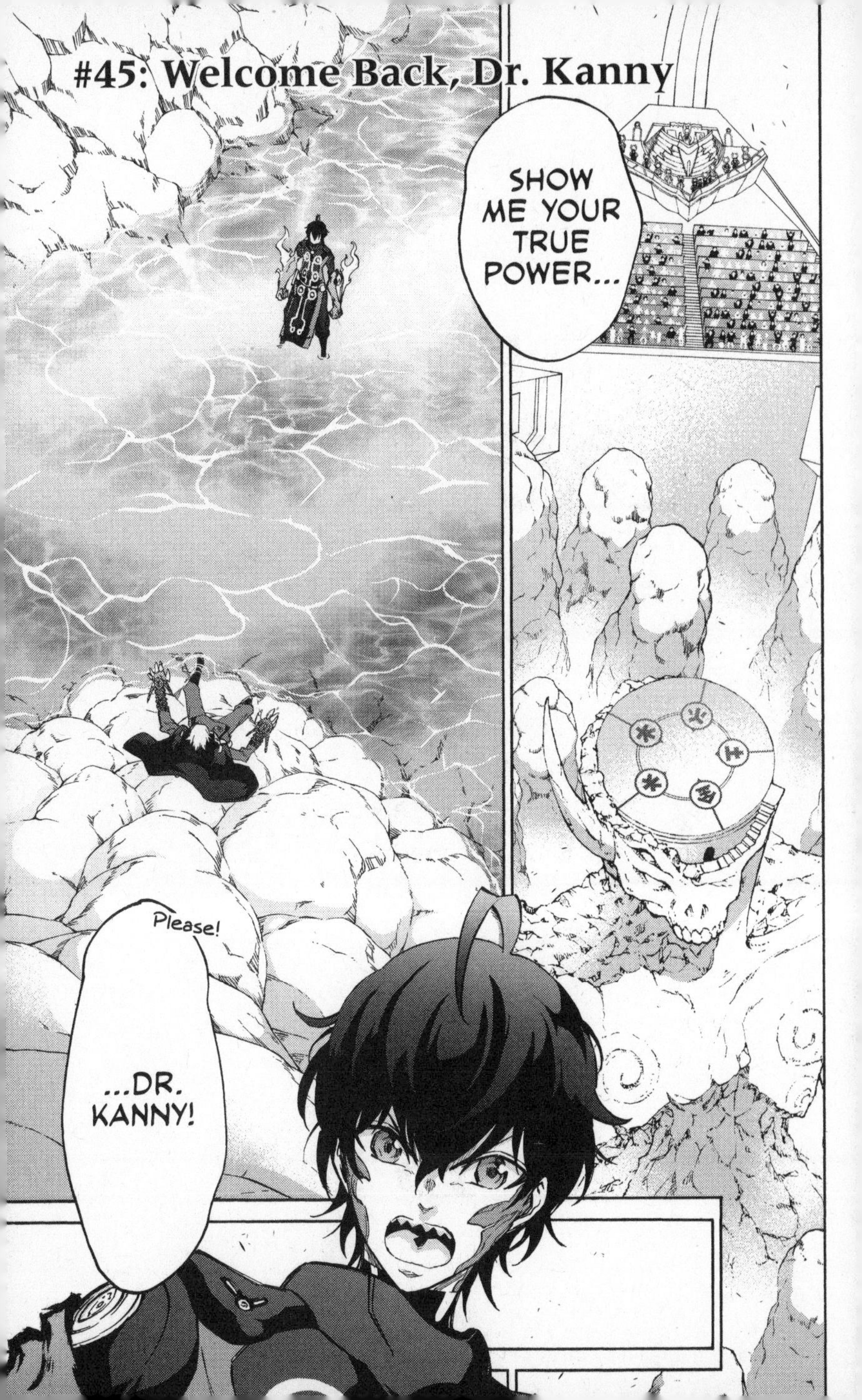
SHOW ME YOUR TRUE POWER...
Please!
...DR. KANNY!

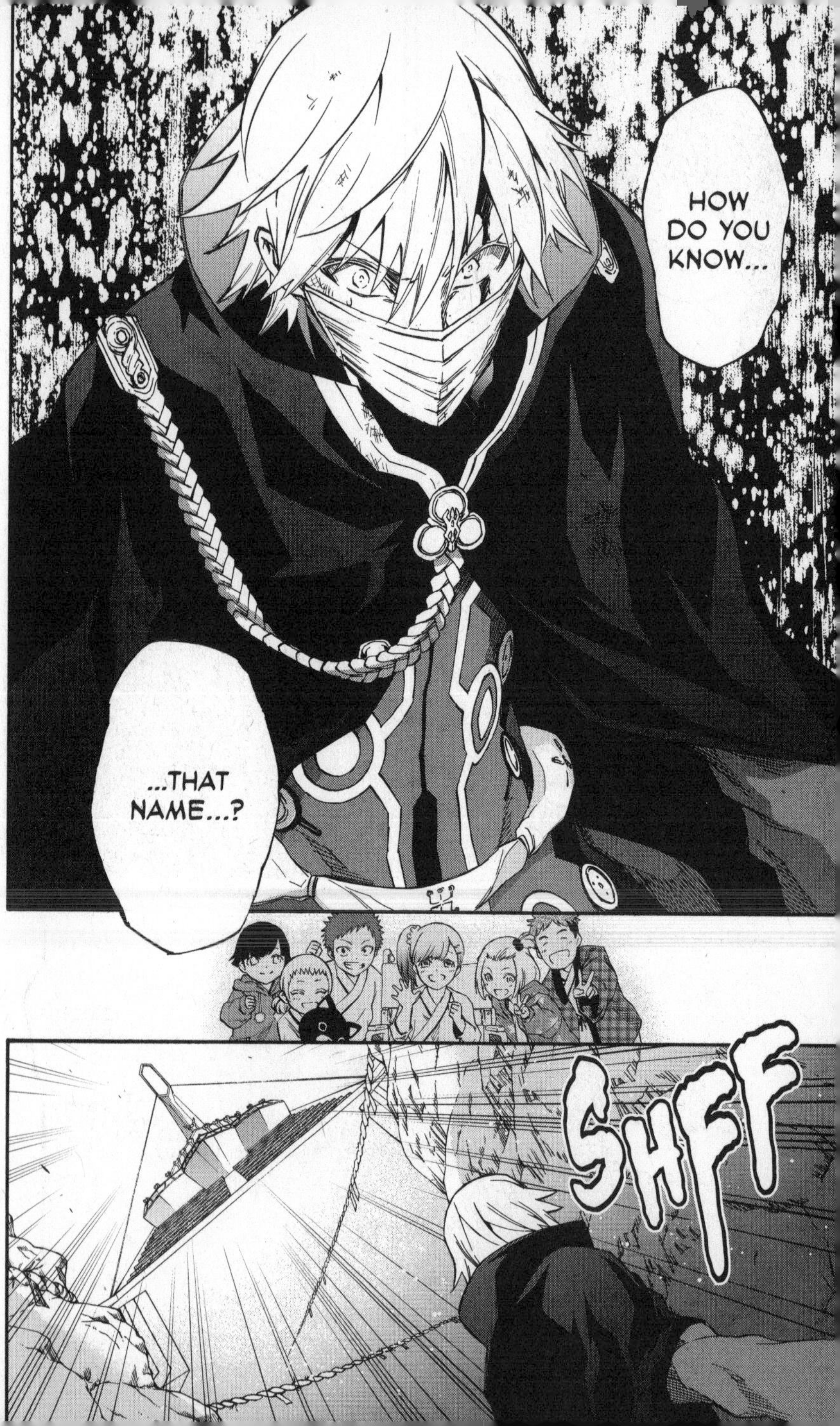
HOW DO YOU KNOW...
...THAT NAME...?
SHFF

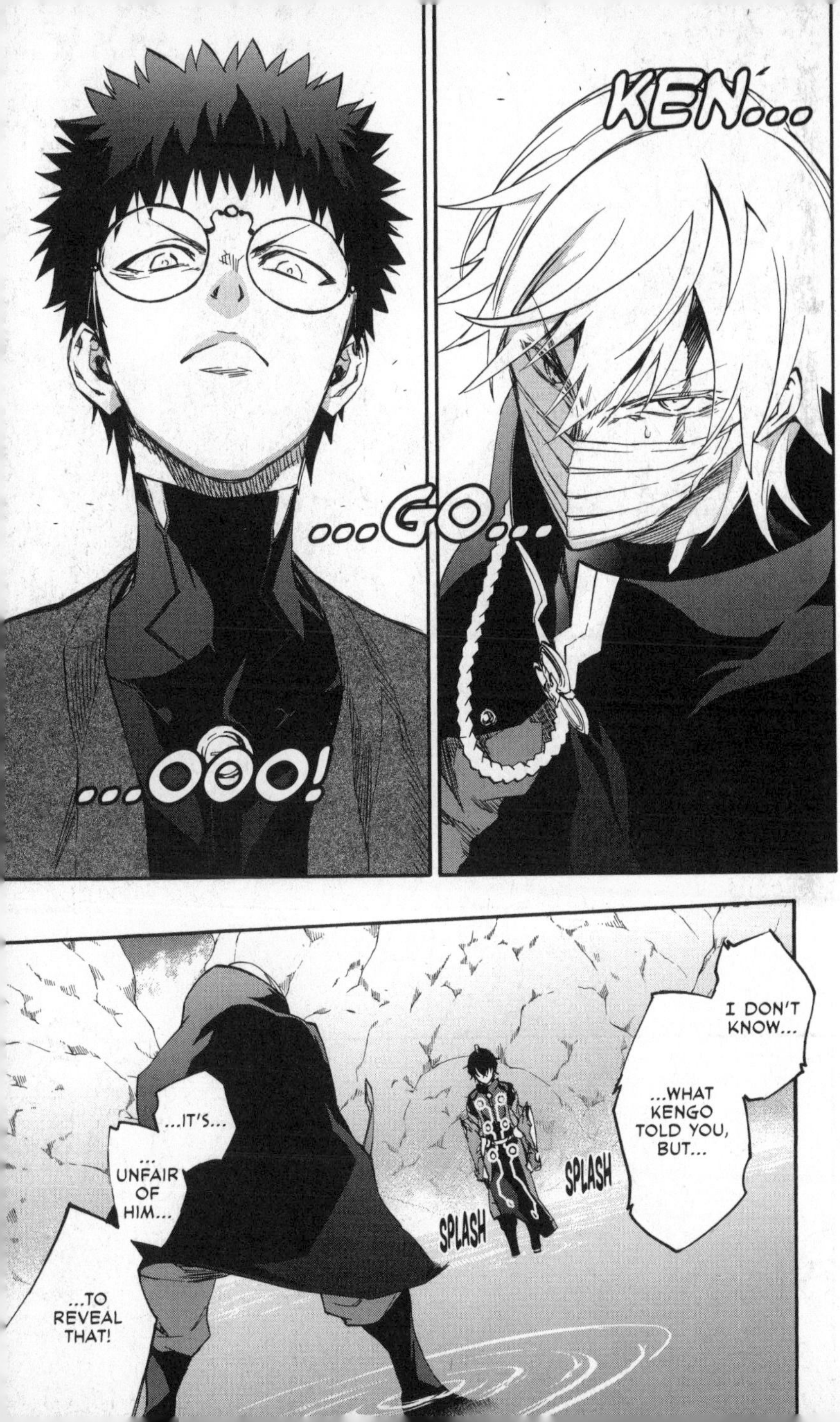
KEN...
...GO...
...OOO!
I DON'T KNOW...
...WHAT KENGO TOLD YOU, BUT...
SPLASH
SPLASH
...IT'S...
...UNFAIR OF HIM...
...TO REVEAL THAT!

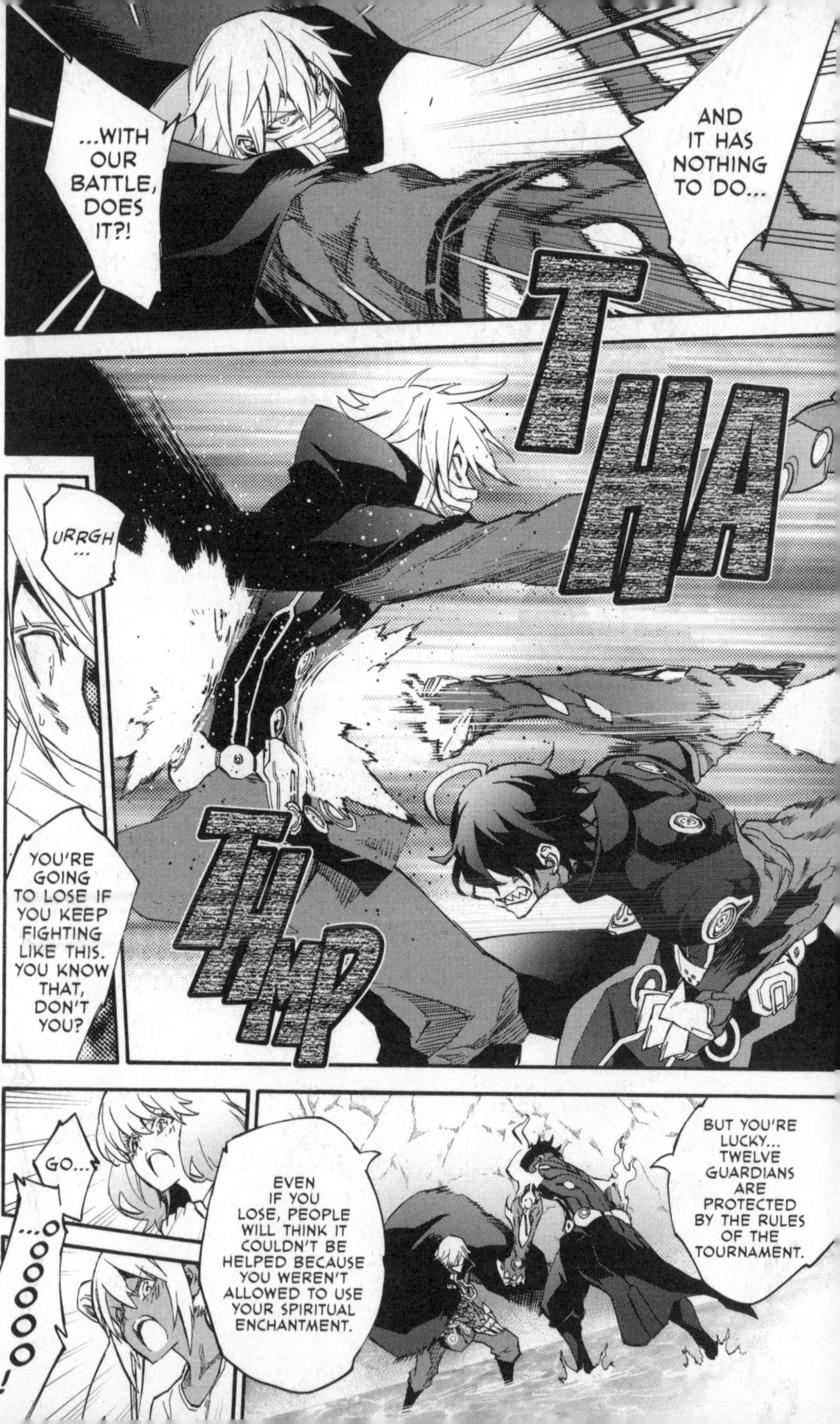
AND IT HAS NOTHING TO DO...
...WITH OUR BATTLE, DOES IT?!
THA
THUMP
URRGH...
YOU'RE GOING TO LOSE IF YOU KEEP FIGHTING LIKE THIS. YOU KNOW THAT, DON'T YOU?
BUT YOU'RE LUCKY... TWELVE GUARDIANS ARE PROTECTED BY THE RULES OF THE TOURNAMENT.
EVEN IF YOU LOSE, PEOPLE WILL THINK IT COULDN'T BE HELPED BECAUSE YOU WEREN'T ALLOWED TO USE YOUR SPIRITUAL ENCHANTMENT.
GO...
...OOOOOOO!

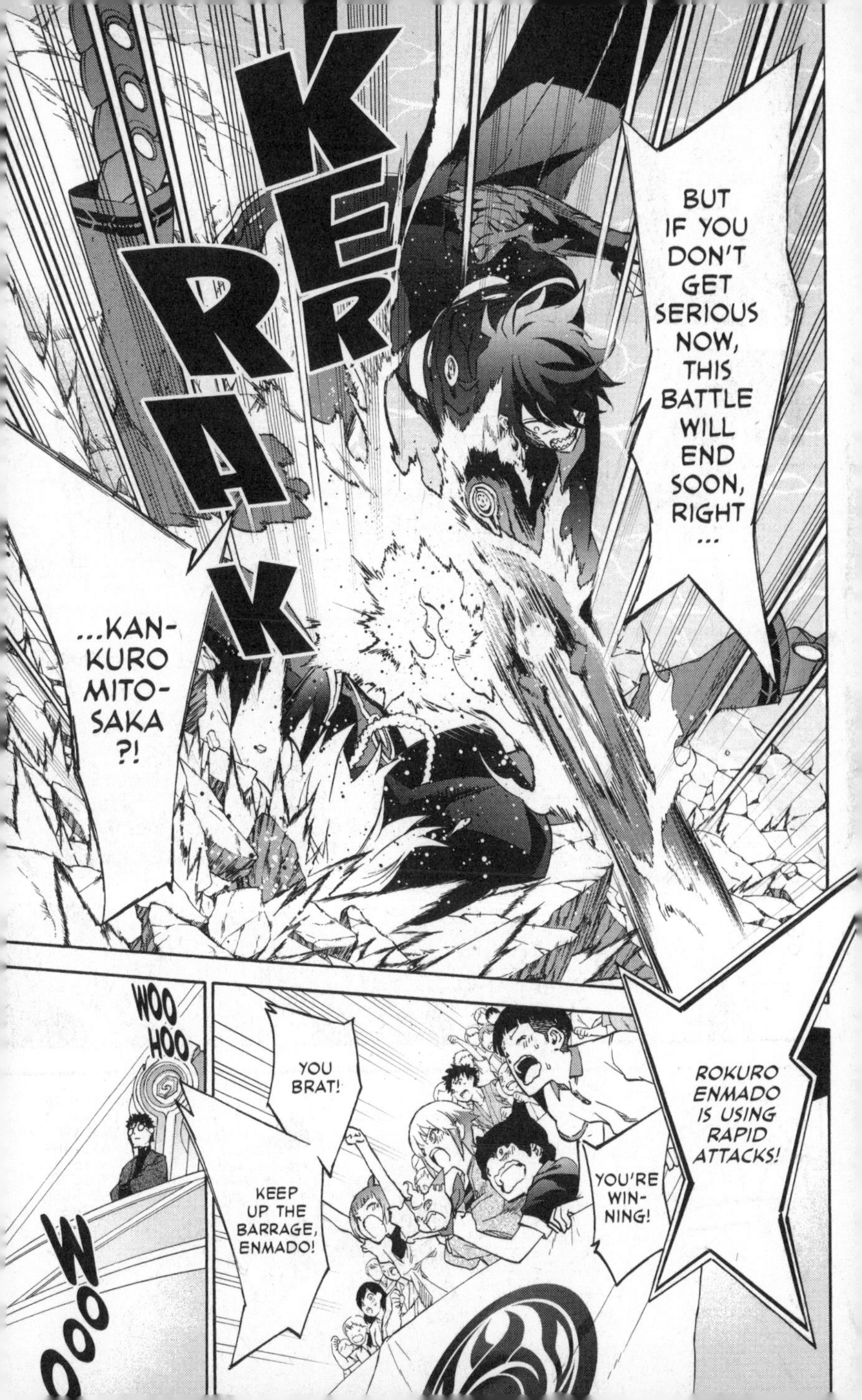
BUT IF YOU DON'T GET SERIOUS NOW, THIS BATTLE WILL END SOON, RIGHT...
KERRAKK
...KANKURO MITOSAKA?!
ROKURO ENMADO IS USING RAPID ATTACKS!
YOU'RE WINNING!
YOU BRAT!
KEEP UP THE BARRAGE, ENMADO!
WOO HOO
WOOOO

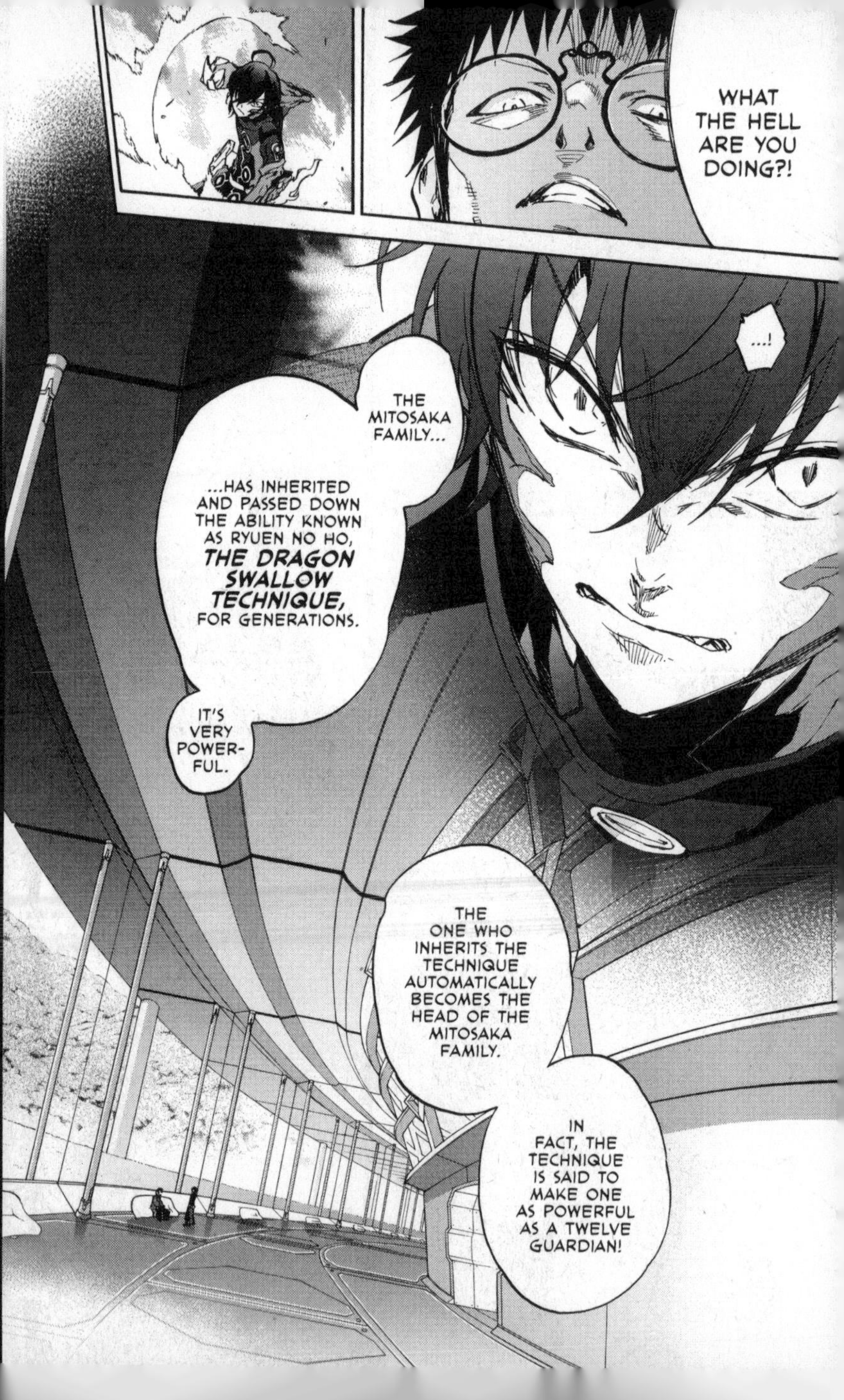
WHAT THE HELL ARE YOU DOING?!
...!
THE MITOSAKA FAMILY...
...HAS INHERITED AND PASSED DOWN THE ABILITY KNOWN AS RYUEN NO HO, ***THE DRAGON SWALLOW TECHNIQUE,*** FOR GENERATIONS.
IT'S VERY POWER-FUL.
THE ONE WHO INHERITS THE TECHNIQUE AUTOMATICALLY BECOMES THE HEAD OF THE MITOSAKA FAMILY.
IN FACT, THE TECHNIQUE IS SAID TO MAKE ONE AS POWERFUL AS A TWELVE GUARDIAN!

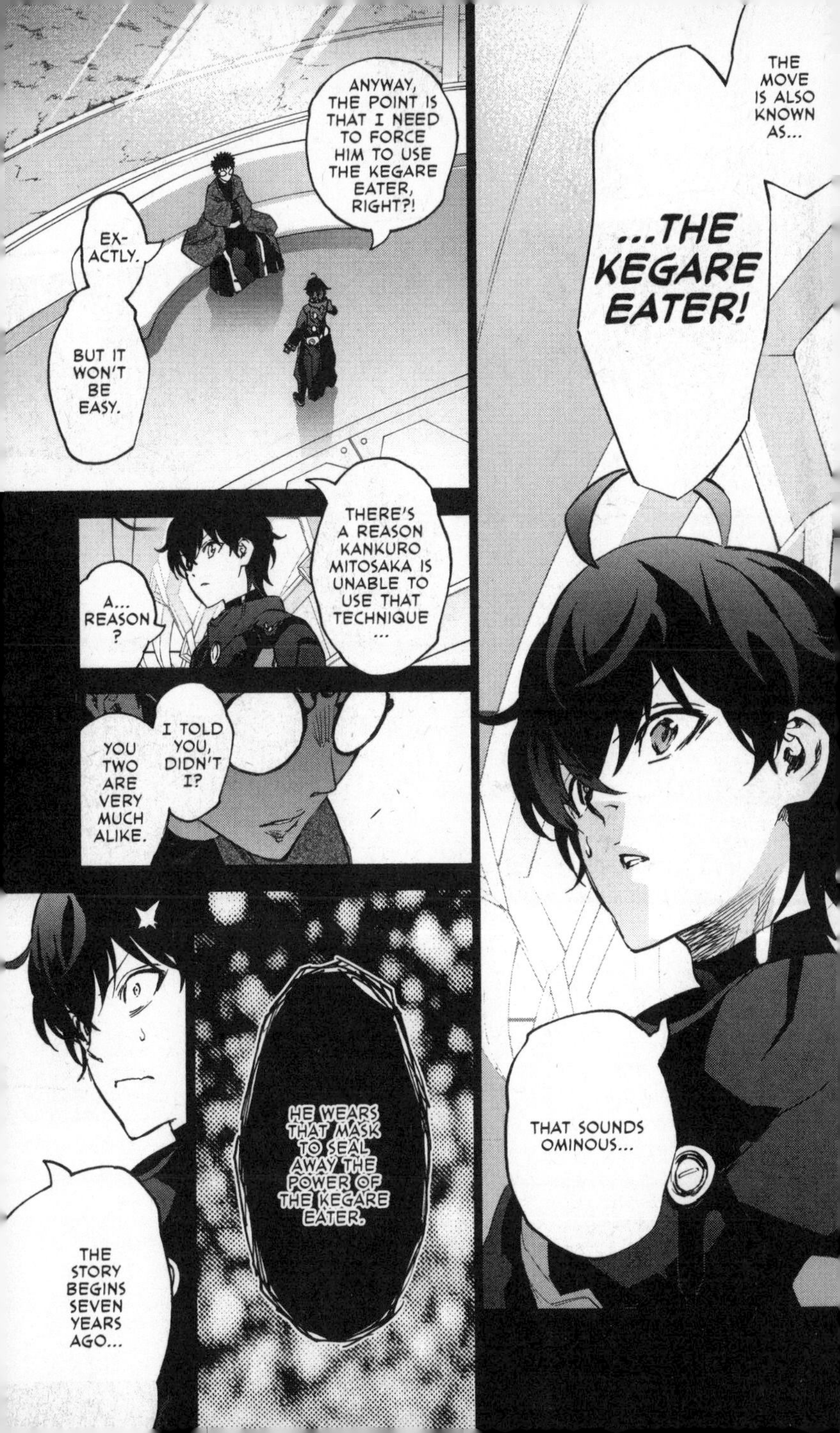
THE MOVE IS ALSO KNOWN AS...
...THE KEGARE EATER!
THAT SOUNDS OMINOUS...
ANYWAY, THE POINT IS THAT I NEED TO FORCE HIM TO USE THE KEGARE EATER, RIGHT?!
EX-ACTLY.
BUT IT WON'T BE EASY.
THERE'S A REASON KANKURO MITOSAKA IS UNABLE TO USE THAT TECHNIQUE...
A... REASON?
I TOLD YOU, DIDN'T I?
YOU TWO ARE VERY MUCH ALIKE.
HE WEARS THAT MASK TO SEAL AWAY THE POWER OF THE KEGARE EATER.
THE STORY BEGINS SEVEN YEARS AGO...

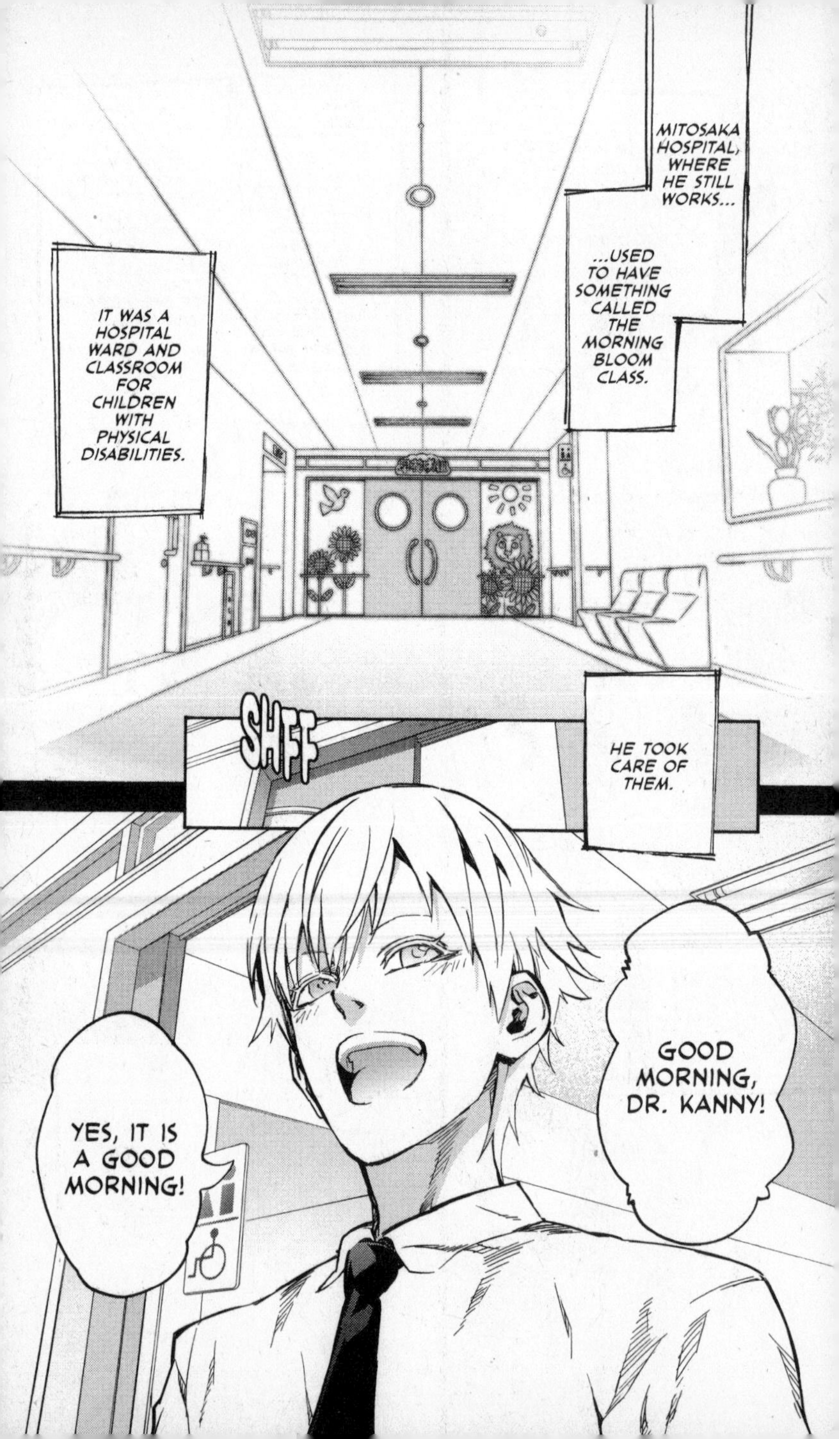
MITOSAKA HOSPITAL, WHERE HE STILL WORKS...
...USED TO HAVE SOMETHING CALLED THE MORNING BLOOM CLASS.
IT WAS A HOSPITAL WARD AND CLASSROOM FOR CHILDREN WITH PHYSICAL DISABILITIES.
HE TOOK CARE OF THEM.
SHFF
GOOD MORNING, DR. KANNY!
YES, IT IS A GOOD MORNING!

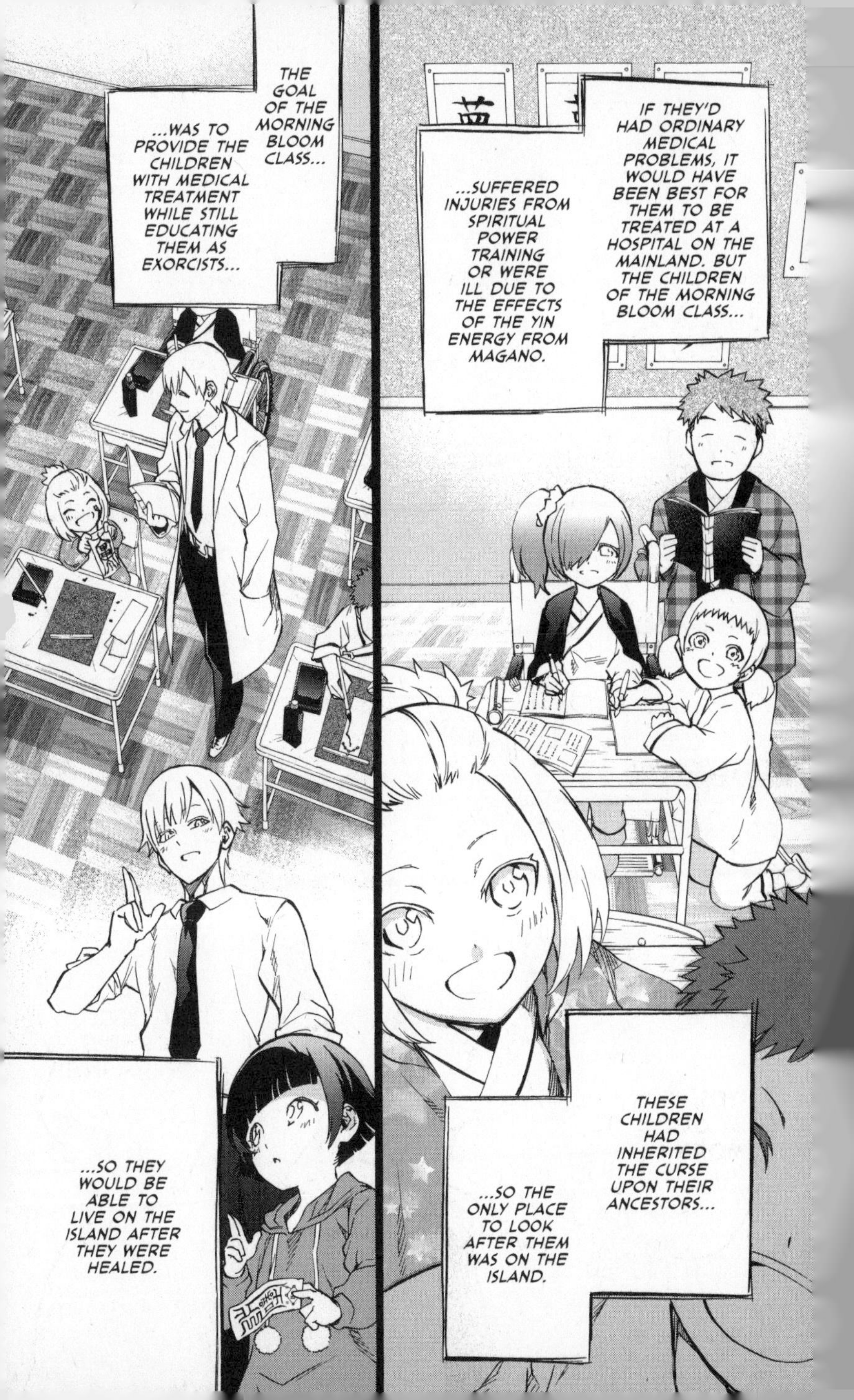
IF THEY'D HAD ORDINARY MEDICAL PROBLEMS, IT WOULD HAVE BEEN BEST FOR THEM TO BE TREATED AT A HOSPITAL ON THE MAINLAND. BUT THE CHILDREN OF THE MORNING BLOOM CLASS...
...SUFFERED INJURIES FROM SPIRITUAL POWER TRAINING OR WERE ILL DUE TO THE EFFECTS OF THE YIN ENERGY FROM MAGANO.
THESE CHILDREN HAD INHERITED THE CURSE UPON THEIR ANCESTORS...
...SO THE ONLY PLACE TO LOOK AFTER THEM WAS ON THE ISLAND.
THE GOAL OF THE MORNING BLOOM CLASS...
...WAS TO PROVIDE THE CHILDREN WITH MEDICAL TREATMENT WHILE STILL EDUCATING THEM AS EXORCISTS...
...SO THEY WOULD BE ABLE TO LIVE ON THE ISLAND AFTER THEY WERE HEALED.

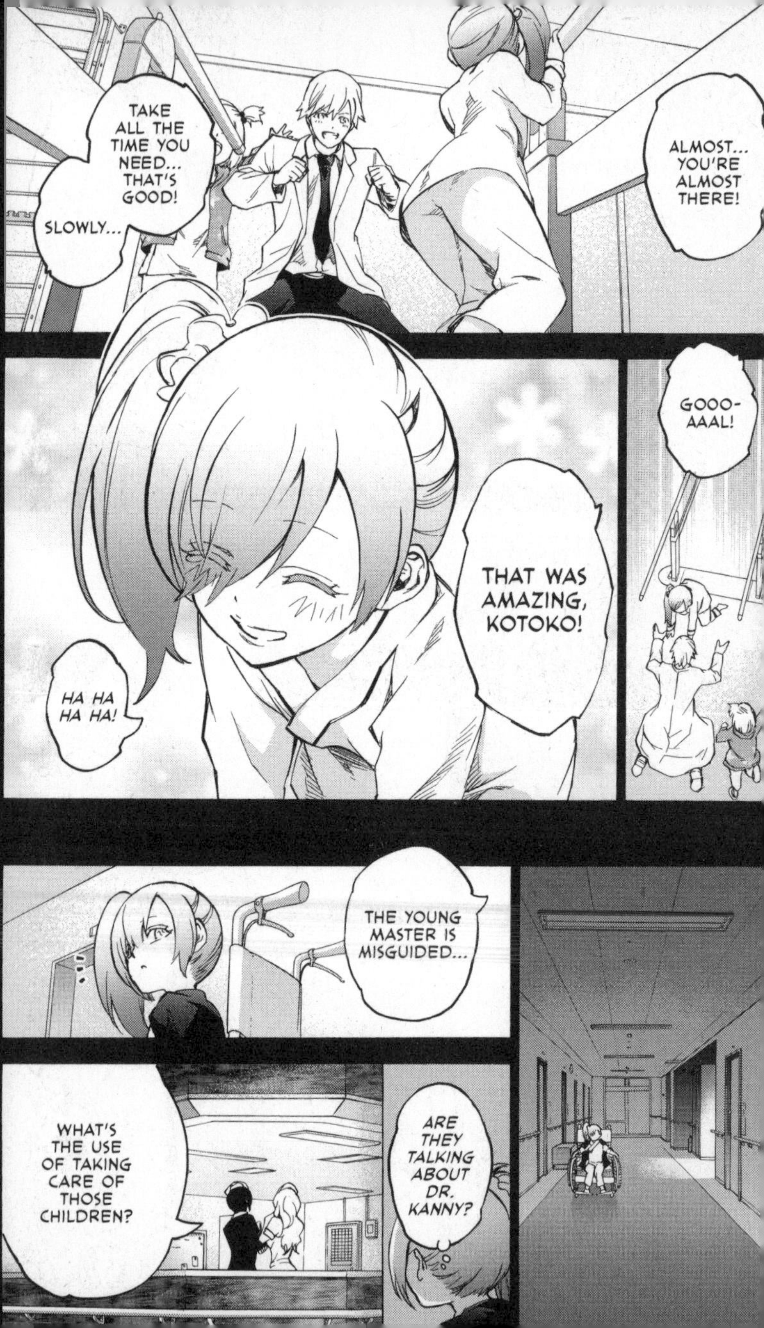
ALMOST... YOU'RE ALMOST THERE!
TAKE ALL THE TIME YOU NEED... THAT'S GOOD!
SLOWLY...
GOOO-AAAL!
THAT WAS AMAZING, KOTOKO!
HA HA HA HA!
THE YOUNG MASTER IS MISGUIDED...
ARE THEY TALKING ABOUT DR. KANNY?
WHAT'S THE USE OF TAKING CARE OF THOSE CHILDREN?

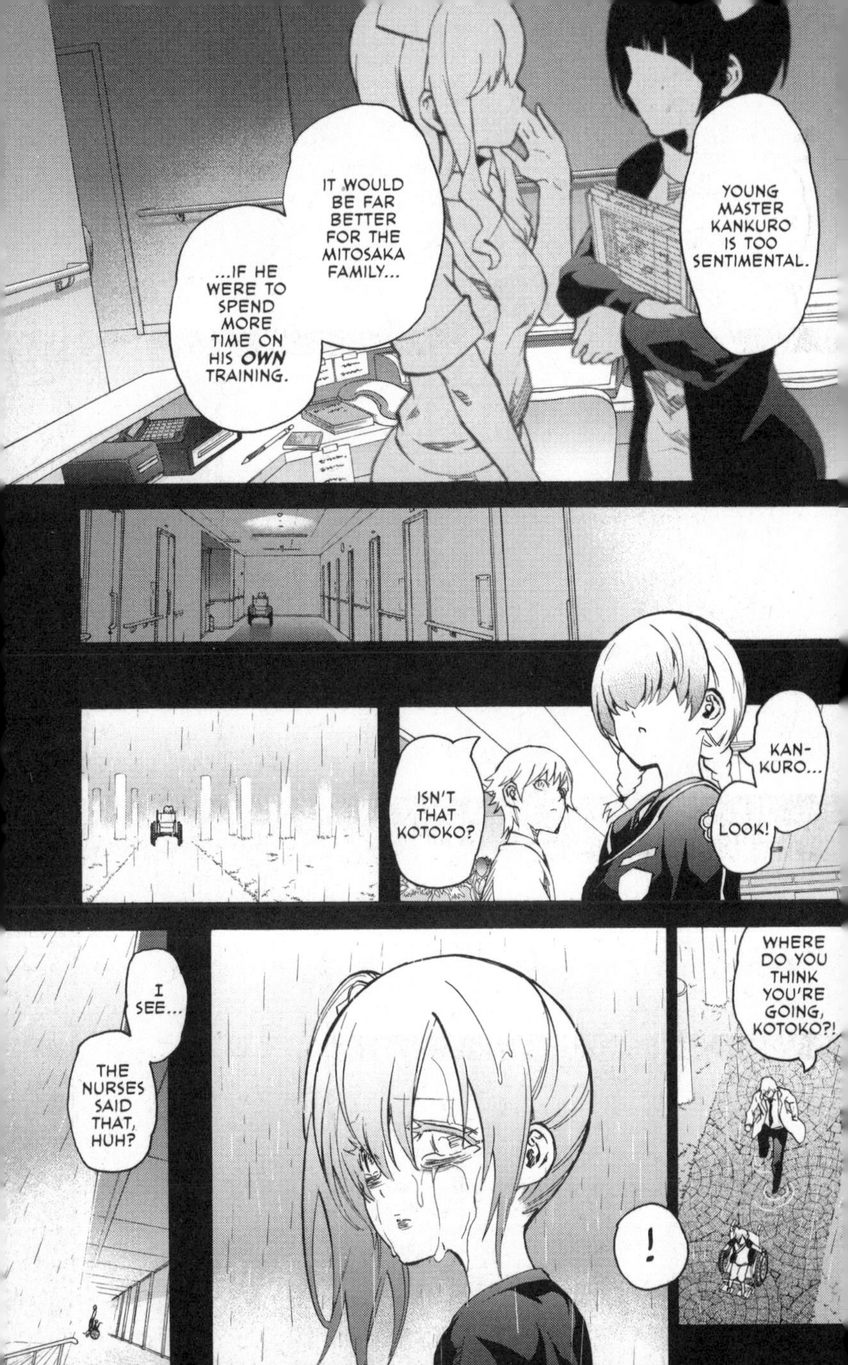
YOUNG MASTER KANKURO IS TOO SENTIMENTAL.
IT WOULD BE FAR BETTER FOR THE MITOSAKA FAMILY...
...IF HE WERE TO SPEND MORE TIME ON HIS *OWN* TRAINING.
KAN-KURO...
LOOK!
ISN'T THAT KOTOKO?
WHERE DO YOU THINK YOU'RE GOING, KOTOKO?!
!
I SEE...
THE NURSES SAID THAT, HUH?

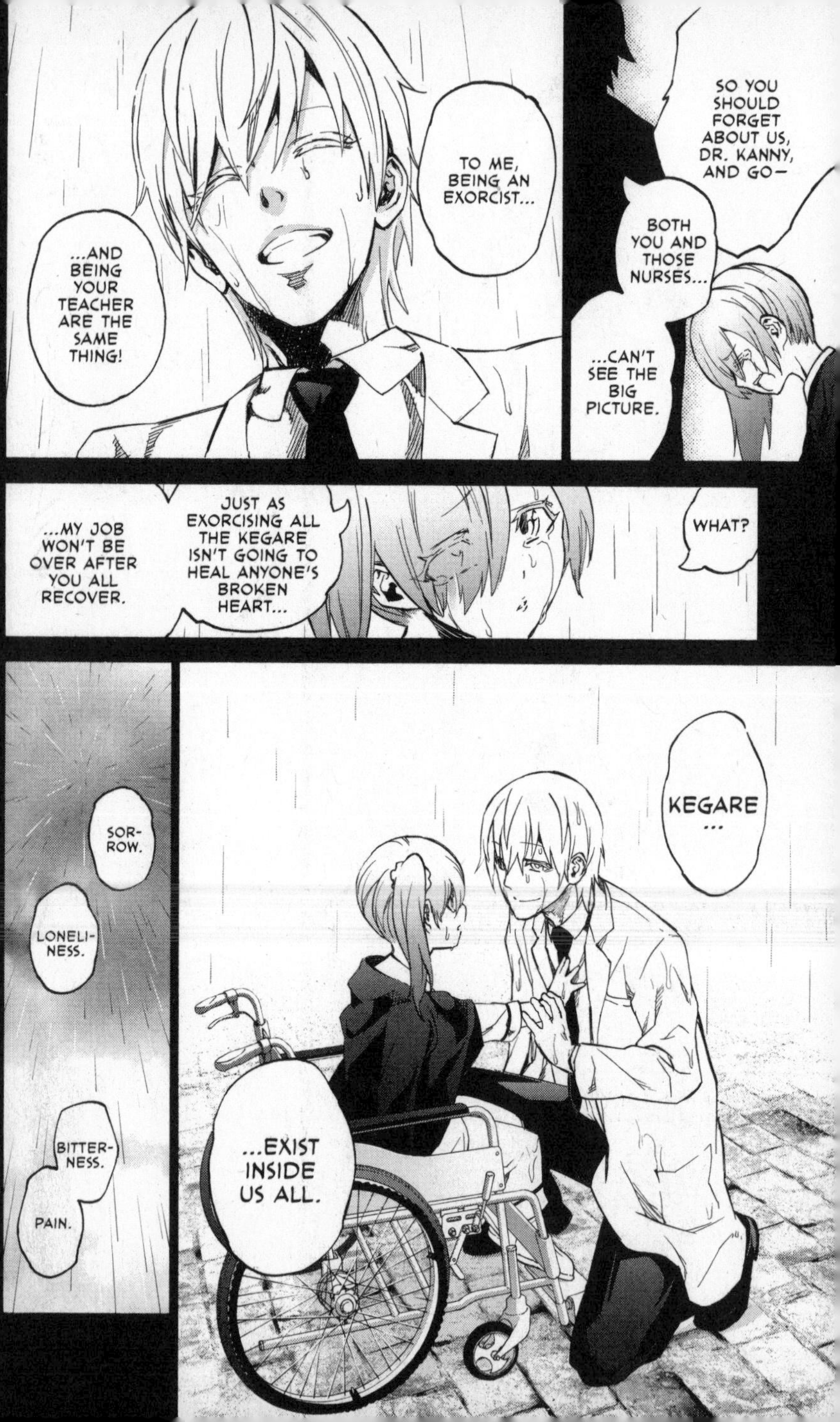
SO YOU SHOULD FORGET ABOUT US, DR. KANNY, AND GO—
BOTH YOU AND THOSE NURSES...
...CAN'T SEE THE BIG PICTURE.
TO ME, BEING AN EXORCIST...
...AND BEING YOUR TEACHER ARE THE SAME THING!
WHAT?
JUST AS EXORCISING ALL THE KEGARE ISN'T GOING TO HEAL ANYONE'S BROKEN HEART...
...MY JOB WON'T BE OVER AFTER YOU ALL RECOVER.
KEGARE...
...EXIST INSIDE US ALL.
SOR-ROW.
LONELI-NESS.
BITTER-NESS.
PAIN.

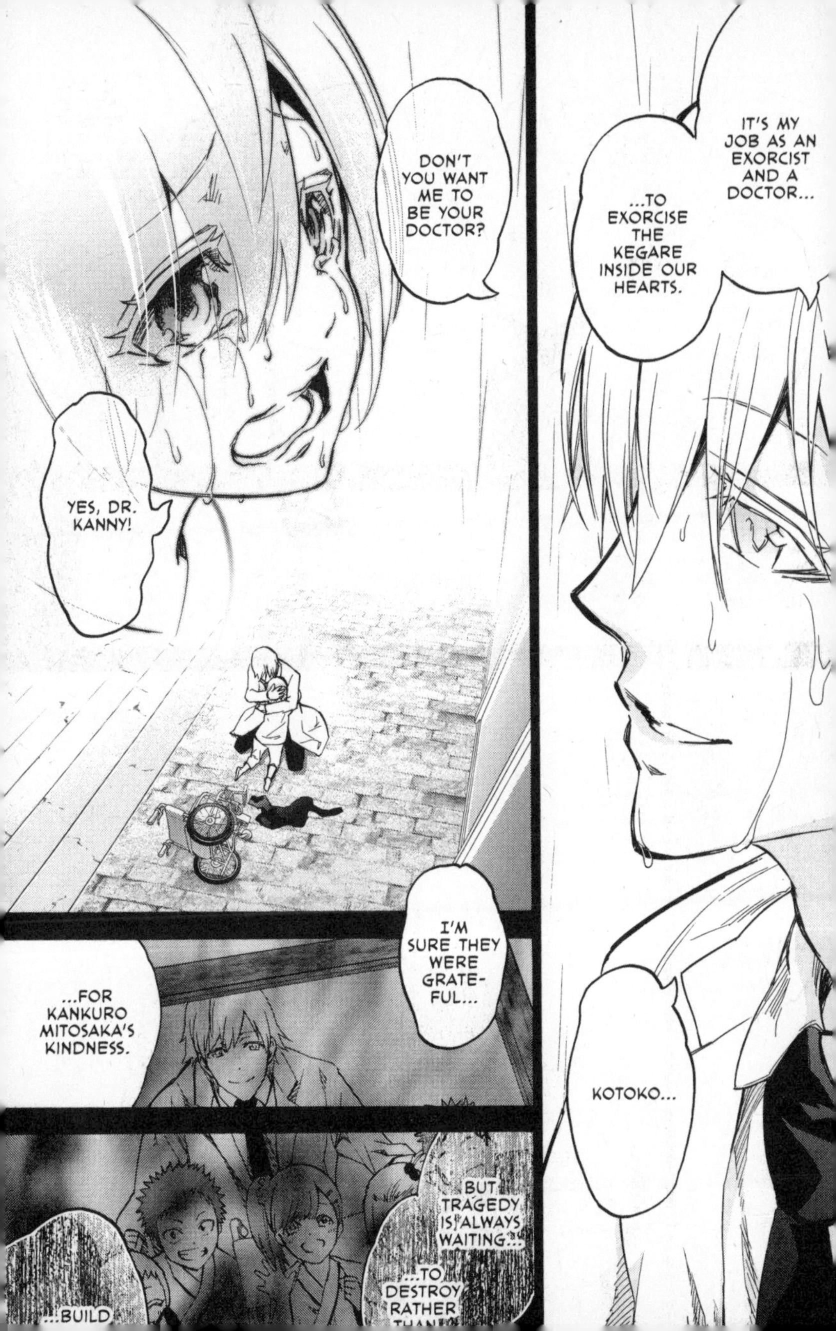
IT'S MY JOB AS AN EXORCIST AND A DOCTOR...
...TO EXORCISE THE KEGARE INSIDE OUR HEARTS.
KOTOKO...
DON'T YOU WANT ME TO BE YOUR DOCTOR?
YES, DR. KANNY!
I'M SURE THEY WERE GRATEFUL...
...FOR KANKURO MITOSAKA'S KINDNESS.
BUT TRAGEDY IS ALWAYS WAITING...
...TO DESTROY RATHER
...BUILD

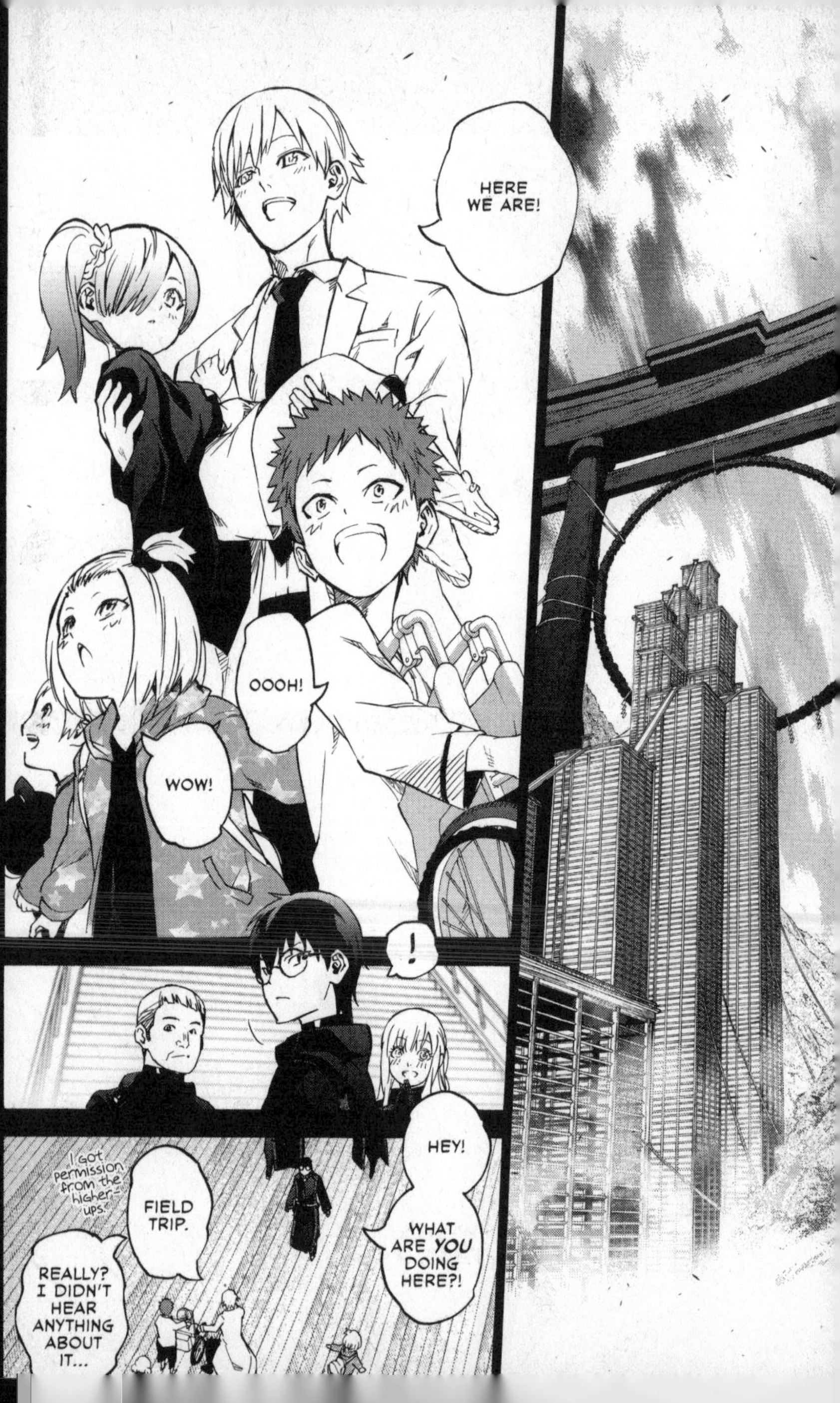
HERE WE ARE!
OOOH!
WOW!
!
HEY!
WHAT ARE YOU DOING HERE?!
FIELD TRIP.
I got permission from the higher-ups.
REALLY? I DIDN'T HEAR ANYTHING ABOUT IT...

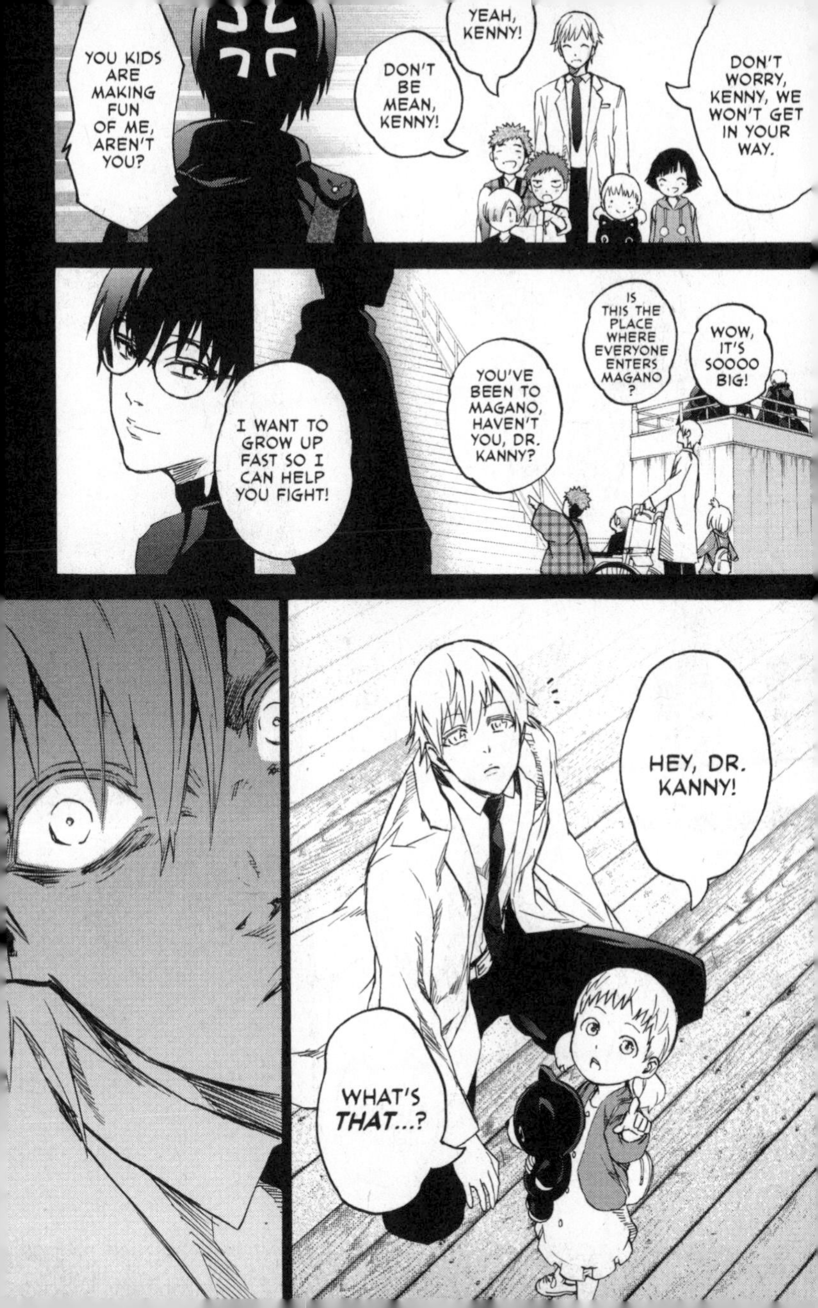
DON'T WORRY, KENNY, WE WON'T GET IN YOUR WAY.
YEAH, KENNY!
DON'T BE MEAN, KENNY!
YOU KIDS ARE MAKING FUN OF ME, AREN'T YOU?
WOW, IT'S SOOOO BIG!
IS THIS THE PLACE WHERE EVERYONE ENTERS MAGANO?
YOU'VE BEEN TO MAGANO, HAVEN'T YOU, DR. KANNY?
I WANT TO GROW UP FAST SO I CAN HELP YOU FIGHT!
HEY, DR. KANNY!
WHAT'S *THAT*...?

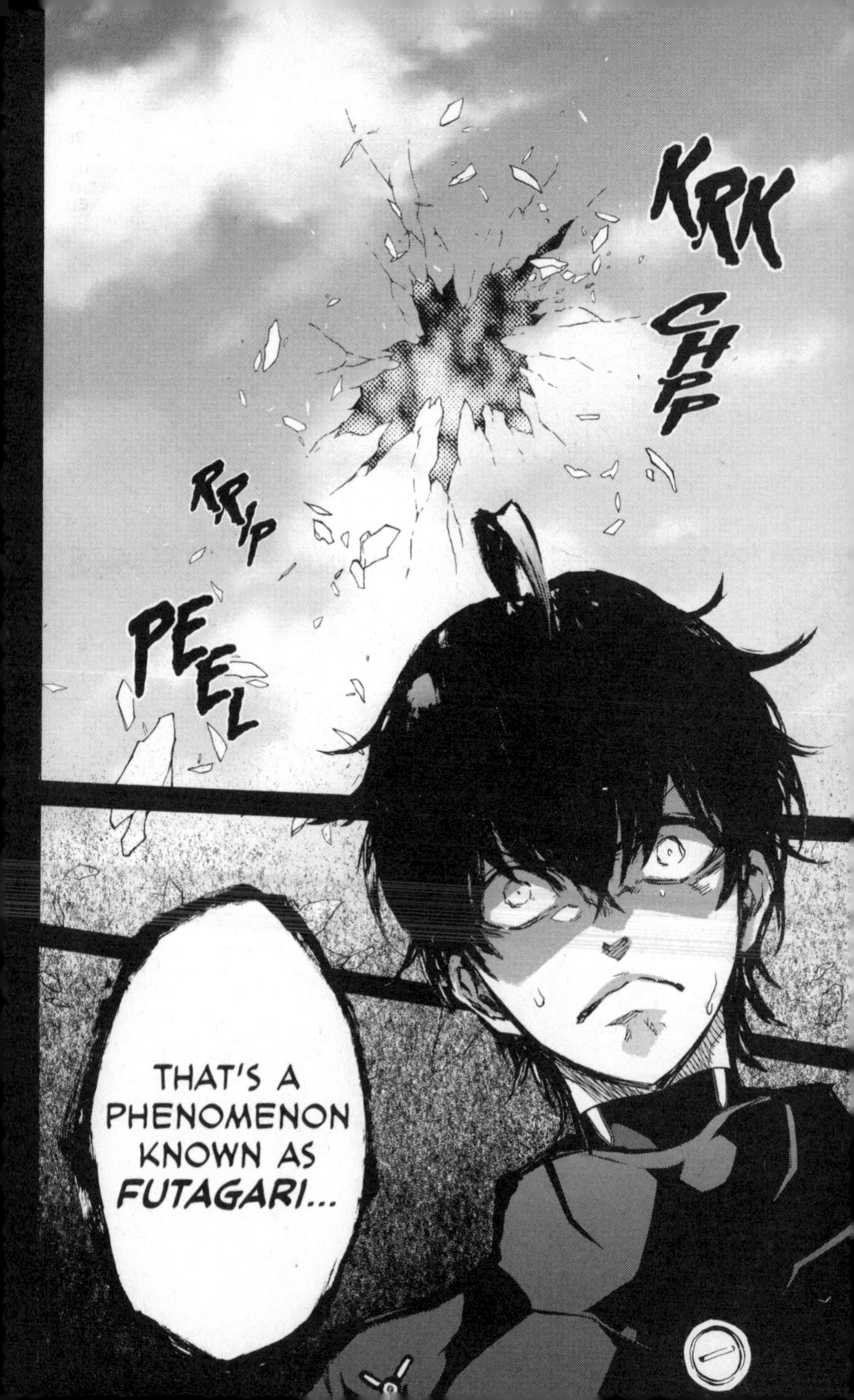
KRK
CHPP
RRIP
PEEL
THAT'S A PHENOMENON KNOWN AS *FUTAGARI*...

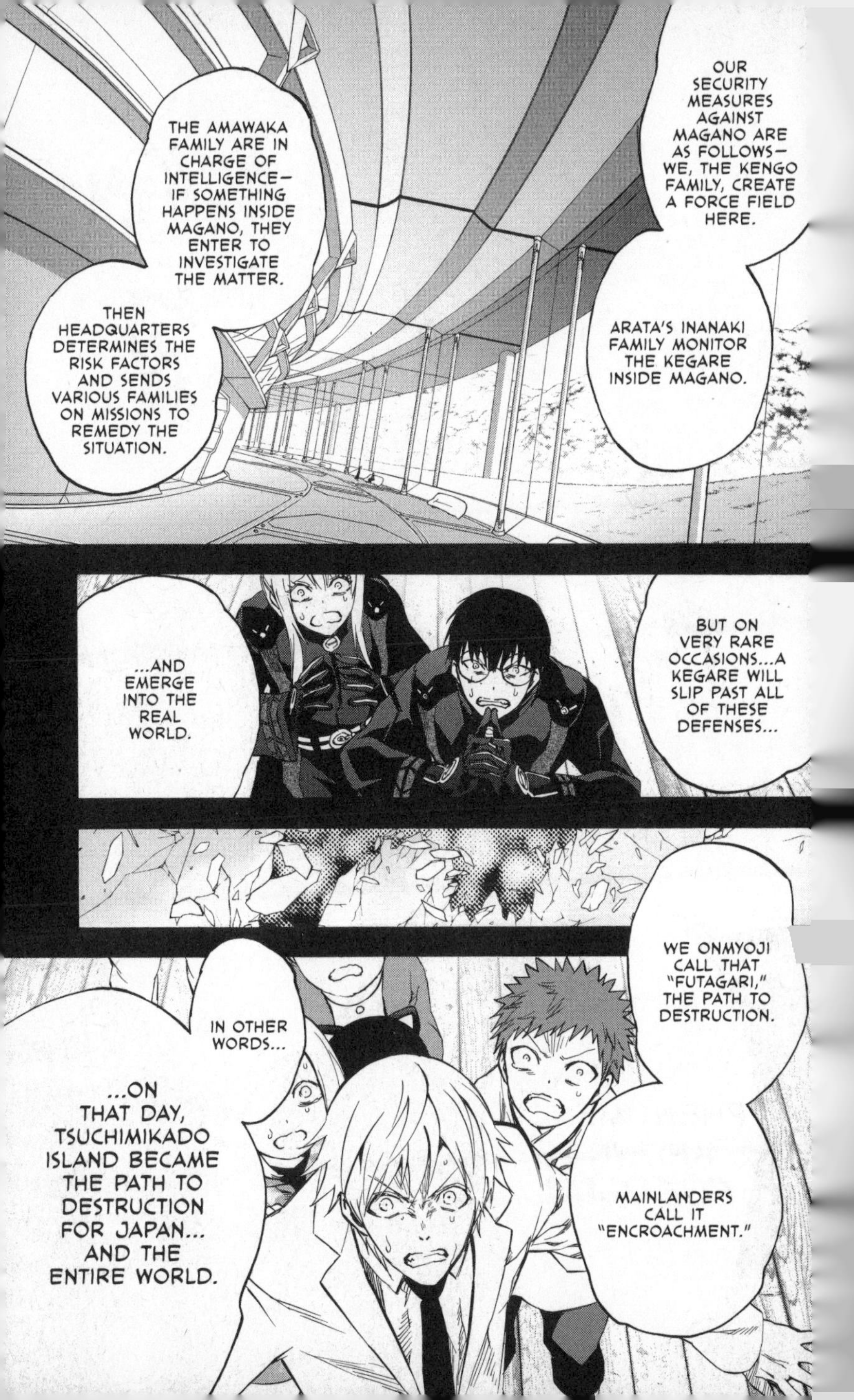
OUR SECURITY MEASURES AGAINST MAGANO ARE AS FOLLOWS—WE, THE KENGO FAMILY, CREATE A FORCE FIELD HERE.
ARATA'S INANAKI FAMILY MONITOR THE KEGARE INSIDE MAGANO.
THE AMAWAKA FAMILY ARE IN CHARGE OF INTELLIGENCE—IF SOMETHING HAPPENS INSIDE MAGANO, THEY ENTER TO INVESTIGATE THE MATTER.
THEN HEADQUARTERS DETERMINES THE RISK FACTORS AND SENDS VARIOUS FAMILIES ON MISSIONS TO REMEDY THE SITUATION.
BUT ON VERY RARE OCCASIONS...A KEGARE WILL SLIP PAST ALL OF THESE DEFENSES...
...AND EMERGE INTO THE REAL WORLD.
WE ONMYOJI CALL THAT "FUTAGARI," THE PATH TO DESTRUCTION.
MAINLANDERS CALL IT "ENCROACHMENT."
IN OTHER WORDS...
...ON THAT DAY, TSUCHIMIKADO ISLAND BECAME THE PATH TO DESTRUCTION FOR JAPAN... AND THE ENTIRE WORLD.

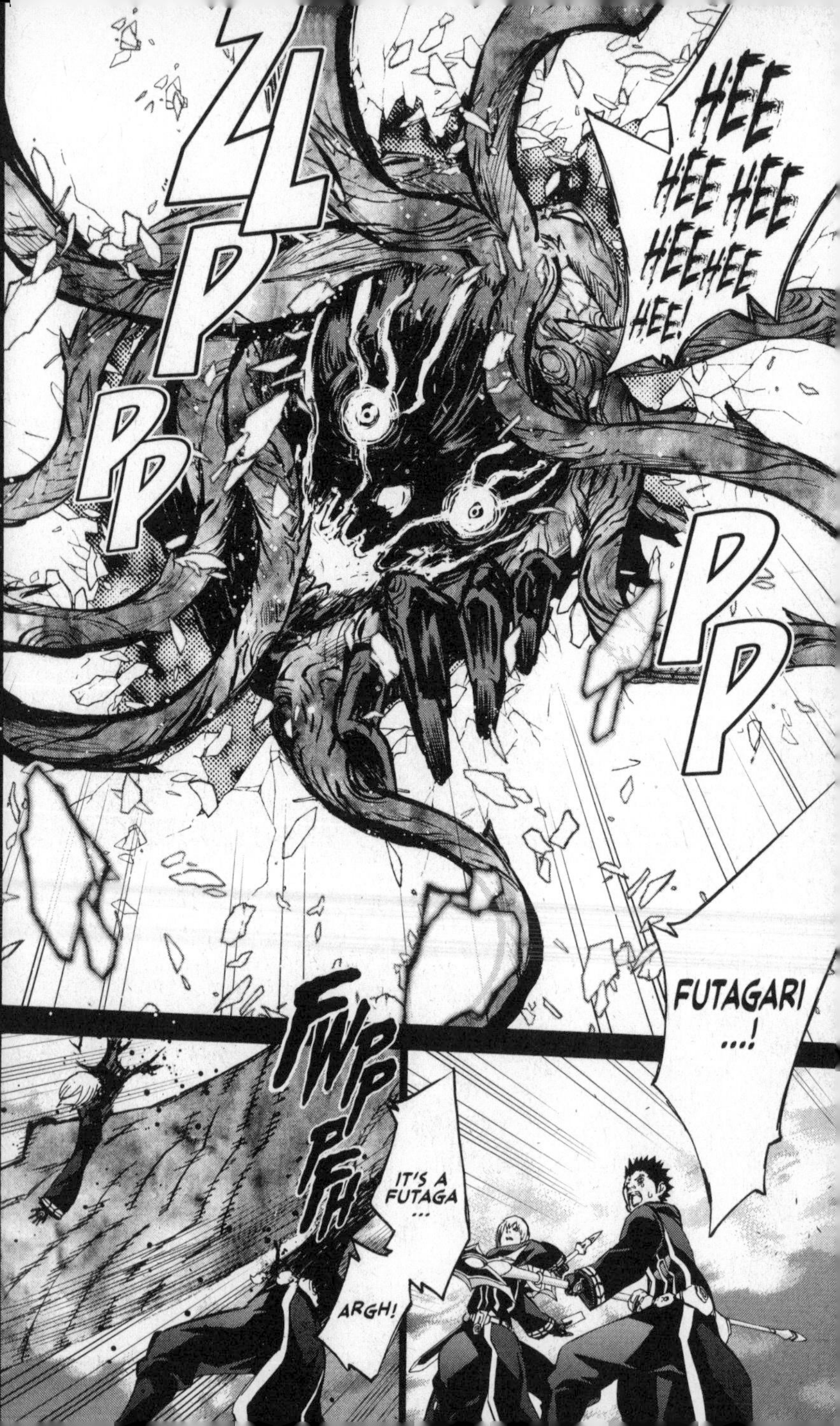
HEE HEE HEE HEE HEE HEE HEE!
PP
ZZPPP
FUTAGARI ...!
FWPPFH
IT'S A FUTAGA ...
ARGH!

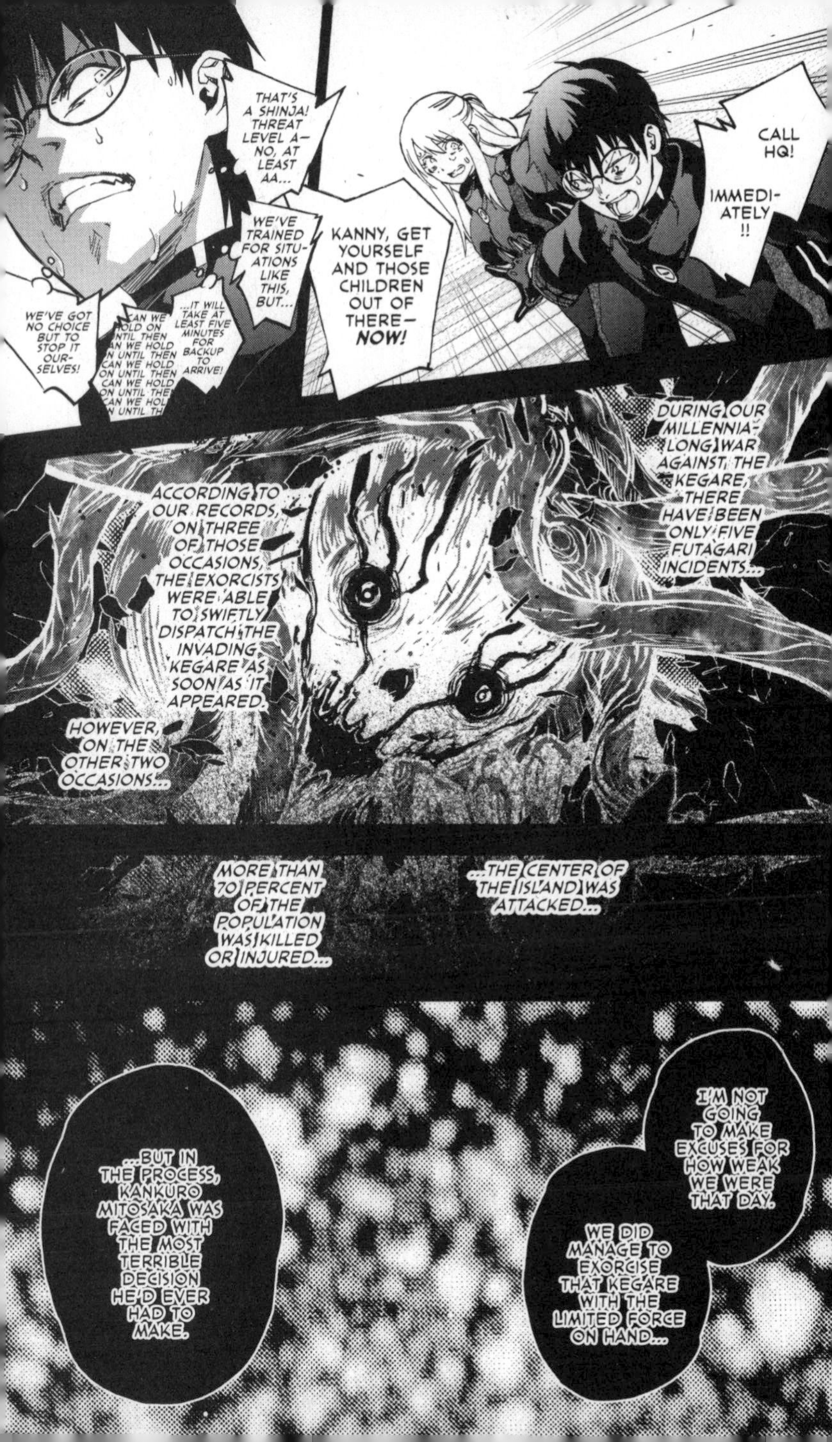
CALL HQ!
IMMEDIATELY!!
KANNY, GET YOURSELF AND THOSE CHILDREN OUT OF THERE—NOW!
THAT'S A SHINJA! THREAT LEVEL A—NO, AT LEAST AA...
WE'VE TRAINED FOR SITUATIONS LIKE THIS, BUT...
...IT WILL TAKE AT LEAST FIVE MINUTES FOR BACKUP TO ARRIVE!
CAN WE HOLD ON UNTIL THEN CAN WE HOLD ON UNTIL THEN CAN WE HOLD ON UNTIL THEN CAN WE HOLD ON UNTIL THE CAN WE HOLD ON UNTIL TH
WE'VE GOT NO CHOICE BUT TO STOP IT OURSELVES!
DURING OUR MILLENNIA-LONG WAR AGAINST THE KEGARE, THERE HAVE BEEN ONLY FIVE FUTAGARI INCIDENTS...
ACCORDING TO OUR RECORDS, ON THREE OF THOSE OCCASIONS, THE EXORCISTS WERE ABLE TO SWIFTLY DISPATCH THE INVADING KEGARE AS SOON AS IT APPEARED.
HOWEVER, ON THE OTHER TWO OCCASIONS...
...THE CENTER OF THE ISLAND WAS ATTACKED...
MORE THAN 70 PERCENT OF THE POPULATION WAS KILLED OR INJURED...
I'M NOT GOING TO MAKE EXCUSES FOR HOW WEAK WE WERE THAT DAY.
WE DID MANAGE TO EXORCISE THAT KEGARE WITH THE LIMITED FORCE ON HAND...
...BUT IN THE PROCESS, KANKURO MITOSAKA WAS FACED WITH THE MOST TERRIBLE DECISION HE'D EVER HAD TO MAKE.

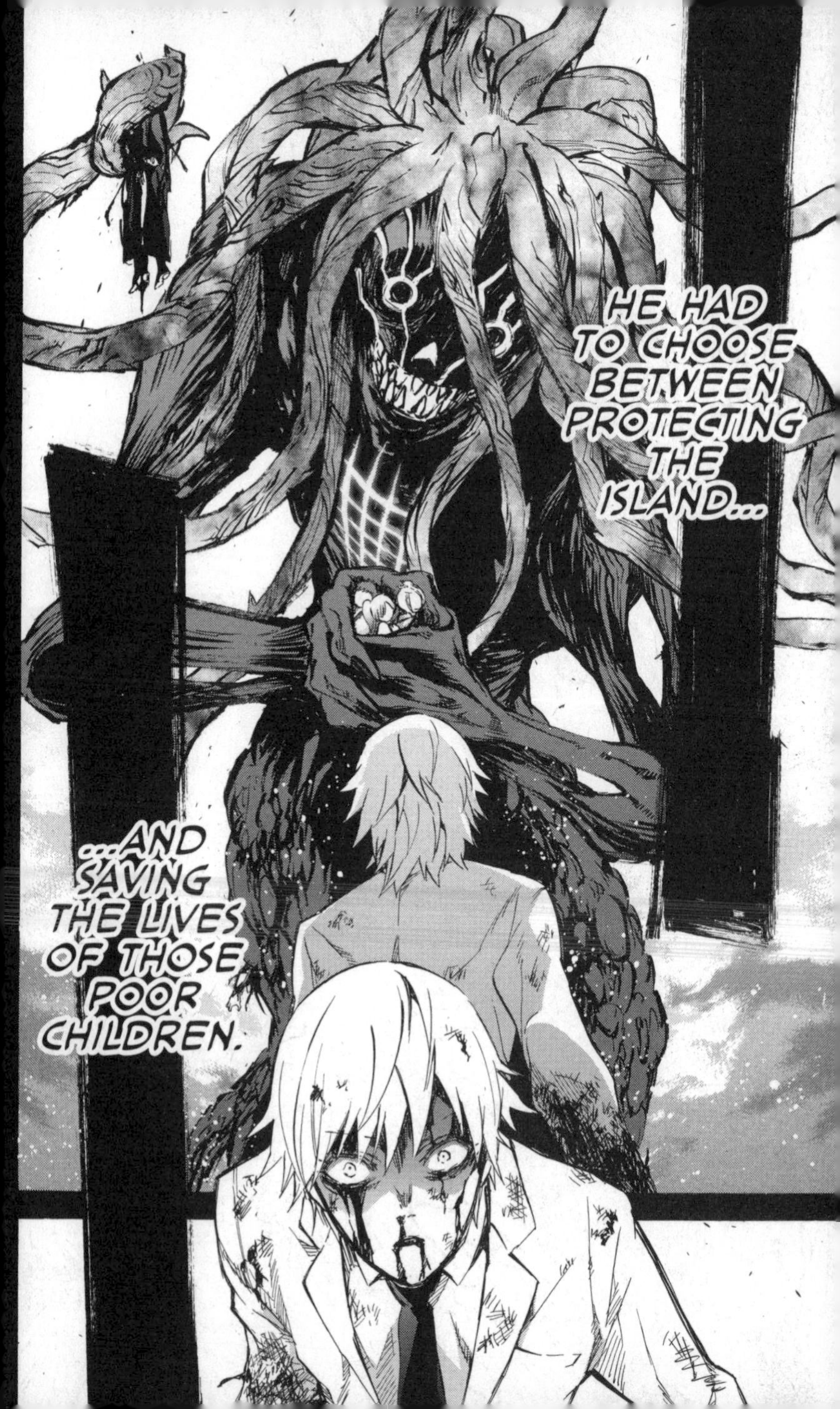
HE HAD TO CHOOSE BETWEEN PROTECTING THE ISLAND...
...AND SAVING THE LIVES OF THOSE POOR CHILDREN.

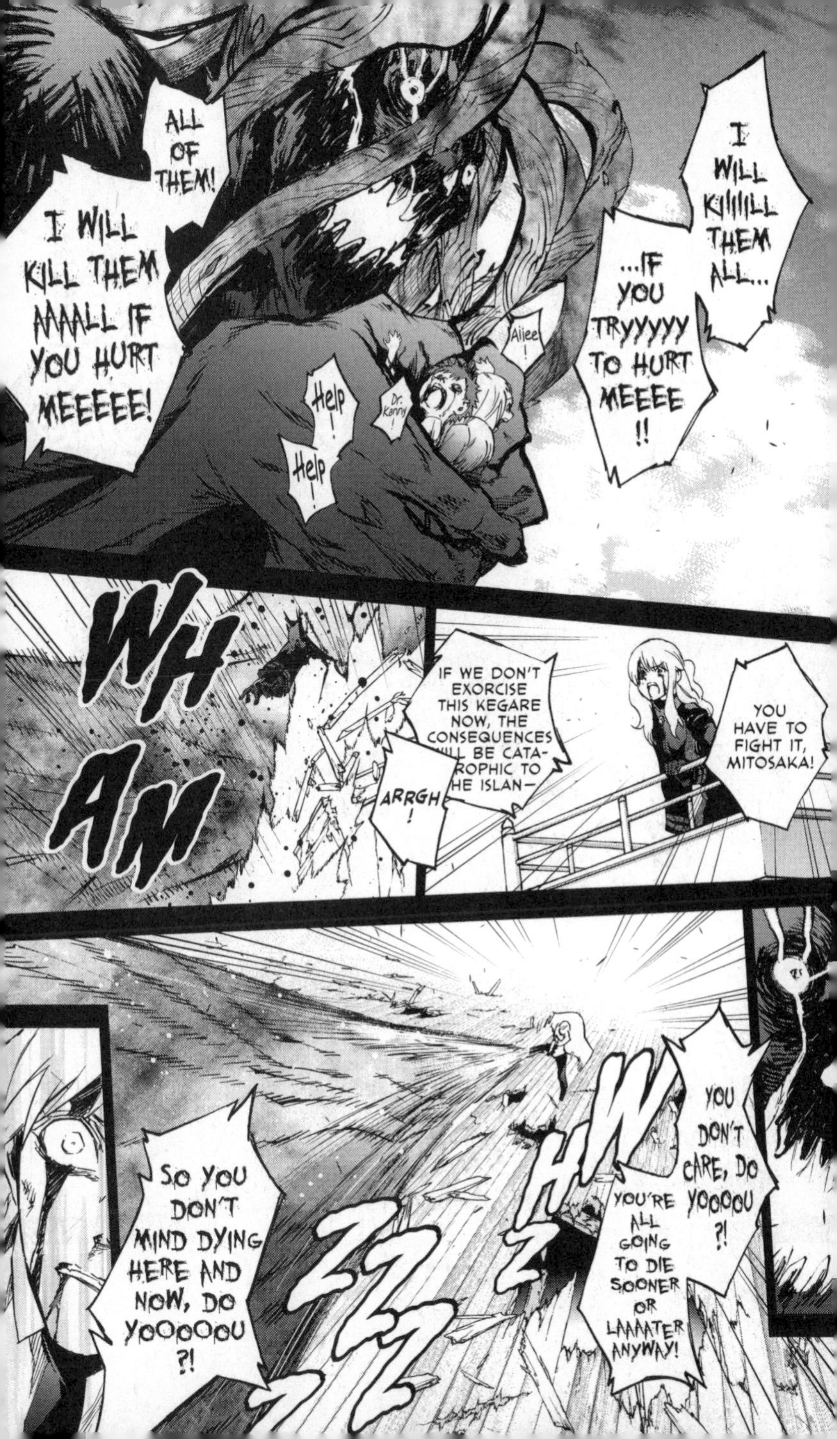
I WILL KIIIIILL THEM ALL...
...IF YOU TRYYYYY TO HURT MEEEE!!
Aiiee!
Dr. Kanny
Help!
Help!
ALL OF THEM!
I WILL KILL THEM MAAALL IF YOU HURT MEEEEE!
YOU HAVE TO FIGHT IT, MITOSAKA!
IF WE DON'T EXORCISE THIS KEGARE NOW, THE CONSEQUENCES ILL BE CATA- ROPHIC TO HE ISLAN—
ARRGH!
WHAM
YOU DON'T CARE, DO YOOOOU?!
YOU'RE ALL GOING TO DIE SOONER OR LAAAATER ANYWAY!
SO YOU DON'T MIND DYING HERE AND NOW, DO YOOOOOU?!

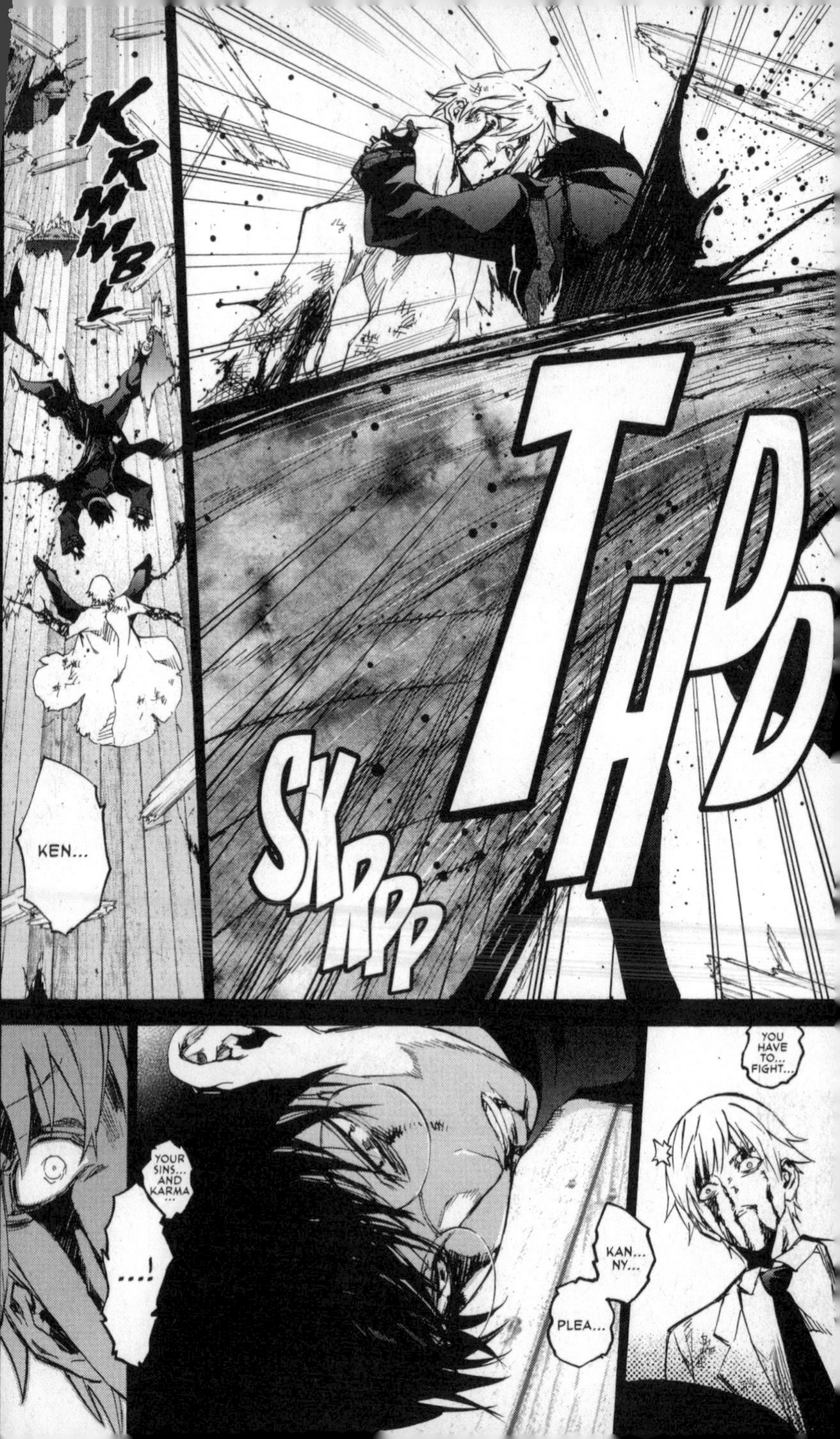
THDD
SKRPP
KRMMBL
KEN...
YOU HAVE TO... FIGHT...
KAN... NY...
PLEA...
YOUR SINS... AND KARMA...
...!

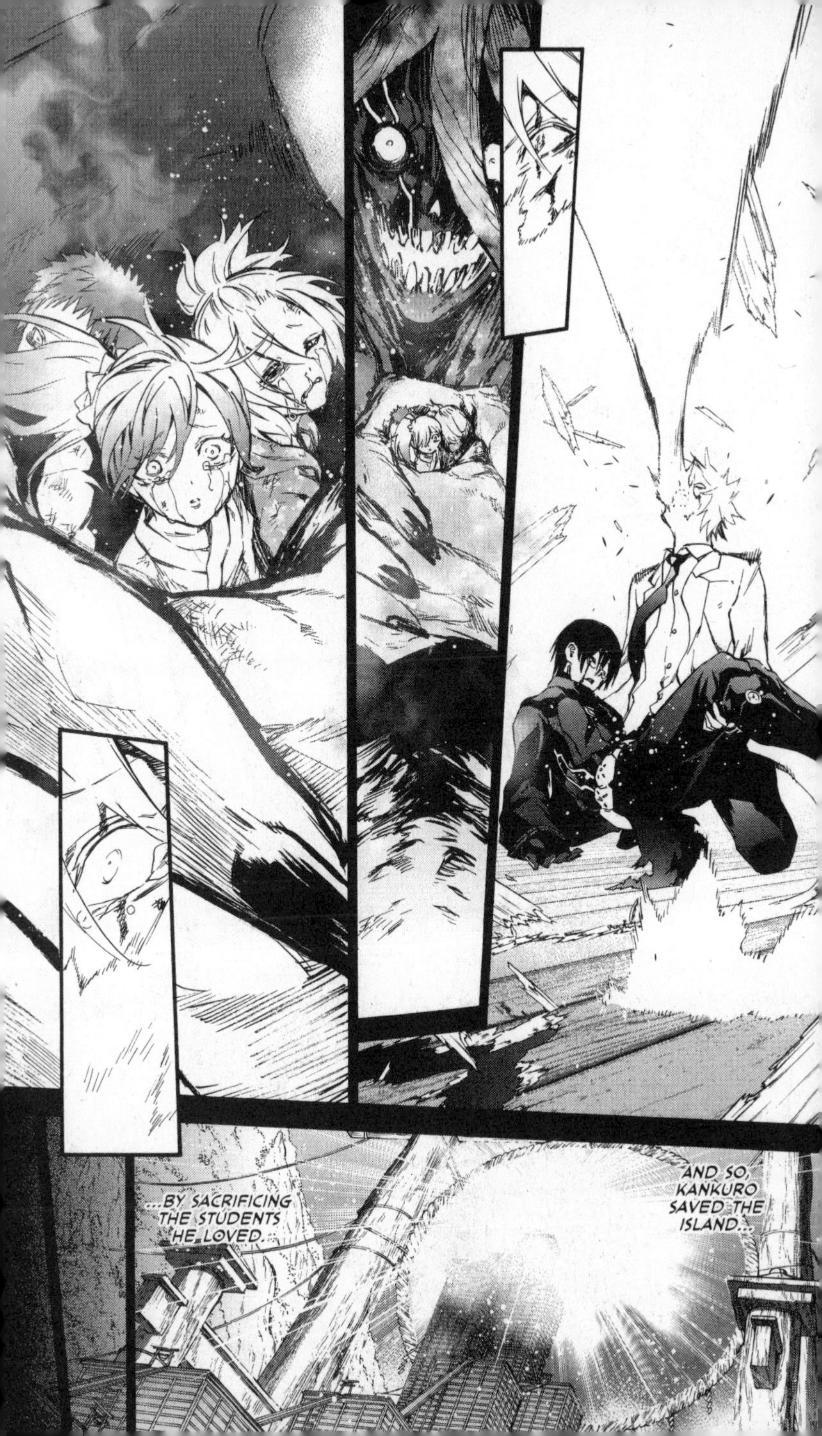
AND SO, KANKURO SAVED THE ISLAND...
...BY SACRIFICING THE STUDENTS HE LOVED...

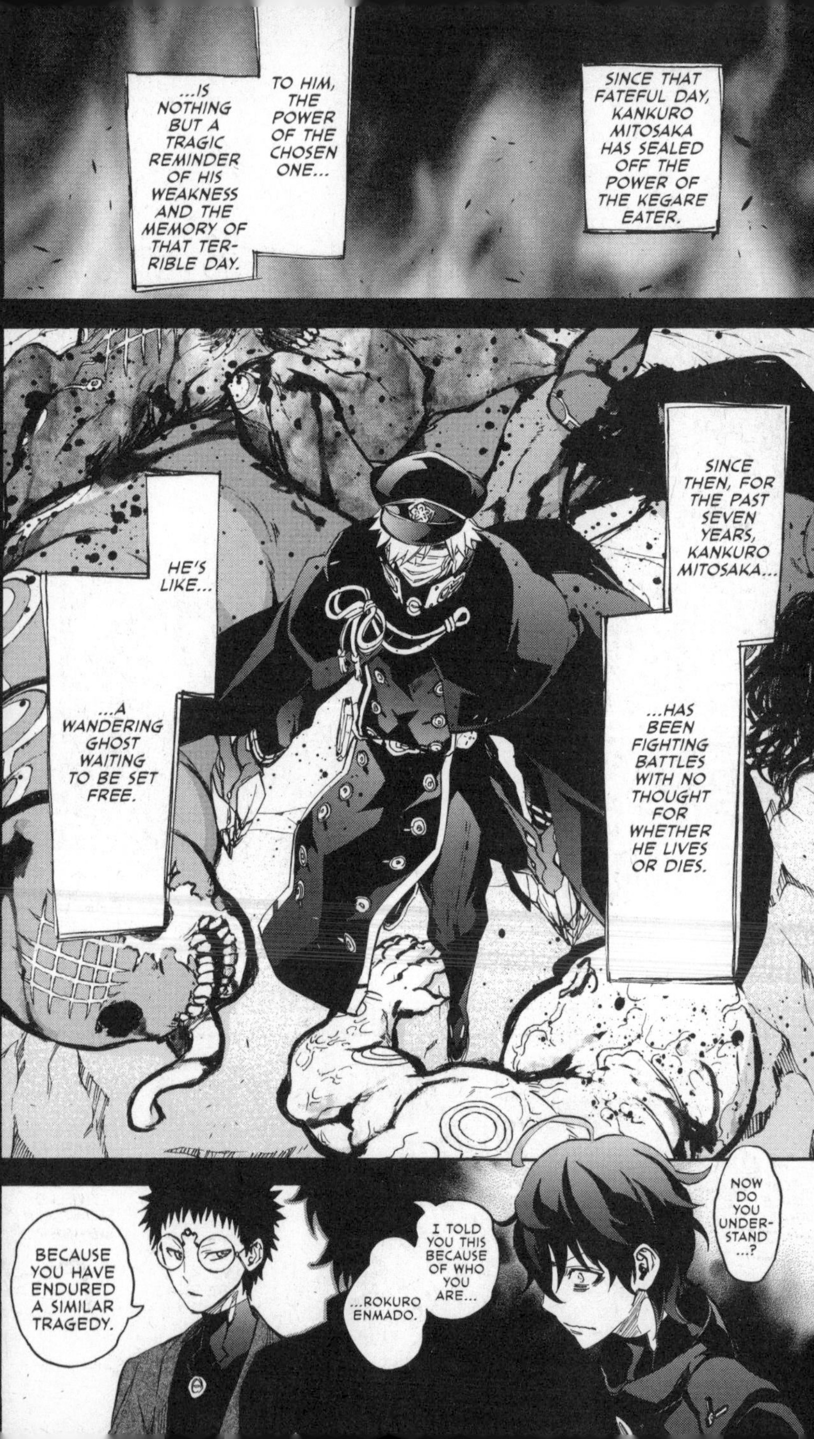
SINCE THAT FATEFUL DAY, KANKURO MITOSAKA HAS SEALED OFF THE POWER OF THE KEGARE EATER.
TO HIM, THE POWER OF THE CHOSEN ONE...
...IS NOTHING BUT A TRAGIC REMINDER OF HIS WEAKNESS AND THE MEMORY OF THAT TER-RIBLE DAY.
SINCE THEN, FOR THE PAST SEVEN YEARS, KANKURO MITOSAKA...
...HAS BEEN FIGHTING BATTLES WITH NO THOUGHT FOR WHETHER HE LIVES OR DIES.
HE'S LIKE...
...A WANDERING GHOST WAITING TO BE SET FREE.
NOW DO YOU UNDER-STAND...?
I TOLD YOU THIS BECAUSE OF WHO YOU ARE...
...ROKURO ENMADO.
BECAUSE YOU HAVE ENDURED A SIMILAR TRAGEDY.

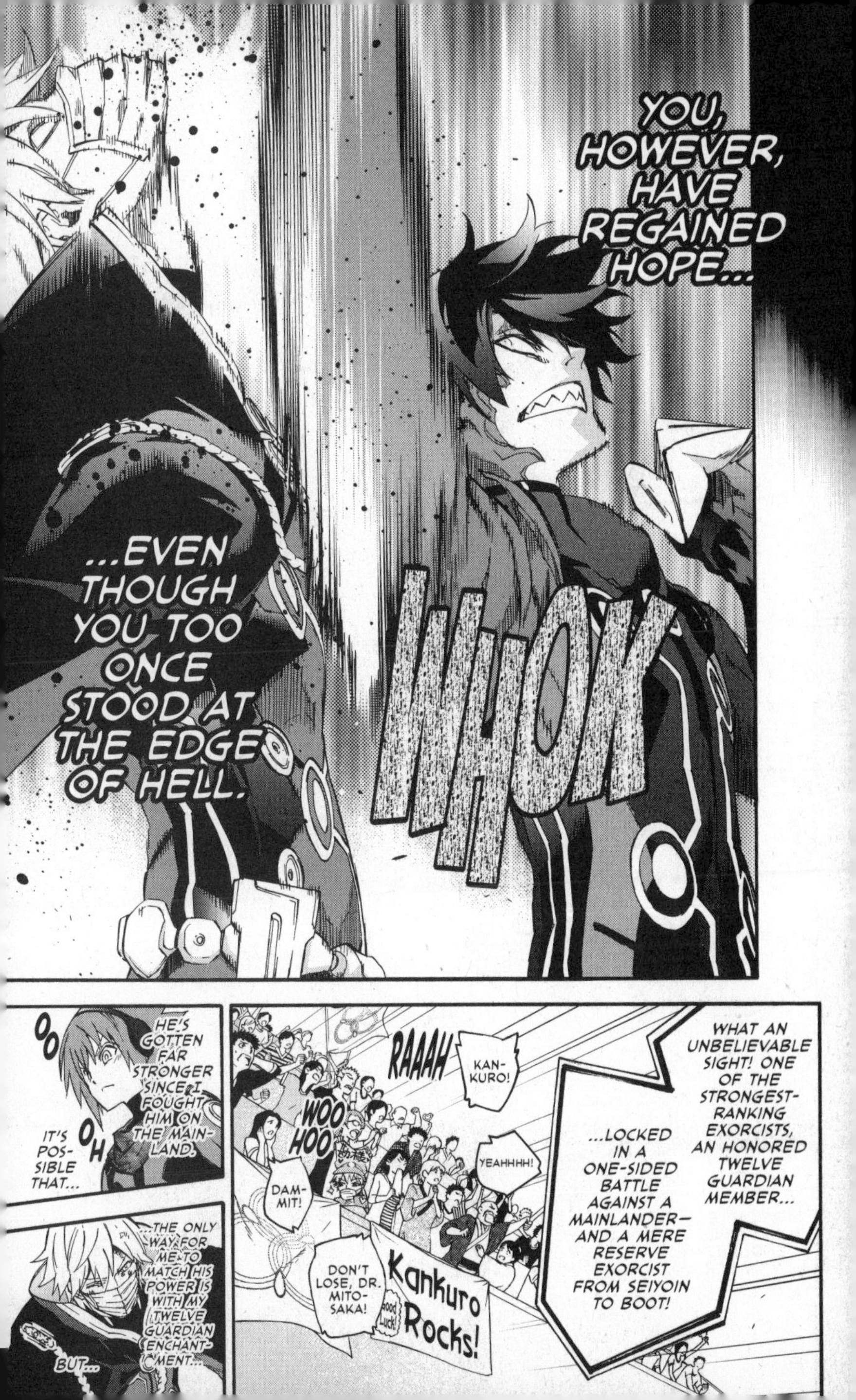
YOU, HOWEVER, HAVE REGAINED HOPE...
...EVEN THOUGH YOU TOO ONCE STOOD AT THE EDGE OF HELL.
WHOK
WHAT AN UNBELIEVABLE SIGHT! ONE OF THE STRONGEST-RANKING EXORCISTS, AN HONORED TWELVE GUARDIAN MEMBER...
...LOCKED IN A ONE-SIDED BATTLE AGAINST A MAINLANDER—AND A MERE RESERVE EXORCIST FROM SEIYOIN TO BOOT!
KAN-KURO!
RAAAH
YEAHHHH!
WOO HOO
DAM-MIT!
DON'T LOSE, DR. MITO-SAKA!
Kankuro Rocks!
Good Luck!
HE'S GOTTEN FAR STRONGER SINCE I FOUGHT HIM ON THE MAINLAND.
OH
IT'S POS-SIBLE THAT...
...THE ONLY WAY FOR ME TO MATCH HIS POWER IS WITH MY TWELVE GUARDIAN ENCHANT-MENT...
BUT...

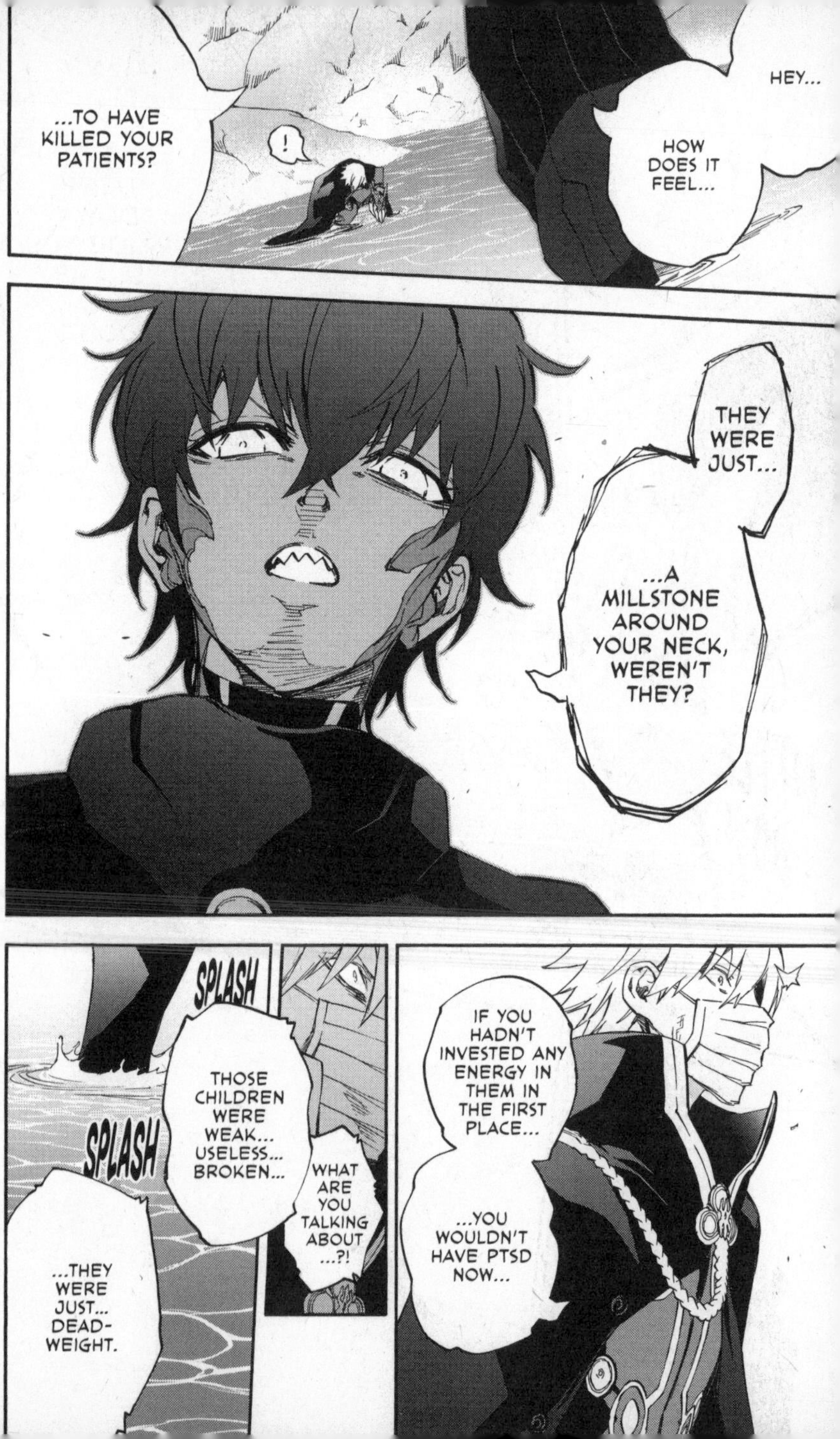
HEY...
HOW DOES IT FEEL...
...TO HAVE KILLED YOUR PATIENTS?
!
THEY WERE JUST...
...A MILLSTONE AROUND YOUR NECK, WEREN'T THEY?
IF YOU HADN'T INVESTED ANY ENERGY IN THEM IN THE FIRST PLACE...
...YOU WOULDN'T HAVE PTSD NOW...
WHAT ARE YOU TALKING ABOUT ...?!
SPLASH
THOSE CHILDREN WERE WEAK... USELESS... BROKEN...
SPLASH
...THEY WERE JUST... DEAD-WEIGHT.

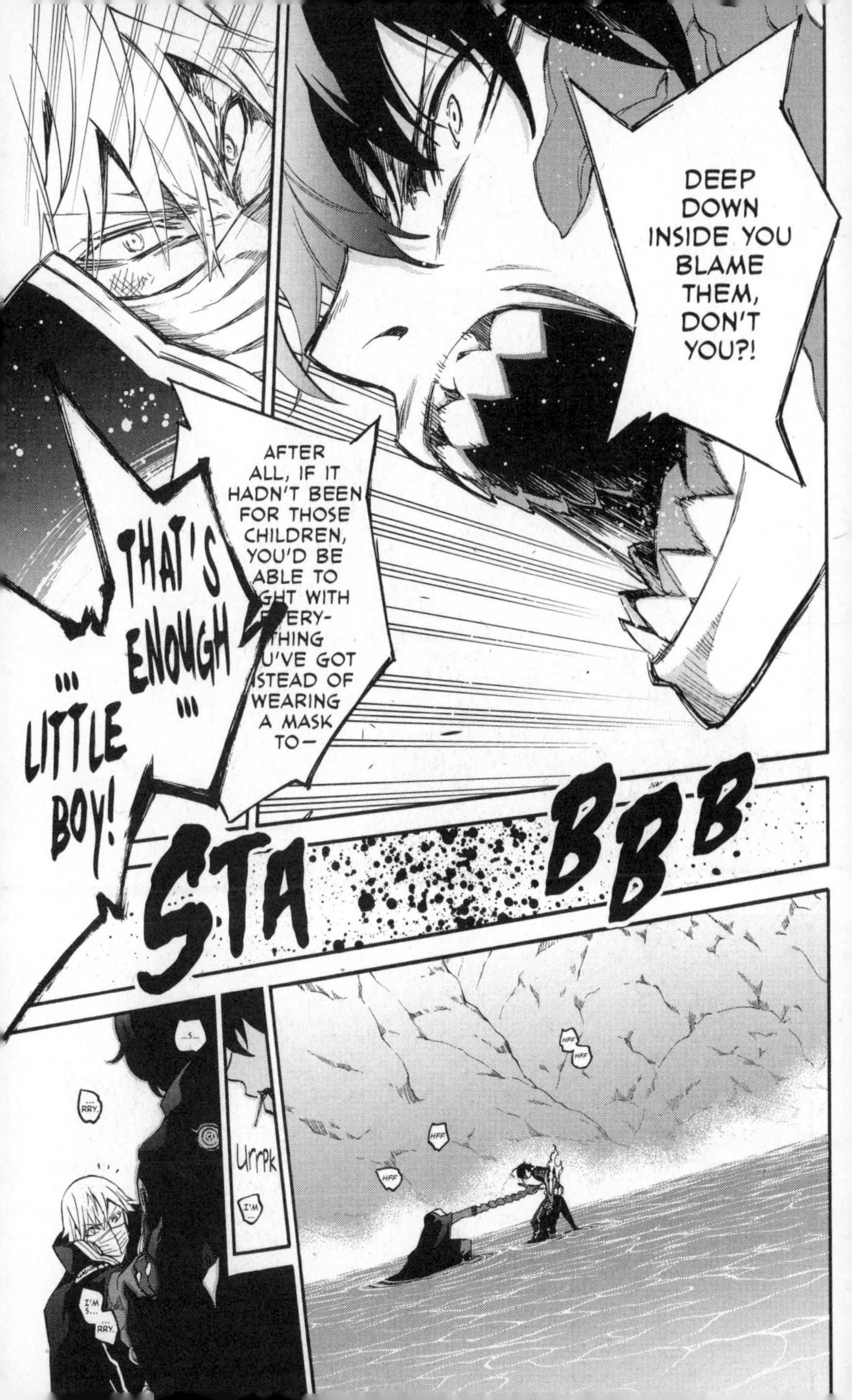
DEEP DOWN INSIDE YOU BLAME THEM, DON'T YOU?!
AFTER ALL, IF IT HADN'T BEEN FOR THOSE CHILDREN, YOU'D BE ABLE TO GHT WITH ERY-THING U'VE GOT STEAD OF WEARING A MASK TO—
THAT'S ENOUGH...
...LITTLE BOY!
STA BBB
HFF
HFF
HFF
HFF
...S...
...RRY.
Urrpk
I'M
I'M S... ...RRY.

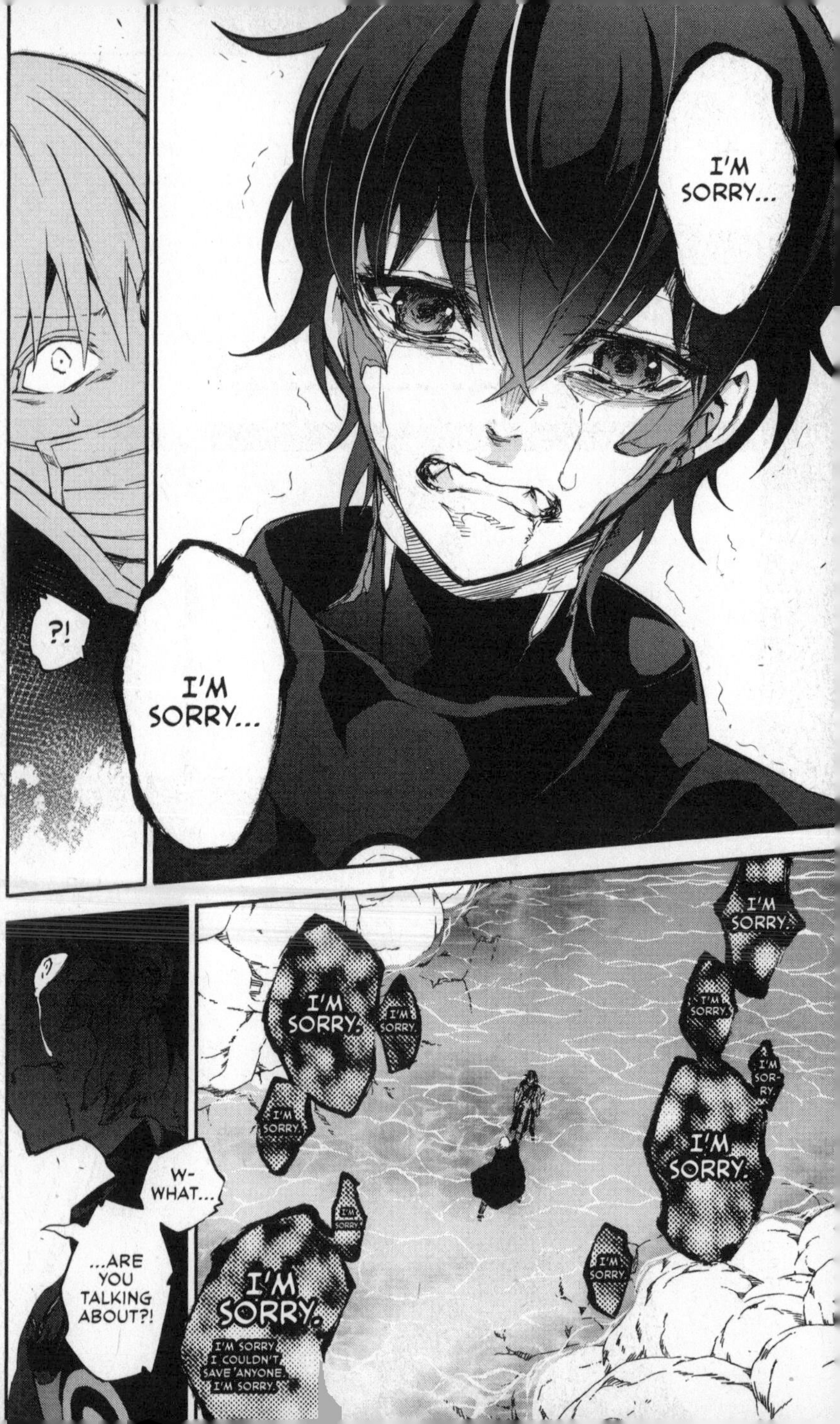
I'M SORRY...
I'M SORRY...
?!
I'M SORRY.
I'M SORRY.
I'M SORRY.
I'M SORRY.
I'M SORRY.
I'M SOR-RY.
I'M SORRY.
I'M SORRY.
I'M SORRY.
I'M SORRY.
I'M SORRY.
I'M SORRY I COULDN'T SAVE ANYONE. I'M SORRY.
W-WHAT...
...ARE YOU TALKING ABOUT?!

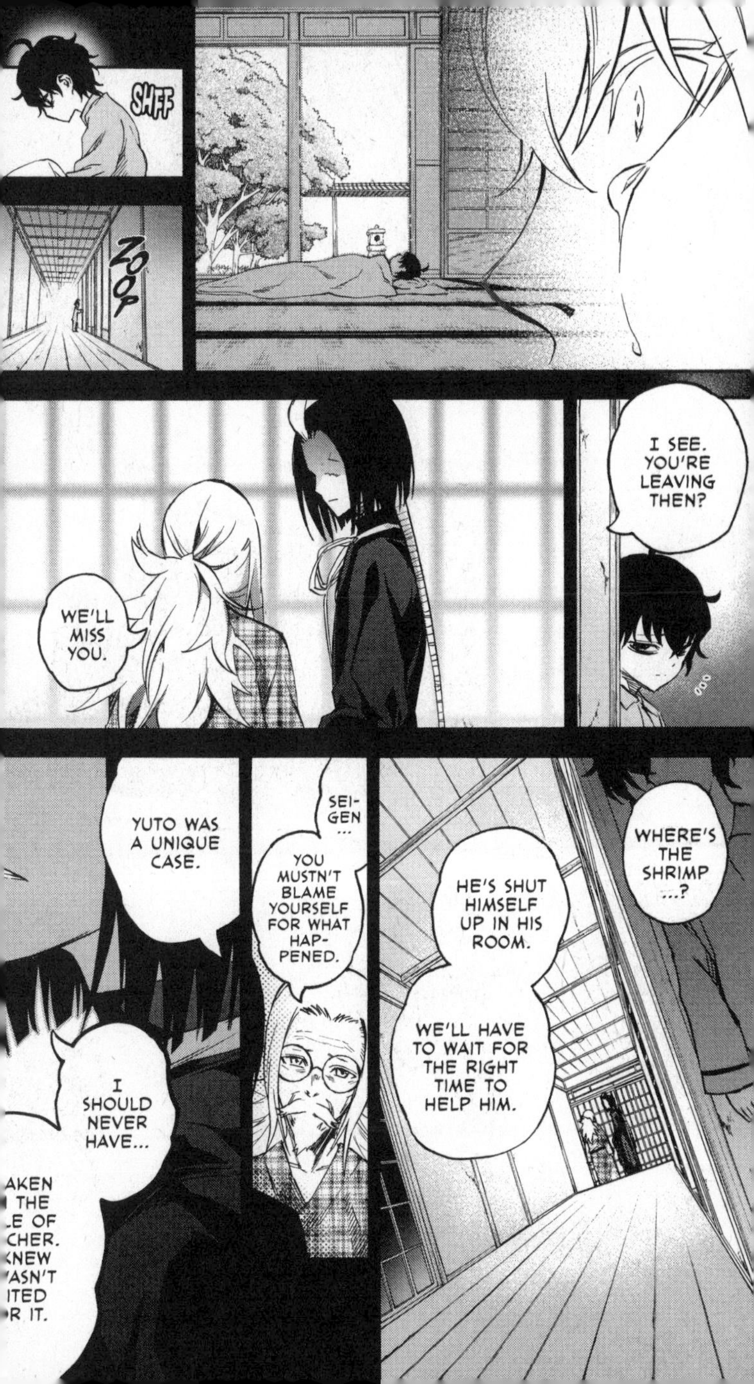
SHFF
ZOOP
I SEE. YOU'RE LEAVING THEN?
WE'LL MISS YOU.
WHERE'S THE SHRIMP ...?
HE'S SHUT HIMSELF UP IN HIS ROOM.
WE'LL HAVE TO WAIT FOR THE RIGHT TIME TO HELP HIM.
SEI-GEN ...
YOU MUSTN'T BLAME YOURSELF FOR WHAT HAP-PENED.
YUTO WAS A UNIQUE CASE.
I SHOULD NEVER HAVE...

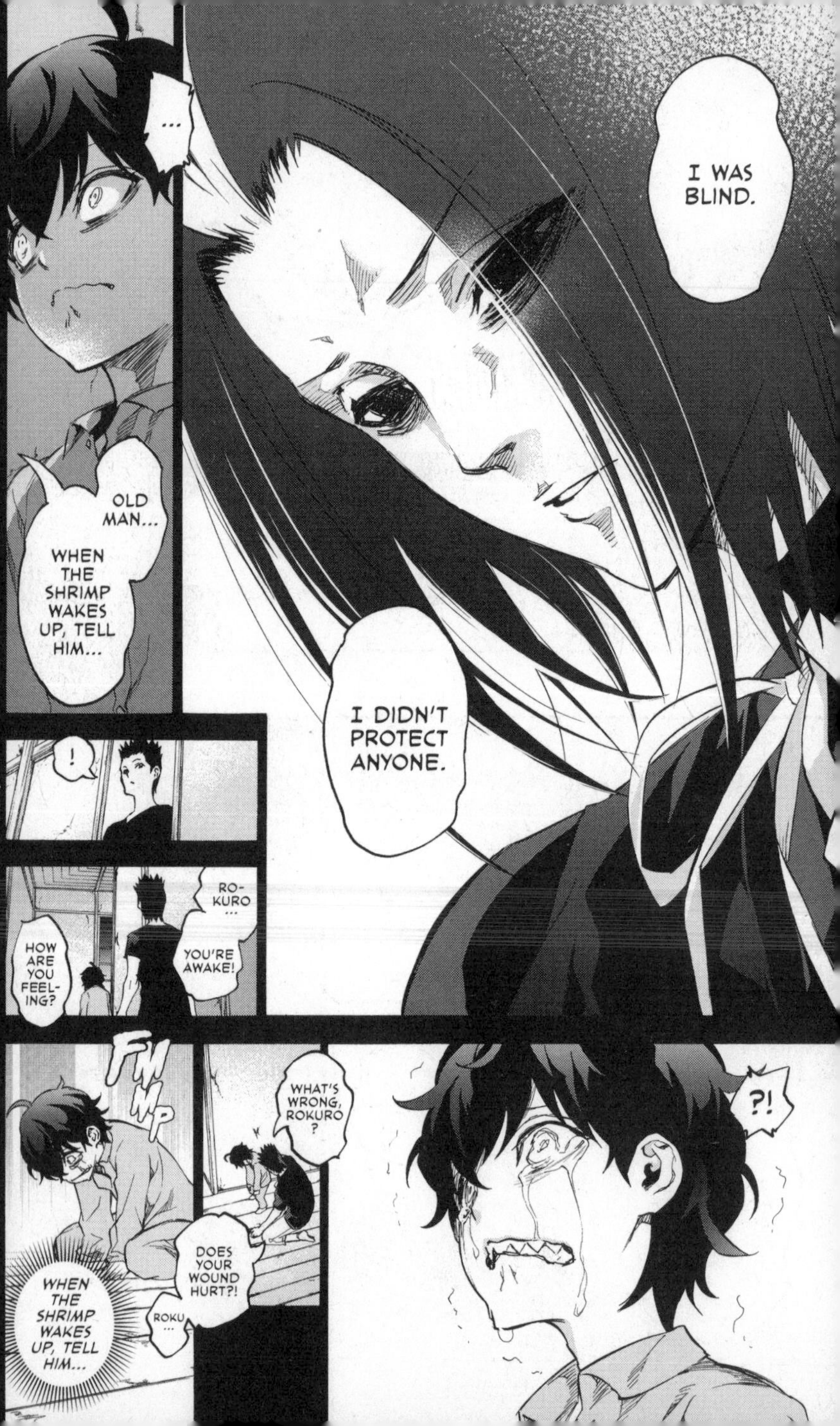
I WAS BLIND.
I DIDN'T PROTECT ANYONE.
...
OLD MAN...
WHEN THE SHRIMP WAKES UP, TELL HIM...
!
RO-KURO...
YOU'RE AWAKE!
HOW ARE YOU FEEL-ING?
?!
WHAT'S WRONG, ROKURO?
DOES YOUR WOUND HURT?!
ROKU...
FMMP
WHEN THE SHRIMP WAKES UP, TELL HIM...

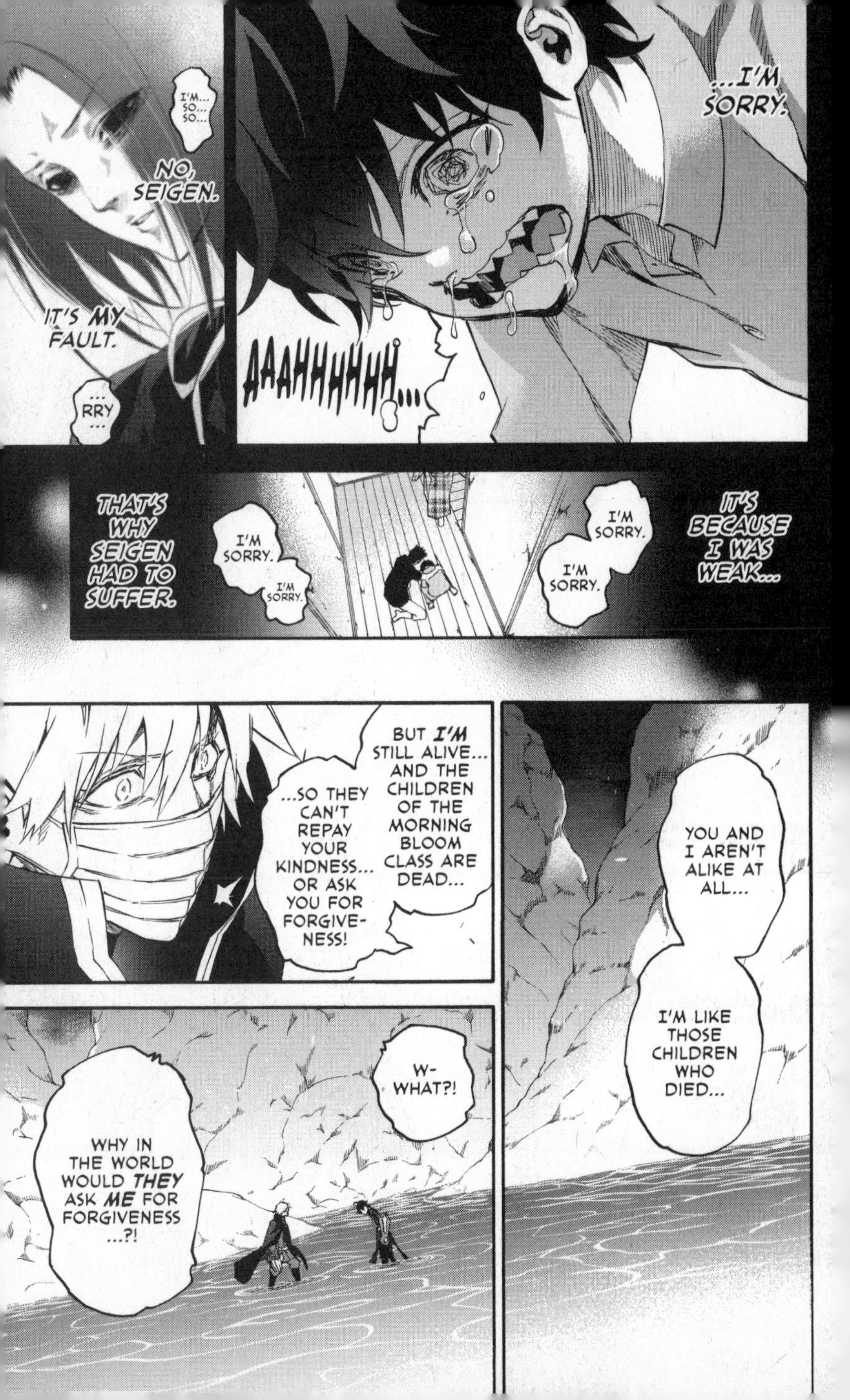
...I'M SORRY.
AAAHHHHHH....
I'M... SO... SO...
NO, SEIGEN.
IT'S MY FAULT.
...RRY...
IT'S BECAUSE I WAS WEAK...
I'M SORRY.
I'M SORRY.
I'M SORRY.
I'M SORRY.
THAT'S WHY SEIGEN HAD TO SUFFER.
YOU AND I AREN'T ALIKE AT ALL...
I'M LIKE THOSE CHILDREN WHO DIED...
BUT *I'M* STILL ALIVE... AND THE CHILDREN OF THE MORNING BLOOM CLASS ARE DEAD...
...SO THEY CAN'T REPAY YOUR KINDNESS... OR ASK YOU FOR FORGIVENESS!
W-WHAT?!
WHY IN THE WORLD WOULD *THEY* ASK *ME* FOR FORGIVENESS...?!

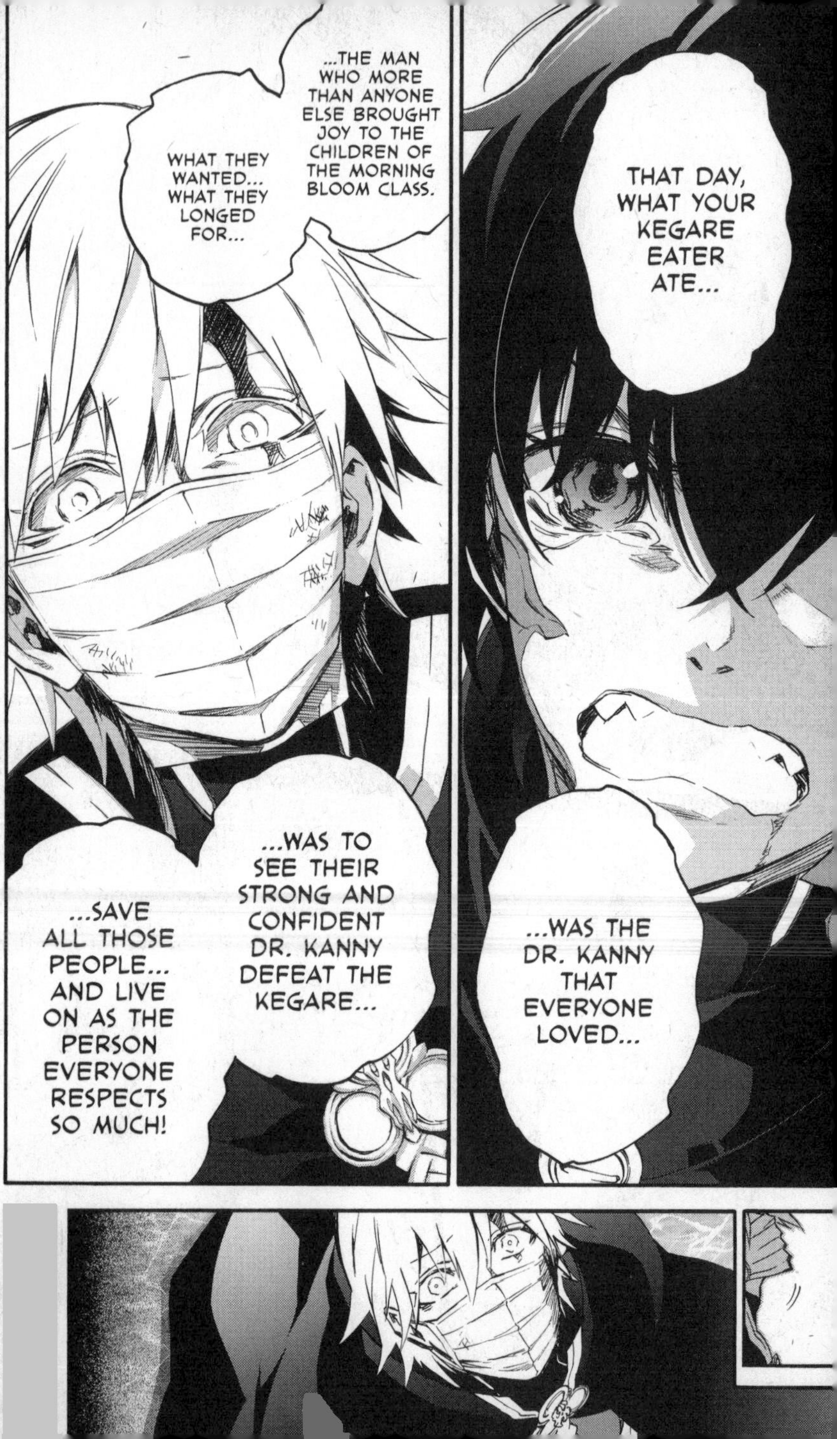
THAT DAY, WHAT YOUR KEGARE EATER ATE...
...WAS THE DR. KANNY THAT EVERYONE LOVED...
...THE MAN WHO MORE THAN ANYONE ELSE BROUGHT JOY TO THE CHILDREN OF THE MORNING BLOOM CLASS.
WHAT THEY WANTED... WHAT THEY LONGED FOR...
...WAS TO SEE THEIR STRONG AND CONFIDENT DR. KANNY DEFEAT THE KEGARE...
...SAVE ALL THOSE PEOPLE... AND LIVE ON AS THE PERSON EVERYONE RESPECTS SO MUCH!

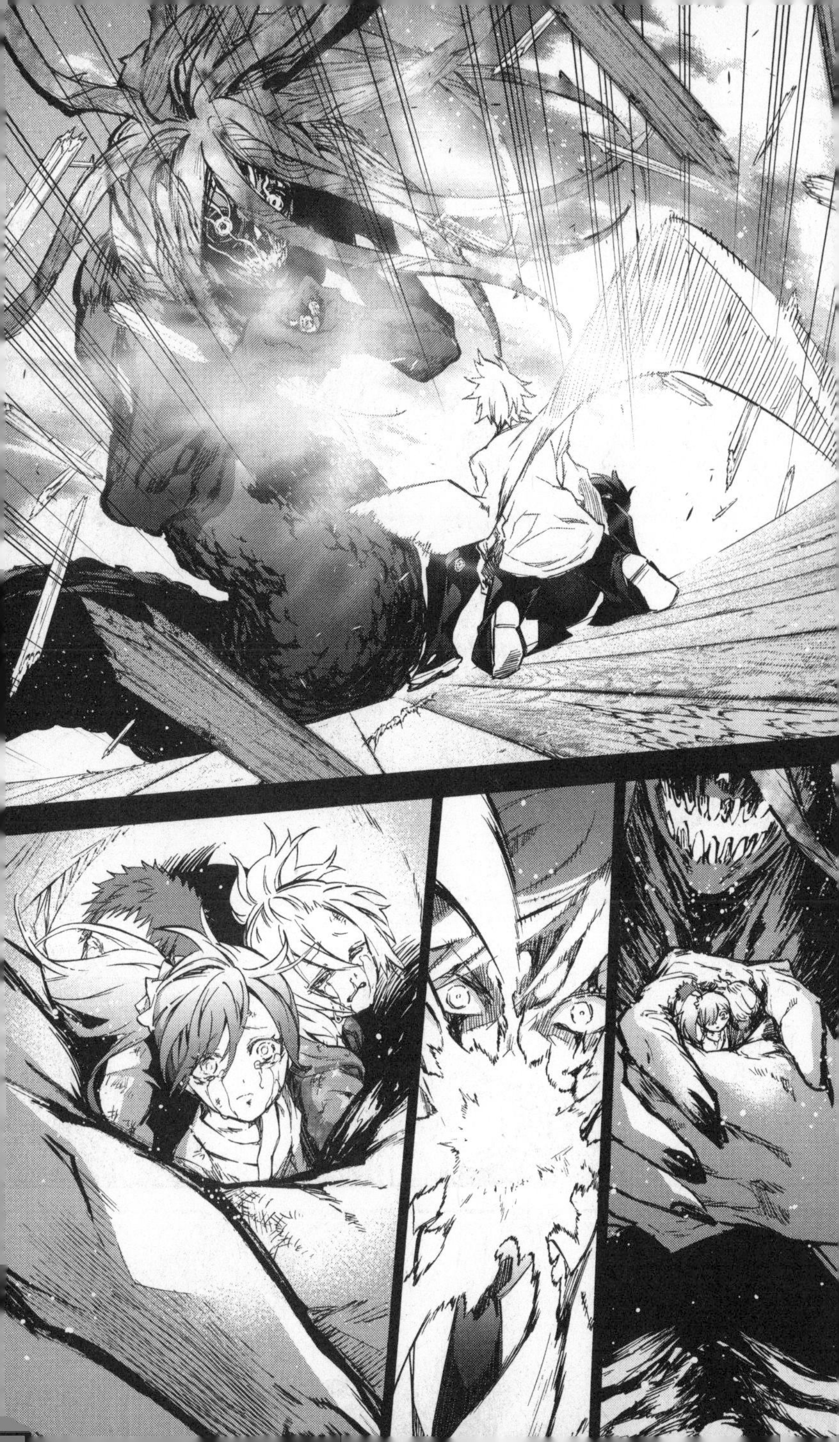

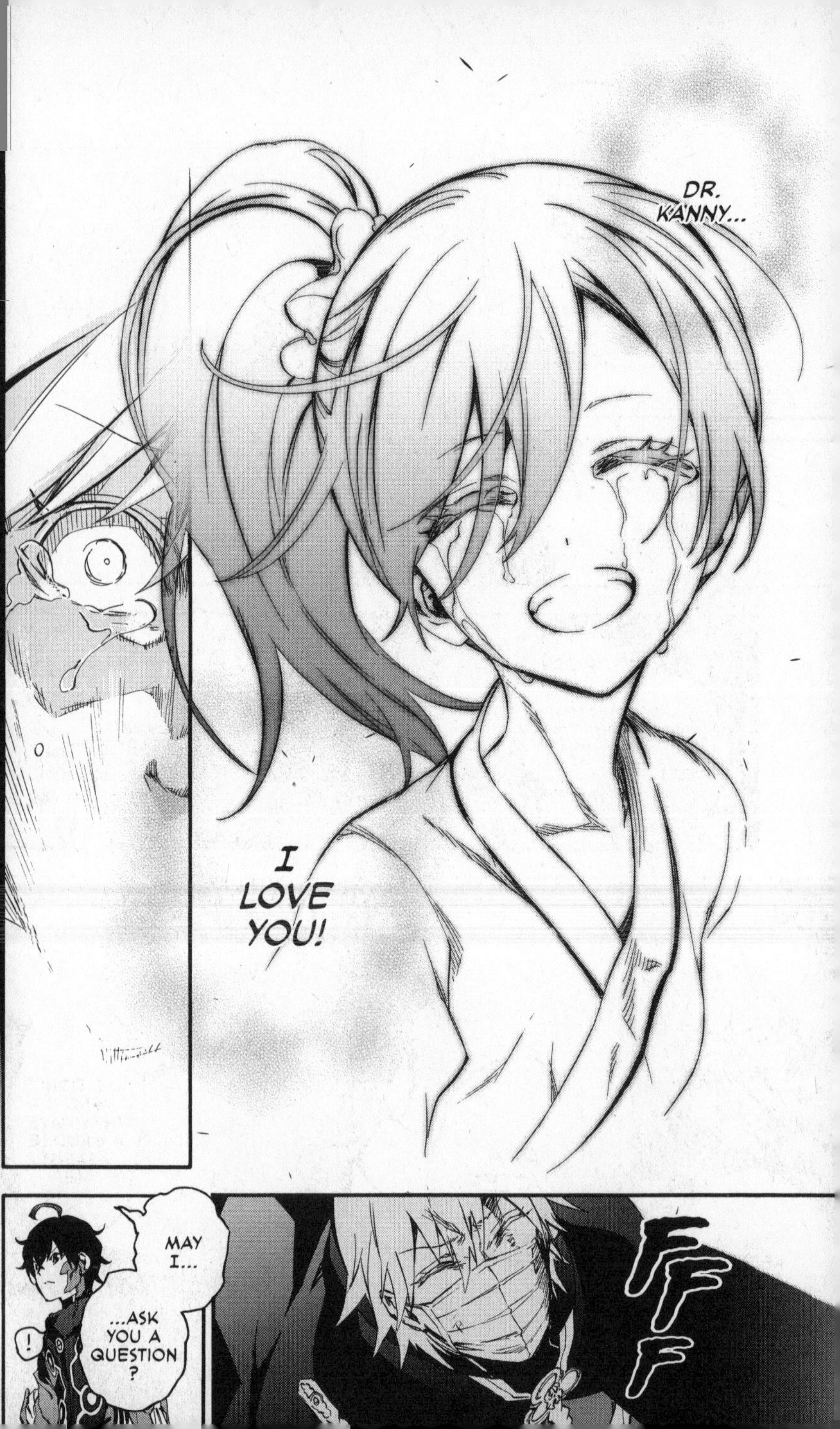
DR. KANNY...
I LOVE YOU!
FFF
MAY I...
...ASK YOU A QUESTION?
!

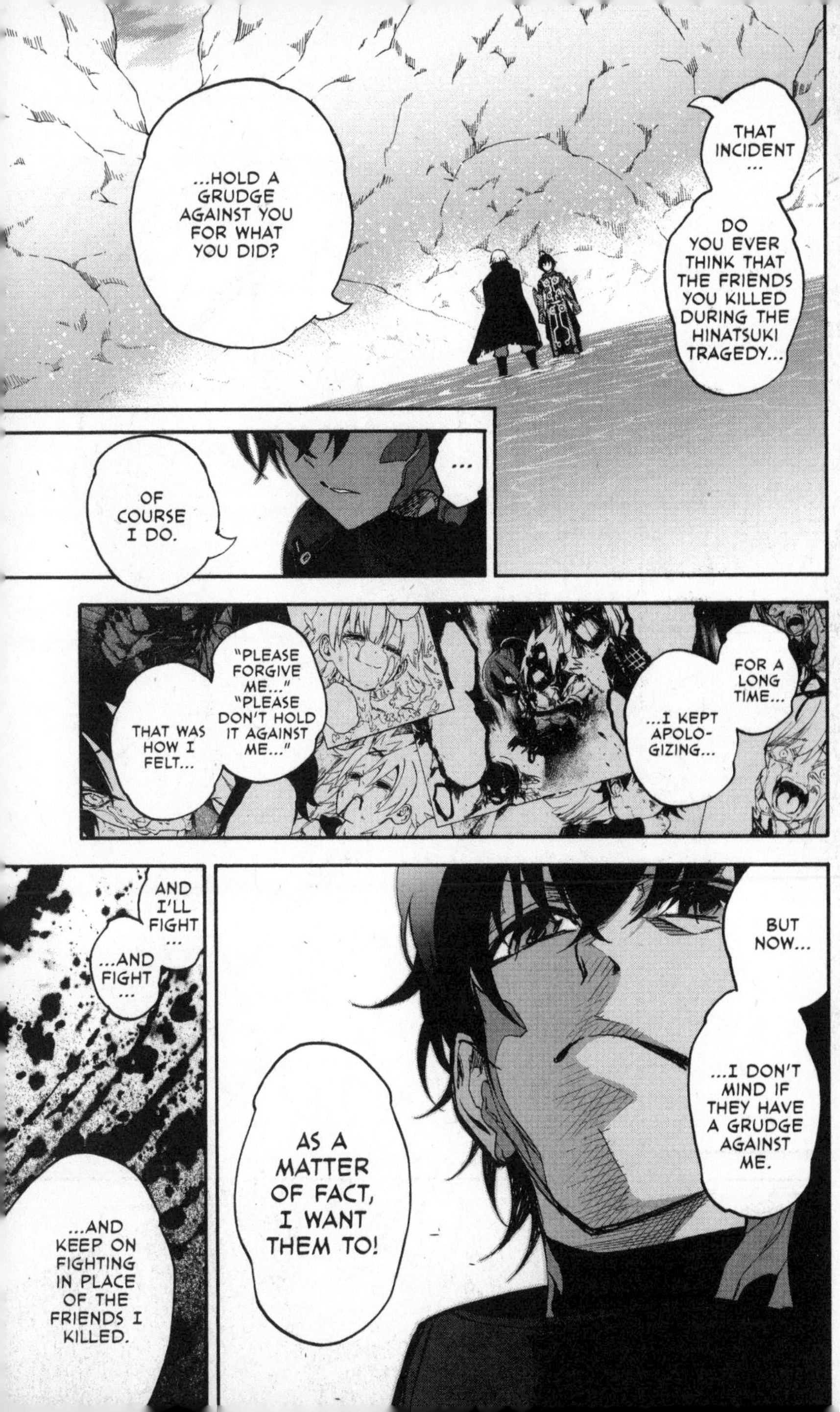
THAT INCIDENT...
DO YOU EVER THINK THAT THE FRIENDS YOU KILLED DURING THE HINATSUKI TRAGEDY...
...HOLD A GRUDGE AGAINST YOU FOR WHAT YOU DID?
...
OF COURSE I DO.
FOR A LONG TIME...
...I KEPT APOLOGIZING...
"PLEASE FORGIVE ME..." "PLEASE DON'T HOLD IT AGAINST ME..."
THAT WAS HOW I FELT...
BUT NOW...
...I DON'T MIND IF THEY HAVE A GRUDGE AGAINST ME.
AS A MATTER OF FACT, I WANT THEM TO!
AND I'LL FIGHT...
...AND FIGHT...
...AND KEEP ON FIGHTING IN PLACE OF THE FRIENDS I KILLED.

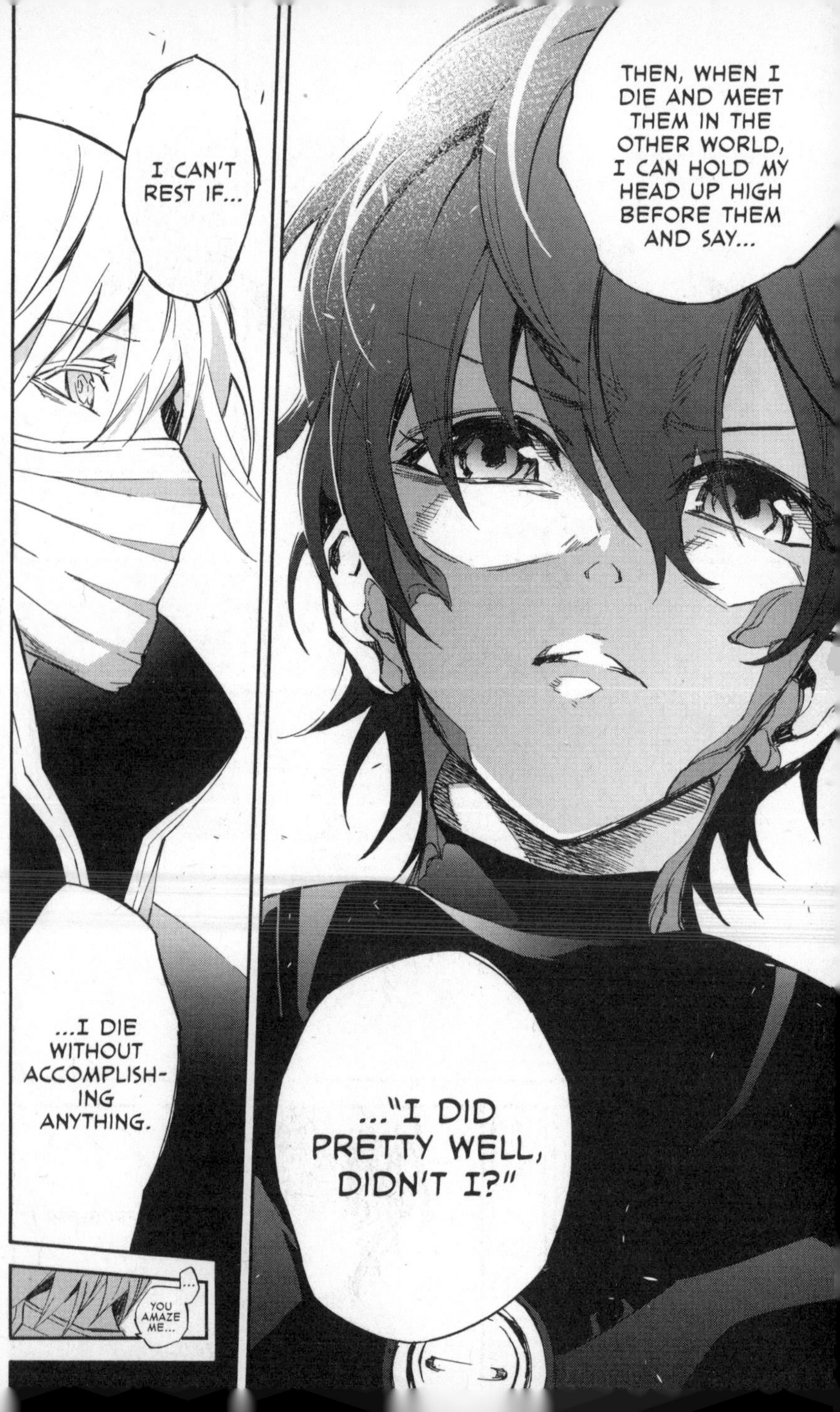
I CAN'T REST IF...
...I DIE WITHOUT ACCOMPLISHING-ING ANYTHING.
THEN, WHEN I DIE AND MEET THEM IN THE OTHER WORLD, I CAN HOLD MY HEAD UP HIGH BEFORE THEM AND SAY...
..."I DID PRETTY WELL, DIDN'T I?"
...
YOU AMAZE ME...

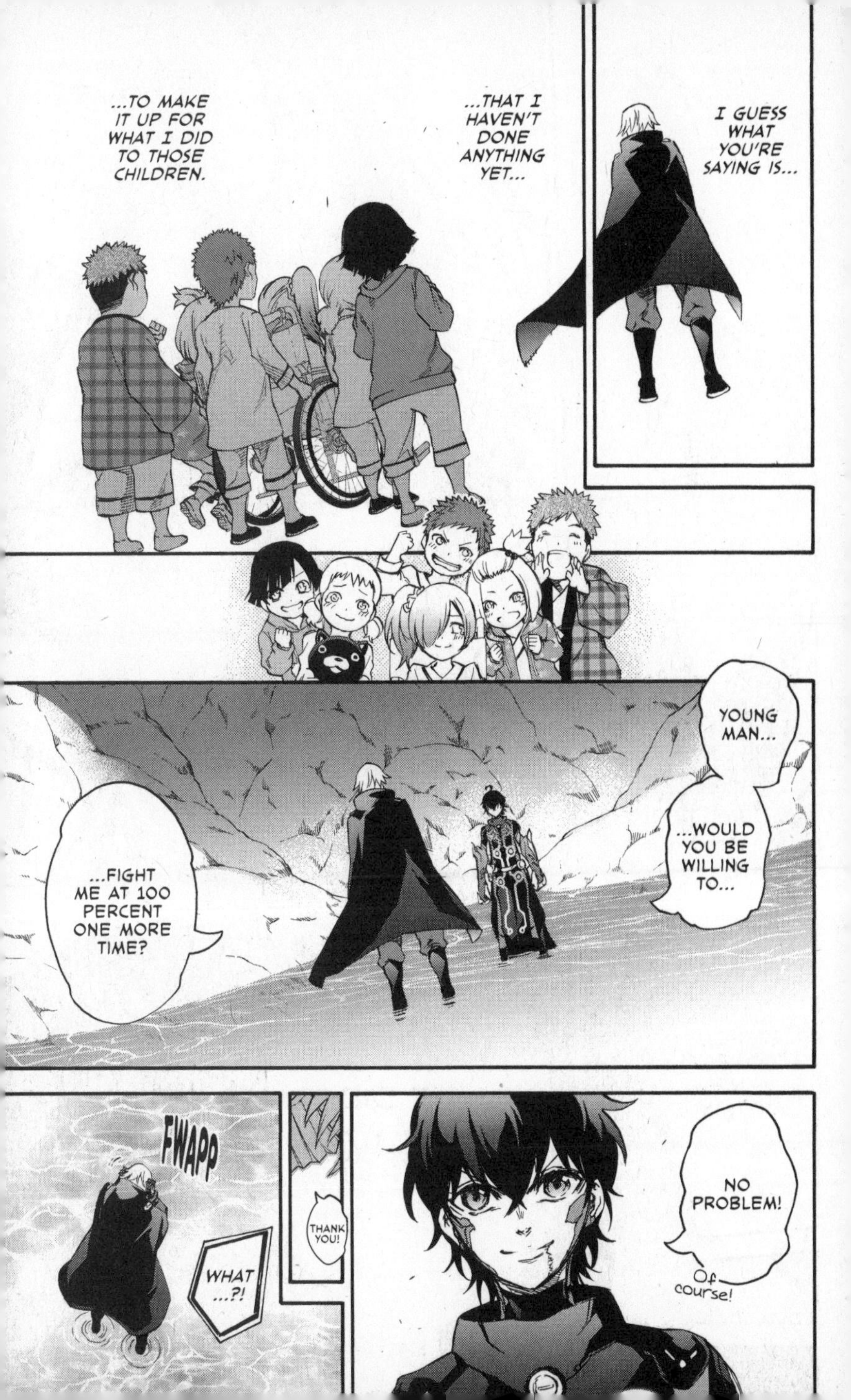
I GUESS WHAT YOU'RE SAYING IS...
...THAT I HAVEN'T DONE ANYTHING YET...
...TO MAKE IT UP FOR WHAT I DID TO THOSE CHILDREN.
YOUNG MAN...
...WOULD YOU BE WILLING TO...
...FIGHT ME AT 100 PERCENT ONE MORE TIME?
NO PROBLEM!
Of course!
THANK YOU!
FWAPP
WHAT ...?!

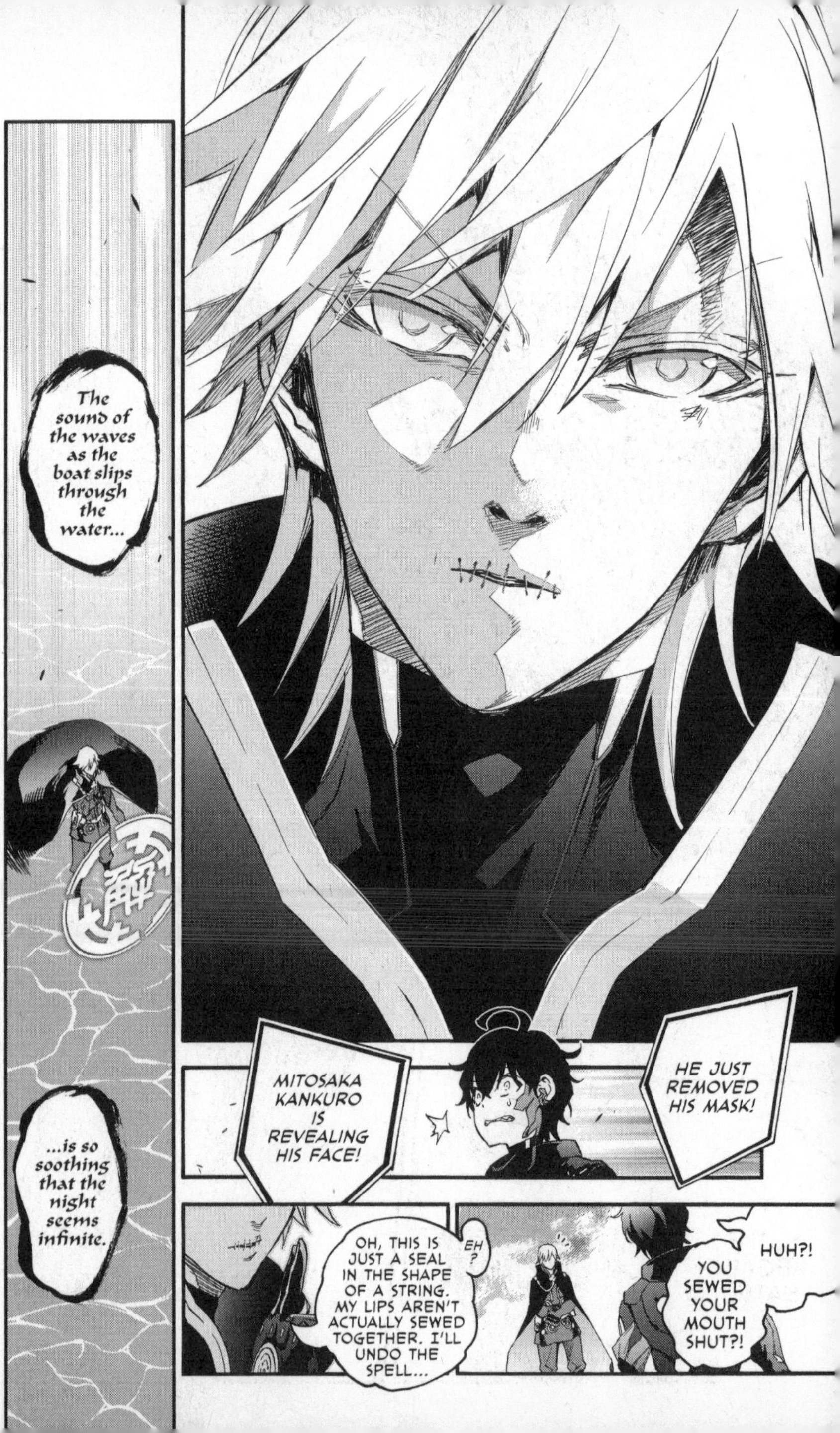
HE JUST REMOVED HIS MASK!
MITOSAKA KANKURO IS REVEALING HIS FACE!
HUH?!
YOU SEWED YOUR MOUTH SHUT?!
EH?
OH, THIS IS JUST A SEAL IN THE SHAPE OF A STRING. MY LIPS AREN'T ACTUALLY SEWED TOGETHER. I'LL UNDO THE SPELL...
The sound of the waves as the boat slips through the water...
...is so soothing that the night seems infinite.

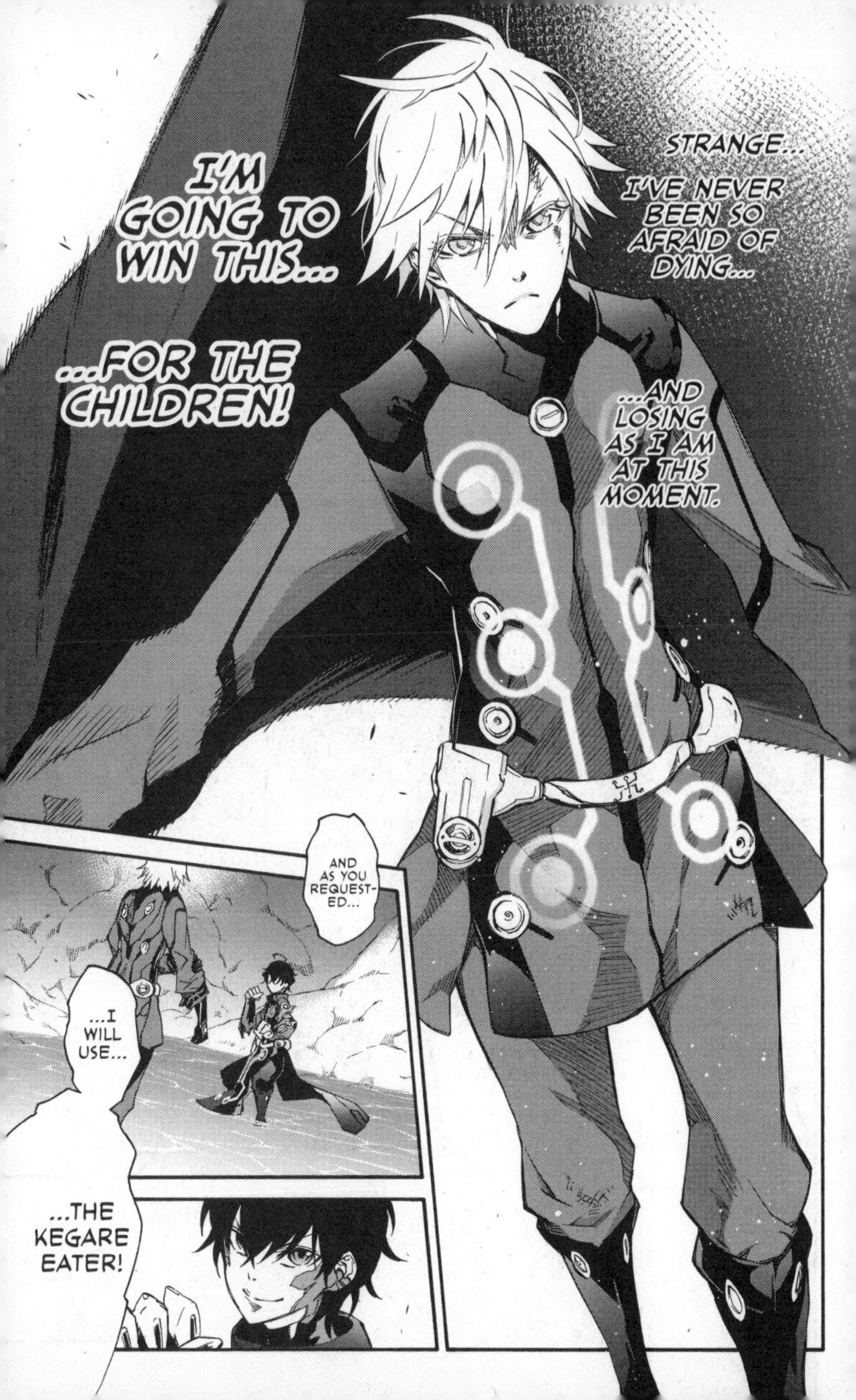
STRANGE...
I'VE NEVER BEEN SO AFRAID OF DYING...
...AND LOSING AS I AM AT THIS MOMENT.
I'M GOING TO WIN THIS...
...FOR THE CHILDREN!
AND AS YOU REQUEST-ED...
...I WILL USE...
...THE KEGARE EATER!

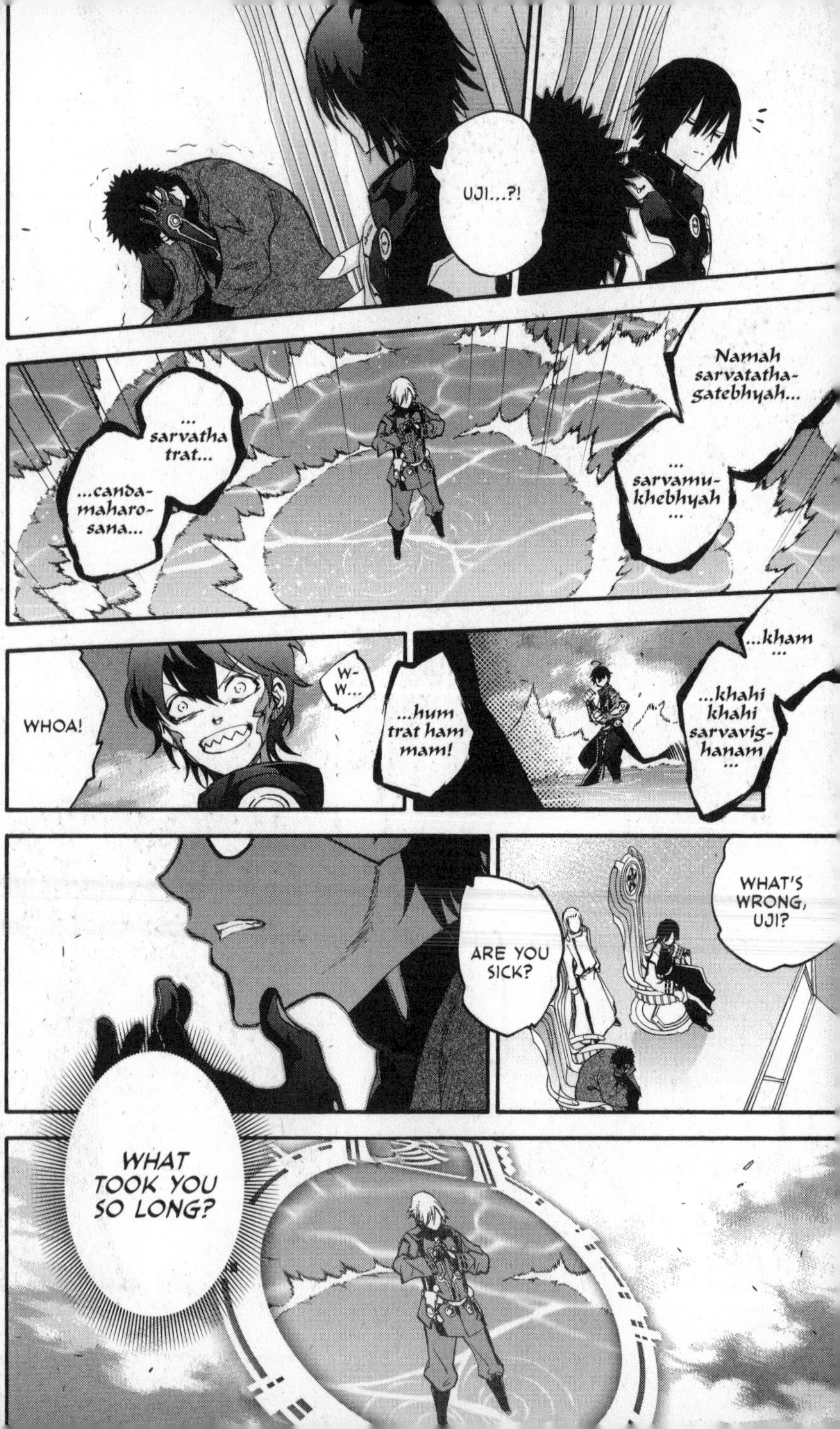
UJI...?!
Namah sarvatatha-gatebhyah...
...sarvamu-khebhyah...
...sarvatha trat...
...canda-maharo-sana...
...kham...
...khahi khahi sarvavig-hanam...
...hum trat ham mam!
W-W...
WHOA!
WHAT'S WRONG, UJI?
ARE YOU SICK?
WHAT TOOK YOU SO LONG?

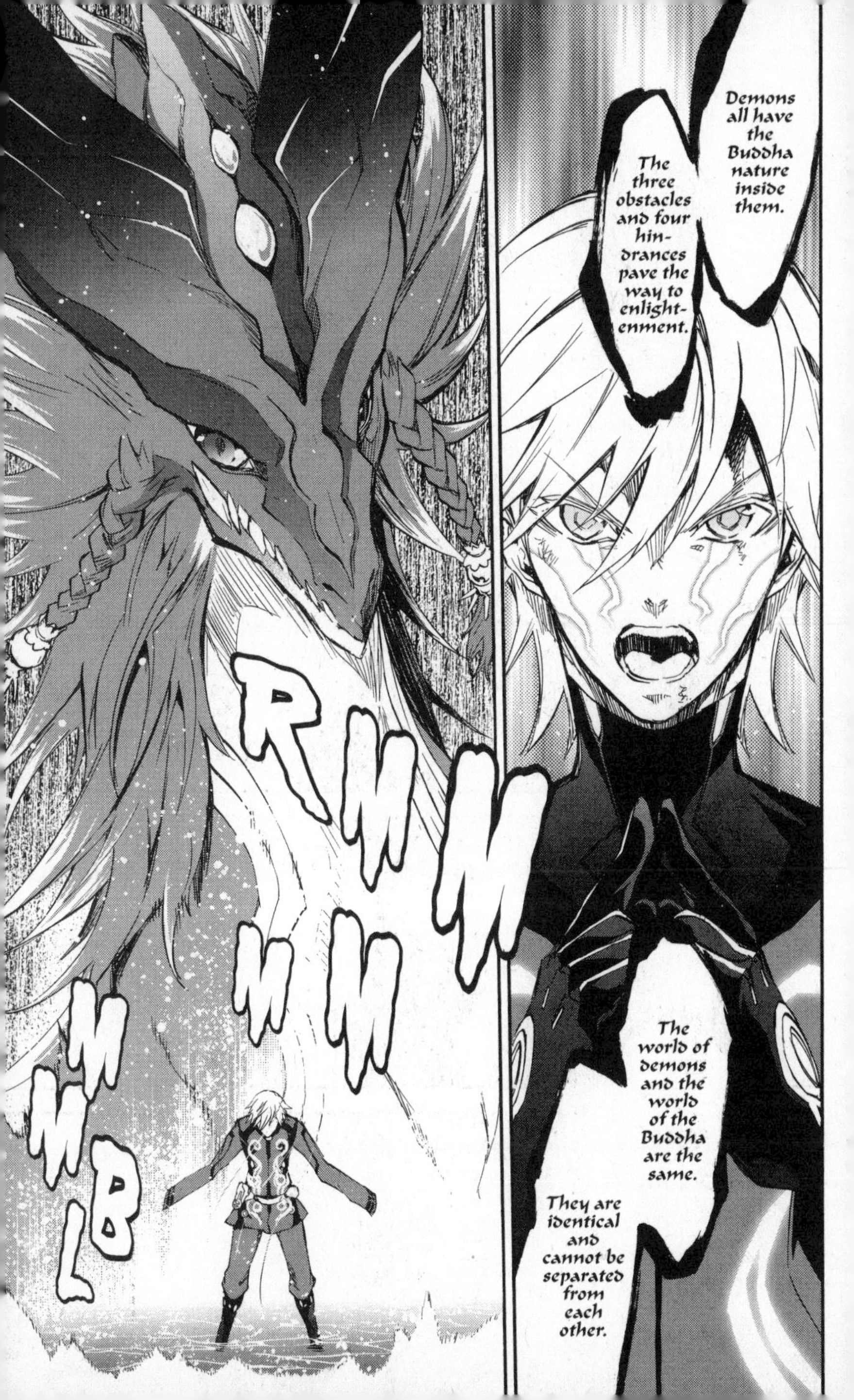
Demons all have the Buddha nature inside them.
The three obstacles and four hin-drances pave the way to enlight-enment.
The world of demons and the world of the Buddha are the same.
They are identical and cannot be separated from each other.
RMMMMM
MMMBL

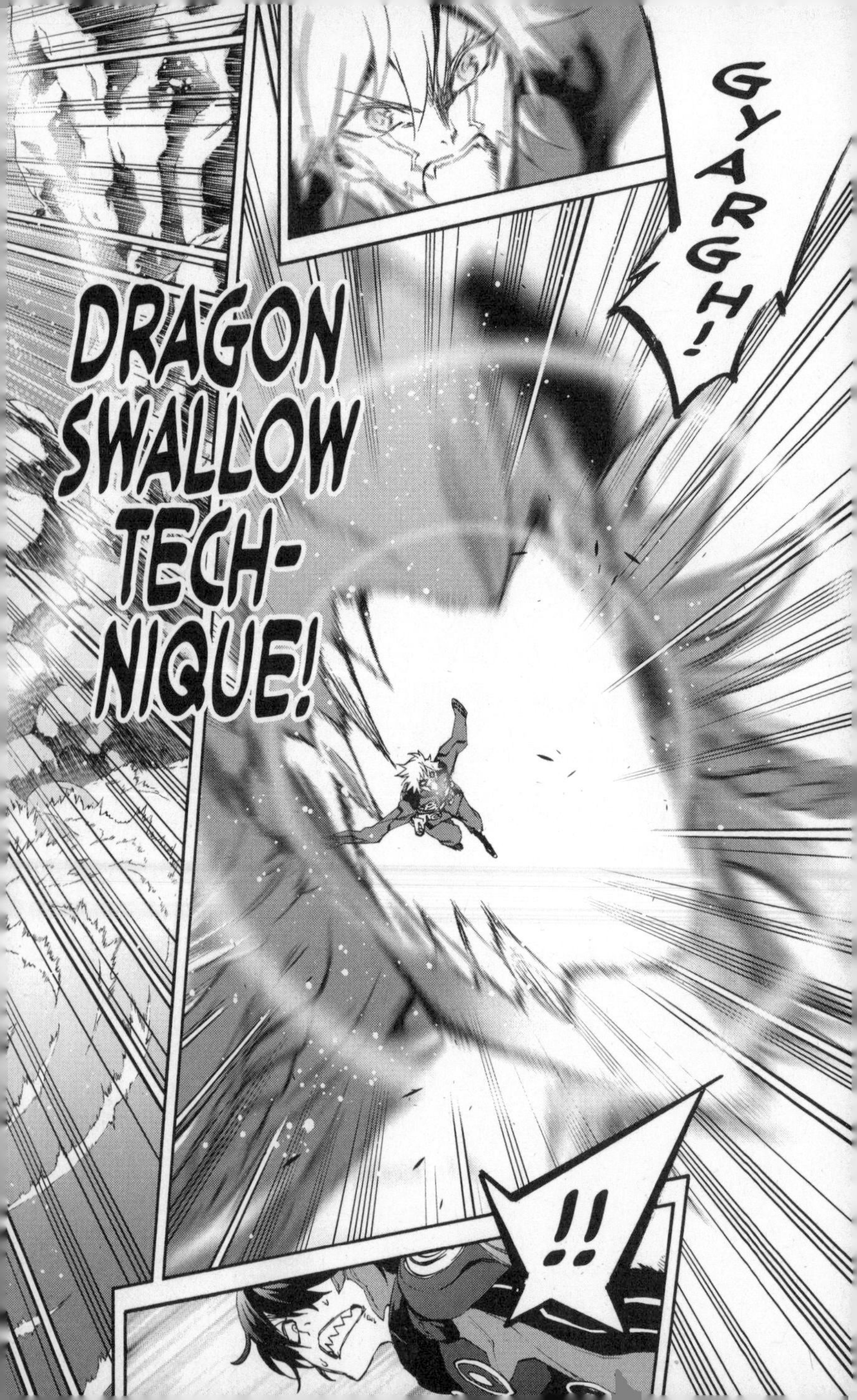
GYARGH!
DRAGON SWALLOW TECH-NIQUE!
!!

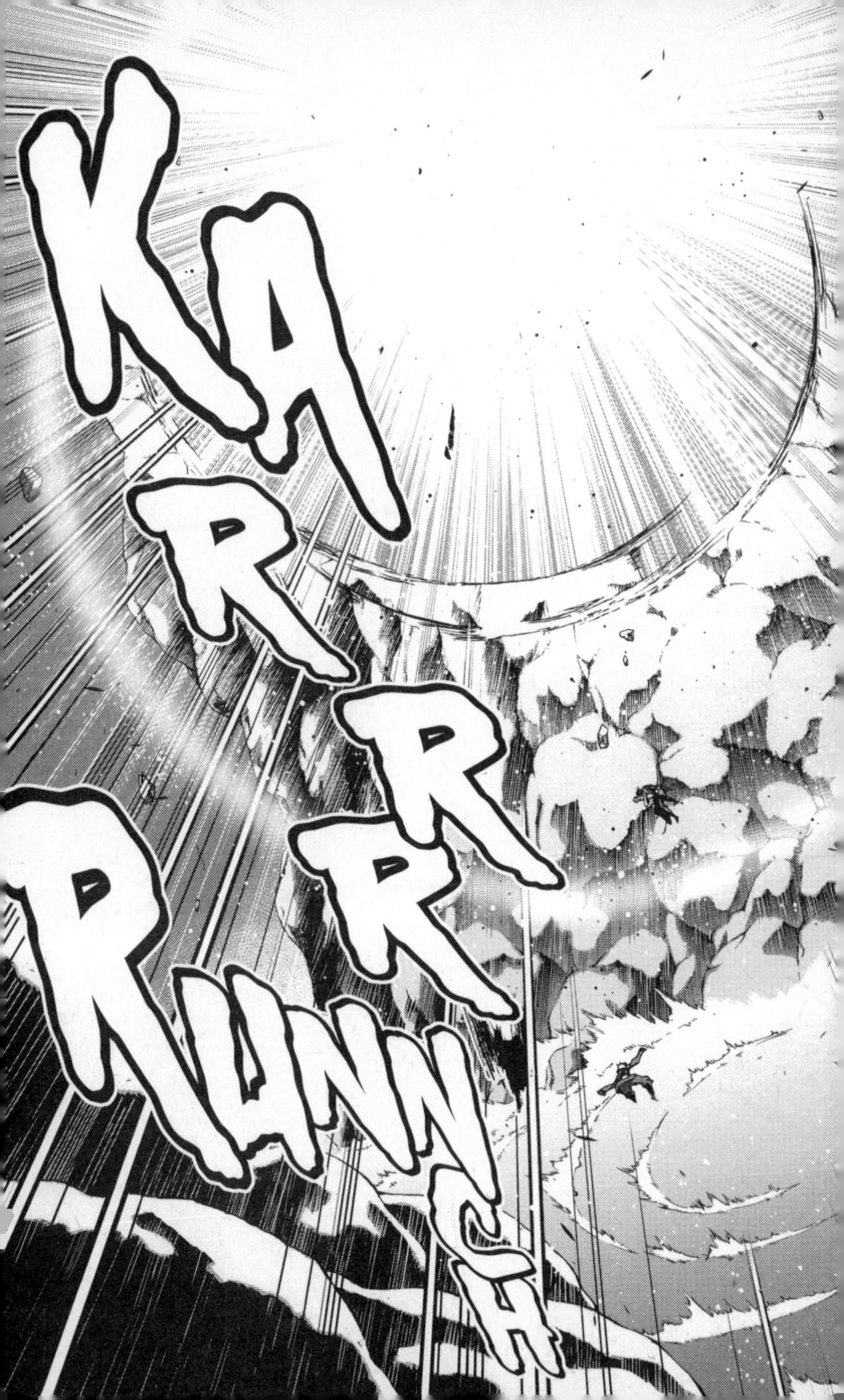
KARRRRUNNCH

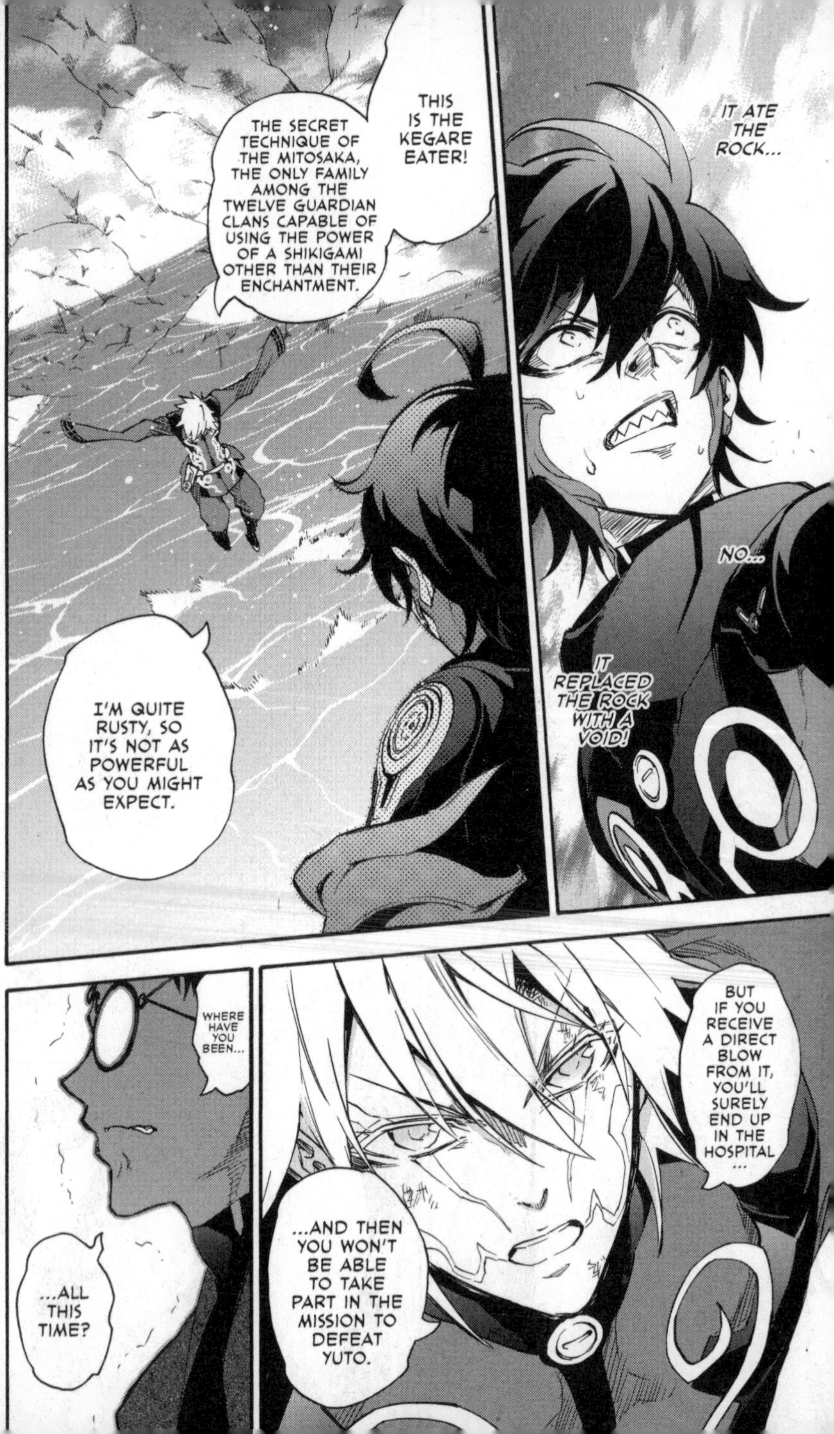
IT ATE THE ROCK...
NO...
IT REPLACED THE ROCK WITH A VOID!
THIS IS THE KEGARE EATER!
THE SECRET TECHNIQUE OF THE MITOSAKA, THE ONLY FAMILY AMONG THE TWELVE GUARDIAN CLANS CAPABLE OF USING THE POWER OF A SHIKIGAMI OTHER THAN THEIR ENCHANTMENT.
I'M QUITE RUSTY, SO IT'S NOT AS POWERFUL AS YOU MIGHT EXPECT.
BUT IF YOU RECEIVE A DIRECT BLOW FROM IT, YOU'LL SURELY END UP IN THE HOSPITAL ...
...AND THEN YOU WON'T BE ABLE TO TAKE PART IN THE MISSION TO DEFEAT YUTO.
WHERE HAVE YOU BEEN...
...ALL THIS TIME?

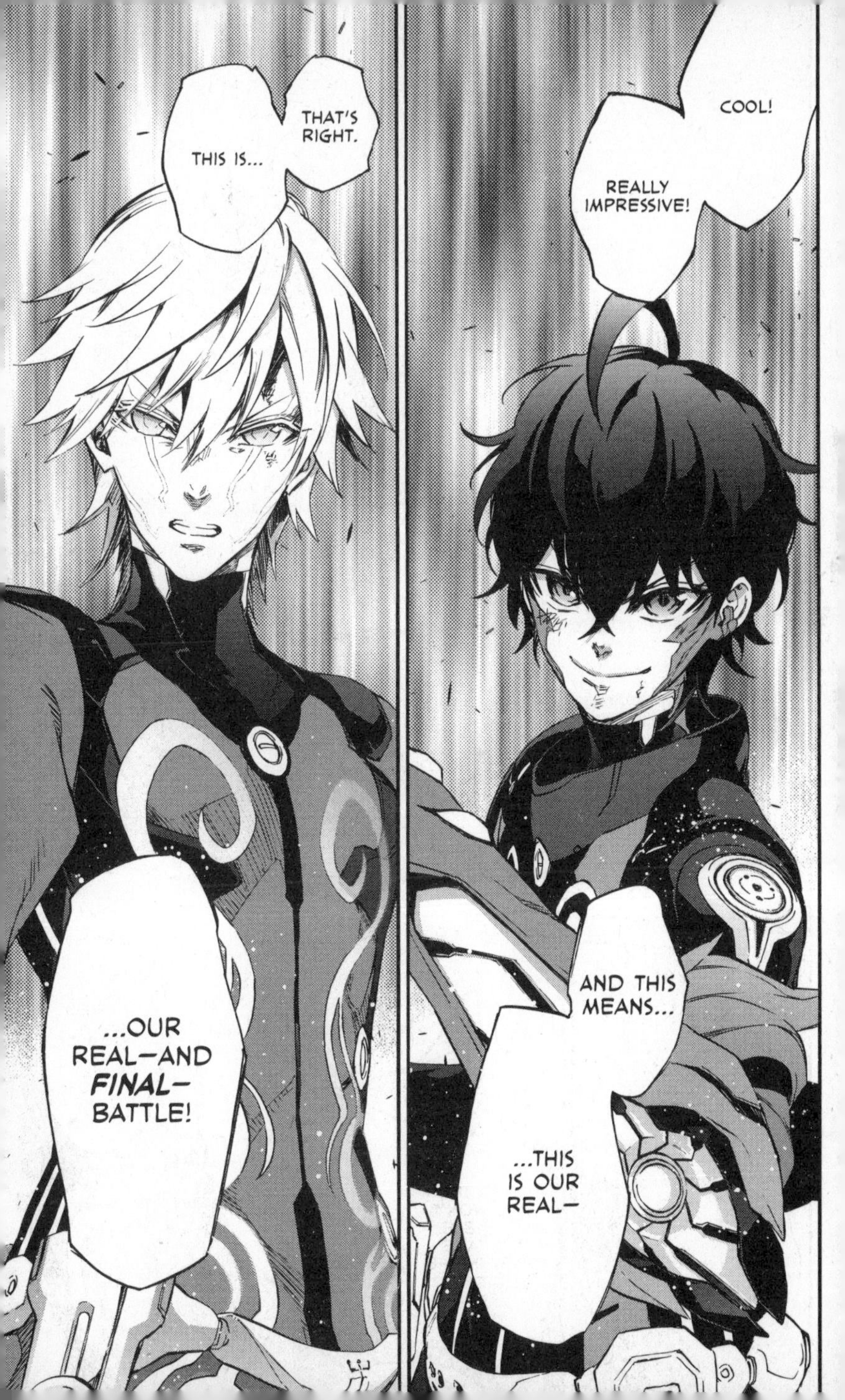
COOL!
REALLY IMPRESSIVE!
AND THIS MEANS...
...THIS IS OUR REAL—
THAT'S RIGHT.
THIS IS...
...OUR REAL—AND *FINAL*—BATTLE!

QQnyoritsuryo!
Question Corner

KRKK
GYRAAGH...
KRKKL
KRKKL

Q Wouldn't the burning version of Ohagi Dumpling Man get scorched and turn to ashes? Can it turn itself back to normal afterwards?
(From Chinu)

A It's a shikigami, so it's fine.

FROM THIS DAY ON, I'M GONNA TAKE THIS GIRL ON AS MY DISCIPLE...
...AND TRAIN HER MYSELF!!

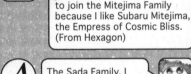

Q Which of the Twelve Guardian Families would you want to join, Sukeno Sensei? I want to join the Mitejima Family because I like Subaru Mitejima, the Empress of Cosmic Bliss.
(From Hexagon)

A The Sada Family, I think... I'd like to hand towels and sports drinks to Sakura.
(I wouldn't fight.)

CHIKO?
HUH?
BIG BROTHER!

Q Why does Shimon call Sayo "Chiko"? (From Kaedebato)

A Shimon misread Sayo's name as Chiyo, so he called her Chiyo for a while. Because of that, Baby Sayo started calling herself Chi...which eventually morphed into the nickname Chiko.

Request R I love Kamui, so could you make January 15 the day he became a Kegare, please? By the way, that's my birthday.
(From Haruka Arita)

A Sure!

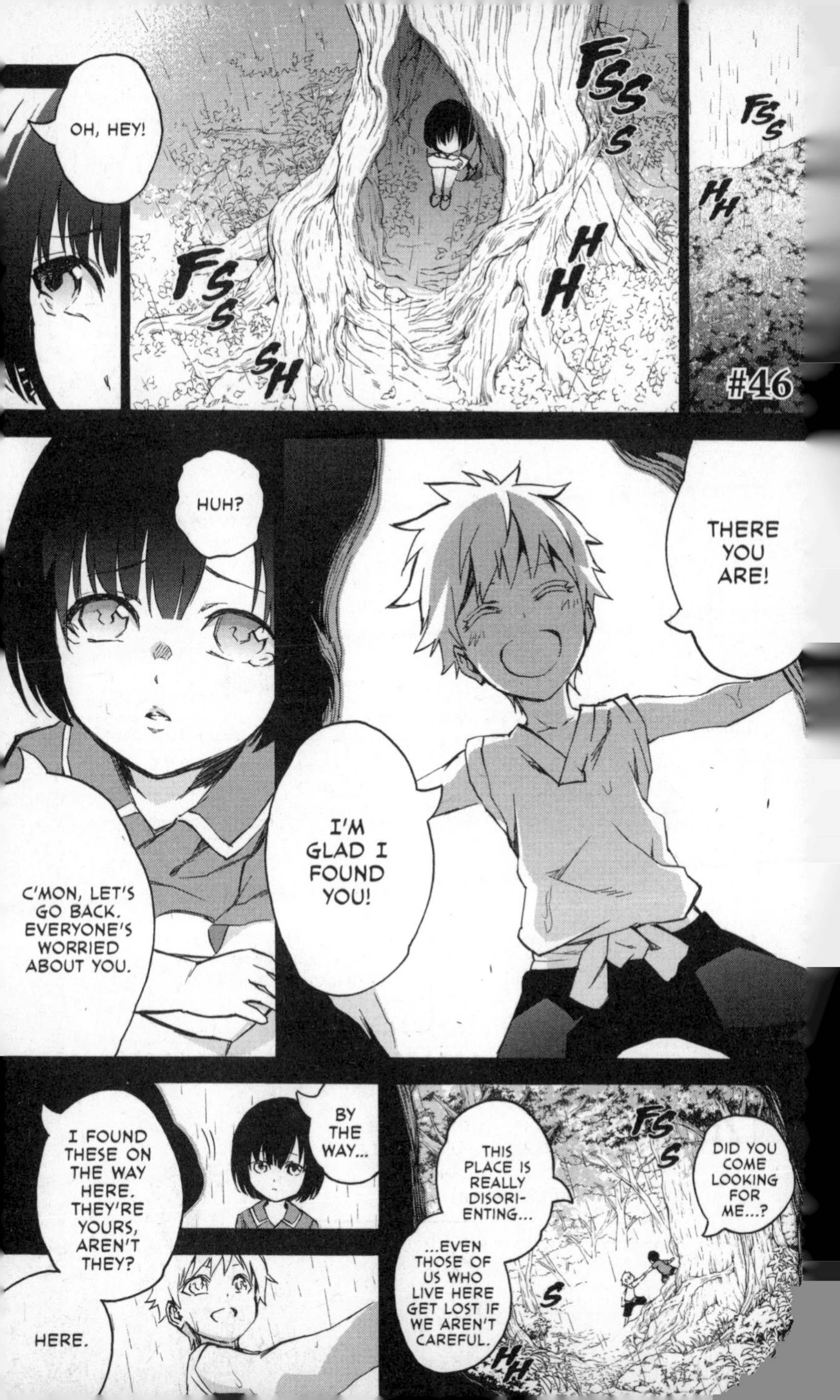
FSS
HH
#46
FSSS
HHH
FSS
SH
OH, HEY!
THERE YOU ARE!
I'M GLAD I FOUND YOU!
HUH?
C'MON, LET'S GO BACK. EVERYONE'S WORRIED ABOUT YOU.
DID YOU COME LOOKING FOR ME...?
FSS
THIS PLACE IS REALLY DISORI-ENTING...
...EVEN THOSE OF US WHO LIVE HERE GET LOST IF WE AREN'T CAREFUL.
S
HH
BY THE WAY...
I FOUND THESE ON THE WAY HERE. THEY'RE YOURS, AREN'T THEY?
HERE.

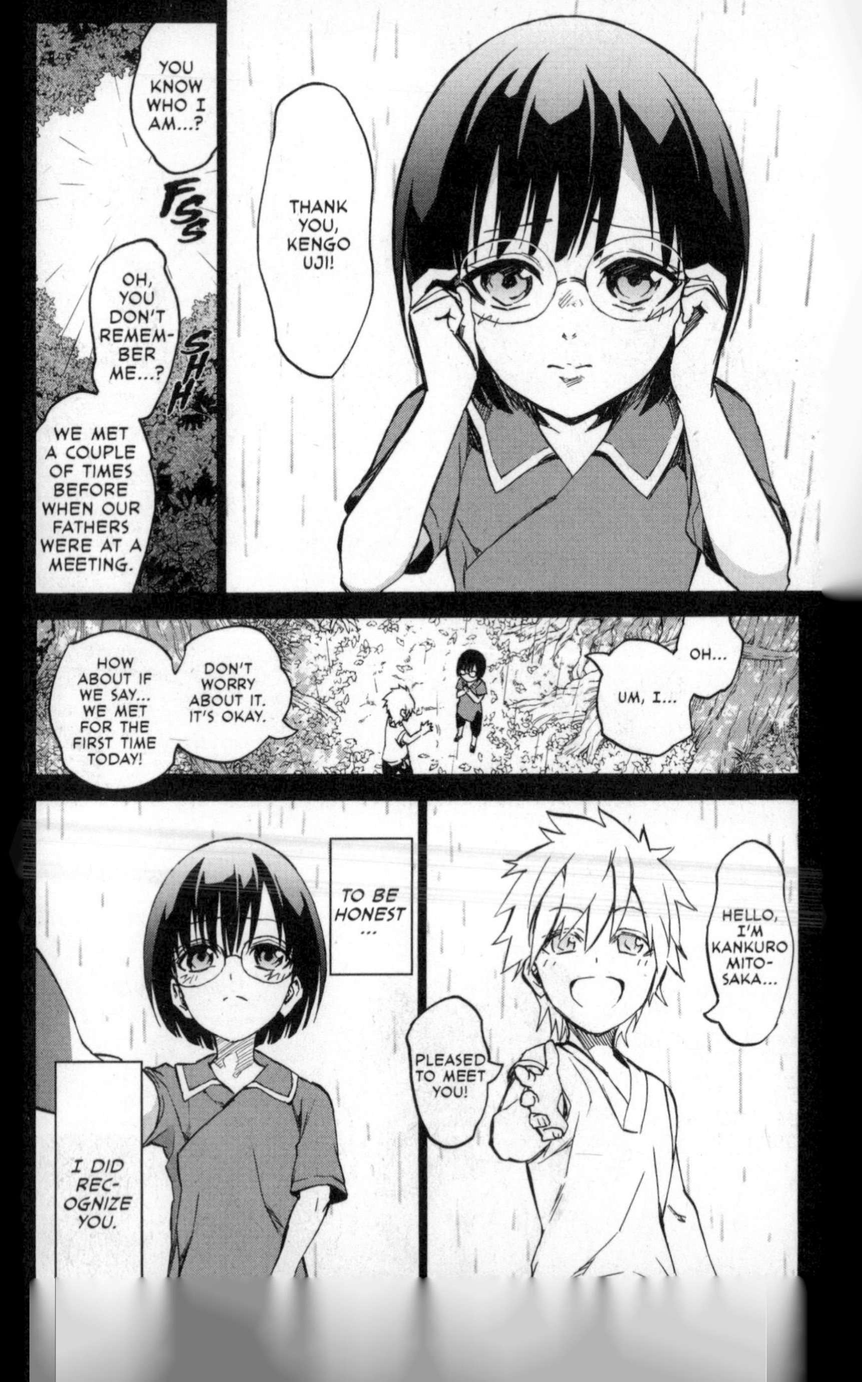
THANK YOU, KENGO UJI!
YOU KNOW WHO I AM...?
FSS
OH, YOU DON'T REMEMBER ME...?
SHH
WE MET A COUPLE OF TIMES BEFORE WHEN OUR FATHERS WERE AT A MEETING.
OH...
UM, I...
DON'T WORRY ABOUT IT. IT'S OKAY.
HOW ABOUT IF WE SAY... WE MET FOR THE FIRST TIME TODAY!
HELLO, I'M KANKURO MITOSAKA...
PLEASED TO MEET YOU!
TO BE HONEST...
I DID RECOGNIZE YOU.

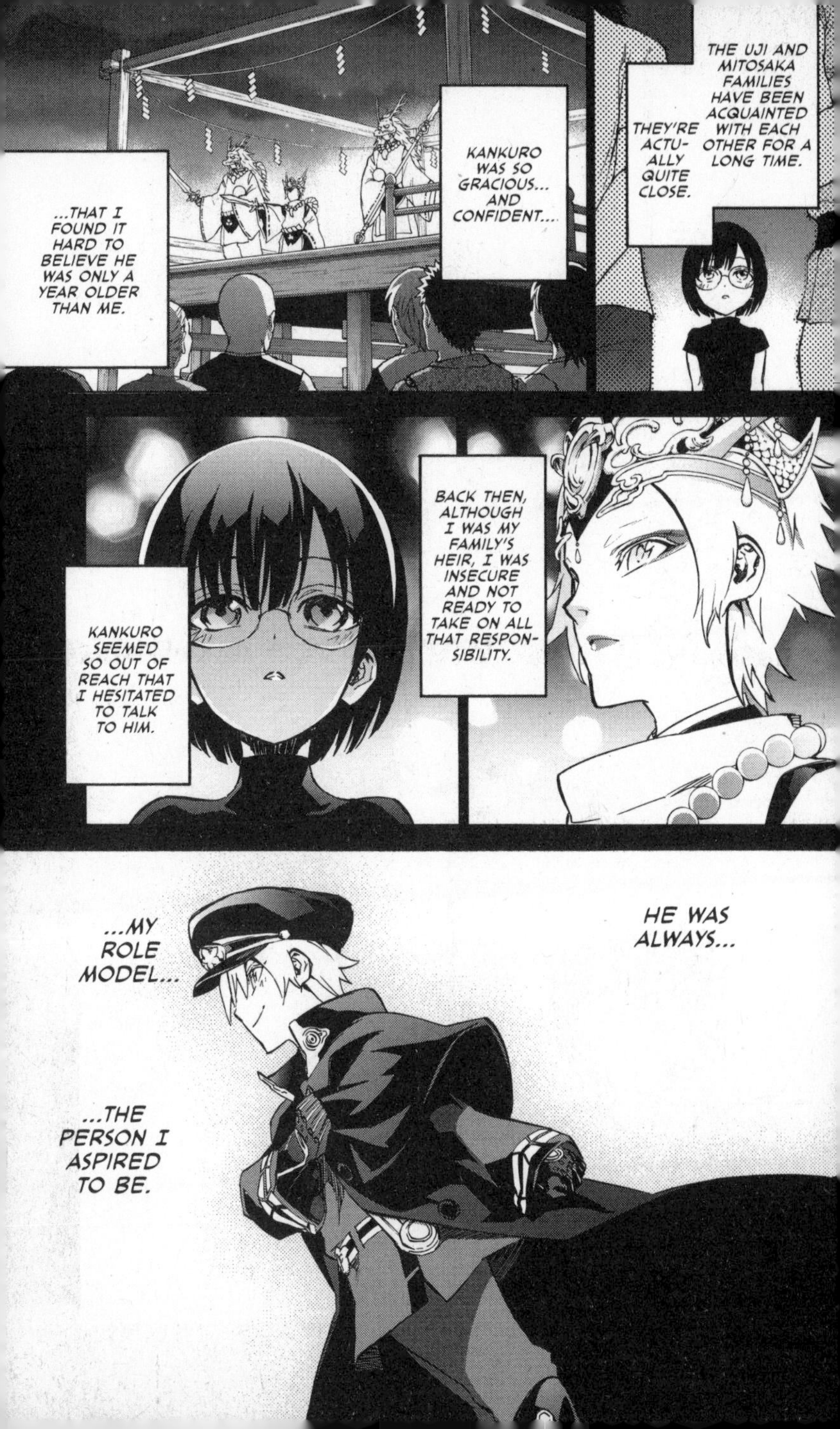
THE UJI AND MITOSAKA FAMILIES HAVE BEEN ACQUAINTED WITH EACH OTHER FOR A LONG TIME.
THEY'RE ACTU-ALLY QUITE CLOSE.
KANKURO WAS SO GRACIOUS... AND CONFIDENT...
...THAT I FOUND IT HARD TO BELIEVE HE WAS ONLY A YEAR OLDER THAN ME.
BACK THEN, ALTHOUGH I WAS MY FAMILY'S HEIR, I WAS INSECURE AND NOT READY TO TAKE ON ALL THAT RESPON-SIBILITY.
KANKURO SEEMED SO OUT OF REACH THAT I HESITATED TO TALK TO HIM.
HE WAS ALWAYS...
...MY ROLE MODEL...
...THE PERSON I ASPIRED TO BE.

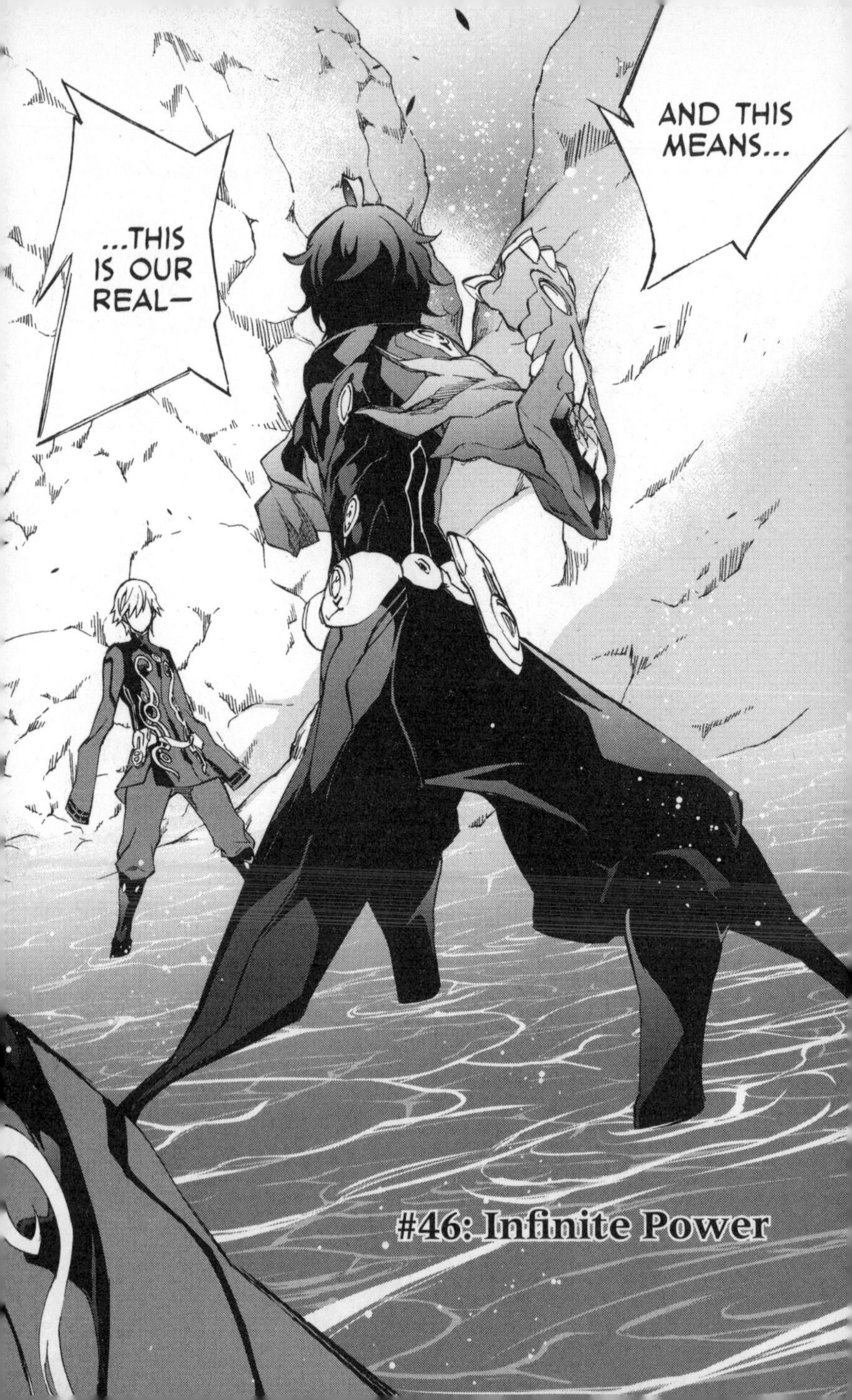
AND THIS MEANS...
...THIS IS OUR REAL—
#46: Infinite Power

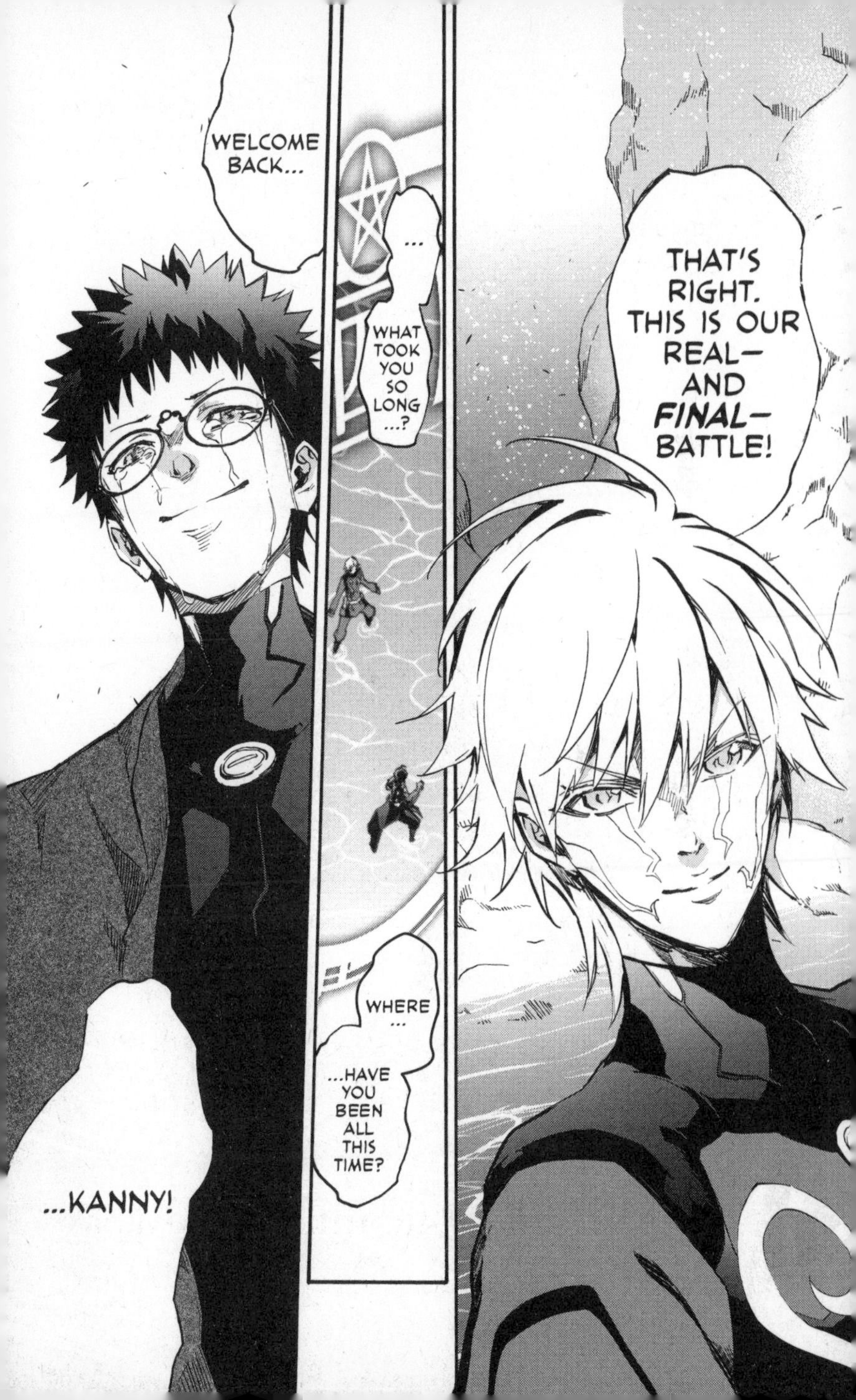
THAT'S RIGHT. THIS IS OUR REAL— AND *FINAL*— BATTLE!
...
WHAT TOOK YOU SO LONG ...?
WHERE ...
...HAVE YOU BEEN ALL THIS TIME?
WELCOME BACK...
...KANNY!

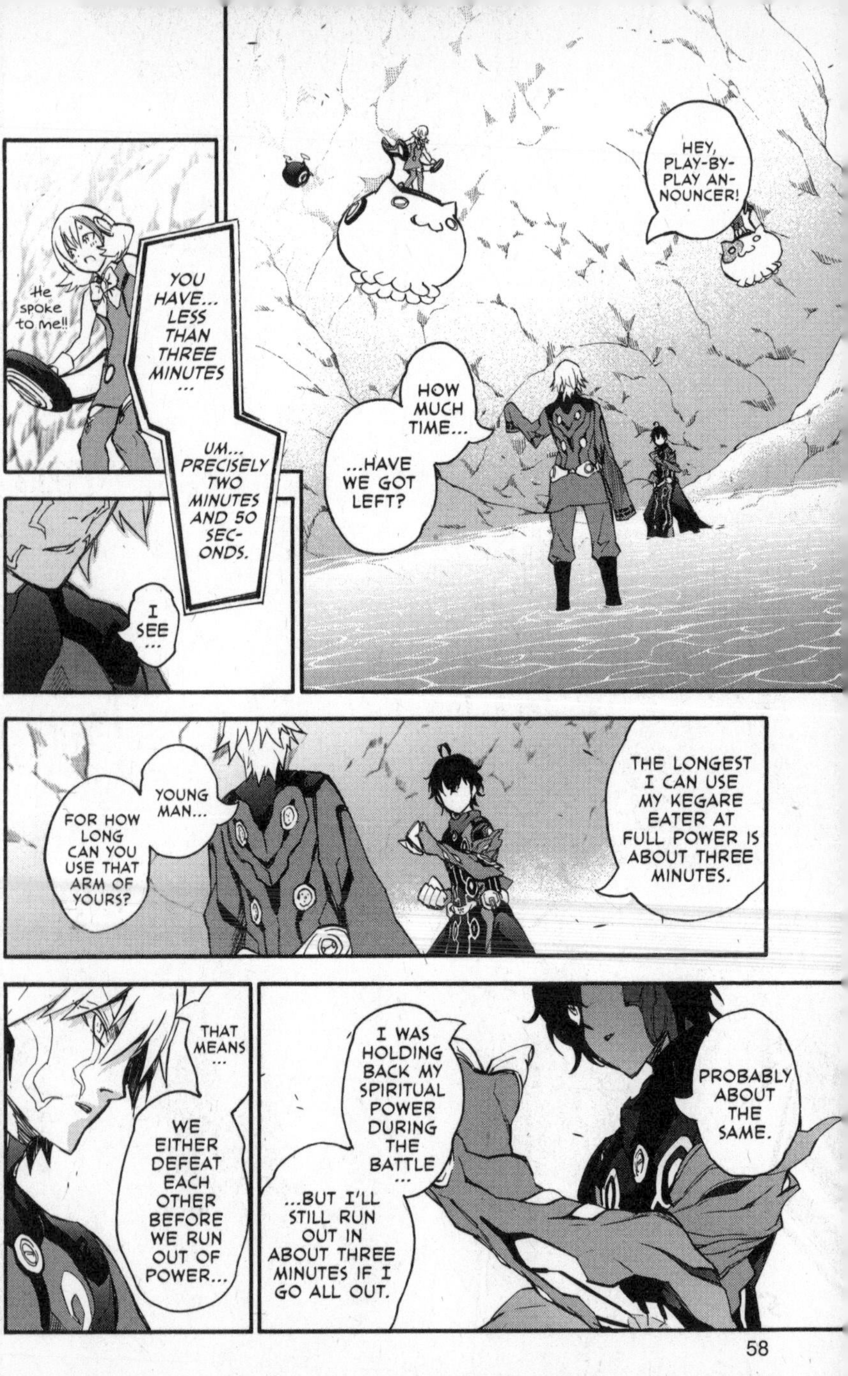
HEY, PLAY-BY-PLAY AN-NOUNCER!
HOW MUCH TIME...
...HAVE WE GOT LEFT?
YOU HAVE... LESS THAN THREE MINUTES...
He spoke to me!!
UM... PRECISELY TWO MINUTES AND 50 SEC-ONDS.
I SEE...
YOUNG MAN...
FOR HOW LONG CAN YOU USE THAT ARM OF YOURS?
THE LONGEST I CAN USE MY KEGARE EATER AT FULL POWER IS ABOUT THREE MINUTES.
PROBABLY ABOUT THE SAME.
I WAS HOLDING BACK MY SPIRITUAL POWER DURING THE BATTLE...
...BUT I'LL STILL RUN OUT IN ABOUT THREE MINUTES IF I GO ALL OUT.
THAT MEANS...
WE EITHER DEFEAT EACH OTHER BEFORE WE RUN OUT OF POWER...

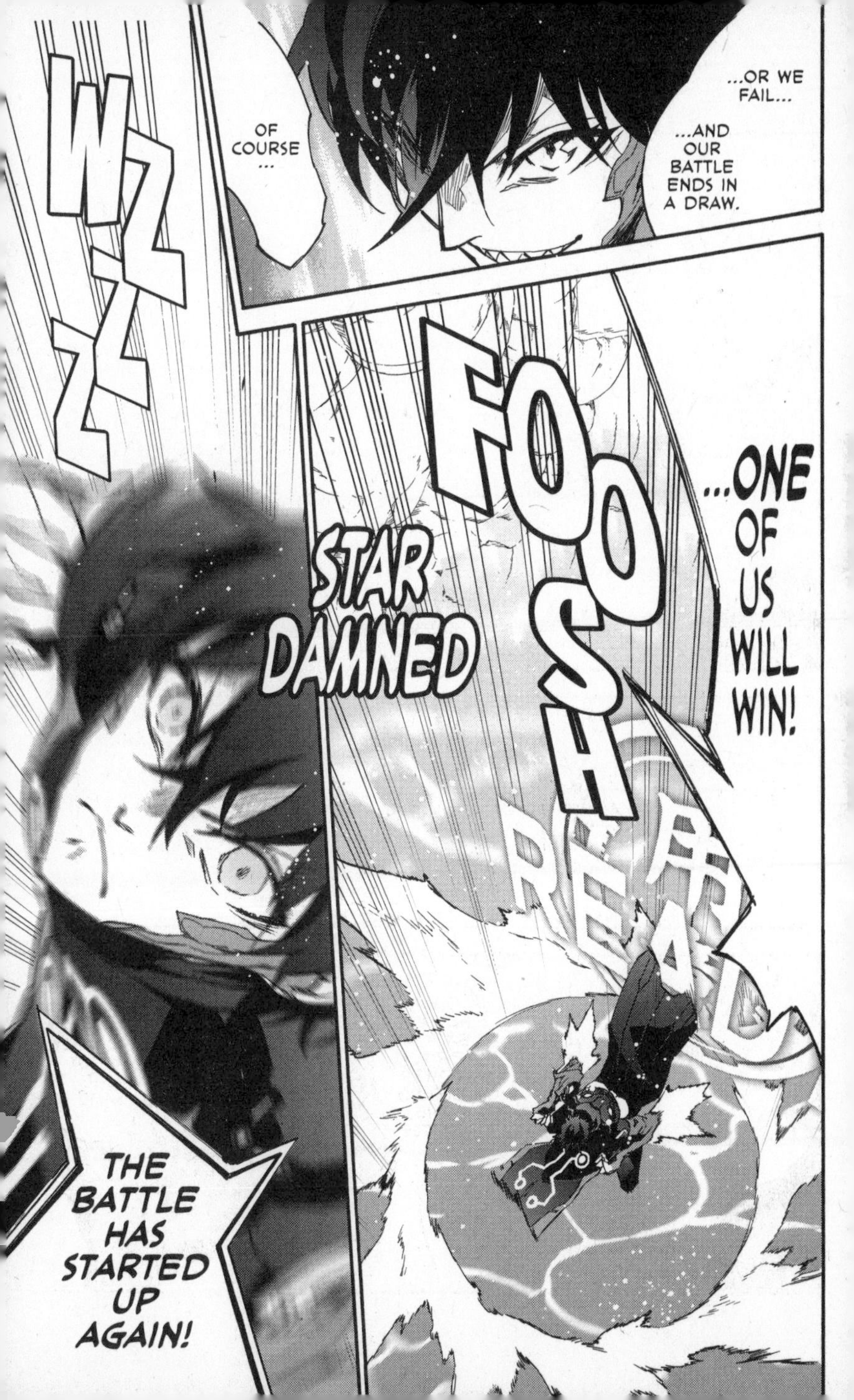
...OR WE FAIL...
...AND OUR BATTLE ENDS IN A DRAW.
OF COURSE ...
...ONE OF US WILL WIN!
FOOSH
STAR DAMNED
WZZZ
THE BATTLE HAS STARTED UP AGAIN!

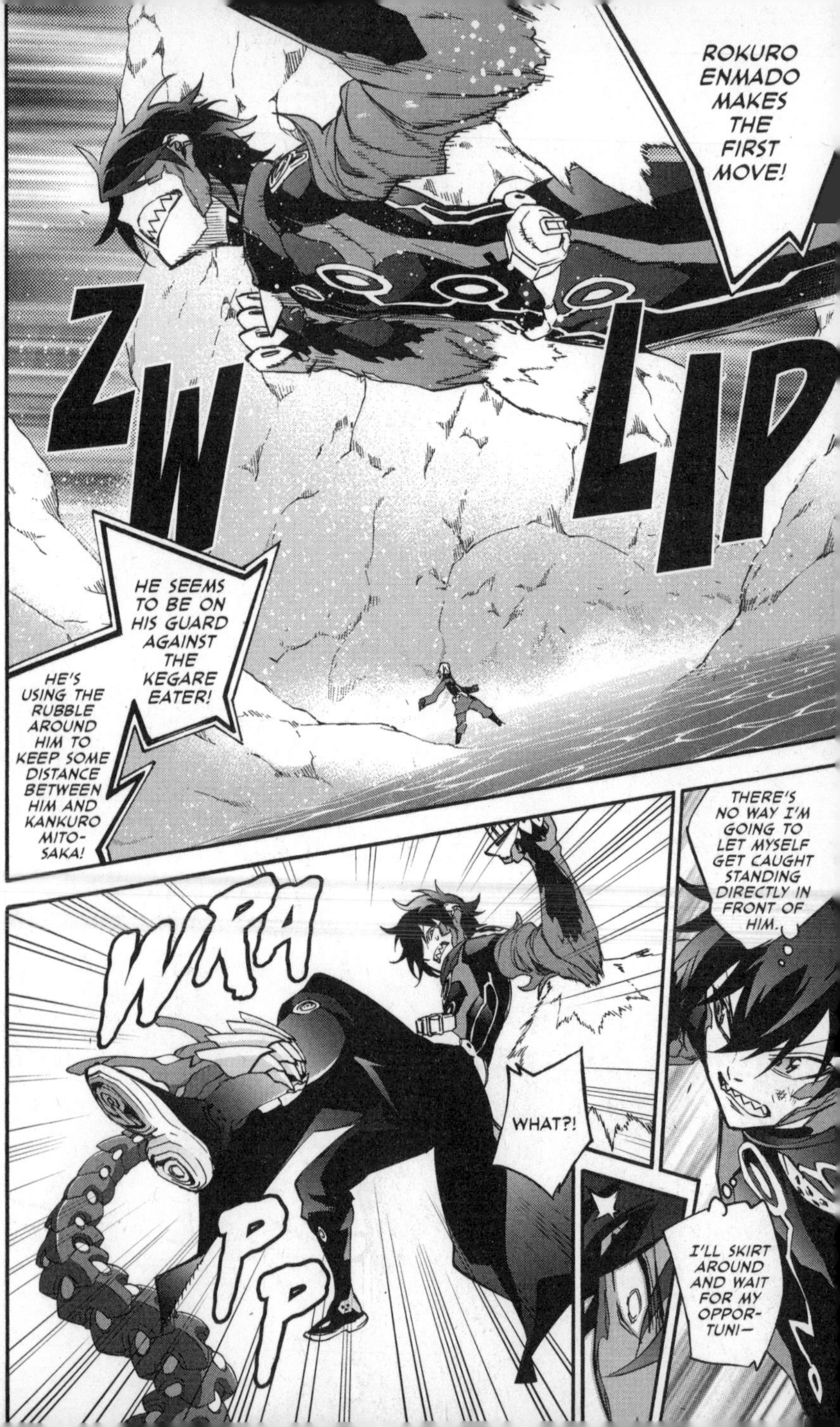
ROKURO ENMADO MAKES THE FIRST MOVE!
ZWLIP
HE SEEMS TO BE ON HIS GUARD AGAINST THE KEGARE EATER!
HE'S USING THE RUBBLE AROUND HIM TO KEEP SOME DISTANCE BETWEEN HIM AND KANKURO MITO-SAKA!
THERE'S NO WAY I'M GOING TO LET MYSELF GET CAUGHT STANDING DIRECTLY IN FRONT OF HIM.
I'LL SKIRT AROUND AND WAIT FOR MY OPPOR-TUNI—
WRAP
WHAT?!
P
P

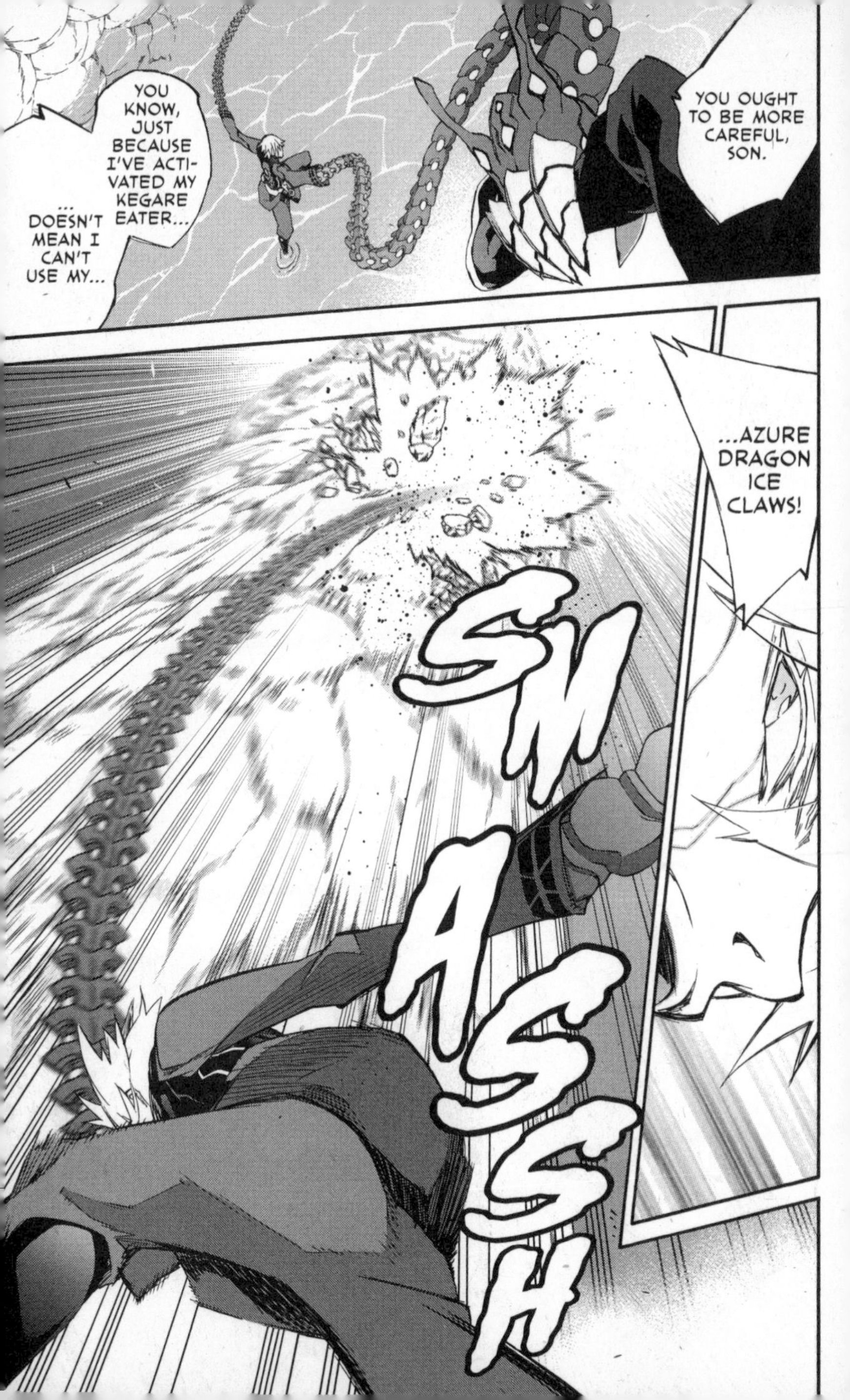
YOU OUGHT TO BE MORE CAREFUL, SON.
YOU KNOW, JUST BECAUSE I'VE ACTIVATED MY KEGARE EATER...
...DOESN'T MEAN I CAN'T USE MY...
...AZURE DRAGON ICE CLAWS!
SMASSH

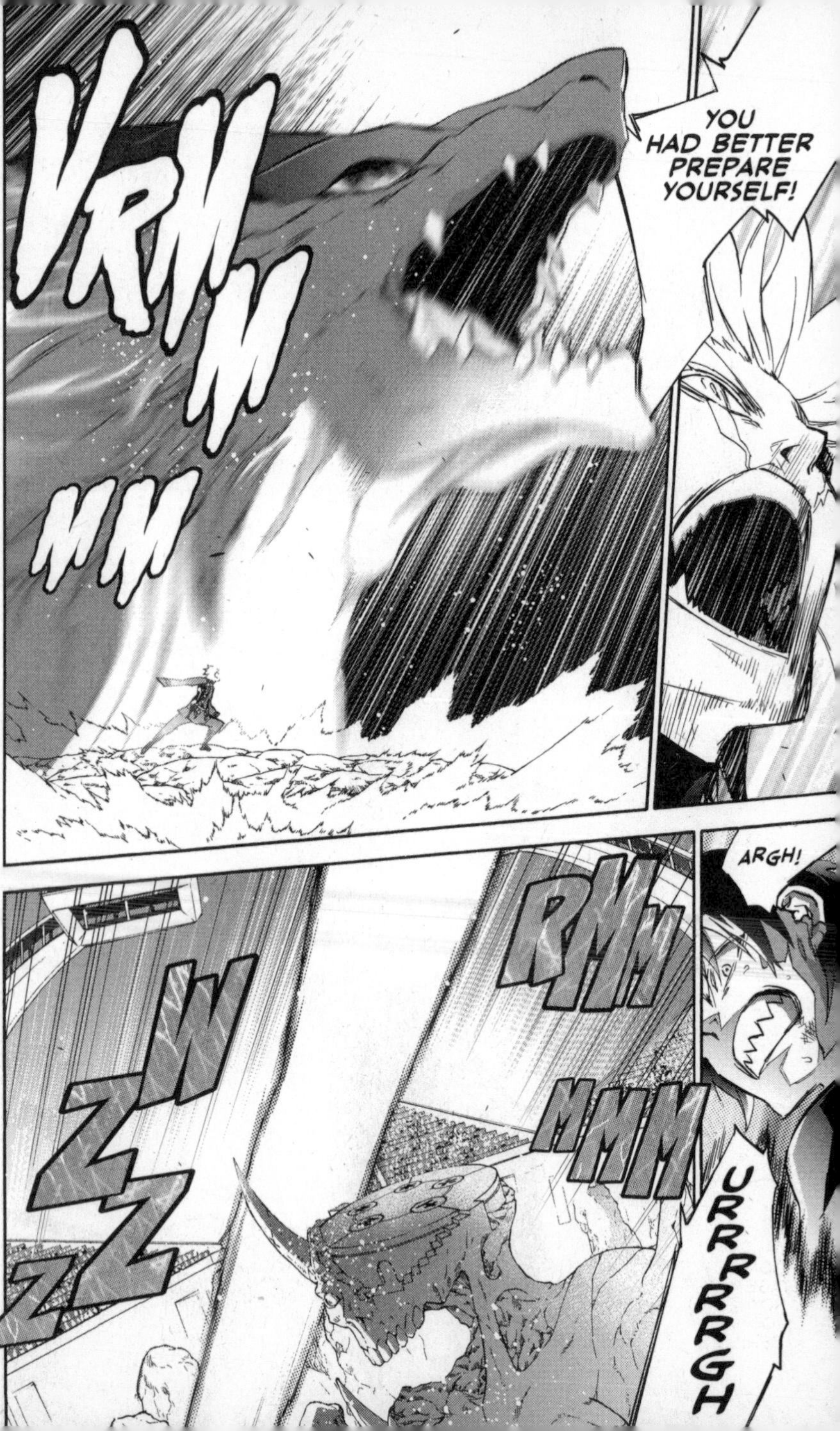
YOU HAD BETTER PREPARE YOURSELF!
VRMMMM
ARGH!
URRRRRGH
RMMMMM
ZZZIN

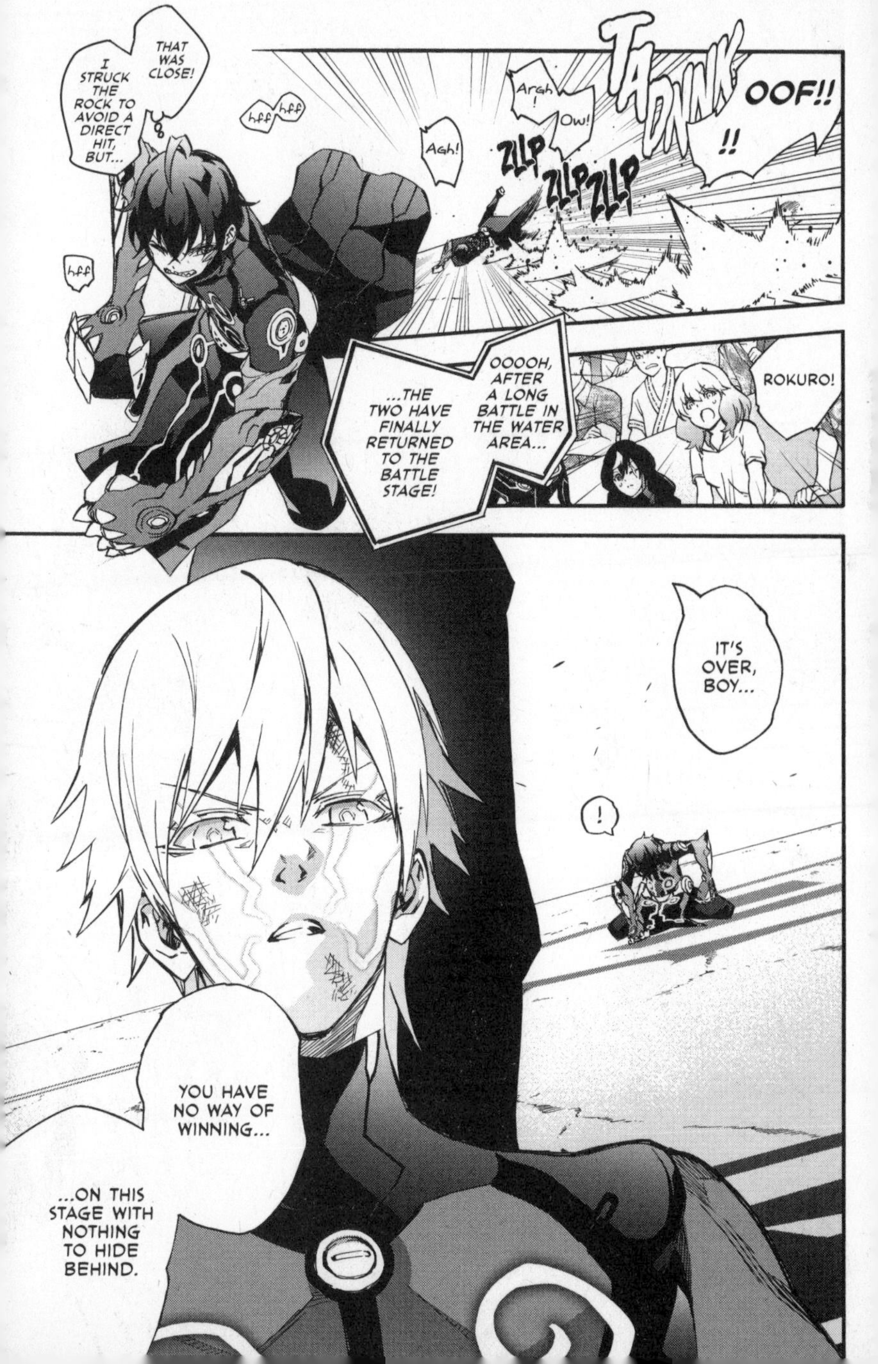
OOF!!
!!
TADNNK
Argh!
Ow!
ZLLP ZLLP ZLLP
Agh!
hff hff
THAT WAS CLOSE!
I STRUCK THE ROCK TO AVOID A DIRECT HIT, BUT...
hff
ROKURO!
OOOOH, AFTER A LONG BATTLE IN THE WATER AREA...
...THE TWO HAVE FINALLY RETURNED TO THE BATTLE STAGE!
IT'S OVER, BOY...
!
YOU HAVE NO WAY OF WINNING...
...ON THIS STAGE WITH NOTHING TO HIDE BEHIND.

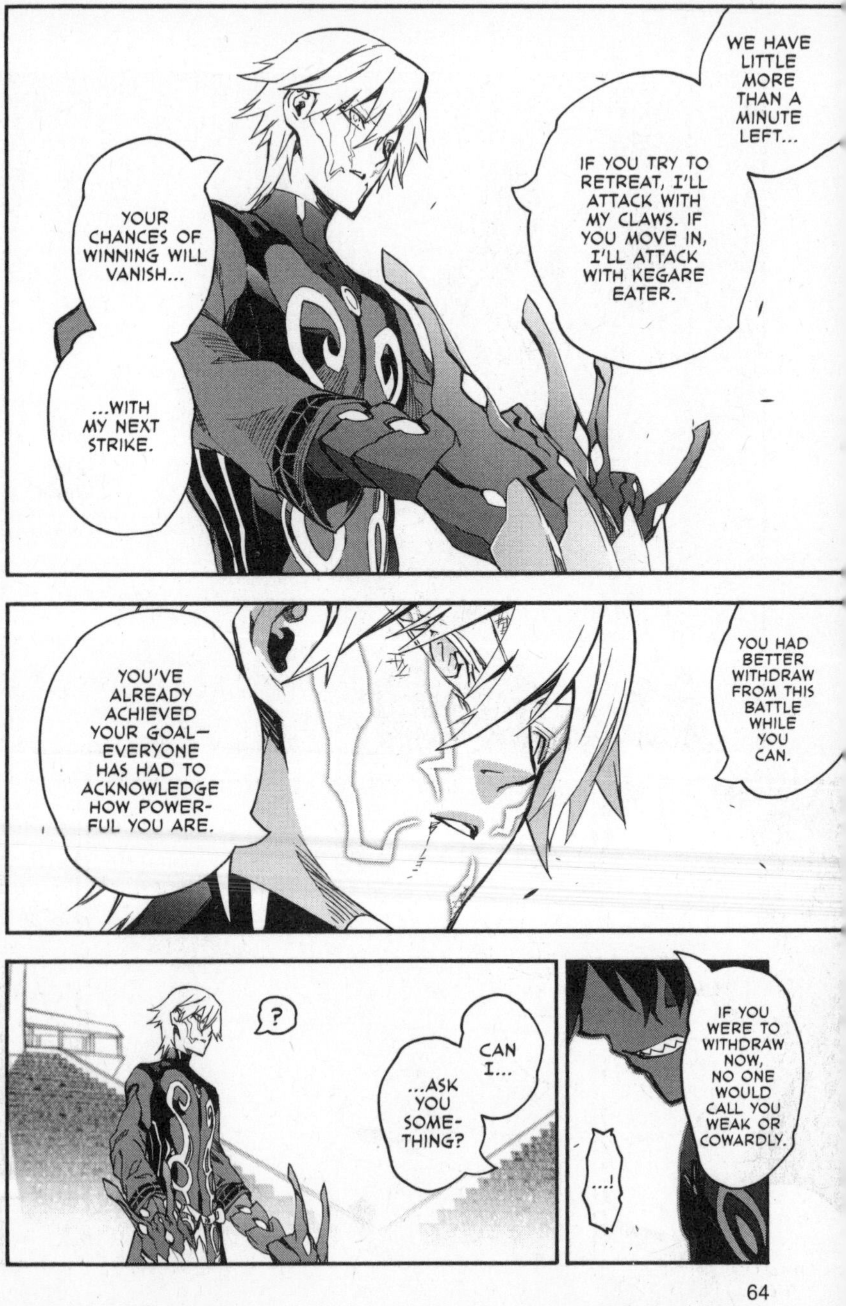
WE HAVE LITTLE MORE THAN A MINUTE LEFT...
IF YOU TRY TO RETREAT, I'LL ATTACK WITH MY CLAWS. IF YOU MOVE IN, I'LL ATTACK WITH KEGARE EATER.
YOUR CHANCES OF WINNING WILL VANISH...
...WITH MY NEXT STRIKE.
YOU HAD BETTER WITHDRAW FROM THIS BATTLE WHILE YOU CAN.
YOU'VE ALREADY ACHIEVED YOUR GOAL—EVERYONE HAS HAD TO ACKNOWLEDGE HOW POWER-FUL YOU ARE.
IF YOU WERE TO WITHDRAW NOW, NO ONE WOULD CALL YOU WEAK OR COWARDLY.
...!
CAN I...
...ASK YOU SOMETHING?
?

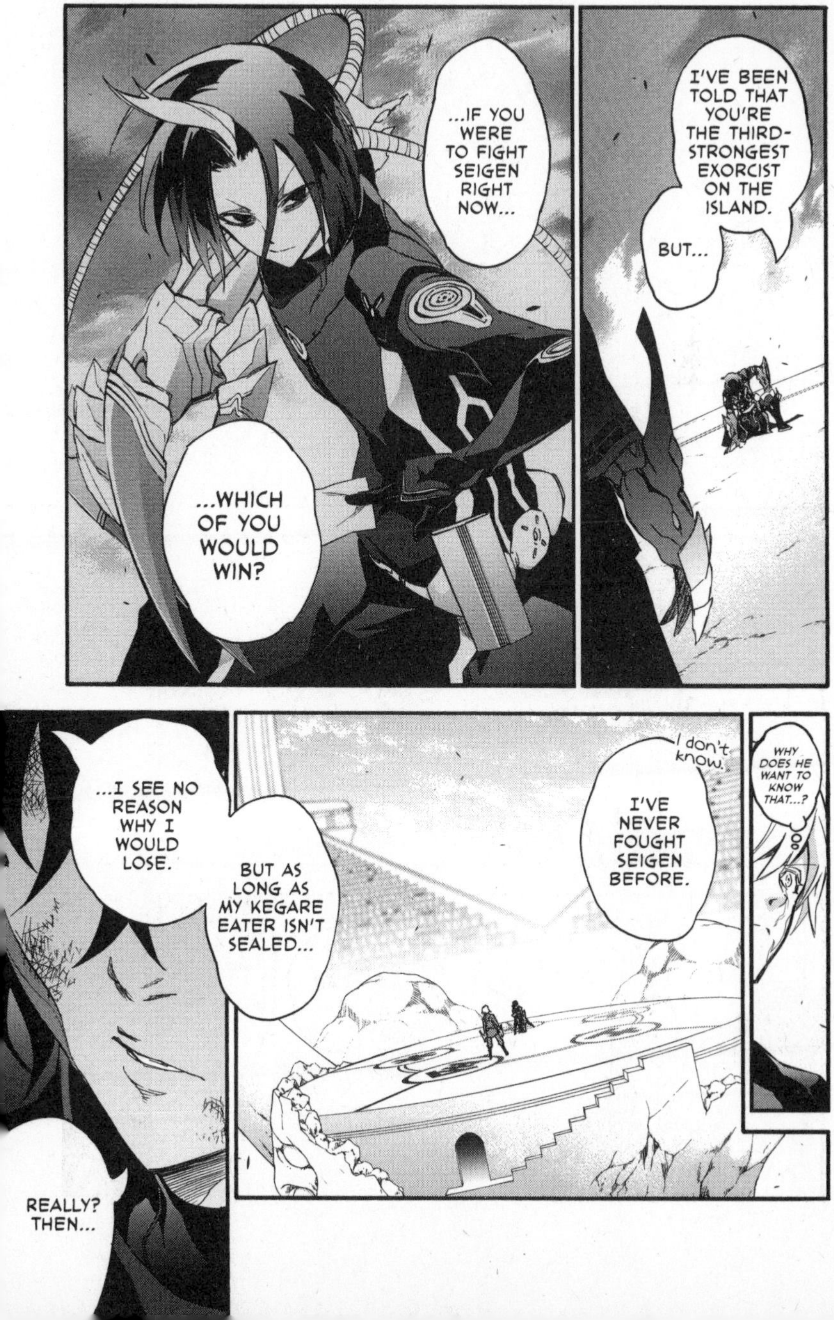
I'VE BEEN TOLD THAT YOU'RE THE THIRD-STRONGEST EXORCIST ON THE ISLAND.
BUT...
...IF YOU WERE TO FIGHT SEIGEN RIGHT NOW...
...WHICH OF YOU WOULD WIN?
WHY DOES HE WANT TO KNOW THAT...?
I don't know.
I'VE NEVER FOUGHT SEIGEN BEFORE.
BUT AS LONG AS MY KEGARE EATER ISN'T SEALED...
...I SEE NO REASON WHY I WOULD LOSE.
REALLY? THEN...

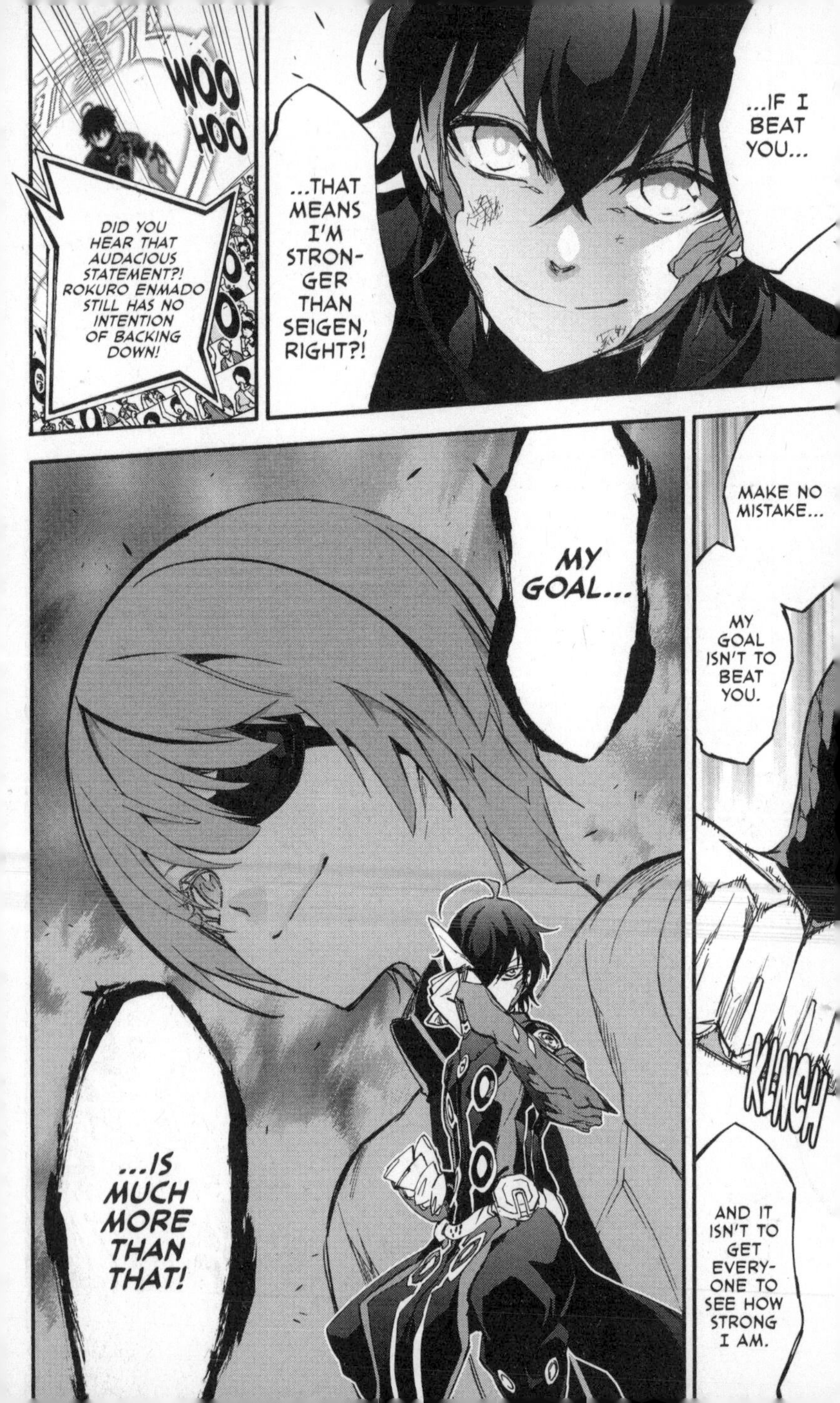

...IF I BEAT YOU...
...THAT MEANS I'M STRON-GER THAN SEIGEN, RIGHT?!
WOO HOO
DID YOU HEAR THAT AUDACIOUS STATEMENT?! ROKURO ENMADO STILL HAS NO INTENTION OF BACKING DOWN!
MAKE NO MISTAKE...
MY GOAL ISN'T TO BEAT YOU.
KLINCH
AND IT ISN'T TO GET EVERY-ONE TO SEE HOW STRONG I AM.
MY GOAL...
...IS MUCH MORE THAN THAT!

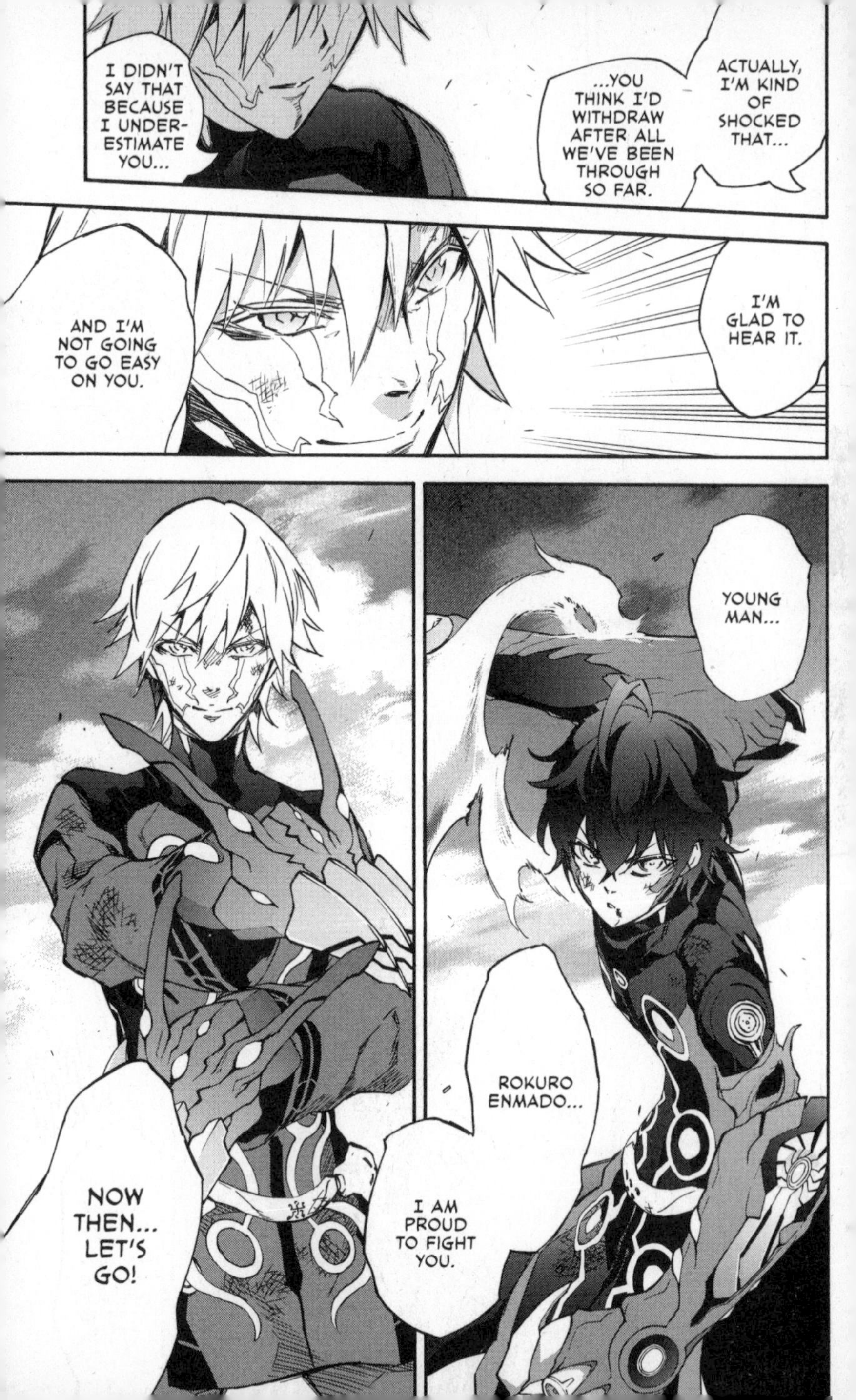
ACTUALLY, I'M KIND OF SHOCKED THAT...
...YOU THINK I'D WITHDRAW AFTER ALL WE'VE BEEN THROUGH SO FAR.
I DIDN'T SAY THAT BECAUSE I UNDERESTIMATE YOU...
I'M GLAD TO HEAR IT.
AND I'M NOT GOING TO GO EASY ON YOU.
YOUNG MAN...
ROKURO ENMADO...
I AM PROUD TO FIGHT YOU.
NOW THEN... LET'S GO!

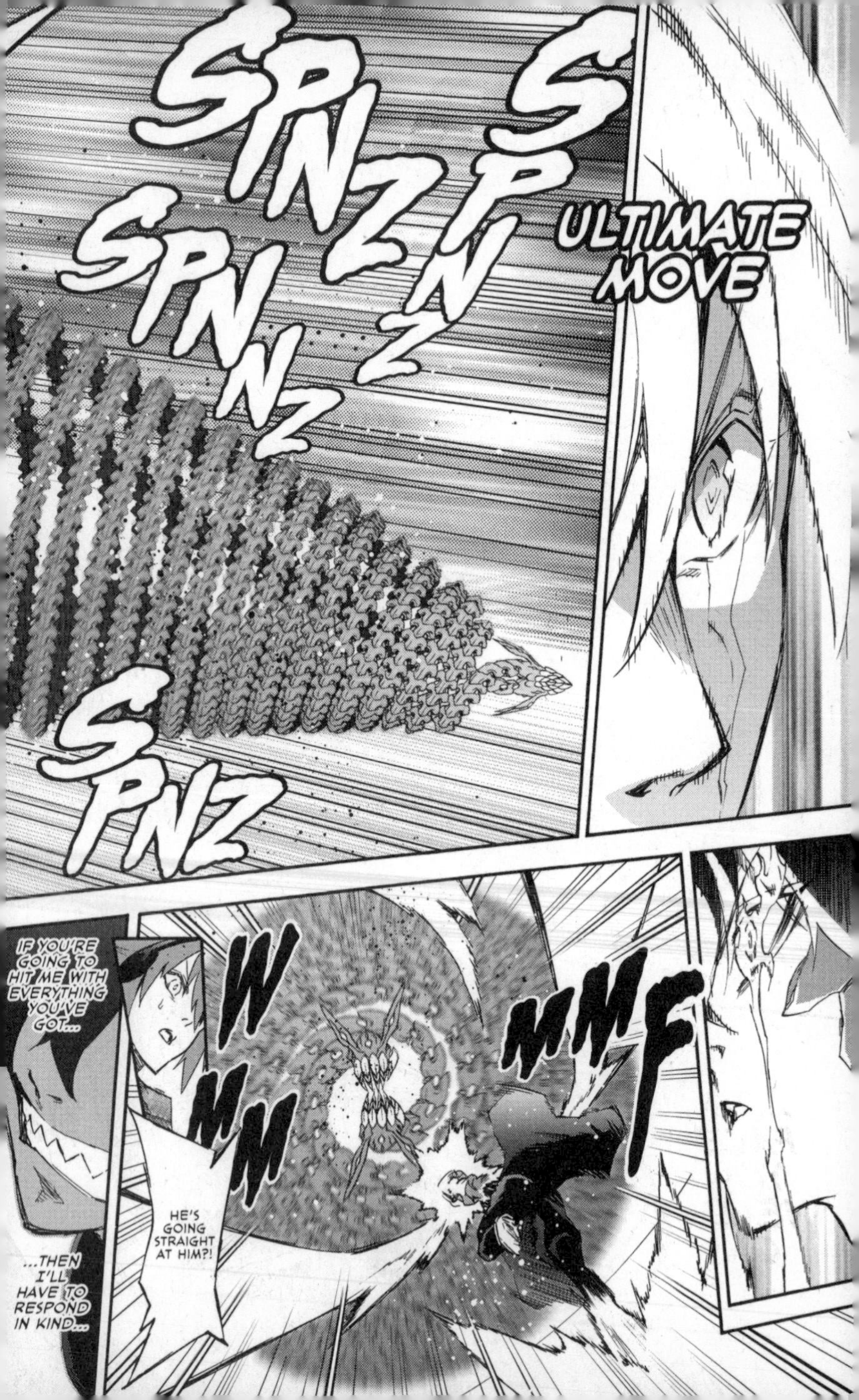
ULTIMATE MOVE
SPNZ
SPNZ
SPNZ
SPNZ
SPNZ
WMMM
MMF
HE'S GOING STRAIGHT AT HIM?!
IF YOU'RE GOING TO HIT ME WITH EVERYTHING YOU'VE GOT...
...THEN I'LL HAVE TO RESPOND IN KIND...

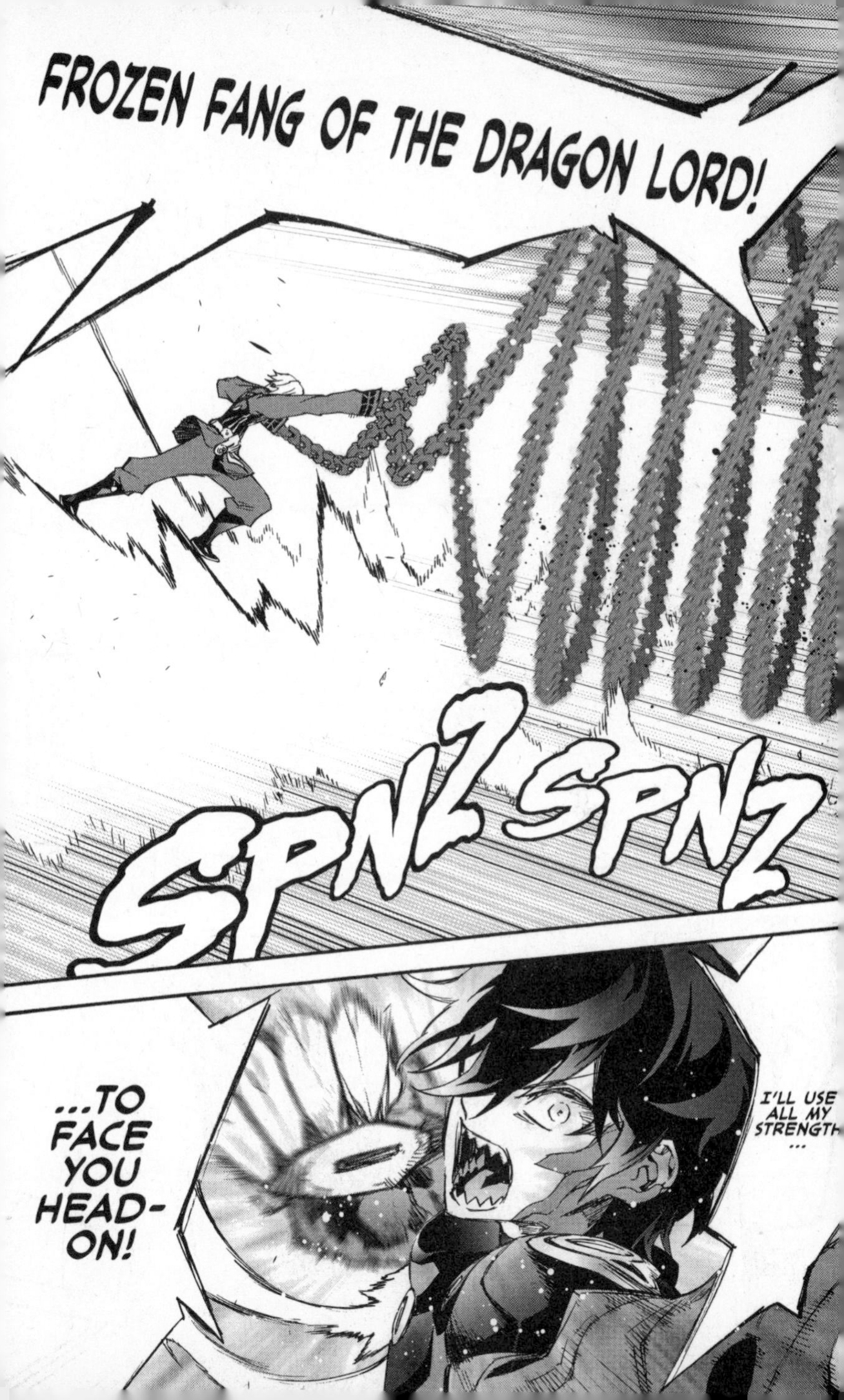
FROZEN FANG OF THE DRAGON LORD!
SPNZ SPNZ
I'LL USE ALL MY STRENGTH...
...TO FACE YOU HEAD-ON!

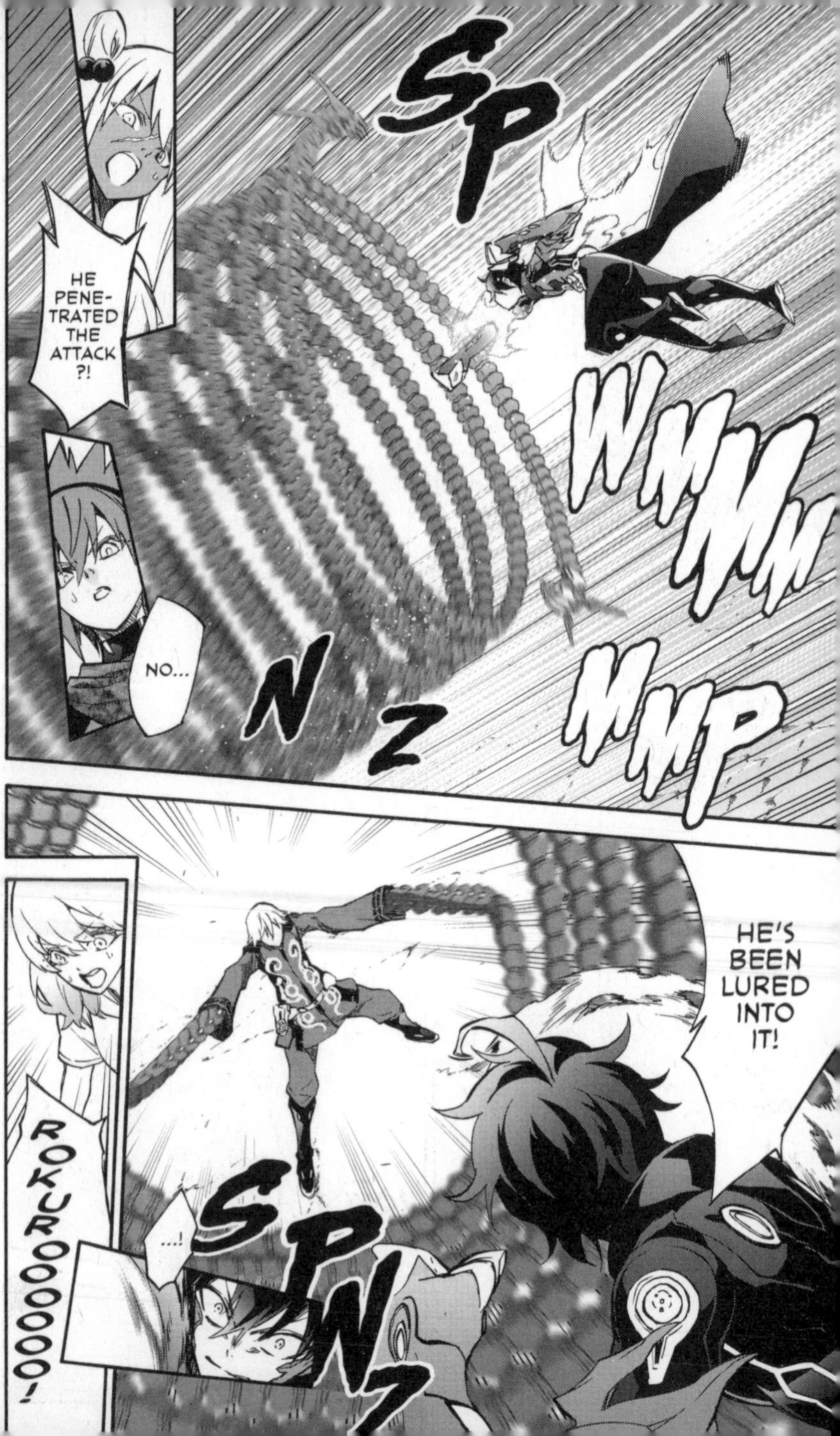
SP
WMMMM
HE PENE-TRATED THE ATTACK?!
MMP
NZ
NO...
HE'S BEEN LURED INTO IT!
SPN
...!
ROKUROOOOOOO!

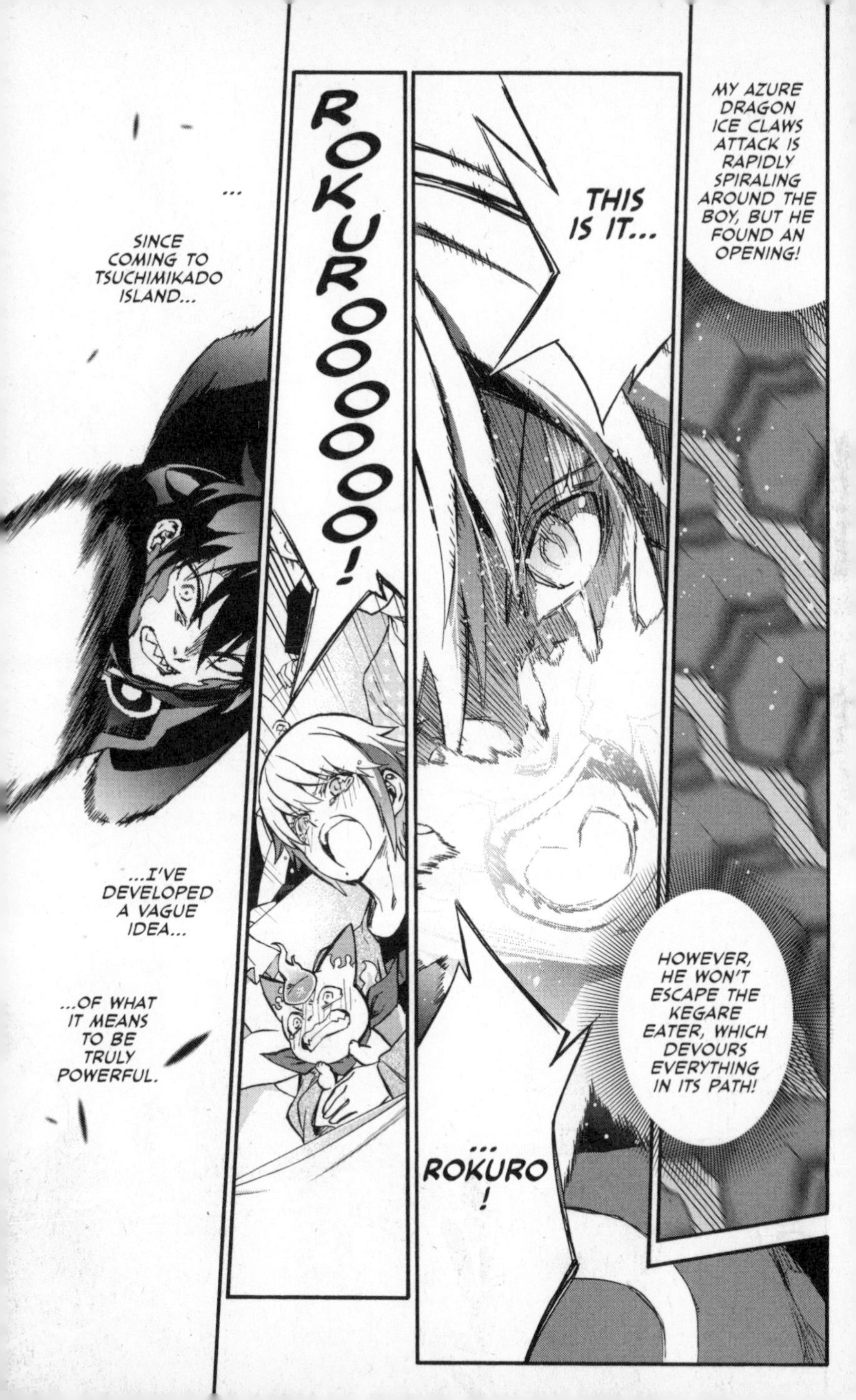
MY AZURE DRAGON ICE CLAWS ATTACK IS RAPIDLY SPIRALING AROUND THE BOY, BUT HE FOUND AN OPENING!
HOWEVER, HE WON'T ESCAPE THE KEGARE EATER, WHICH DEVOURS EVERYTHING IN ITS PATH!
THIS IS IT...
...ROKURO!
ROKUROOOOOOOO!
...
SINCE COMING TO TSUCHIMIKADO ISLAND...
...I'VE DEVELOPED A VAGUE IDEA...
...OF WHAT IT MEANS TO BE TRULY POWERFUL.

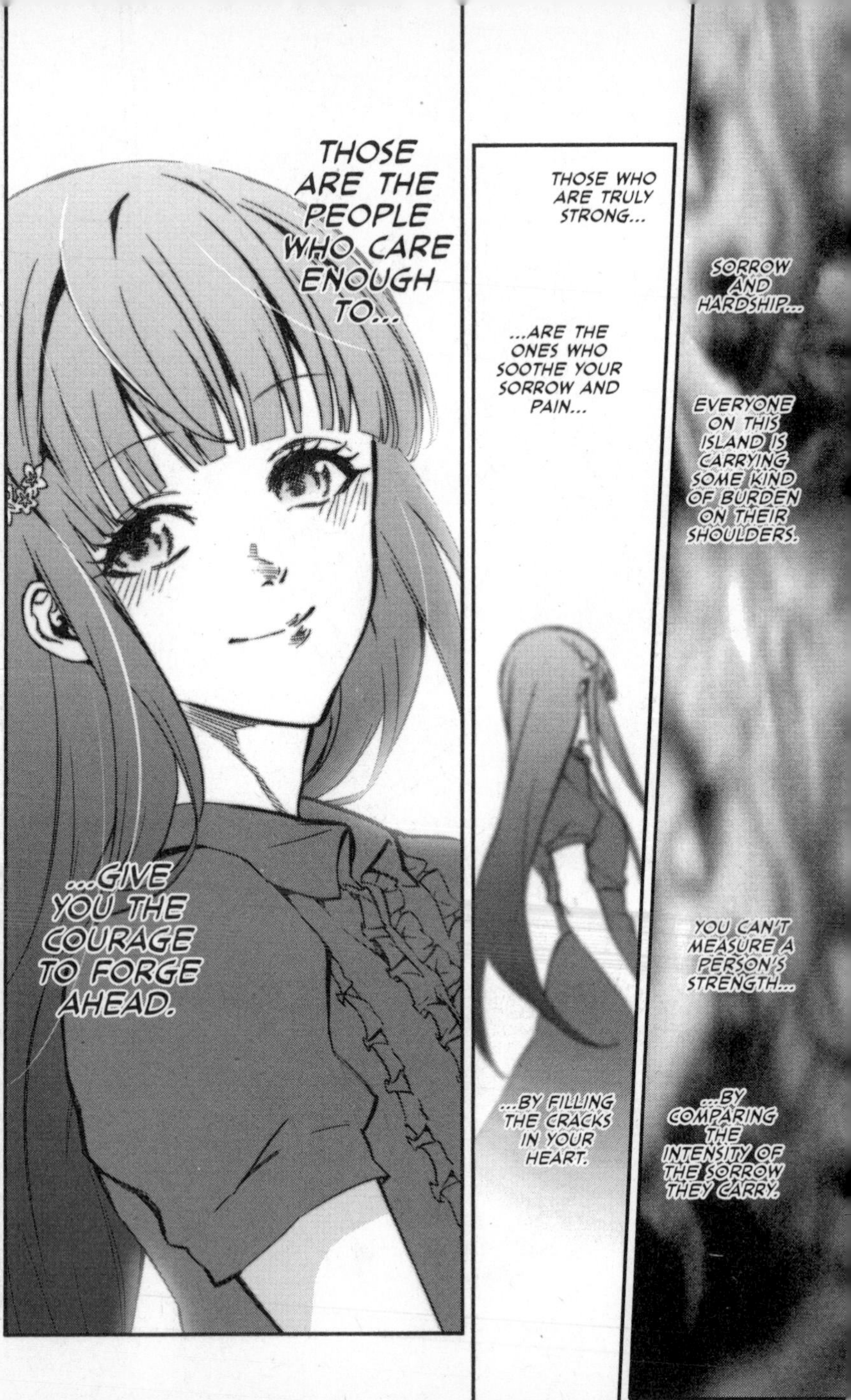
SORROW AND HARDSHIP...
EVERYONE ON THIS ISLAND IS CARRYING SOME KIND OF BURDEN ON THEIR SHOULDERS.
YOU CAN'T MEASURE A PERSON'S STRENGTH...
...BY COMPARING THE INTENSITY OF THE SORROW THEY CARRY.
THOSE WHO ARE TRULY STRONG...
...ARE THE ONES WHO SOOTHE YOUR SORROW AND PAIN...
...BY FILLING THE CRACKS IN YOUR HEART.
THOSE ARE THE PEOPLE WHO CARE ENOUGH TO...
...GIVE YOU THE COURAGE TO FORGE AHEAD.

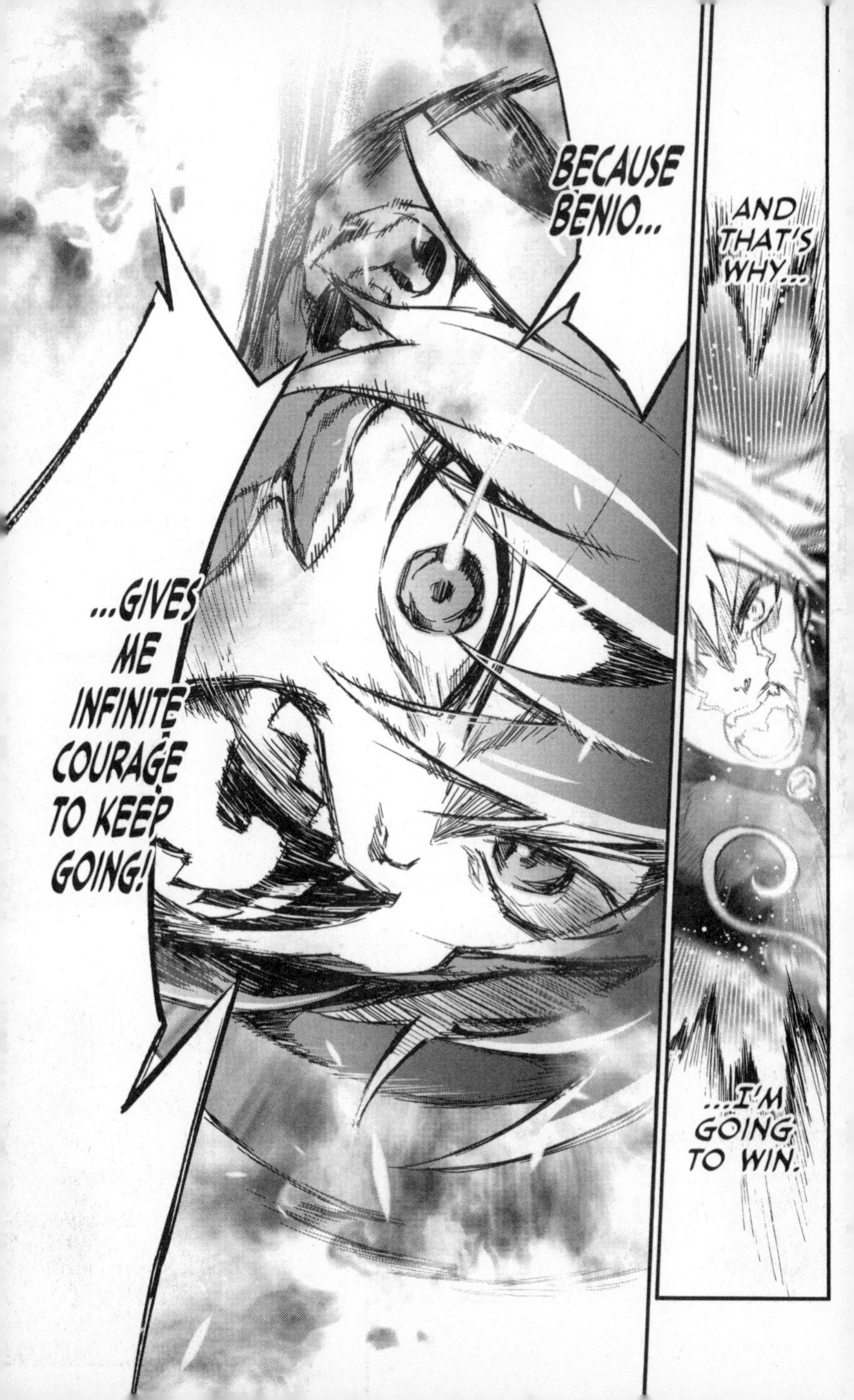
AND THAT'S WHY...
...I'M GOING TO WIN.
BECAUSE BENIO...
...GIVES ME INFINITE COURAGE TO KEEP GOING!

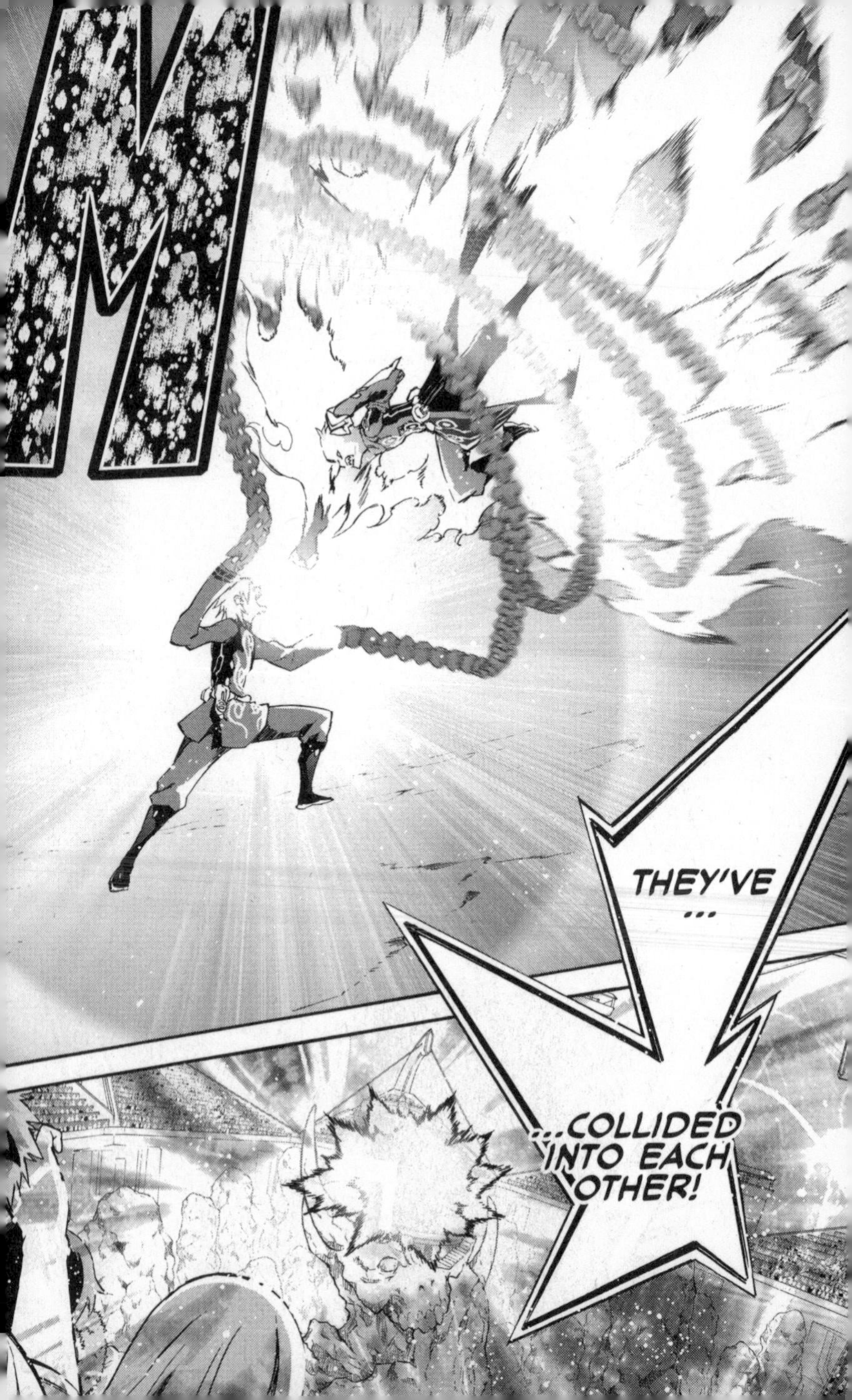
M
THEY'VE...
...COLLIDED INTO EACH OTHER!

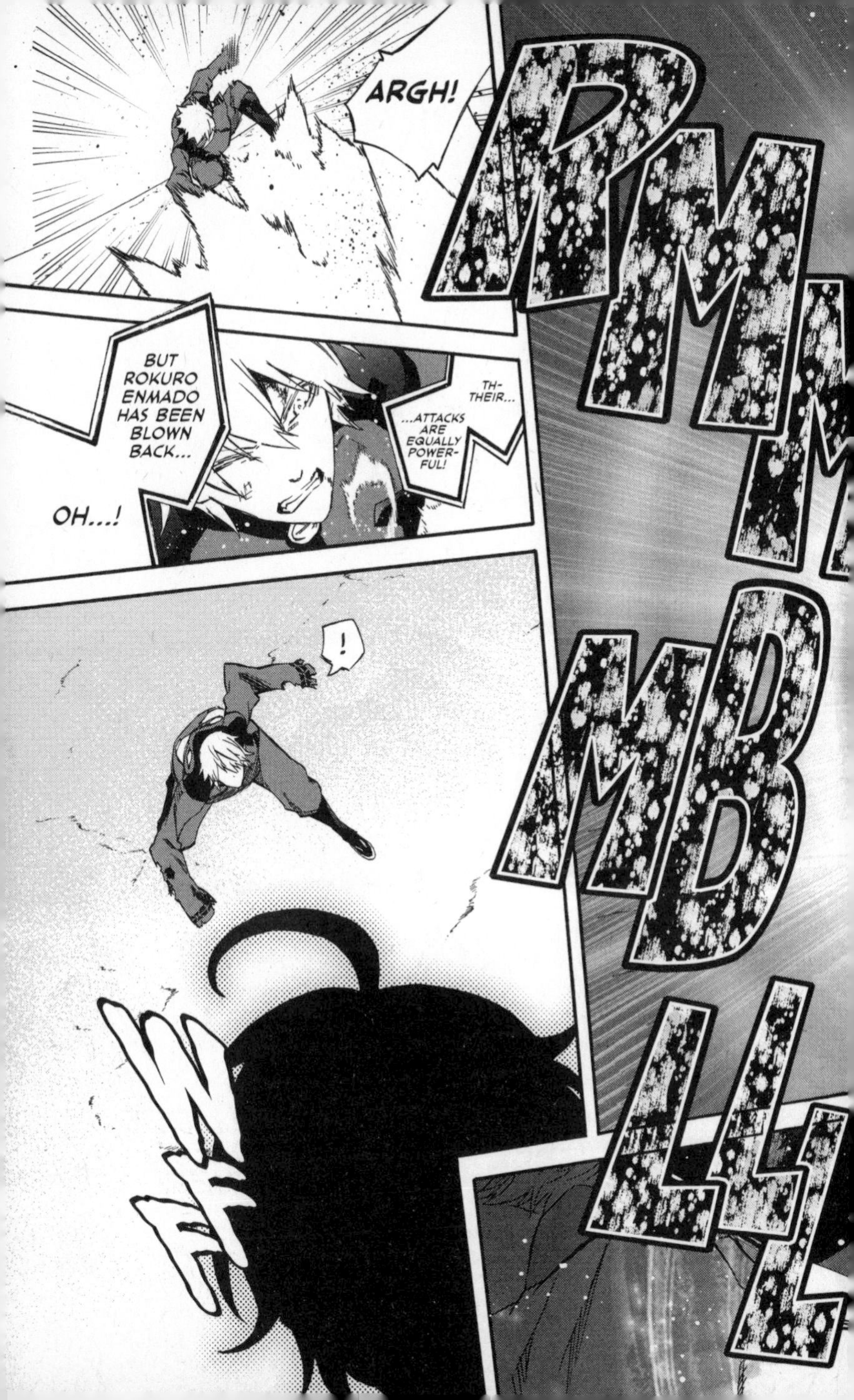
RMMMBLL
ARGH!
TH- THEIR...
...ATTACKS ARE EQUALLY POWERFUL!
BUT ROKURO ENMADO HAS BEEN BLOWN BACK...
OH...!
!

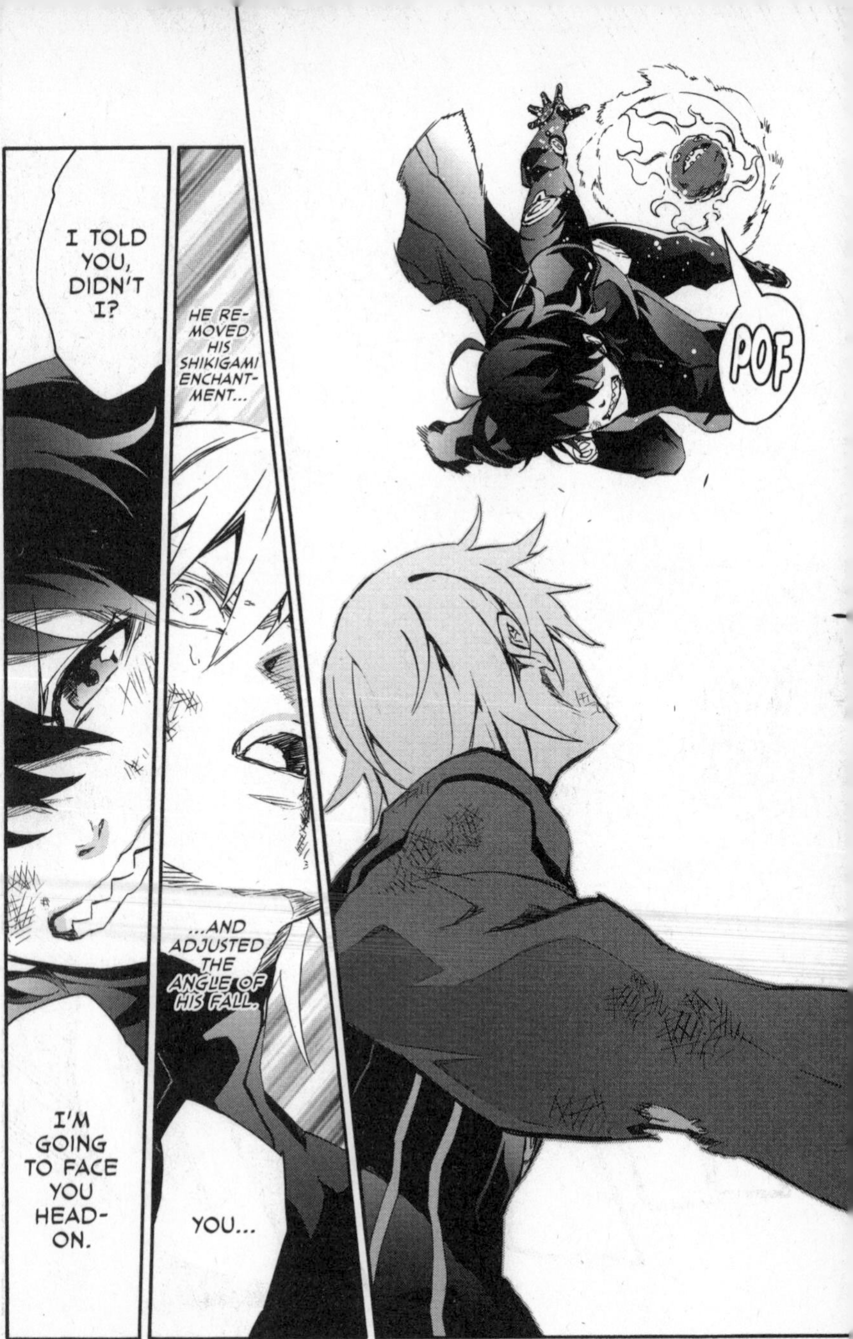
POF
HE REMOVED HIS SHIKIGAMI ENCHANTMENT...
...AND ADJUSTED THE ANGLE OF HIS FALL.
YOU...
I TOLD YOU, DIDN'T I?
I'M GOING TO FACE YOU HEAD-ON.

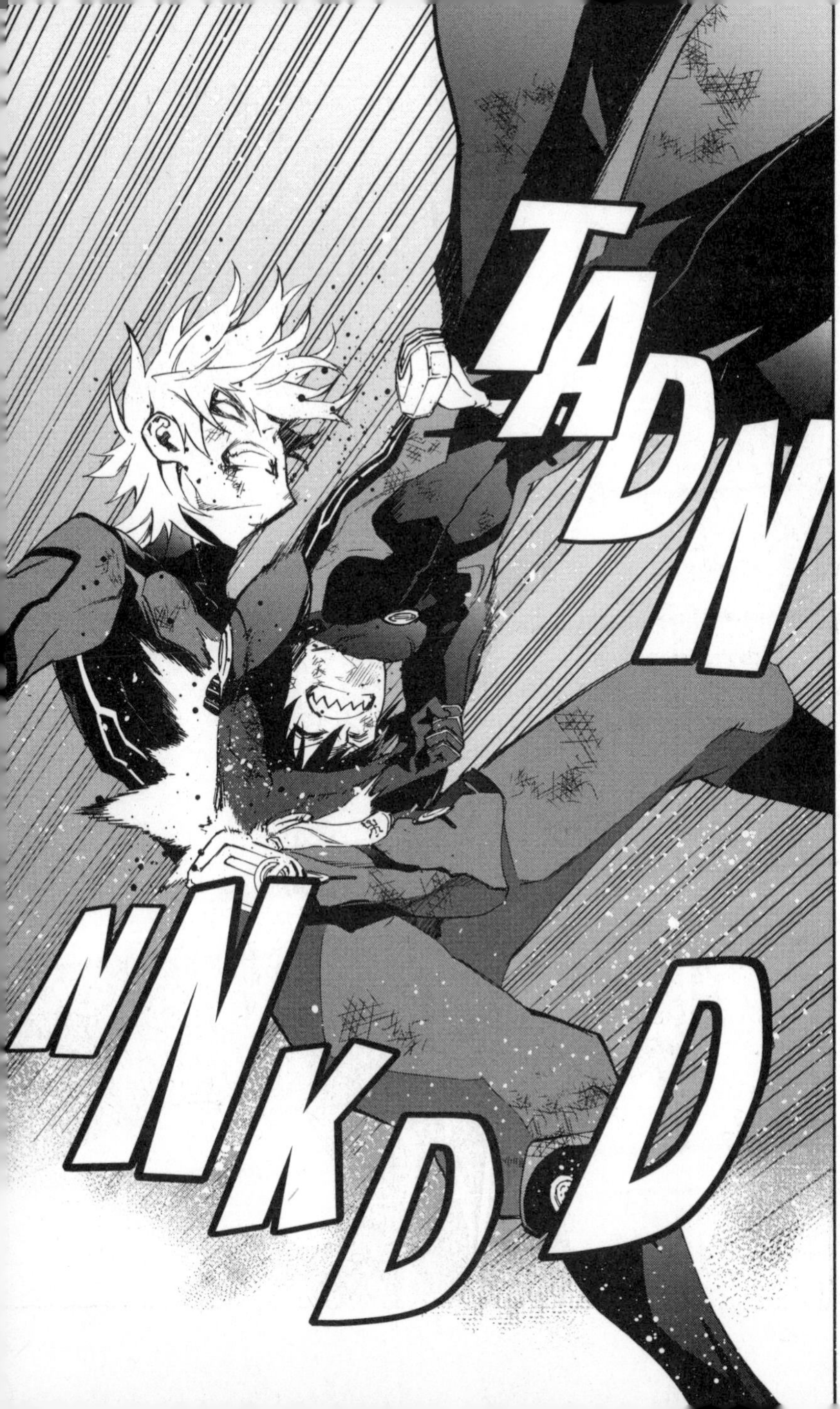
TADN
NNKDD

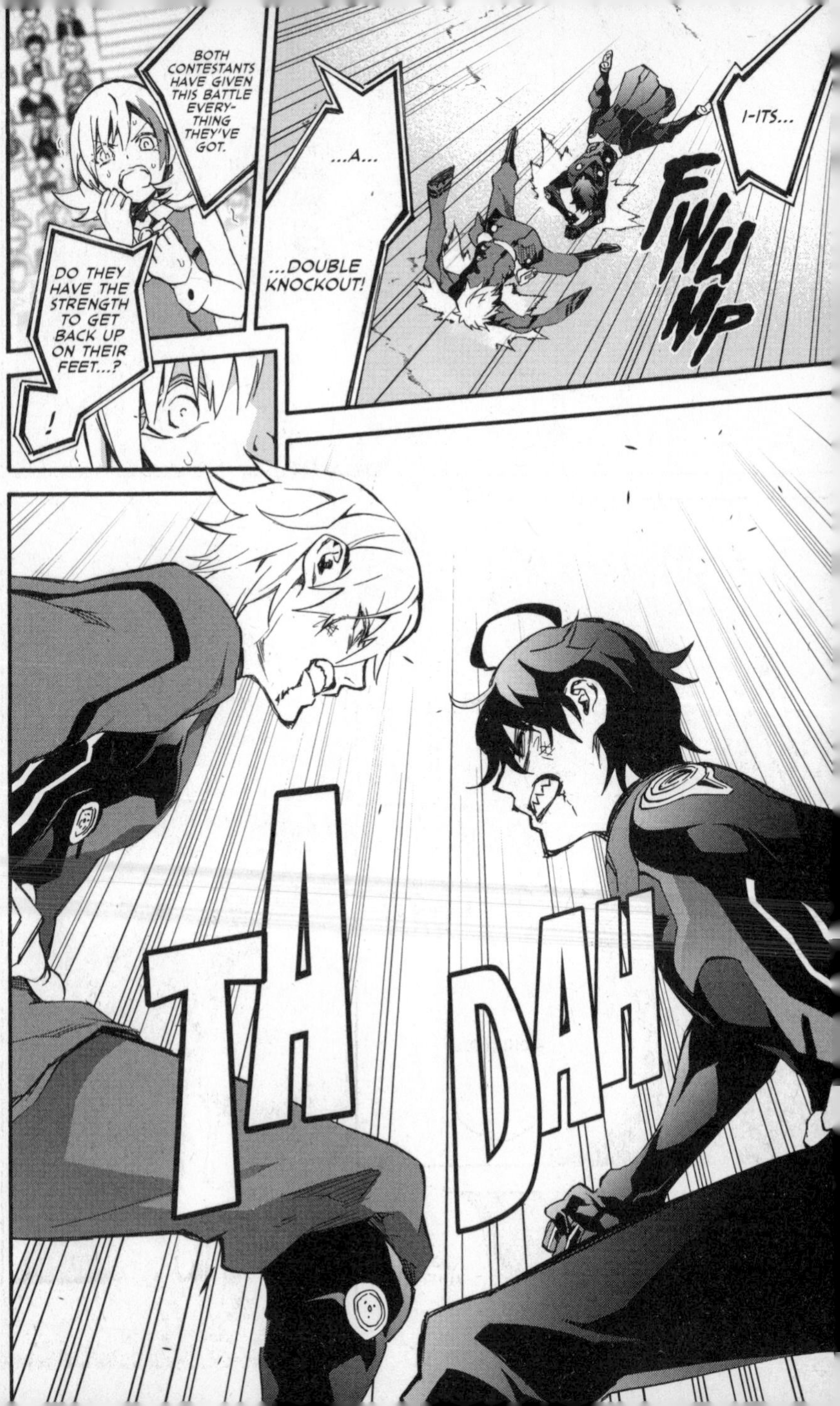
I-ITS...
FWUMP
...A...
...DOUBLE KNOCKOUT!
BOTH CONTESTANTS HAVE GIVEN THIS BATTLE EVERYTHING THEY'VE GOT.
DO THEY HAVE THE STRENGTH TO GET BACK UP ON THEIR FEET...?
!
TA DAH

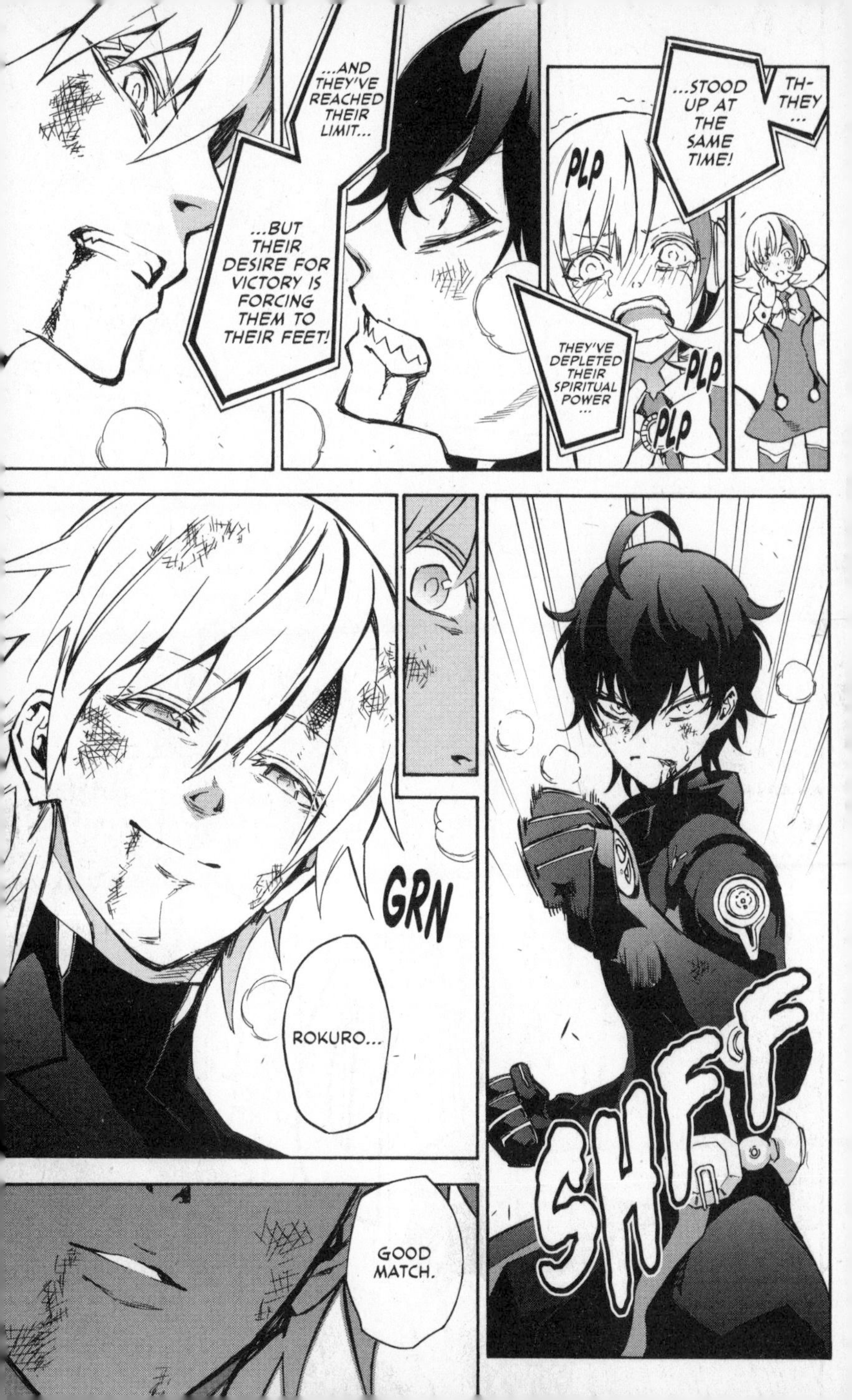
TH-THEY...
...STOOD UP AT THE SAME TIME!
PLP
PLP
PLP
THEY'VE DEPLETED THEIR SPIRITUAL POWER...
...AND THEY'VE REACHED THEIR LIMIT...
...BUT THEIR DESIRE FOR VICTORY IS FORCING THEM TO THEIR FEET!
SHF!
GRN
ROKURO...
GOOD MATCH.

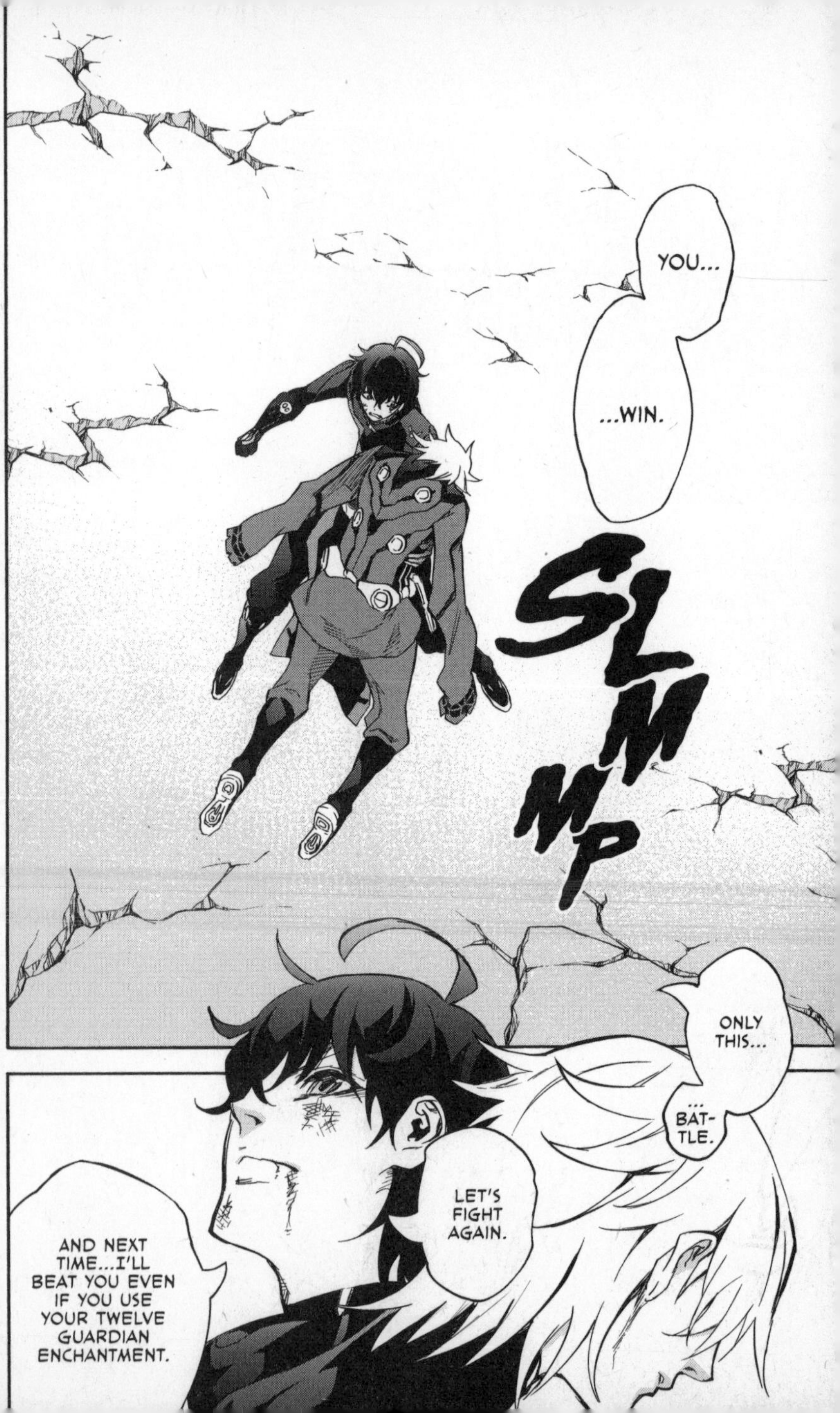
YOU...
...WIN.
SLMMP
ONLY THIS...
...BAT-TLE.
LET'S FIGHT AGAIN.
AND NEXT TIME...I'LL BEAT YOU EVEN IF YOU USE YOUR TWELVE GUARDIAN ENCHANTMENT.

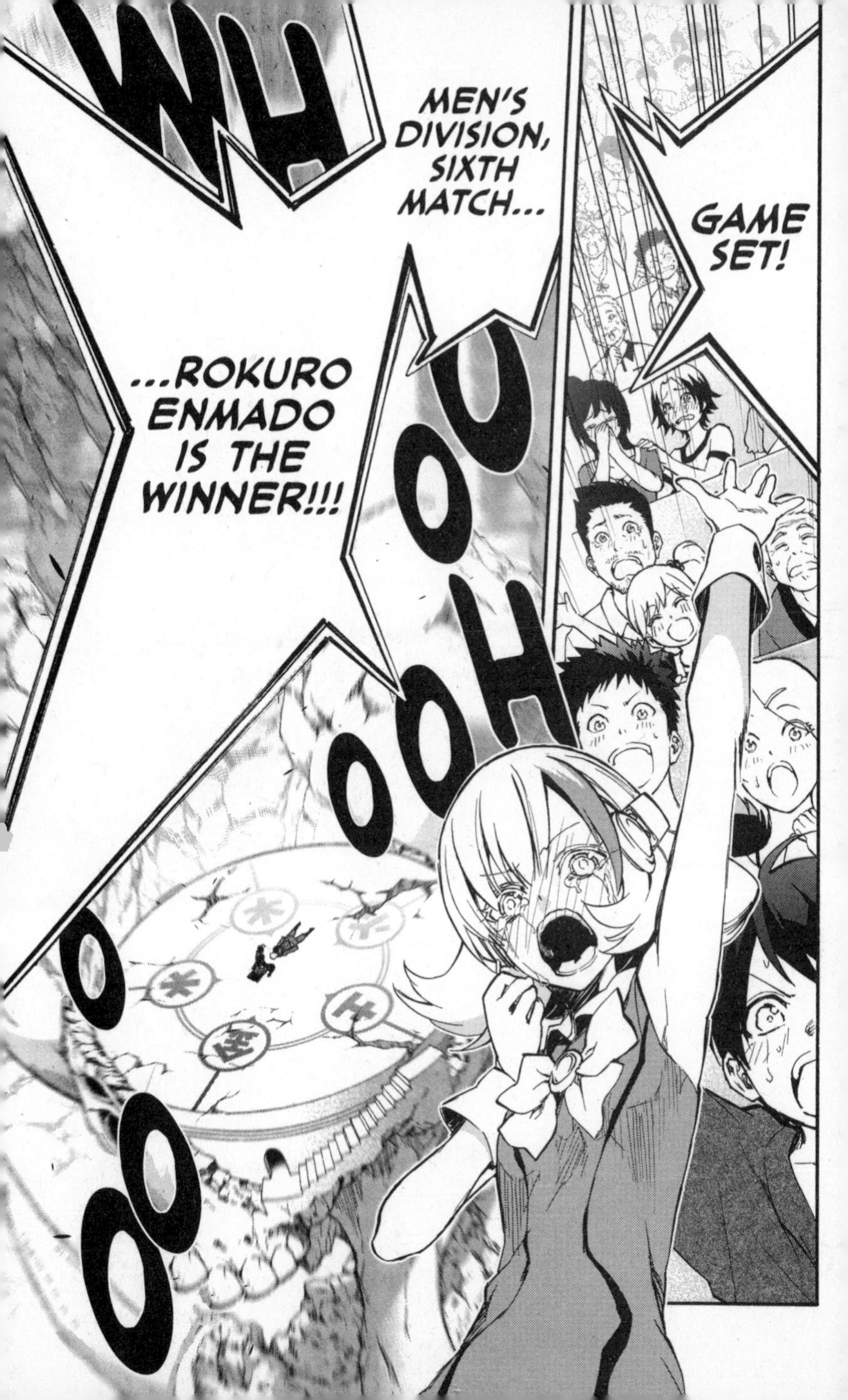
MEN'S DIVISION, SIXTH MATCH...
GAME SET!
...ROKURO ENMADO IS THE WINNER!!!

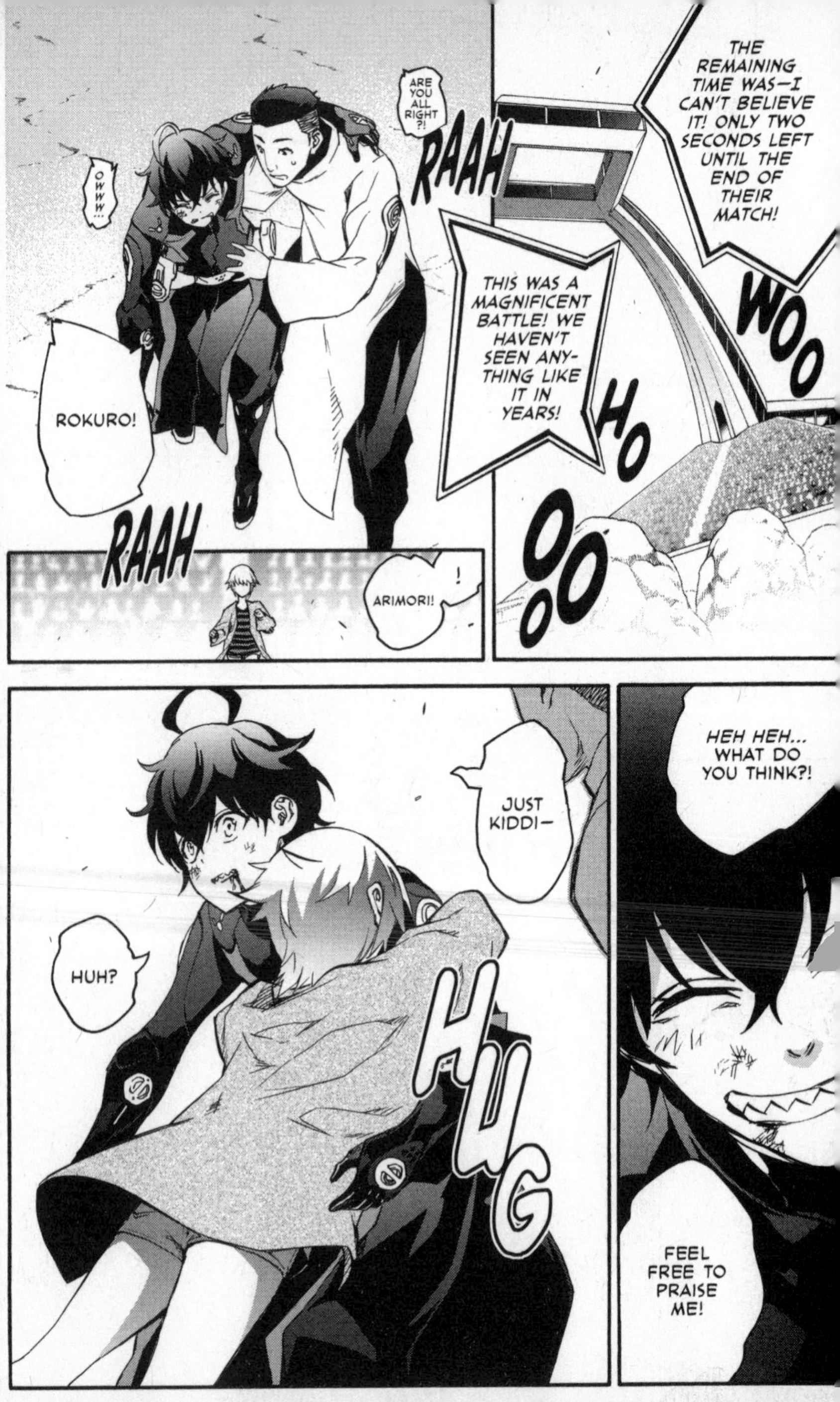
THE REMAINING TIME WAS—I CAN'T BELIEVE IT! ONLY TWO SECONDS LEFT UNTIL THE END OF THEIR MATCH!
THIS WAS A MAGNIFICENT BATTLE! WE HAVEN'T SEEN ANY-THING LIKE IT IN YEARS!
WOO HO OOO
RAAH
ARE YOU ALL RIGHT?!
OWWW...
ROKURO!
RAAH
!
ARIMORI!
HEH HEH... WHAT DO YOU THINK?!
FEEL FREE TO PRAISE ME!
JUST KIDDI—
HUH?
HUG

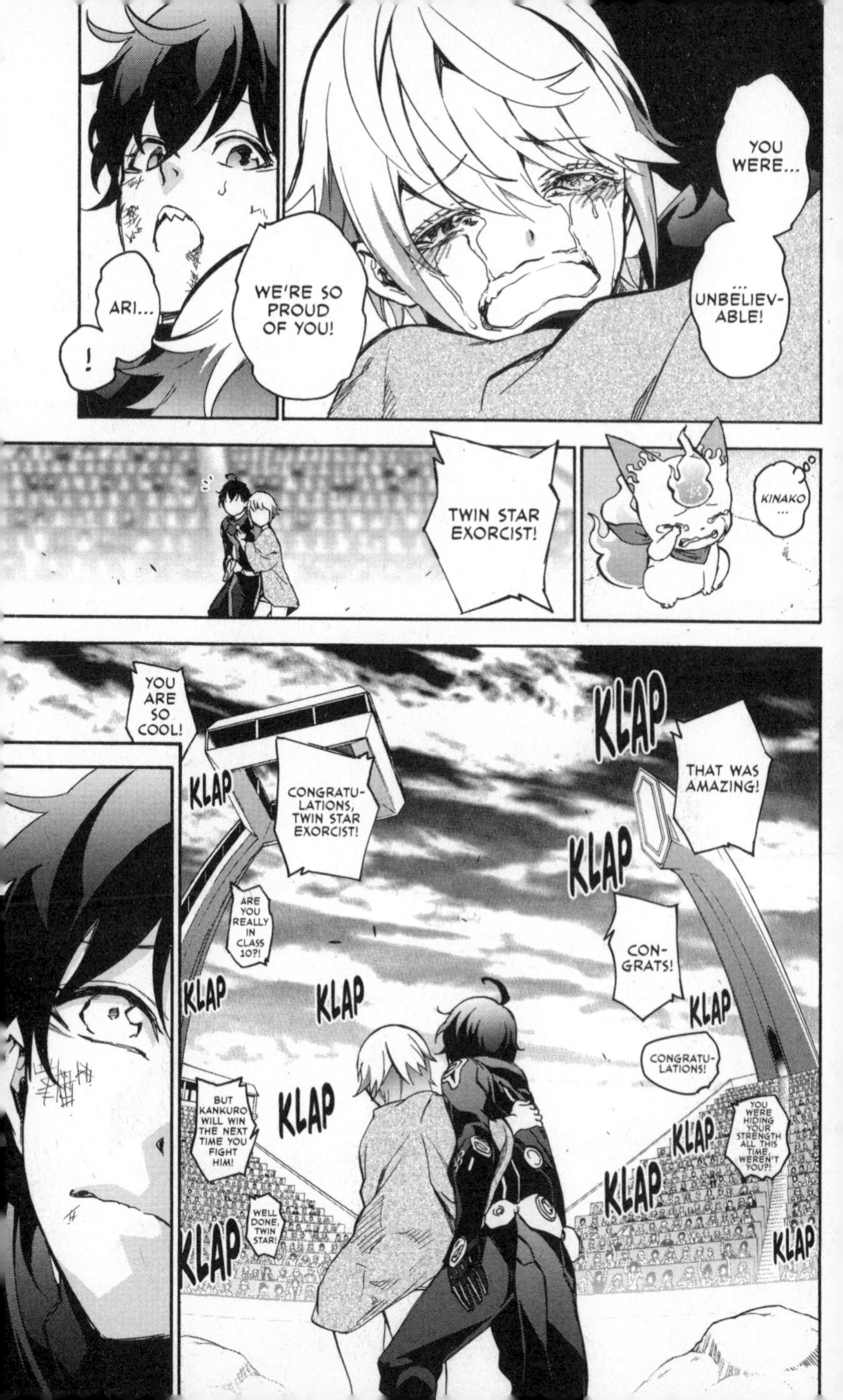
YOU WERE...
...UNBELIEVABLE!
WE'RE SO PROUD OF YOU!
ARI...
!
KINAKO...
TWIN STAR EXORCIST!
KLAP
THAT WAS AMAZING!
KLAP
CONGRATULATIONS, TWIN STAR EXORCIST!
YOU ARE SO COOL!
KLAP
CON-GRATS!
ARE YOU REALLY IN CLASS 10?!
KLAP
KLAP
KLAP
CONGRATULATIONS!
YOU WERE HIDING YOUR STRENGTH ALL THIS TIME, WEREN'T YOU?!
KLAP
KLAP
KLAP
BUT KANKURO WILL WIN THE NEXT TIME YOU FIGHT HIM!
WELL DONE, TWIN STAR!
KLAP

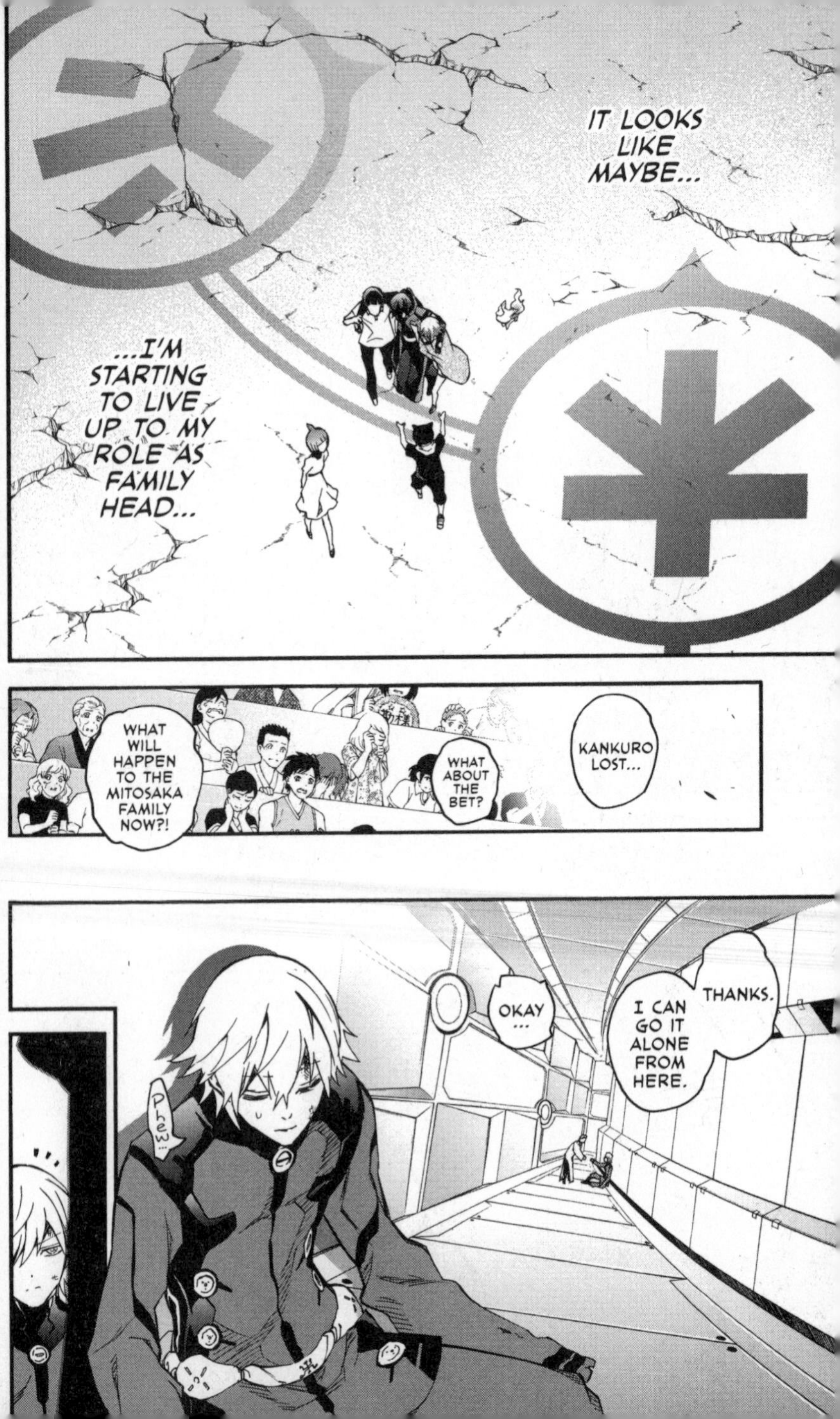
IT LOOKS LIKE MAYBE...
...I'M STARTING TO LIVE UP TO MY ROLE AS FAMILY HEAD...
KANKURO LOST...
WHAT ABOUT THE BET?
WHAT WILL HAPPEN TO THE MITOSAKA FAMILY NOW?!
THANKS.
I CAN GO IT ALONE FROM HERE.
OKAY ...
Phew...

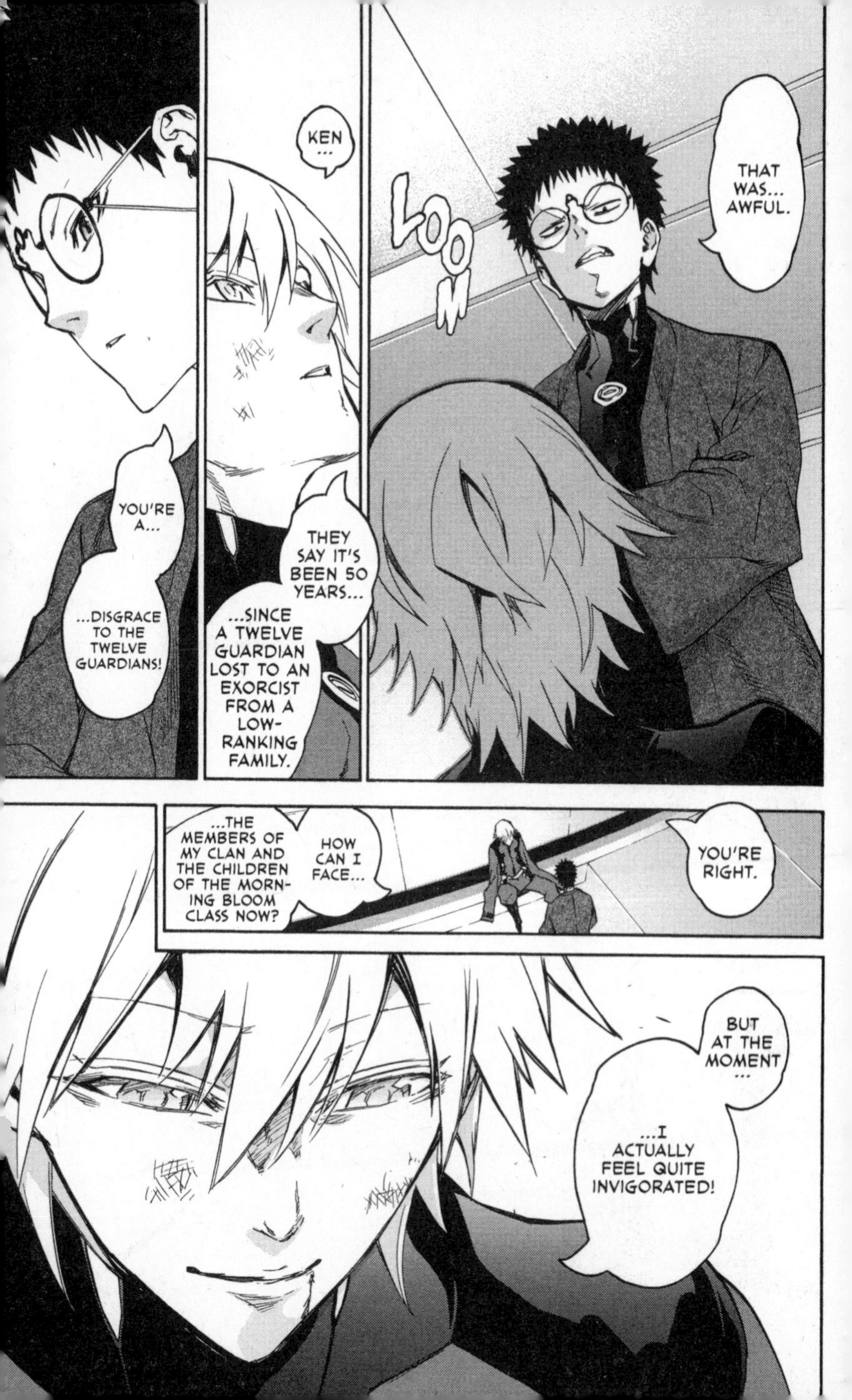
THAT WAS... AWFUL.
LOOM
KEN ...
THEY SAY IT'S BEEN 50 YEARS...
...SINCE A TWELVE GUARDIAN LOST TO AN EXORCIST FROM A LOW-RANKING FAMILY.
YOU'RE A...
...DISGRACE TO THE TWELVE GUARDIANS!
YOU'RE RIGHT.
HOW CAN I FACE...
...THE MEMBERS OF MY CLAN AND THE CHILDREN OF THE MORNING BLOOM CLASS NOW?
BUT AT THE MOMENT ...
...I ACTUALLY FEEL QUITE INVIGORATED!

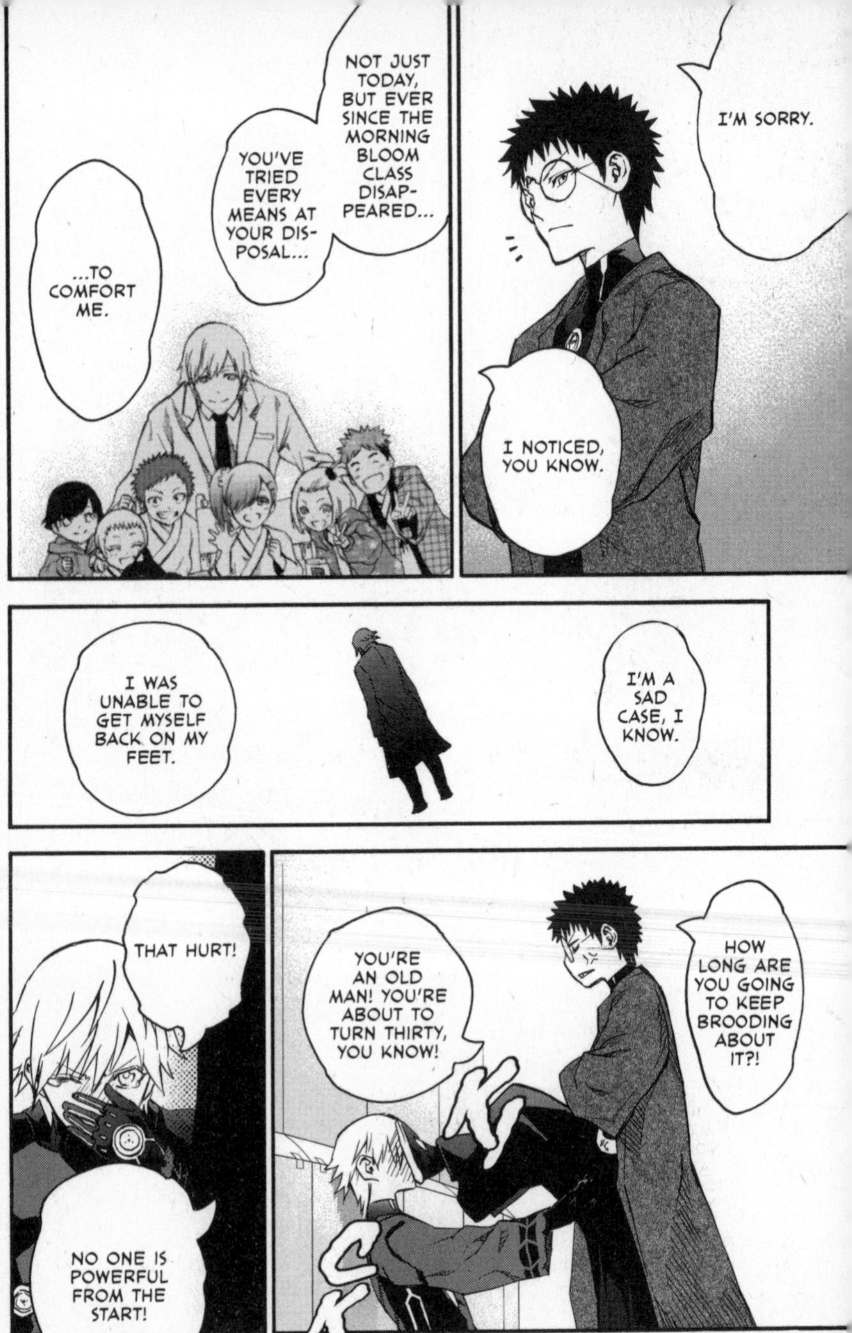
I'M SORRY.
I NOTICED, YOU KNOW.
NOT JUST TODAY, BUT EVER SINCE THE MORNING BLOOM CLASS DISAPPEARED...
YOU'VE TRIED EVERY MEANS AT YOUR DISPOSAL...
...TO COMFORT ME.
I'M A SAD CASE, I KNOW.
I WAS UNABLE TO GET MYSELF BACK ON MY FEET.
HOW LONG ARE YOU GOING TO KEEP BROODING ABOUT IT?!
YOU'RE AN OLD MAN! YOU'RE ABOUT TO TURN THIRTY, YOU KNOW!
THAT HURT!
NO ONE IS POWERFUL FROM THE START!

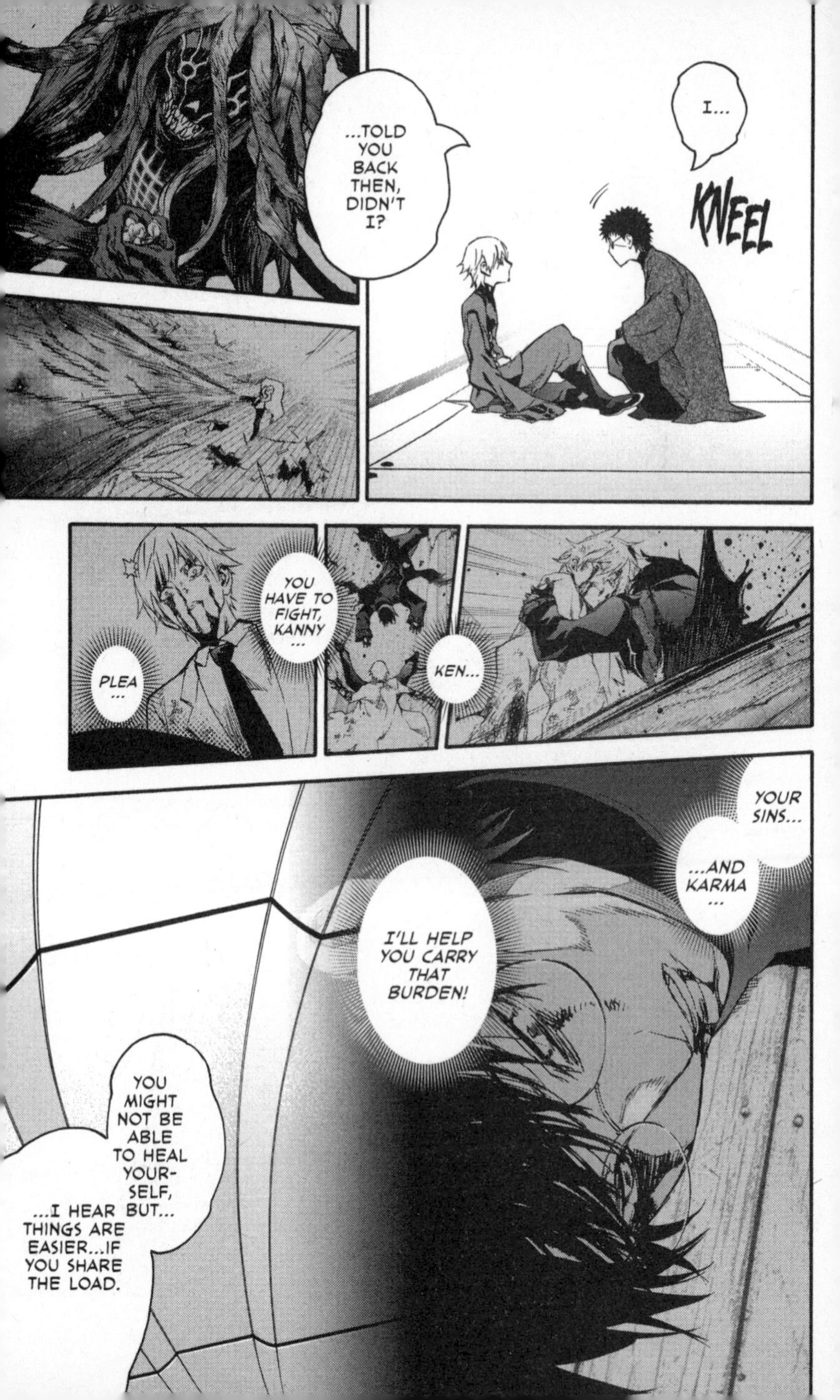
I...
KNEEL
...TOLD YOU BACK THEN, DIDN'T I?
KEN...
YOU HAVE TO FIGHT, KANNY...
PLEA...
YOUR SINS...
...AND KARMA...
I'LL HELP YOU CARRY THAT BURDEN!
YOU MIGHT NOT BE ABLE TO HEAL YOURSELF, BUT...
...I HEAR THINGS ARE EASIER...IF YOU SHARE THE LOAD.

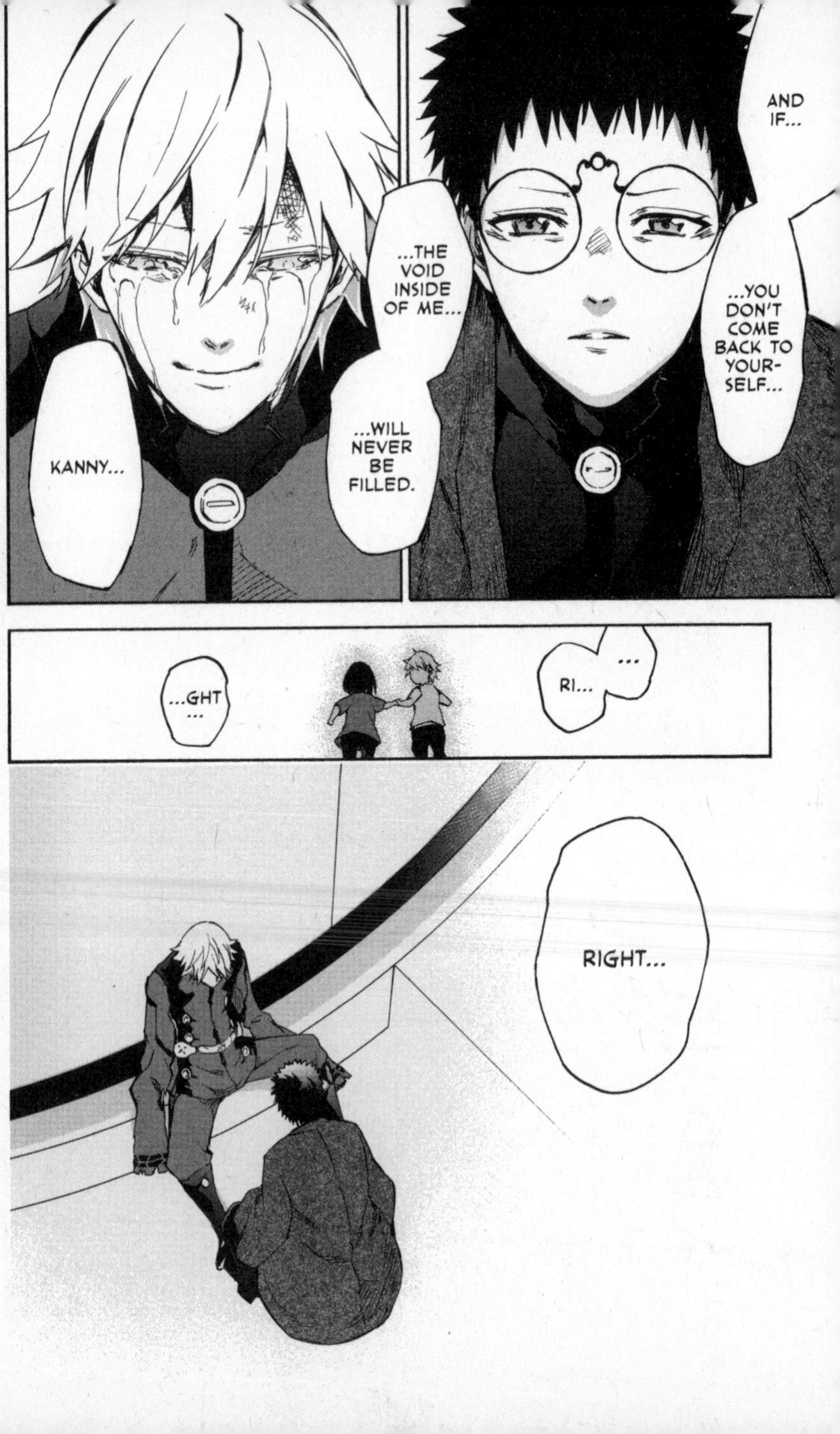
AND IF...
...YOU DON'T COME BACK TO YOUR-SELF...
...THE VOID INSIDE OF ME...
...WILL NEVER BE FILLED.
KANNY...
RI...
...
...GHT
...
RIGHT...

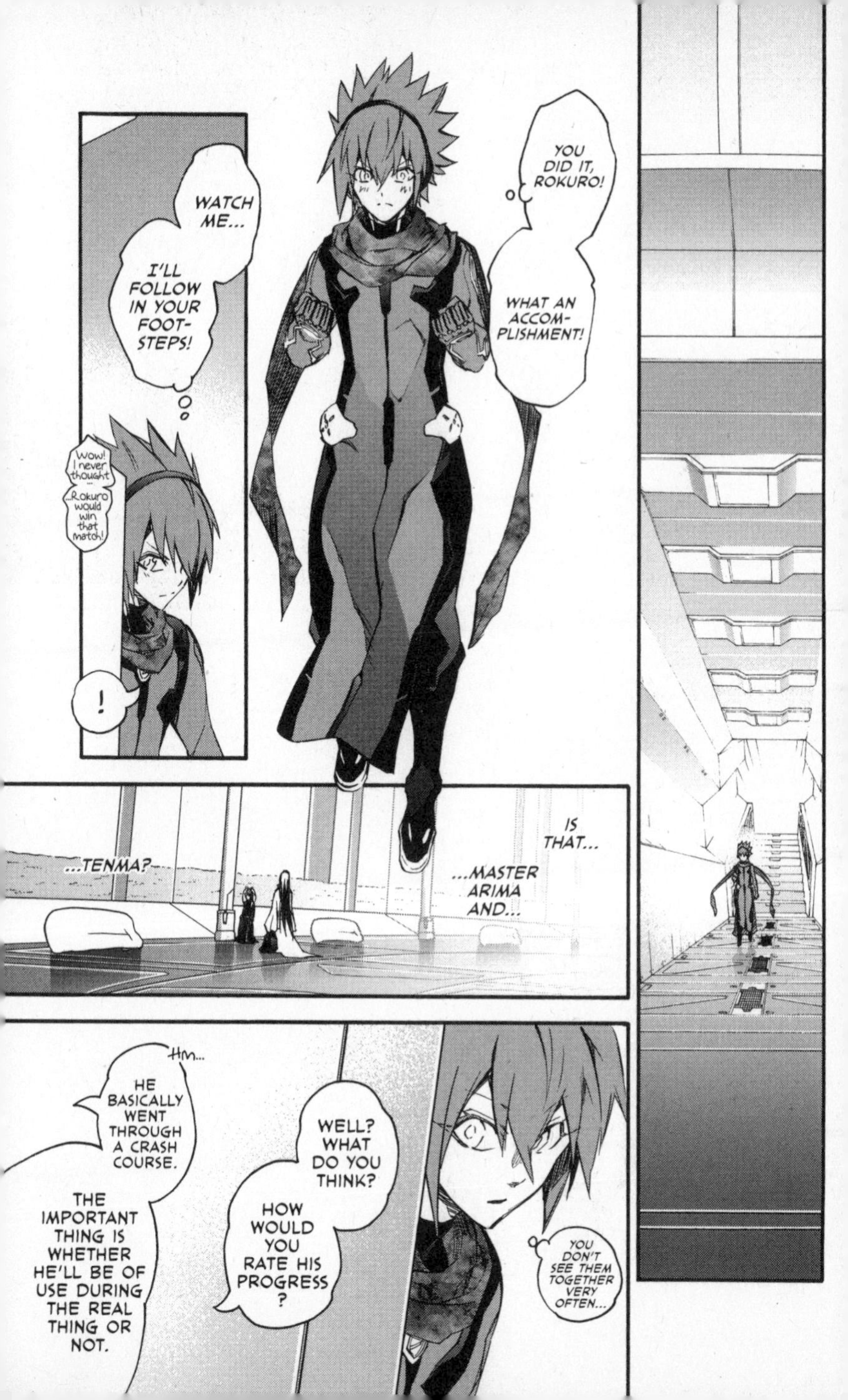
YOU DID IT, ROKURO!
WHAT AN ACCOM-PLISHMENT!
WATCH ME...
I'LL FOLLOW IN YOUR FOOT-STEPS!
Wow! I never thought... ...Rokuro would win that match!
!
IS THAT...
...MASTER ARIMA AND...
...TENMA?
YOU DON'T SEE THEM TOGETHER VERY OFTEN...
WELL? WHAT DO YOU THINK?
HOW WOULD YOU RATE HIS PROGRESS?
Hm...
HE BASICALLY WENT THROUGH A CRASH COURSE.
THE IMPORTANT THING IS WHETHER HE'LL BE OF USE DURING THE REAL THING OR NOT.

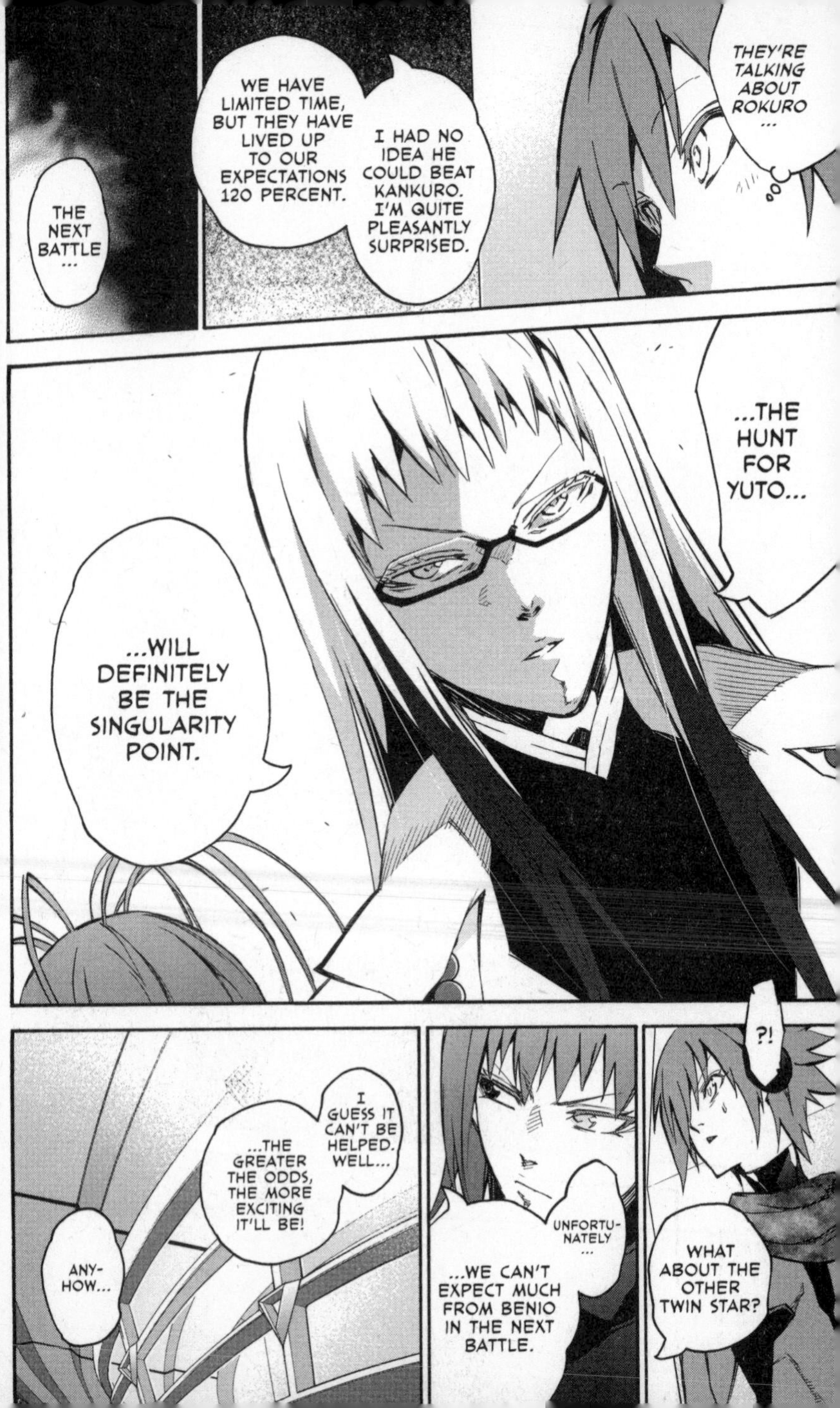
THEY'RE TALKING ABOUT ROKURO...
WE HAVE LIMITED TIME, BUT THEY HAVE LIVED UP TO OUR EXPECTATIONS 120 PERCENT.
I HAD NO IDEA HE COULD BEAT KANKURO. I'M QUITE PLEASANTLY SURPRISED.
THE NEXT BATTLE...
...THE HUNT FOR YUTO...
...WILL DEFINITELY BE THE SINGULARITY POINT.
?!
WHAT ABOUT THE OTHER TWIN STAR?
UNFORTU-NATELY...
...WE CAN'T EXPECT MUCH FROM BENIO IN THE NEXT BATTLE.
I GUESS IT CAN'T BE HELPED. WELL...
...THE GREATER THE ODDS, THE MORE EXCITING IT'LL BE!
ANY-HOW...

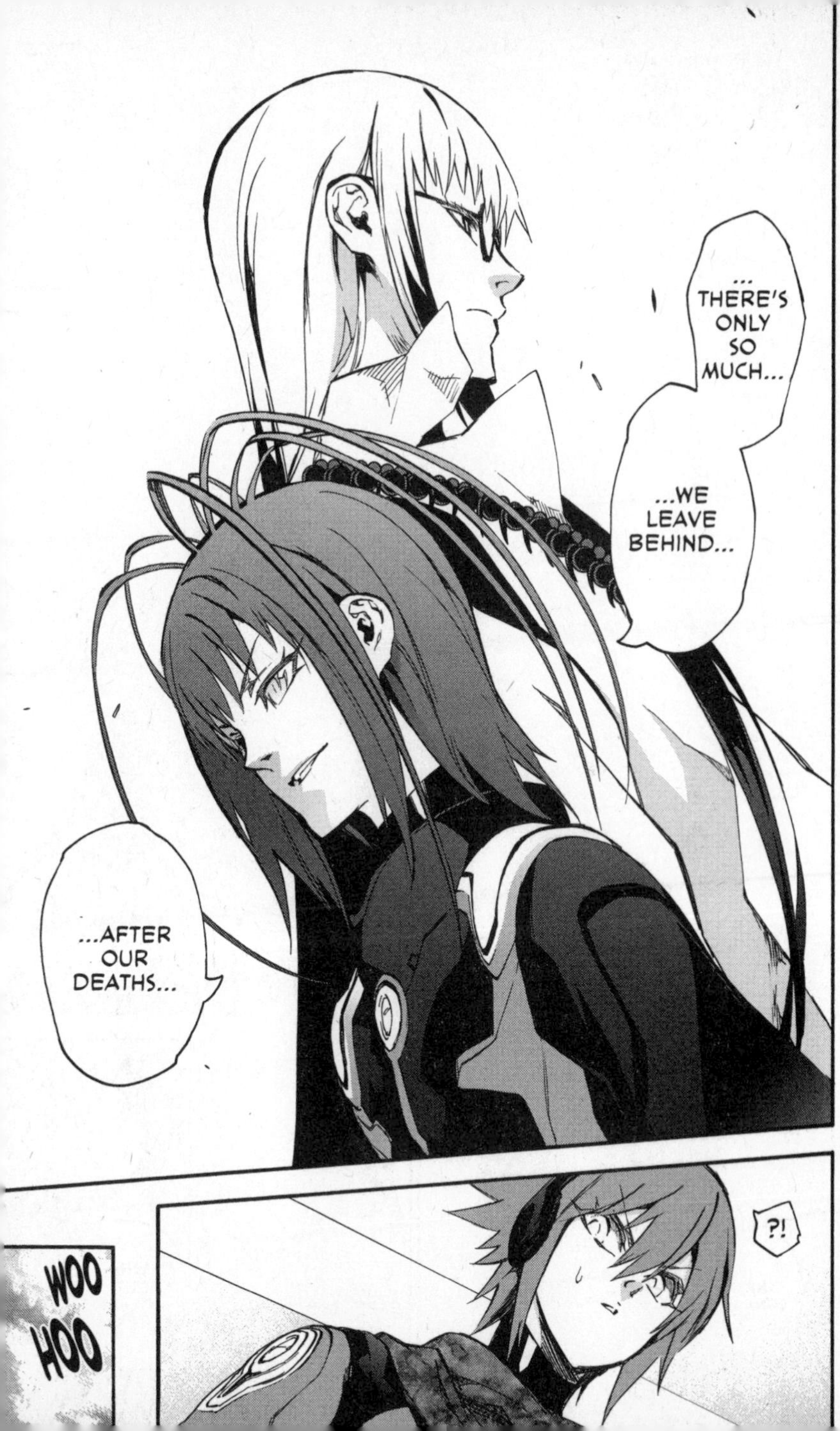
...THERE'S ONLY SO MUCH...
...WE LEAVE BEHIND...
...AFTER OUR DEATHS...
?!
WOO HOO

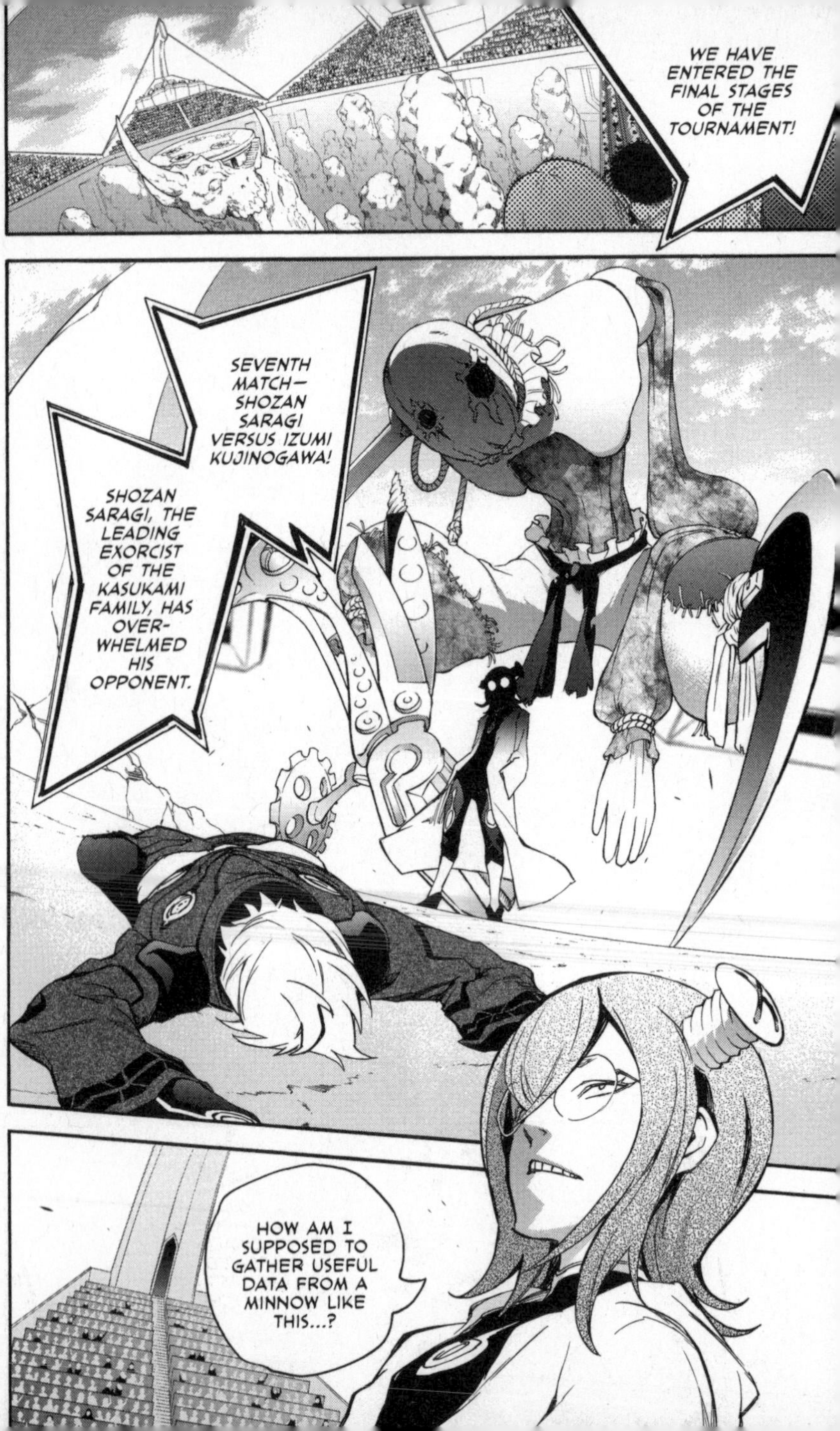
WE HAVE ENTERED THE FINAL STAGES OF THE TOURNAMENT!
SEVENTH MATCH—SHOZAN SARAGI VERSUS IZUMI KUJINOGAWA!
SHOZAN SARAGI, THE LEADING EXORCIST OF THE KASUKAMI FAMILY, HAS OVER-WHELMED HIS OPPONENT.
HOW AM I SUPPOSED TO GATHER USEFUL DATA FROM A MINNOW LIKE THIS...?

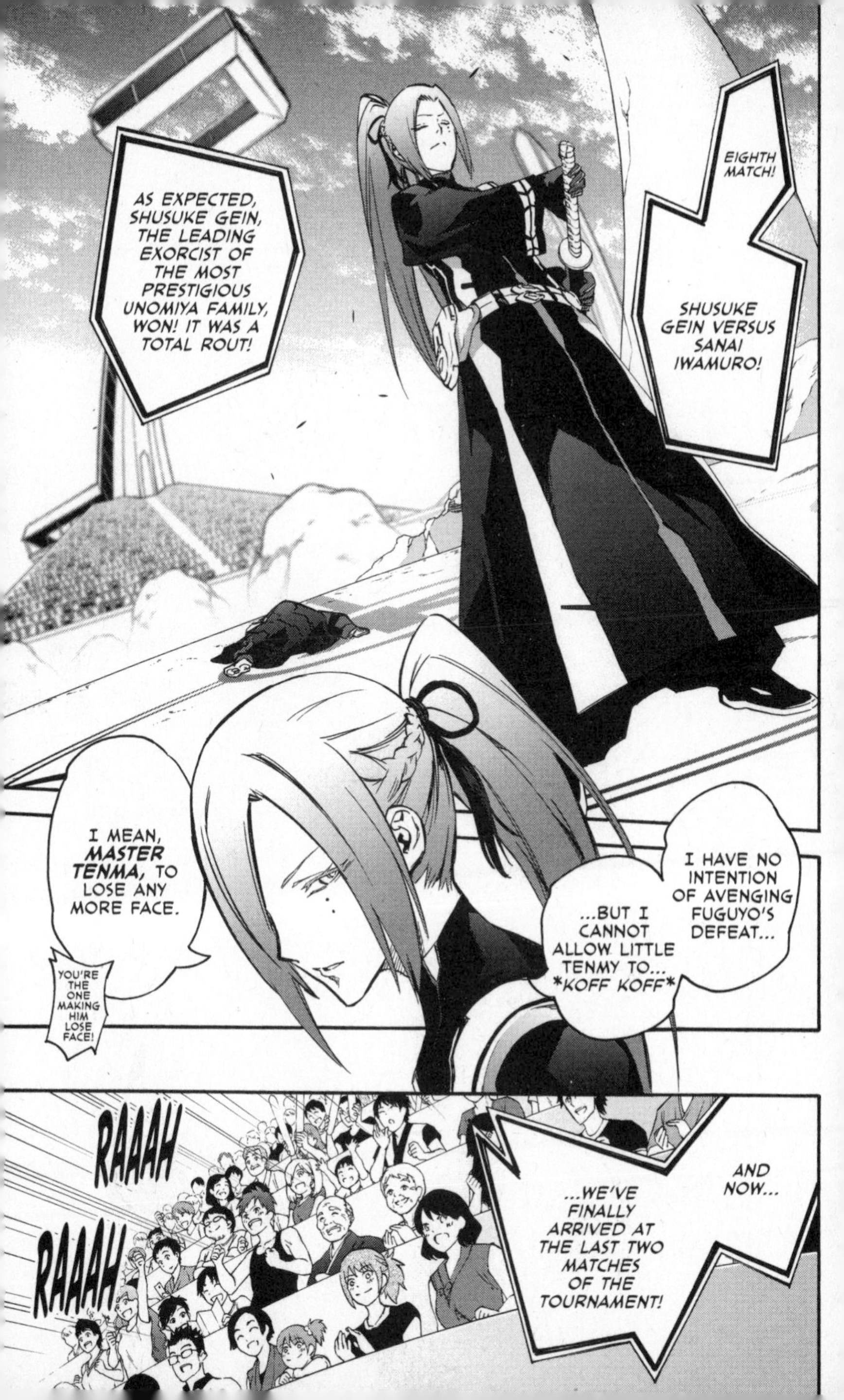

EIGHTH MATCH!
SHUSUKE GEIN VERSUS SANAI IWAMURO!
AS EXPECTED, SHUSUKE GEIN, THE LEADING EXORCIST OF THE MOST PRESTIGIOUS UNOMIYA FAMILY, WON! IT WAS A TOTAL ROUT!
I HAVE NO INTENTION OF AVENGING FUGUYO'S DEFEAT...
...BUT I CANNOT ALLOW LITTLE TENMY TO... *KOFF KOFF*
I MEAN, **MASTER TENMA,** TO LOSE ANY MORE FACE.
YOU'RE THE ONE MAKING HIM LOSE FACE!
AND NOW...
...WE'VE FINALLY ARRIVED AT THE LAST TWO MATCHES OF THE TOURNAMENT!
RAAAH
RAAAH

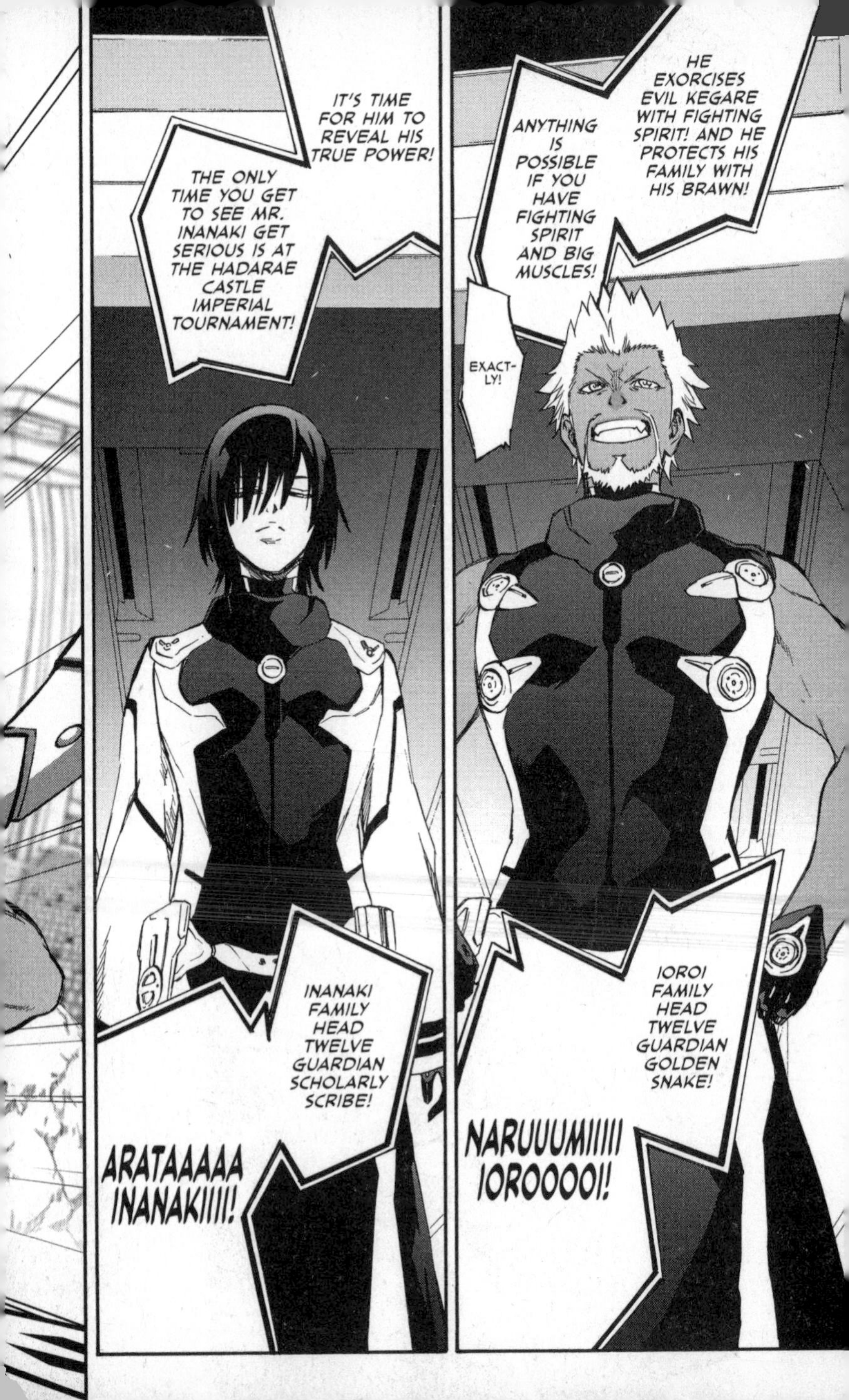
HE EXORCISES EVIL KEGARE WITH FIGHTING SPIRIT! AND HE PROTECTS HIS FAMILY WITH HIS BRAWN!
ANYTHING IS POSSIBLE IF YOU HAVE FIGHTING SPIRIT AND BIG MUSCLES!
EXACTLY!
IOROI FAMILY HEAD TWELVE GUARDIAN GOLDEN SNAKE!
NARUUUMIIIII IOROOOOI!
IT'S TIME FOR HIM TO REVEAL HIS TRUE POWER!
THE ONLY TIME YOU GET TO SEE MR. INANAKI GET SERIOUS IS AT THE HADARAE CASTLE IMPERIAL TOURNAMENT!
INANAKI FAMILY HEAD TWELVE GUARDIAN SCHOLARLY SCRIBE!
ARATAAAAA INANAKIIIII!

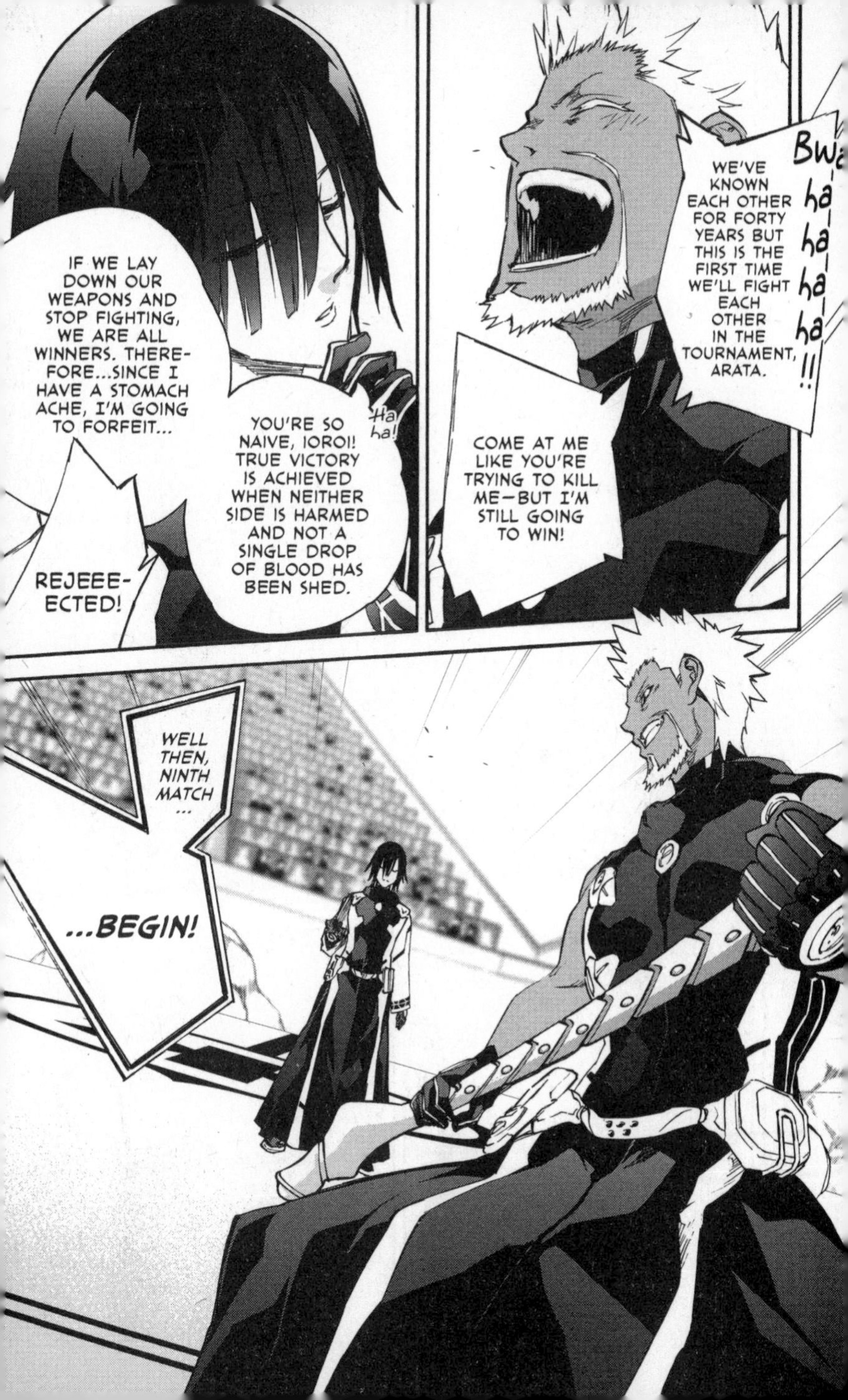

Bwa ha ha ha ha!!
WE'VE KNOWN EACH OTHER FOR FORTY YEARS BUT THIS IS THE FIRST TIME WE'LL FIGHT EACH OTHER IN THE TOURNAMENT, ARATA.
COME AT ME LIKE YOU'RE TRYING TO KILL ME—BUT I'M STILL GOING TO WIN!
IF WE LAY DOWN OUR WEAPONS AND STOP FIGHTING, WE ARE ALL WINNERS. THEREFORE...SINCE I HAVE A STOMACH ACHE, I'M GOING TO FORFEIT...
REJEEE-ECTED!
Ha ha!
YOU'RE SO NAIVE, IOROI! TRUE VICTORY IS ACHIEVED WHEN NEITHER SIDE IS HARMED AND NOT A SINGLE DROP OF BLOOD HAS BEEN SHED.
WELL THEN, NINTH MATCH...
...BEGIN!

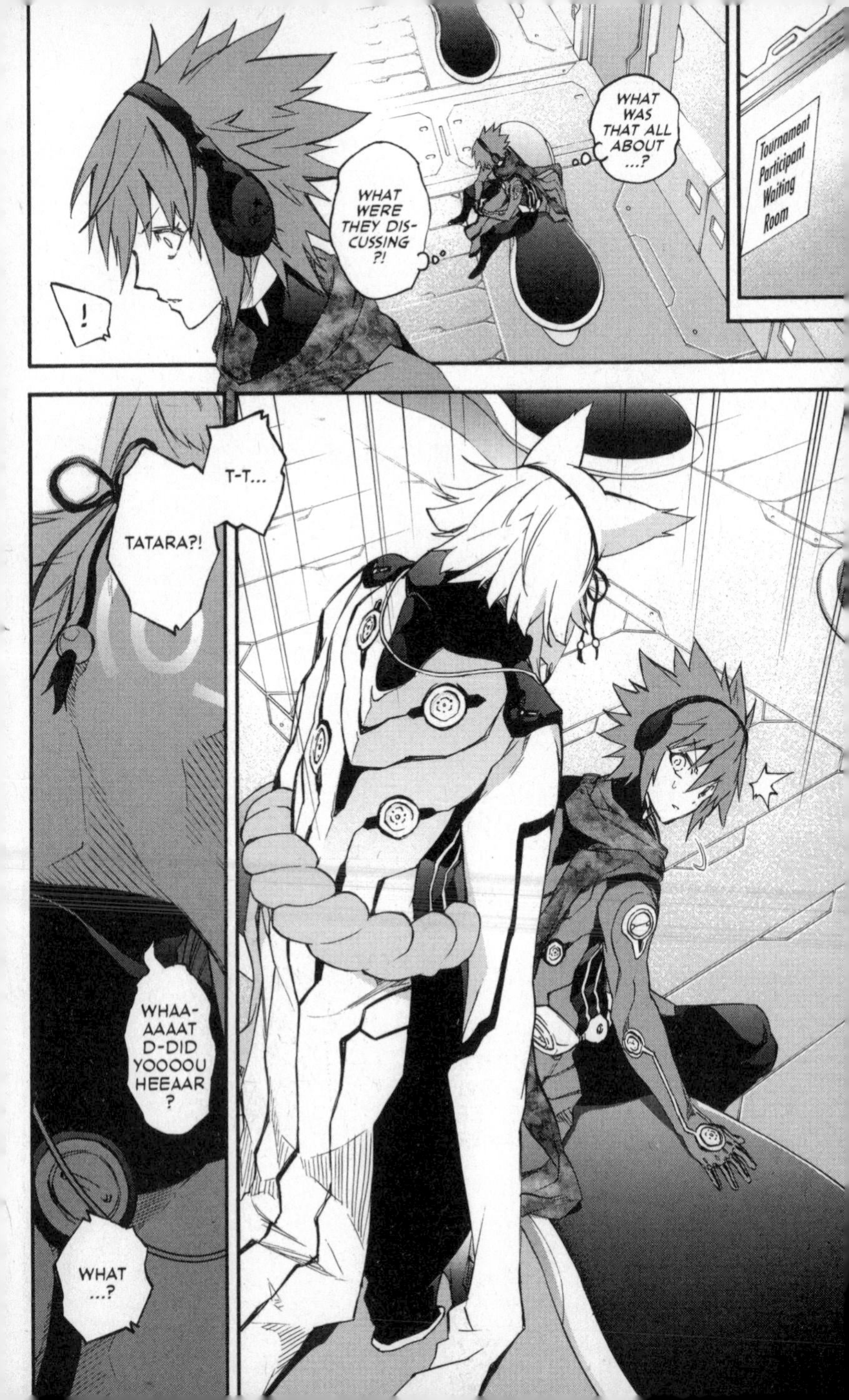
Tournament Participant Waiting Room
WHAT WAS THAT ALL ABOUT ...?
WHAT WERE THEY DIS-CUSSING ?!
!
T-T...
TATARA?!
WHAA-AAAAT D-DID YOOOOU HEEAAR ?
WHAT ...?

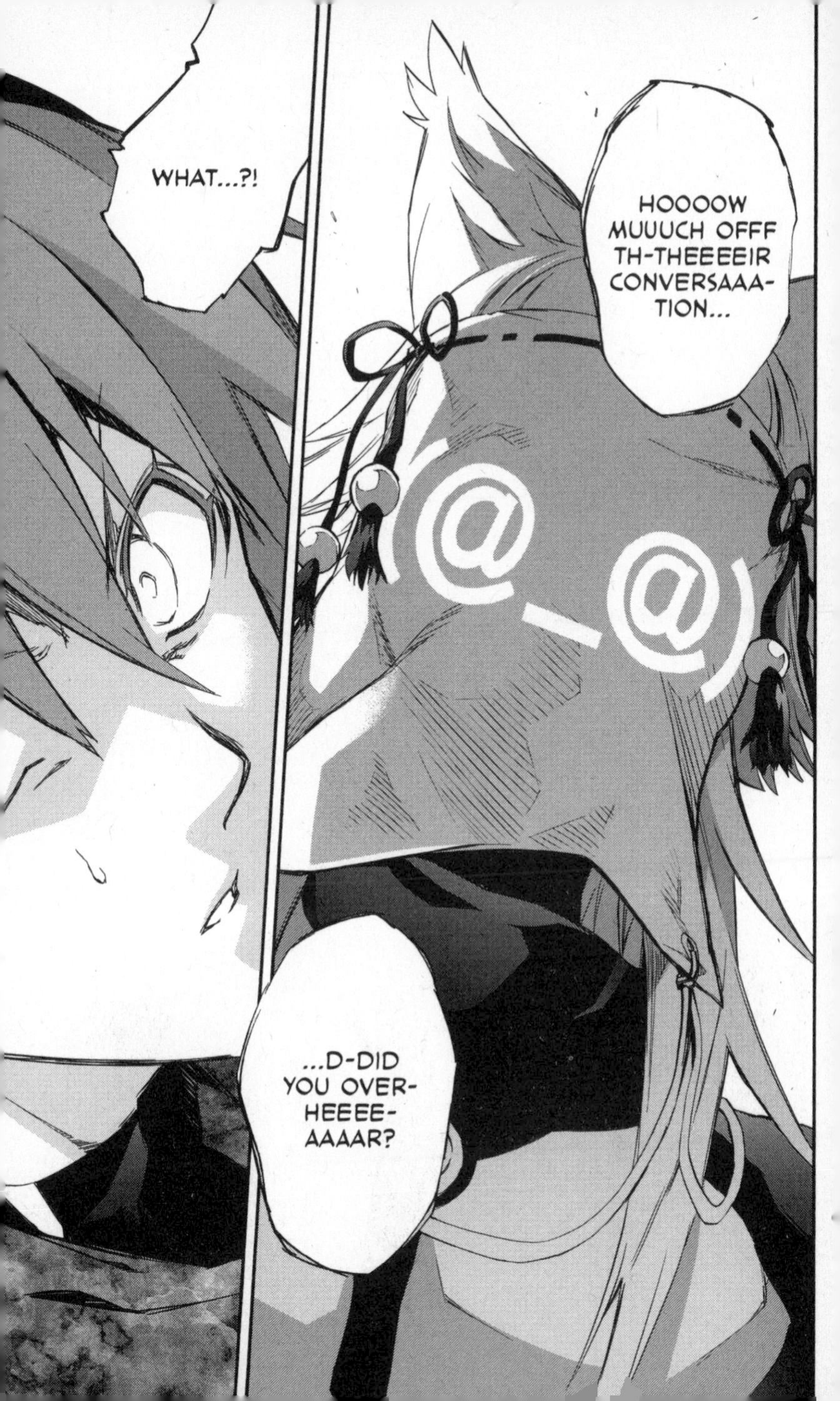
HOOOOW MUUUCH OFFF TH-THEEEEIR CONVERSAAA-TION...
...D-DID YOU OVER-HEEEE-AAAAR?
WHAT...?!

Twin Star Exorcists

ONMYOJI

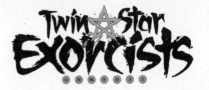

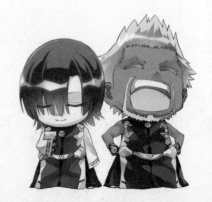

#47: My Name Is Not Bird Boy

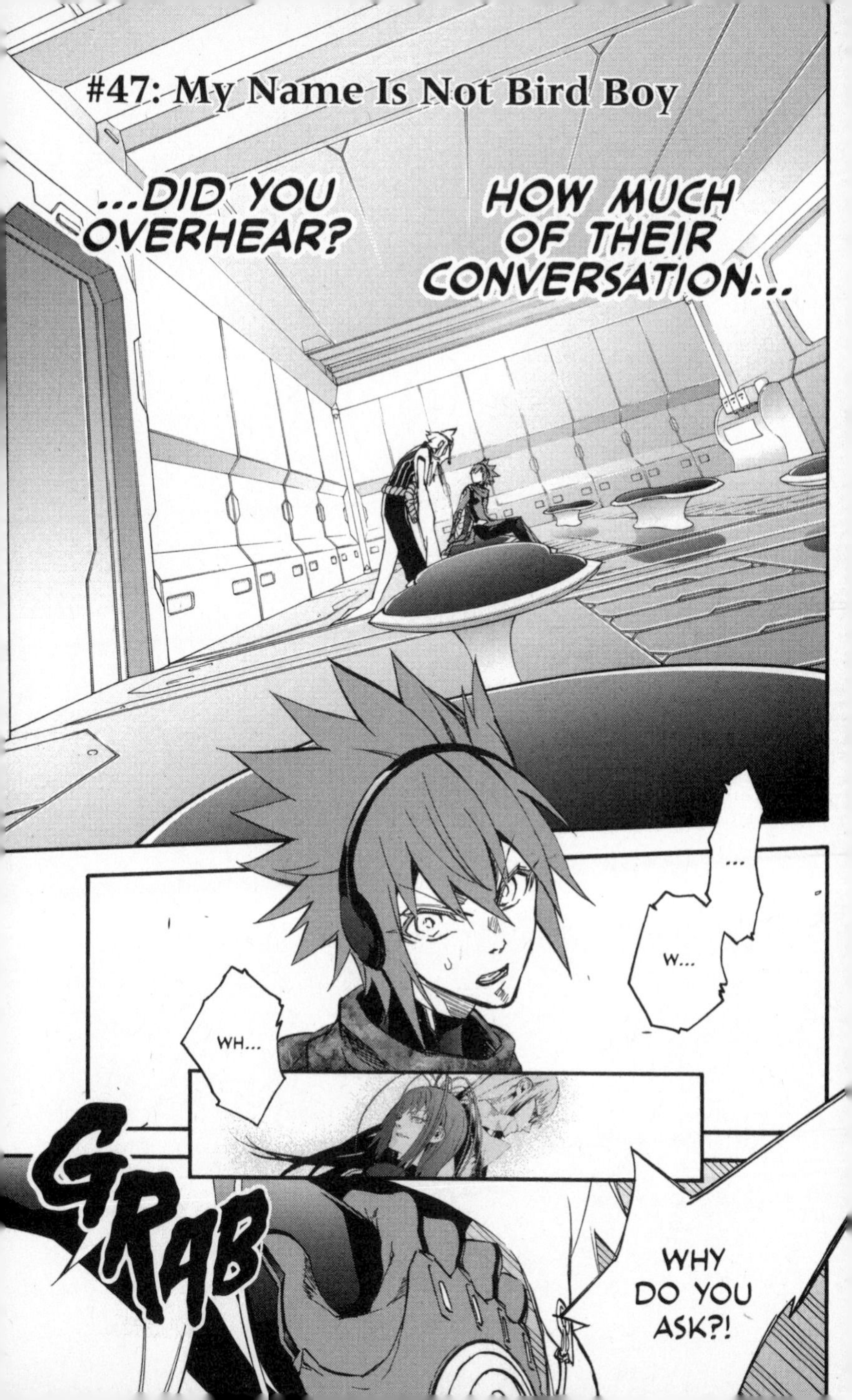
HOW MUCH OF THEIR CONVERSATION...
...DID YOU OVERHEAR?
...
W...
WH...
WHY DO YOU ASK?!
GRAB

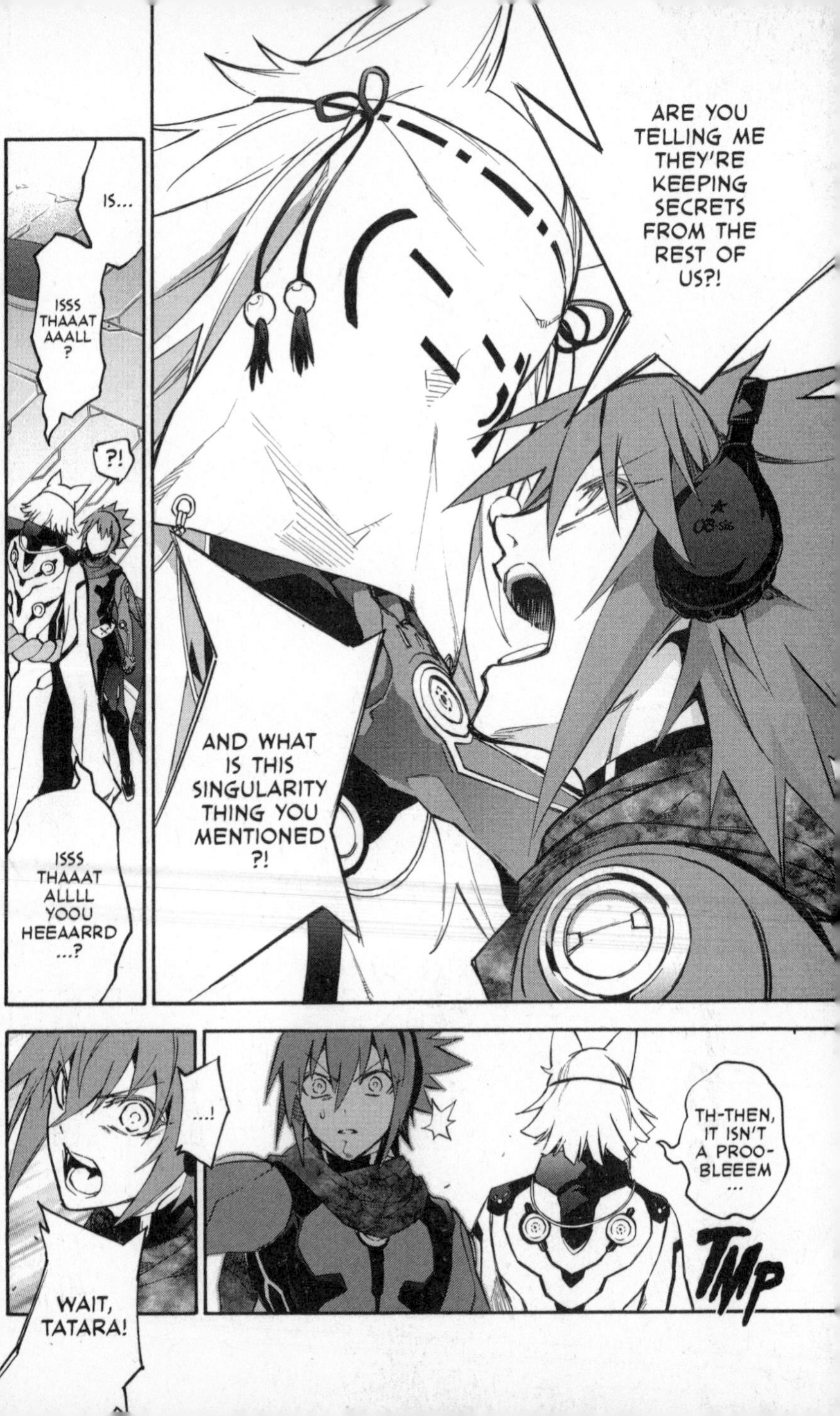
ARE YOU TELLING ME THEY'RE KEEPING SECRETS FROM THE REST OF US?!
AND WHAT IS THIS SINGULARITY THING YOU MENTIONED ?!
IS...
ISSS THAAAT AAALL ?
?!
ISSS THAAAT ALLLL YOOU HEEAARRD ...?
TH-THEN, IT ISN'T A PROO-BLEEEM ...
...!
TMP
WAIT, TATARA!

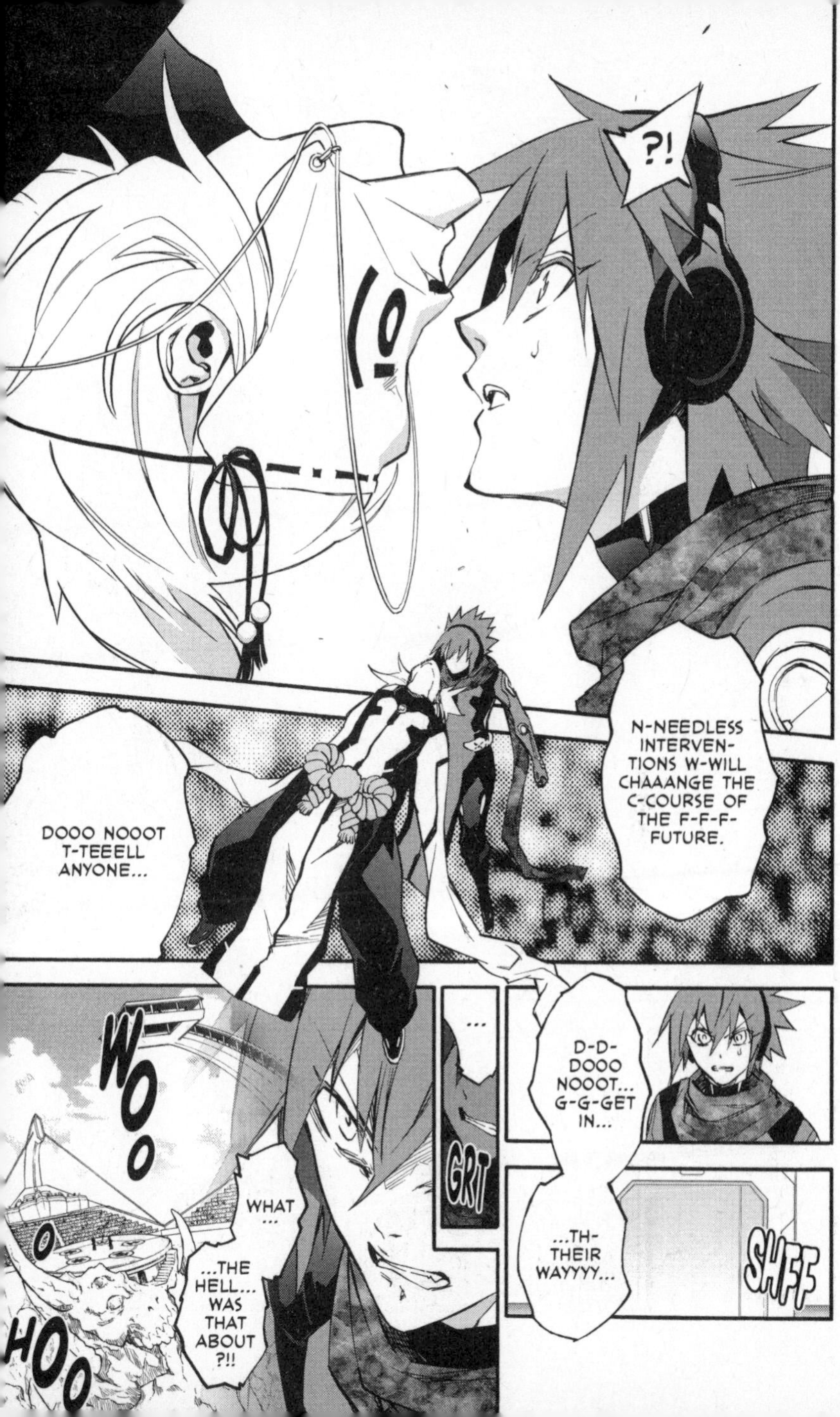
?!
N-NEEDLESS INTERVEN-TIONS W-WILL CHAAANGE THE C-COURSE OF THE F-F-F-FUTURE.
DOOO NOOOT T-TEEELL ANYONE...
D-D-DOOO NOOOT... G-G-GET IN...
...TH-THEIR WAYYYY...
SHFF
...
GRT
WHAT ...
...THE HELL... WAS THAT ABOUT ?!!
WOOO
HOOO

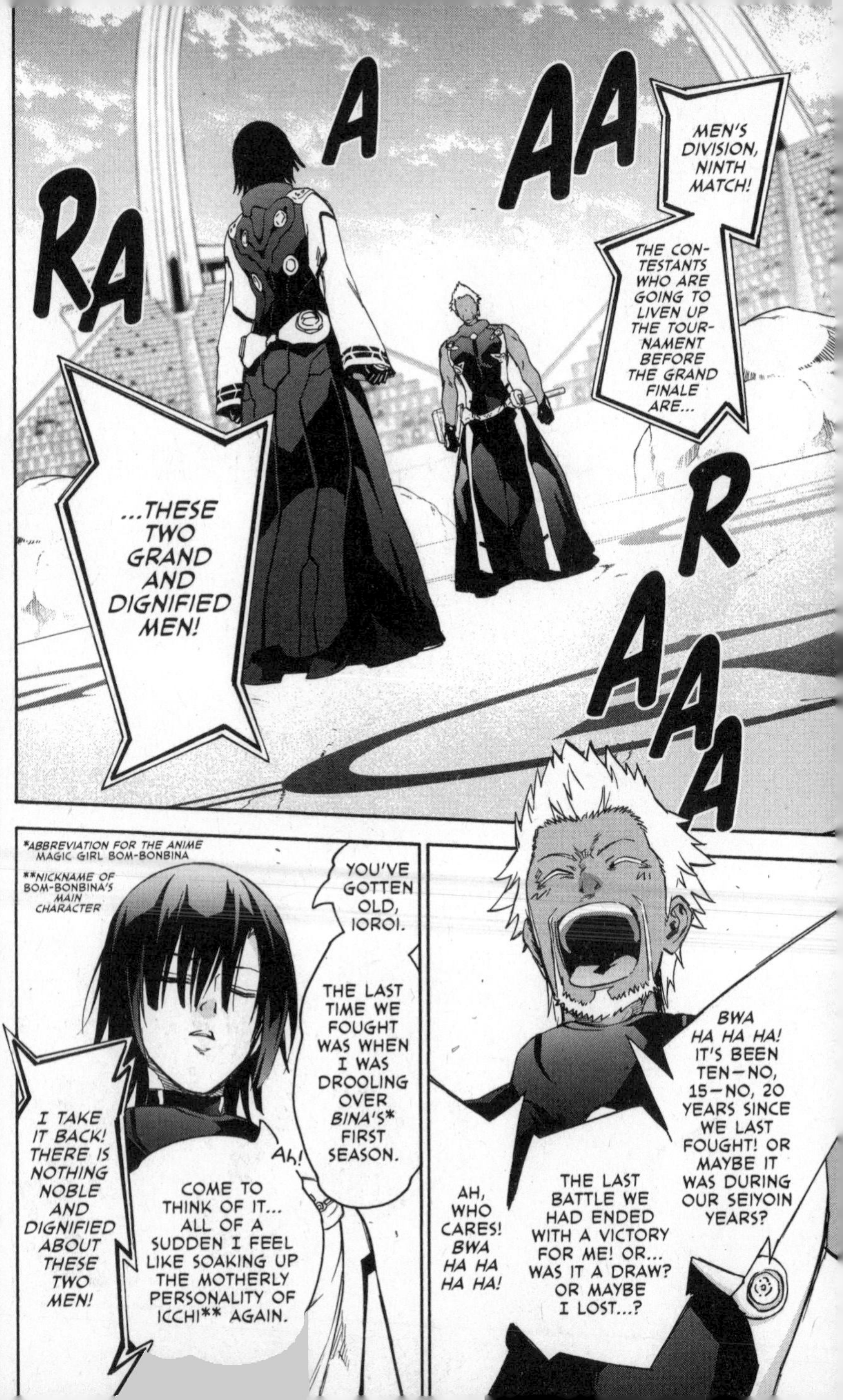
MEN'S DIVISION, NINTH MATCH!
THE CONTESTANTS WHO ARE GOING TO LIVEN UP THE TOURNAMENT BEFORE THE GRAND FINALE ARE...
AA
A
RA
...THESE TWO GRAND AND DIGNIFIED MEN!
RAAAA
BWA HA HA HA! IT'S BEEN TEN—NO, 15—NO, 20 YEARS SINCE WE LAST FOUGHT! OR MAYBE IT WAS DURING OUR SEIYOIN YEARS?
THE LAST BATTLE WE HAD ENDED WITH A VICTORY FOR ME! OR... WAS IT A DRAW? OR MAYBE I LOST...?
AH, WHO CARES! BWA HA HA HA HA!
YOU'VE GOTTEN OLD, IOROI.
THE LAST TIME WE FOUGHT WAS WHEN I WAS DROOLING OVER *BINA'S** FIRST SEASON.
Ah!
COME TO THINK OF IT... ALL OF A SUDDEN I FEEL LIKE SOAKING UP THE MOTHERLY PERSONALITY OF ICCHI** AGAIN.
I TAKE IT BACK! THERE IS NOTHING NOBLE AND DIGNIFIED ABOUT THESE TWO MEN!
*ABBREVIATION FOR THE ANIME MAGIC GIRL BOM-BONBINA
**NICKNAME OF BOM-BONBINA'S MAIN CHARACTER

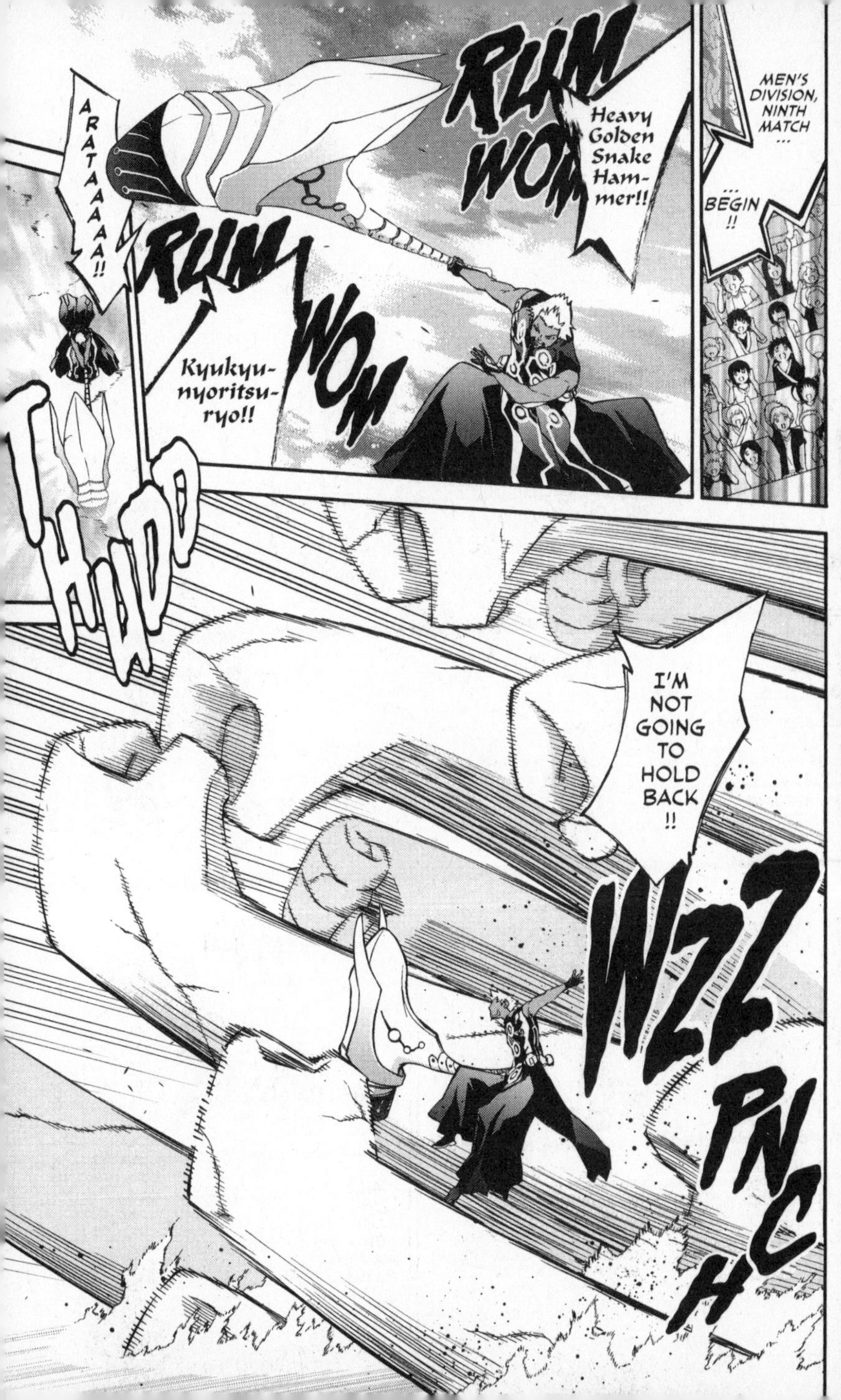
MEN'S DIVISION, NINTH MATCH ...
... BEGIN !!
RUM WOM
Heavy Golden Snake Ham-mer!!
ARATAAAAA!!
RUM WOM
Kyukyu-nyoritsu-ryo!!
THUDD
I'M NOT GOING TO HOLD BACK !!
WZZ PNCH

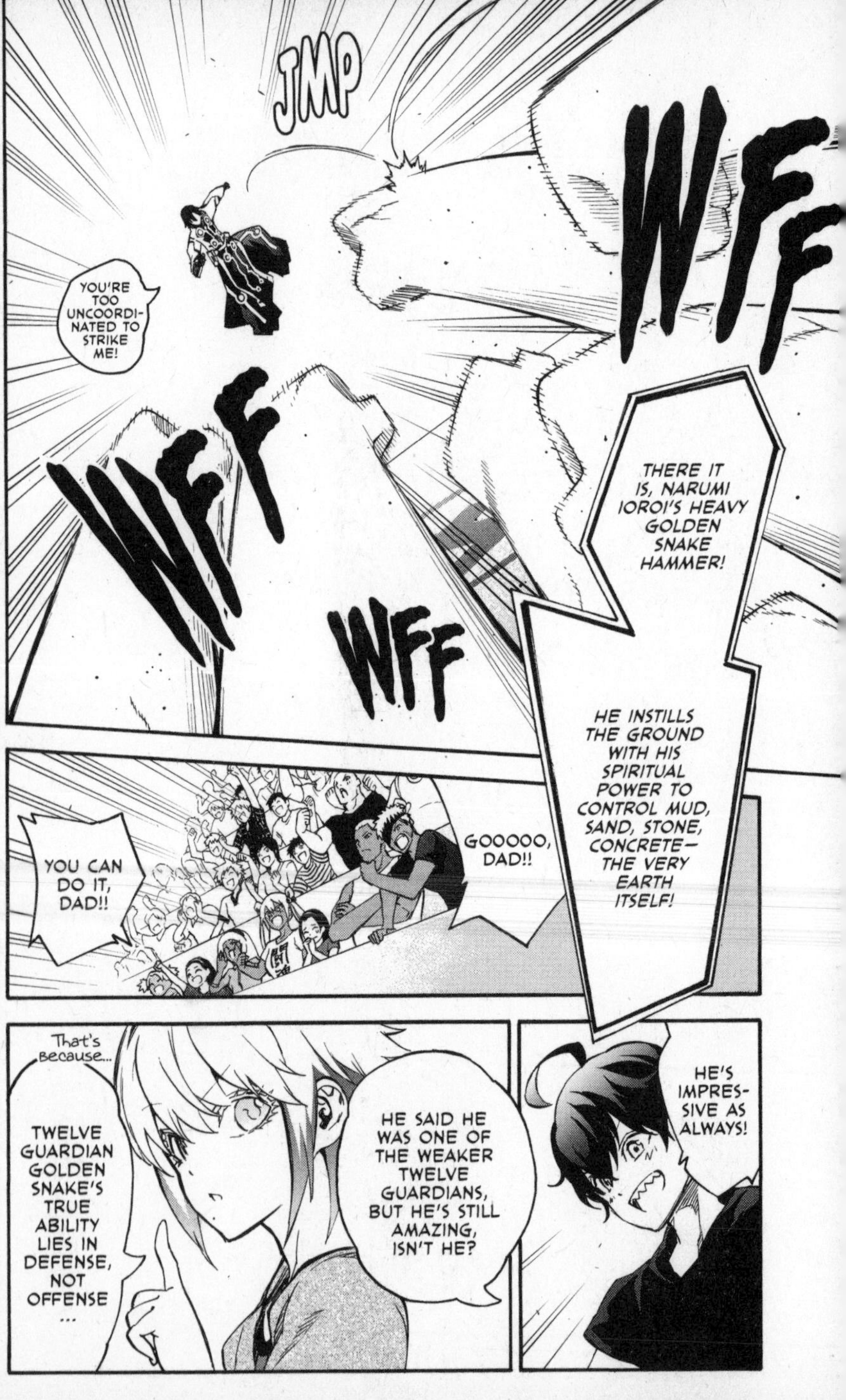
WFF
JMP
THERE IT IS, NARUMI IOROI'S HEAVY GOLDEN SNAKE HAMMER!
YOU'RE TOO UNCOORDI-NATED TO STRIKE ME!
WFF
WFF
HE INSTILLS THE GROUND WITH HIS SPIRITUAL POWER TO CONTROL MUD, SAND, STONE, CONCRETE—THE VERY EARTH ITSELF!
GOOOOO, DAD!!
YOU CAN DO IT, DAD!!
HE'S IMPRES-SIVE AS ALWAYS!
HE SAID HE WAS ONE OF THE WEAKER TWELVE GUARDIANS, BUT HE'S STILL AMAZING, ISN'T HE?
That's because...
TWELVE GUARDIAN GOLDEN SNAKE'S TRUE ABILITY LIES IN DEFENSE, NOT OFFENSE ...

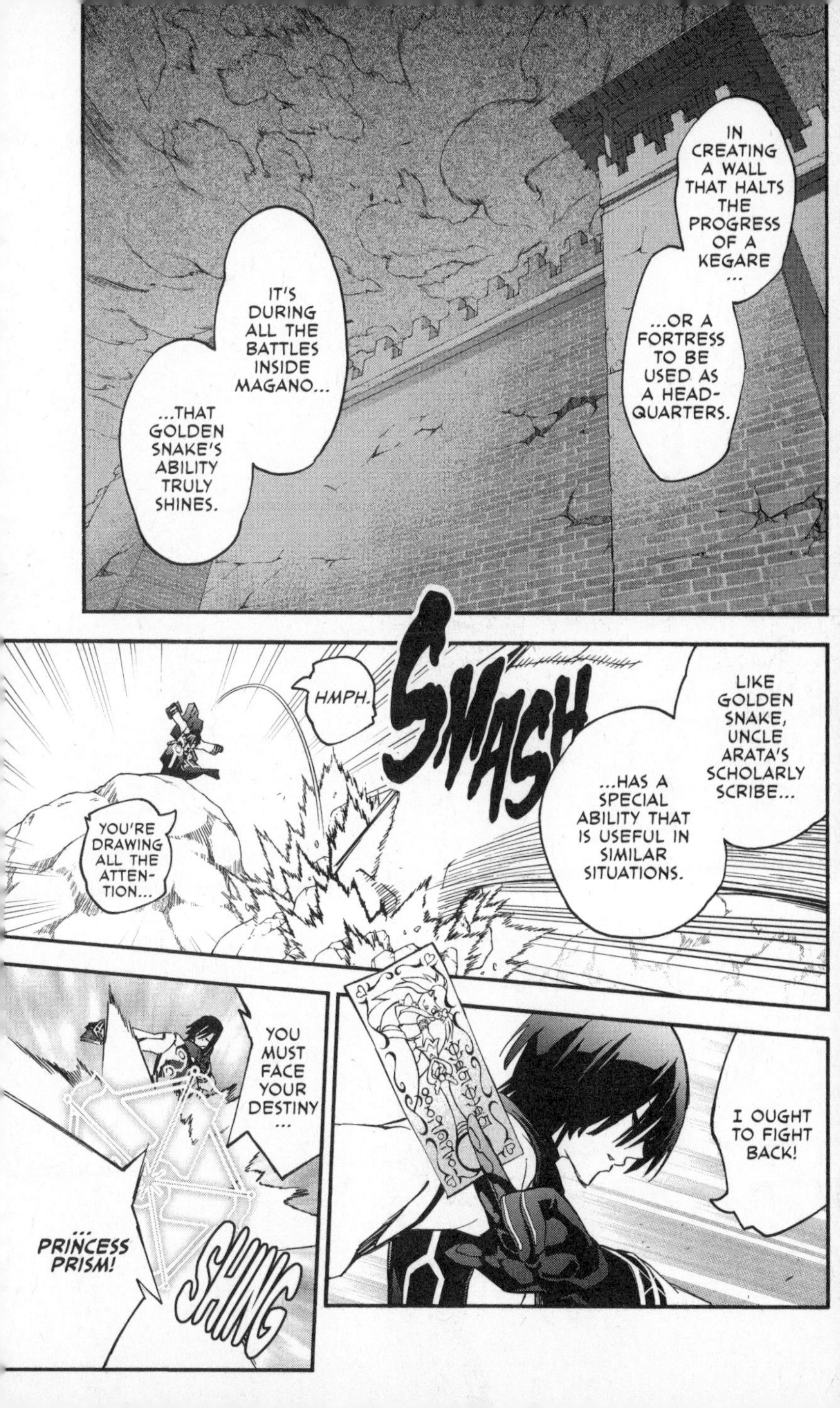
IN CREATING A WALL THAT HALTS THE PROGRESS OF A KEGARE...
...OR A FORTRESS TO BE USED AS A HEAD-QUARTERS.
IT'S DURING ALL THE BATTLES INSIDE MAGANO...
...THAT GOLDEN SNAKE'S ABILITY TRULY SHINES.
LIKE GOLDEN SNAKE, UNCLE ARATA'S SCHOLARLY SCRIBE...
...HAS A SPECIAL ABILITY THAT IS USEFUL IN SIMILAR SITUATIONS.
SMASH
HMPH.
YOU'RE DRAWING ALL THE ATTEN-TION...
I OUGHT TO FIGHT BACK!
YOU MUST FACE YOUR DESTINY...
...PRINCESS PRISM!
SHING

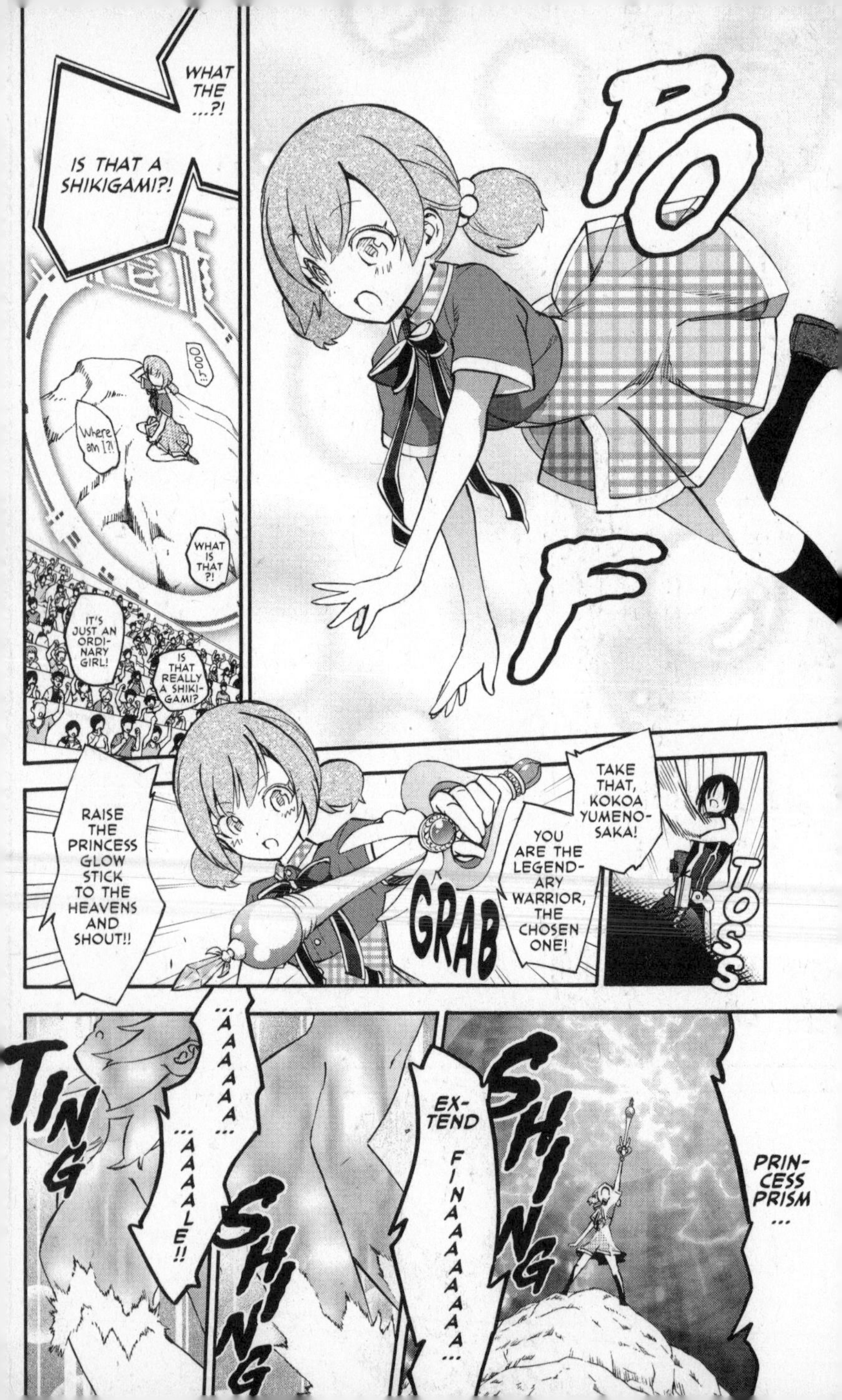
POF
WHAT THE ...?!
IS THAT A SHIKIGAMI?!
Oooh!!
Where am I?!
WHAT IS THAT?!
IT'S JUST AN ORDINARY GIRL!
IS THAT REALLY A SHIKIGAMI?
TAKE THAT, KOKOA YUMENOSAKA!
YOU ARE THE LEGENDARY WARRIOR, THE CHOSEN ONE!
TOSS
GRAB
RAISE THE PRINCESS GLOW STICK TO THE HEAVENS AND SHOUT!!
PRINCESS PRISM ...
SHING
EXTEND FINAAAAAAAAAA...
SHING
...AAAAAA...
...AAAAALE!!
TING

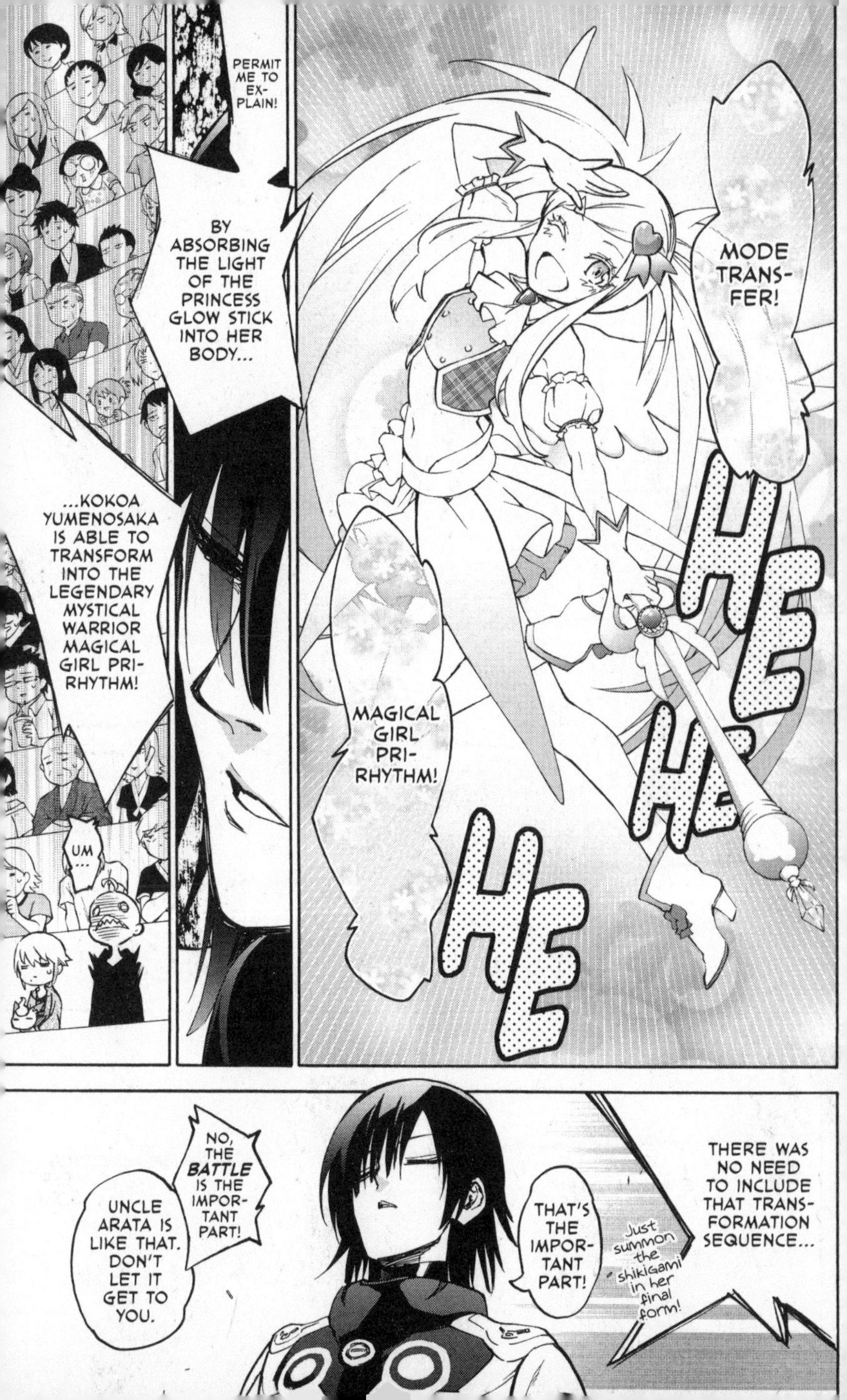
MODE TRANSFER!
MAGICAL GIRL PRI-RHYTHM!
HE HE HE
PERMIT ME TO EXPLAIN!
BY ABSORBING THE LIGHT OF THE PRINCESS GLOW STICK INTO HER BODY...
...KOKOA YUMENOSAKA IS ABLE TO TRANSFORM INTO THE LEGENDARY MYSTICAL WARRIOR MAGICAL GIRL PRI-RHYTHM!
UM ...
THERE WAS NO NEED TO INCLUDE THAT TRANSFORMATION SEQUENCE...
Just summon the shikigami in her final form!
THAT'S THE IMPORTANT PART!
NO, THE BATTLE IS THE IMPORTANT PART!
UNCLE ARATA IS LIKE THAT. DON'T LET IT GET TO YOU.

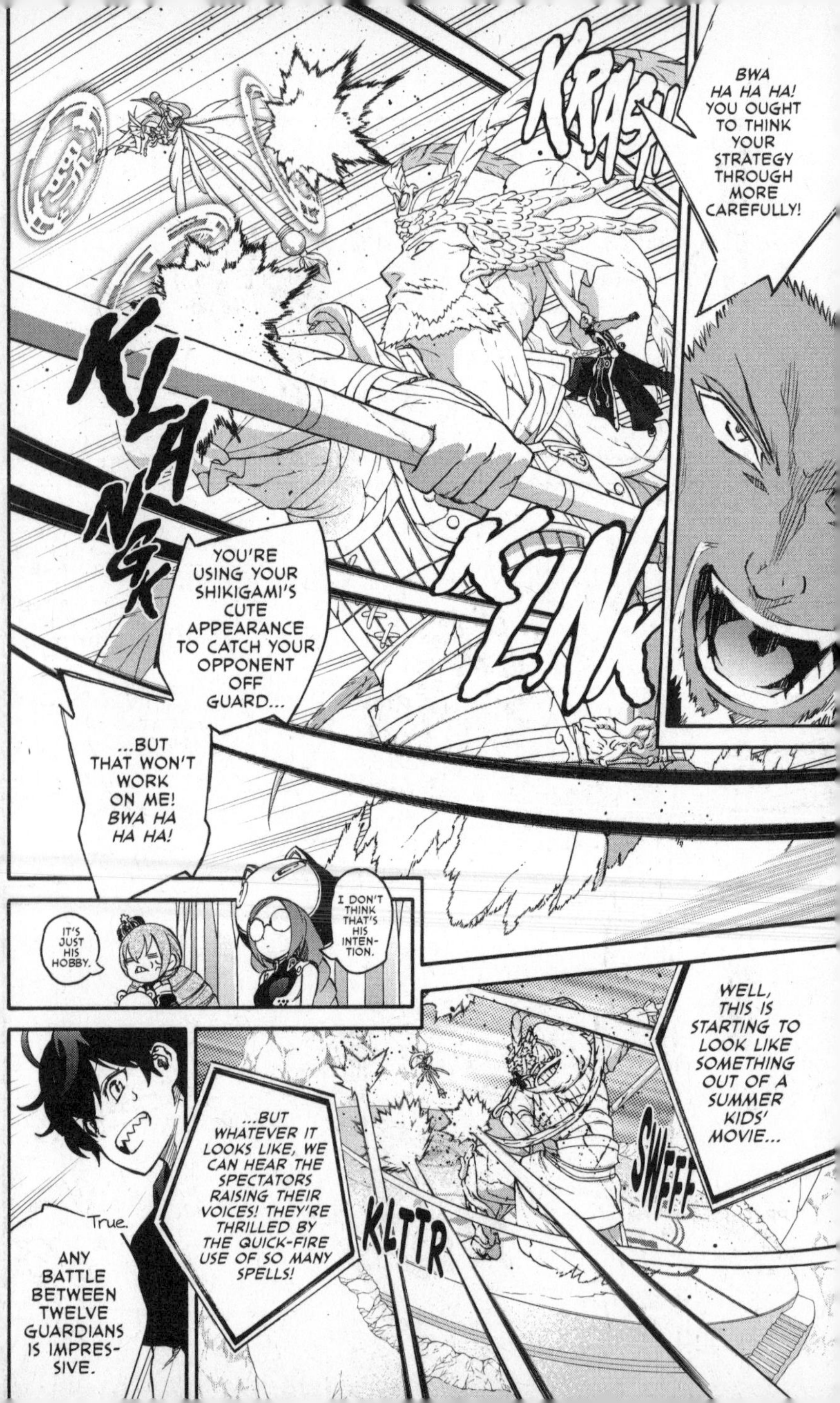
BWA HA HA HA! YOU OUGHT TO THINK YOUR STRATEGY THROUGH MORE CAREFULLY!
KRASH
KLANGK
KLINK
YOU'RE USING YOUR SHIKIGAMI'S CUTE APPEARANCE TO CATCH YOUR OPPONENT OFF GUARD...
...BUT THAT WON'T WORK ON ME! BWA HA HA HA!
I DON'T THINK THAT'S HIS INTEN-TION.
IT'S JUST HIS HOBBY.
WELL, THIS IS STARTING TO LOOK LIKE SOMETHING OUT OF A SUMMER KIDS' MOVIE...
SWFFF
...BUT WHATEVER IT LOOKS LIKE, WE CAN HEAR THE SPECTATORS RAISING THEIR VOICES! THEY'RE THRILLED BY THE QUICK-FIRE USE OF SO MANY SPELLS!
KLTTR
True.
ANY BATTLE BETWEEN TWELVE GUARDIANS IS IMPRES-SIVE.

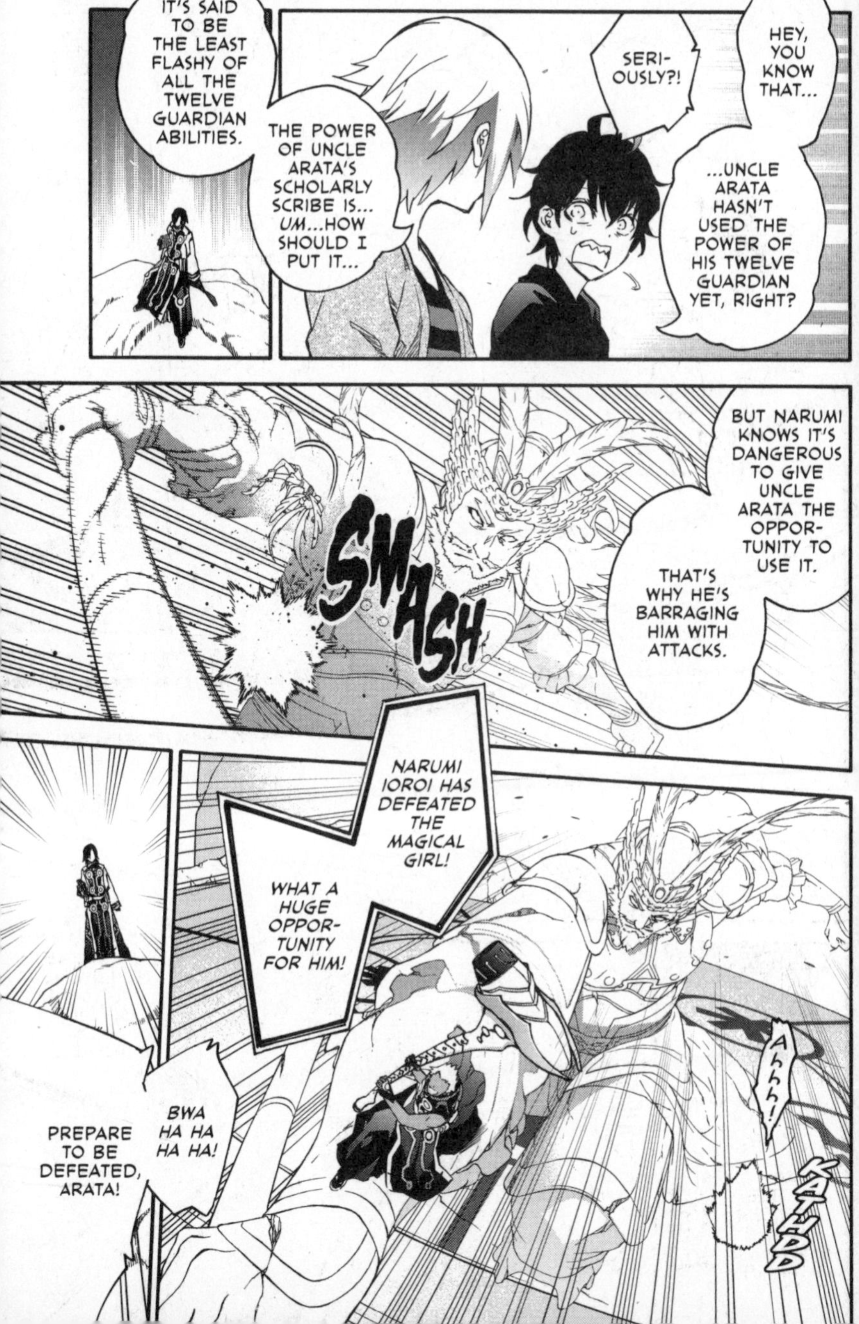
HEY, YOU KNOW THAT...
SERI-OUSLY?!
...UNCLE ARATA HASN'T USED THE POWER OF HIS TWELVE GUARDIAN YET, RIGHT?
THE POWER OF UNCLE ARATA'S SCHOLARLY SCRIBE IS... *UM*...HOW SHOULD I PUT IT...
IT'S SAID TO BE THE LEAST FLASHY OF ALL THE TWELVE GUARDIAN ABILITIES.
BUT NARUMI KNOWS IT'S DANGEROUS TO GIVE UNCLE ARATA THE OPPOR-TUNITY TO USE IT.
THAT'S WHY HE'S BARRAGING HIM WITH ATTACKS.
SMASH
NARUMI IOROI HAS DEFEATED THE MAGICAL GIRL!
WHAT A HUGE OPPOR-TUNITY FOR HIM!
Ahhh!
KATHUDD
BWA HA HA HA HA!
PREPARE TO BE DEFEATED, ARATA!

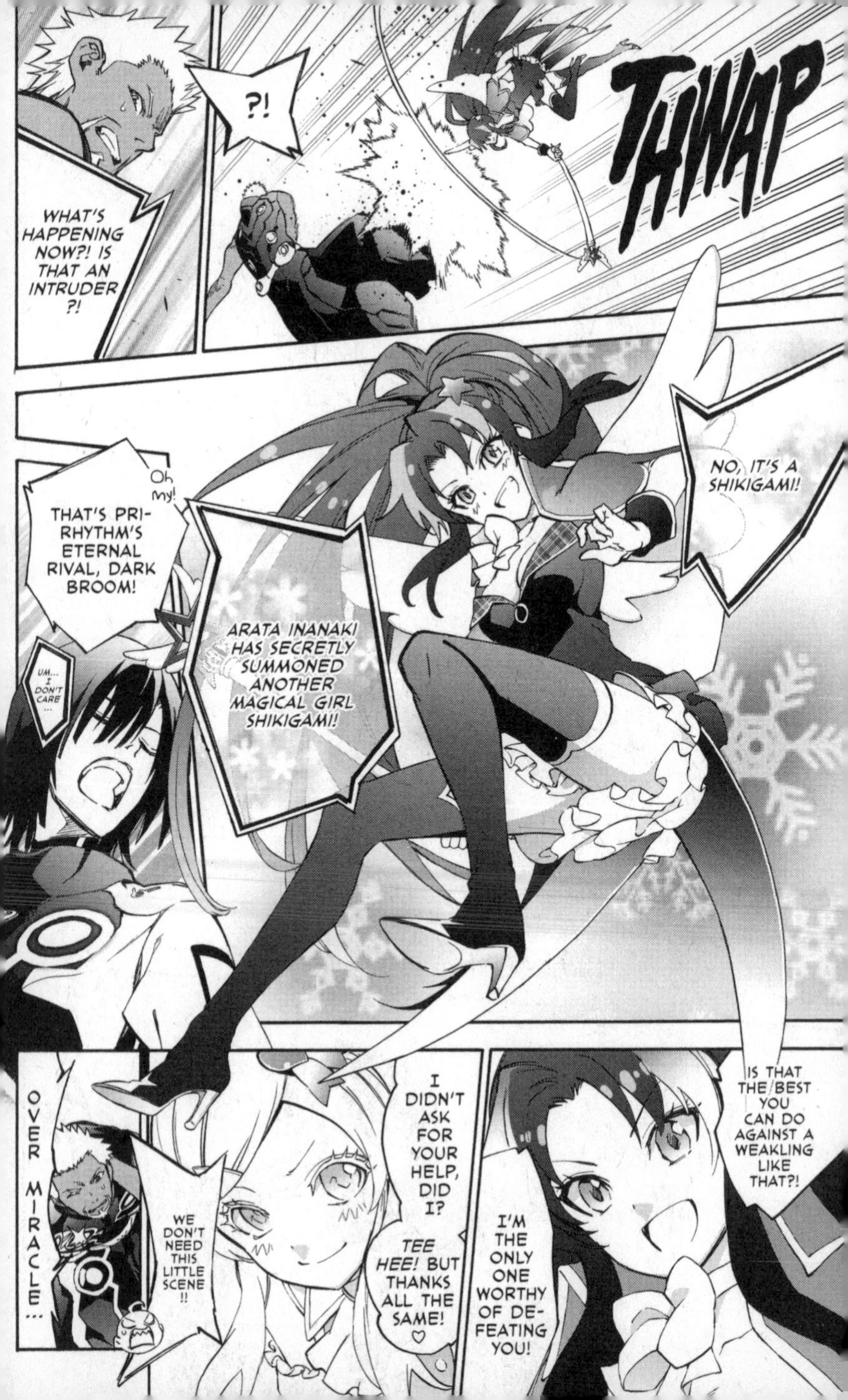
THWAP
?!
WHAT'S HAPPENING NOW?! IS THAT AN INTRUDER ?!
NO, IT'S A SHIKIGAMI!
ARATA INANAKI HAS SECRETLY SUMMONED ANOTHER MAGICAL GIRL SHIKIGAMI!
Oh my!
THAT'S PRI-RHYTHM'S ETERNAL RIVAL, DARK BROOM!
UM... I DON'T CARE ...
IS THAT THE BEST YOU CAN DO AGAINST A WEAKLING LIKE THAT?!
I'M THE ONLY ONE WORTHY OF DE-FEATING YOU!
I DIDN'T ASK FOR YOUR HELP, DID I?
TEE HEE! BUT THANKS ALL THE SAME! ♡
WE DON'T NEED THIS LITTLE SCENE !!
OVER MIRACLE...

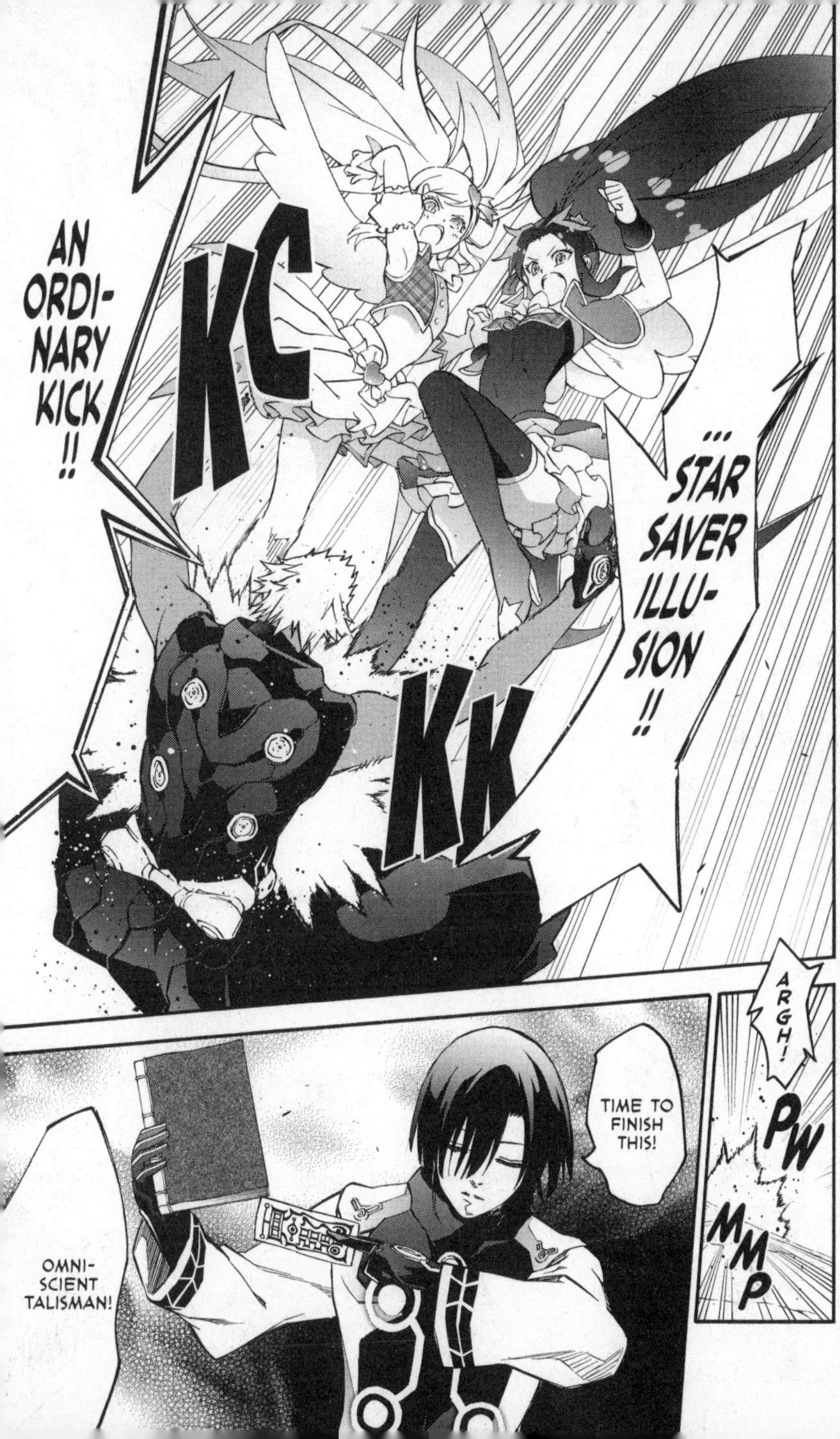
...STAR SAVER ILLUSION!!
KC
AN ORDINARY KICK!!
KK
ARGH!
PWMMP
TIME TO FINISH THIS!
OMNISCIENT TALISMAN!

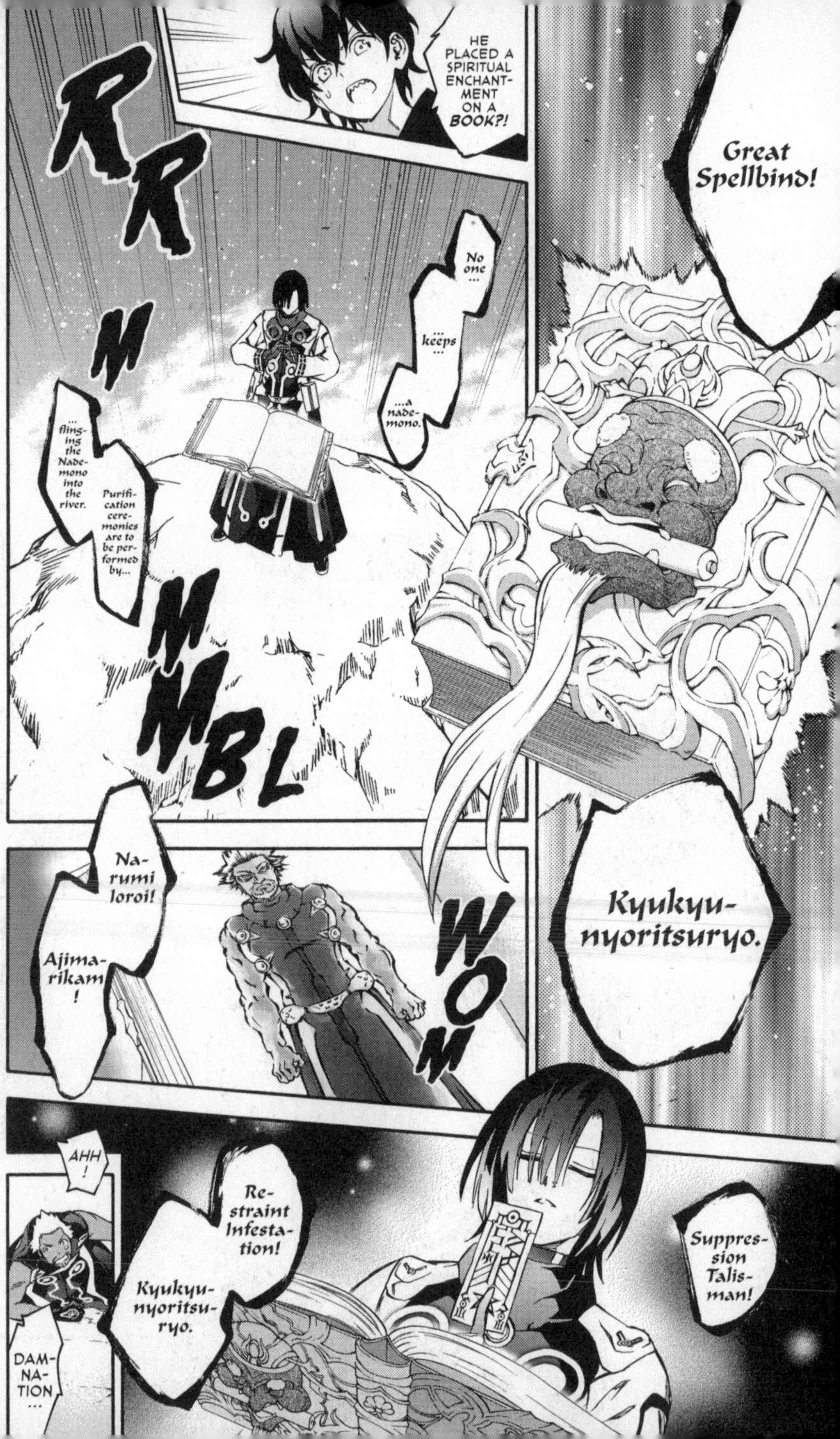
Great Spellbind!
Kyukyu-nyoritsuryo.
HE PLACED A SPIRITUAL ENCHANTMENT ON A BOOK?!
RRRM
No one ...
... keeps ...
...a nademono.
Purification ceremonies are to be performed by...
... flinging the Nademono into the river.
MMMBL
WOM
Narumi loroi!
Ajimarikam!
Suppression Talisman!
Restraint Infestation!
Kyukyunyoritsuryo.
AHH!
DAMNATION ...

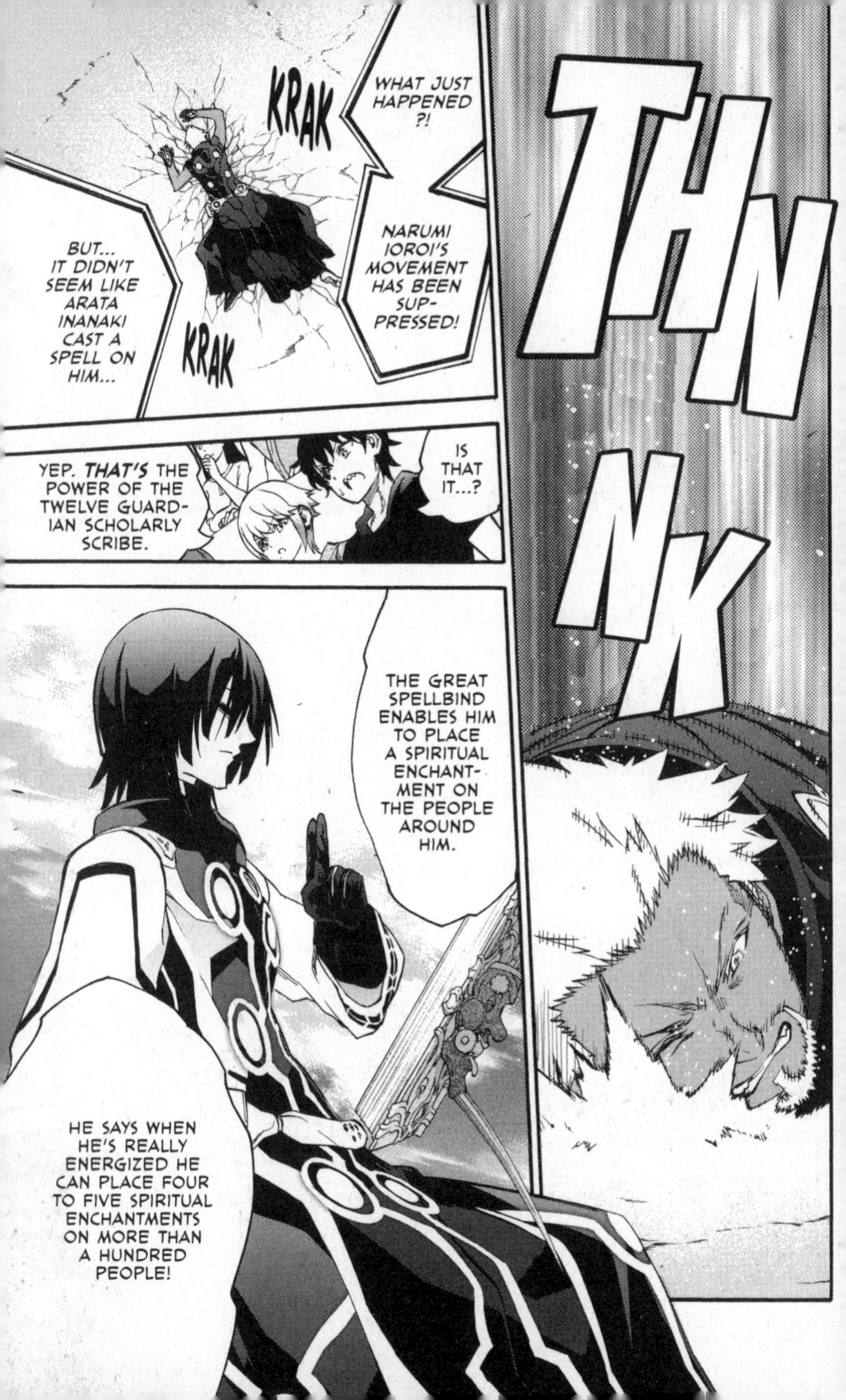
THNNK
WHAT JUST HAPPENED?!
KRAK
NARUMI IOROI'S MOVEMENT HAS BEEN SUP-PRESSED!
BUT... IT DIDN'T SEEM LIKE ARATA INANAKI CAST A SPELL ON HIM...
KRAK
IS THAT IT...?
YEP. *THAT'S* THE POWER OF THE TWELVE GUARD-IAN SCHOLARLY SCRIBE.
THE GREAT SPELLBIND ENABLES HIM TO PLACE A SPIRITUAL ENCHANT-MENT ON THE PEOPLE AROUND HIM.
HE SAYS WHEN HE'S REALLY ENERGIZED HE CAN PLACE FOUR TO FIVE SPIRITUAL ENCHANTMENTS ON MORE THAN A HUNDRED PEOPLE!

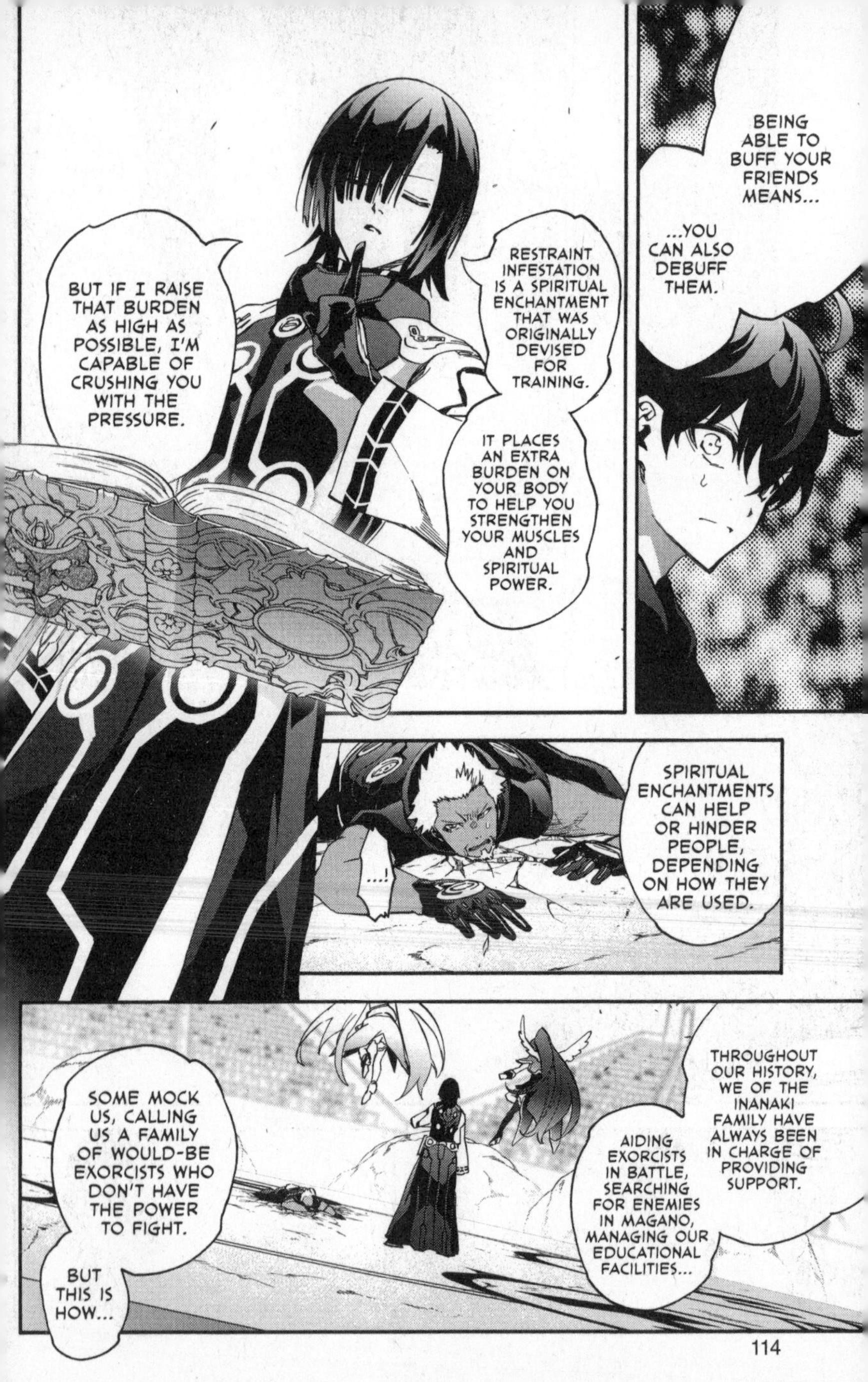
BEING ABLE TO BUFF YOUR FRIENDS MEANS...
...YOU CAN ALSO DEBUFF THEM.
RESTRAINT INFESTATION IS A SPIRITUAL ENCHANTMENT THAT WAS ORIGINALLY DEVISED FOR TRAINING.
IT PLACES AN EXTRA BURDEN ON YOUR BODY TO HELP YOU STRENGTHEN YOUR MUSCLES AND SPIRITUAL POWER.
BUT IF I RAISE THAT BURDEN AS HIGH AS POSSIBLE, I'M CAPABLE OF CRUSHING YOU WITH THE PRESSURE.
SPIRITUAL ENCHANTMENTS CAN HELP OR HINDER PEOPLE, DEPENDING ON HOW THEY ARE USED.
...!
THROUGHOUT OUR HISTORY, WE OF THE INANAKI FAMILY HAVE ALWAYS BEEN IN CHARGE OF PROVIDING SUPPORT.
AIDING EXORCISTS IN BATTLE, SEARCHING FOR ENEMIES IN MAGANO, MANAGING OUR EDUCATIONAL FACILITIES...
SOME MOCK US, CALLING US A FAMILY OF WOULD-BE EXORCISTS WHO DON'T HAVE THE POWER TO FIGHT.
BUT THIS IS HOW...

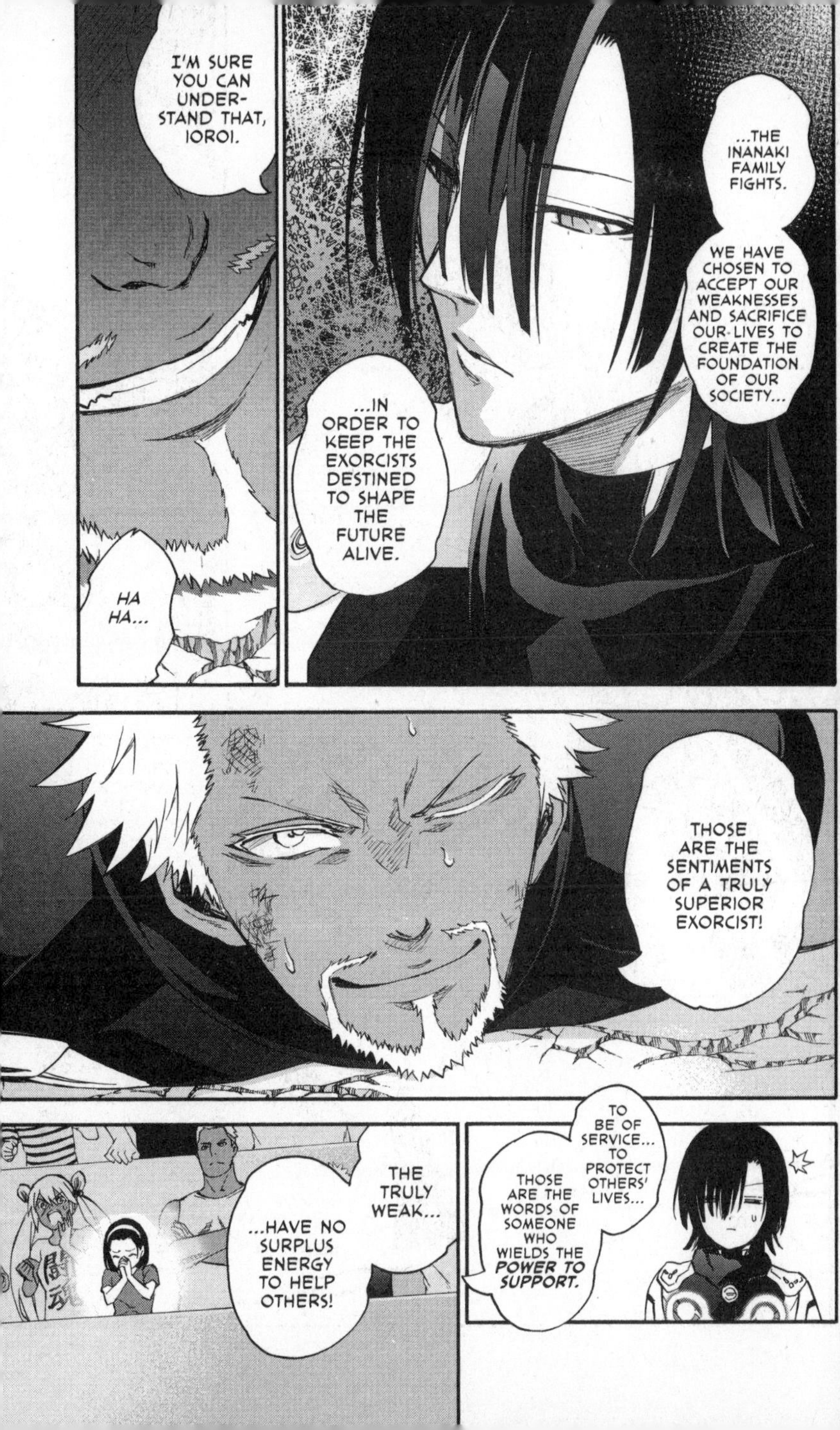
...THE INANAKI FAMILY FIGHTS.
WE HAVE CHOSEN TO ACCEPT OUR WEAKNESSES AND SACRIFICE OUR LIVES TO CREATE THE FOUNDATION OF OUR SOCIETY...
...IN ORDER TO KEEP THE EXORCISTS DESTINED TO SHAPE THE FUTURE ALIVE.
I'M SURE YOU CAN UNDER-STAND THAT, IOROI.
HA HA...
THOSE ARE THE SENTIMENTS OF A TRULY SUPERIOR EXORCIST!
TO BE OF SERVICE... TO PROTECT OTHERS' LIVES...
THOSE ARE THE WORDS OF SOMEONE WHO WIELDS THE ***POWER TO SUPPORT.***
THE TRULY WEAK...
...HAVE NO SURPLUS ENERGY TO HELP OTHERS!

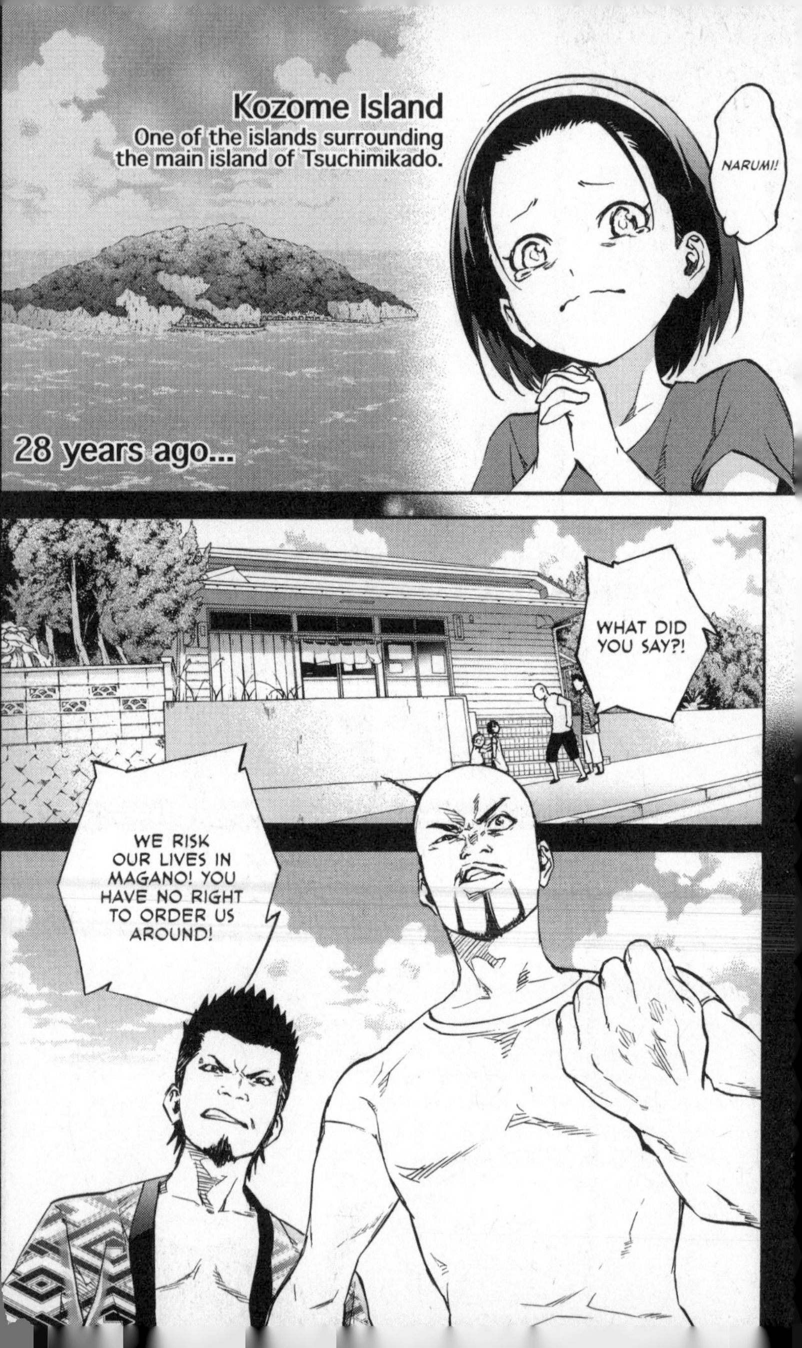

NARUMI!
Kozome Island
One of the islands surrounding the main island of Tsuchimikado.
28 years ago...
WHAT DID YOU SAY?!
WE RISK OUR LIVES IN MAGANO! YOU HAVE NO RIGHT TO ORDER US AROUND!

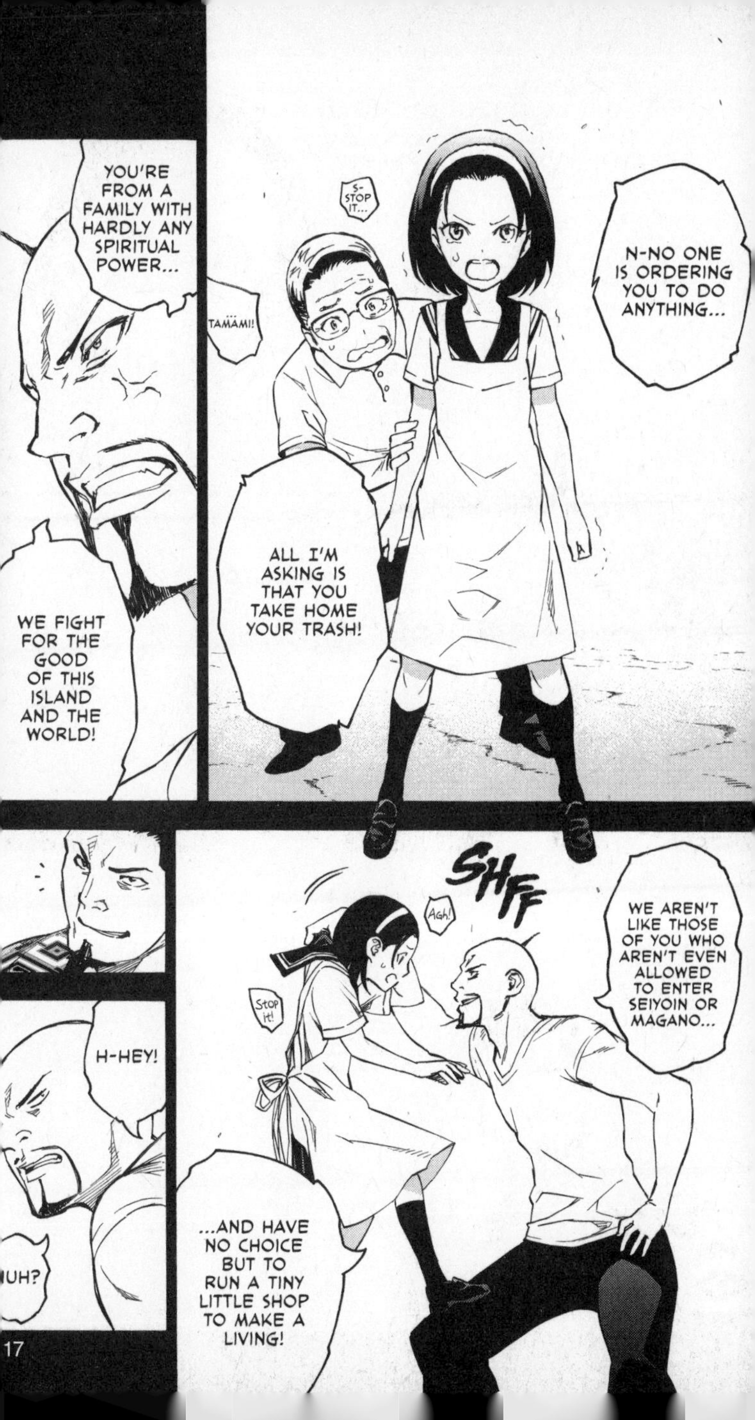
N-NO ONE IS ORDERING YOU TO DO ANYTHING...
S-STOP IT...
...TAMAMI!
ALL I'M ASKING IS THAT YOU TAKE HOME YOUR TRASH!
YOU'RE FROM A FAMILY WITH HARDLY ANY SPIRITUAL POWER...
WE FIGHT FOR THE GOOD OF THIS ISLAND AND THE WORLD!
SHFF
WE AREN'T LIKE THOSE OF YOU WHO AREN'T EVEN ALLOWED TO ENTER SEIYOIN OR MAGANO...
Agh!
Stop it!
...AND HAVE NO CHOICE BUT TO RUN A TINY LITTLE SHOP TO MAKE A LIVING!
H-HEY!
UH?

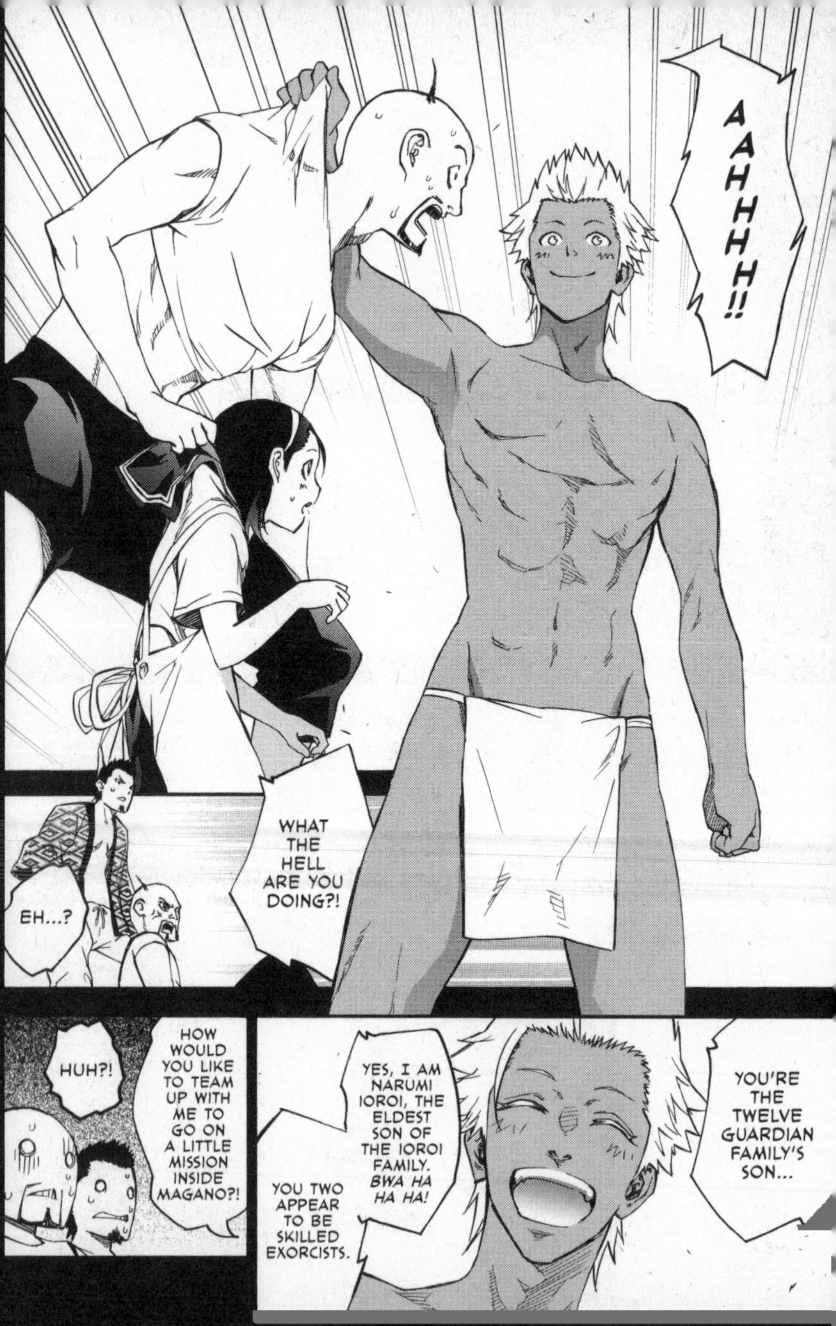
AAHHHH!!
WHAT THE HELL ARE YOU DOING?!
EH...?
YOU'RE THE TWELVE GUARDIAN FAMILY'S SON...
YES, I AM NARUMI IOROI, THE ELDEST SON OF THE IOROI FAMILY. *BWA HA HA HA!*
YOU TWO APPEAR TO BE SKILLED EXORCISTS.
HOW WOULD YOU LIKE TO TEAM UP WITH ME TO GO ON A LITTLE MISSION INSIDE MAGANO?!
HUH?!

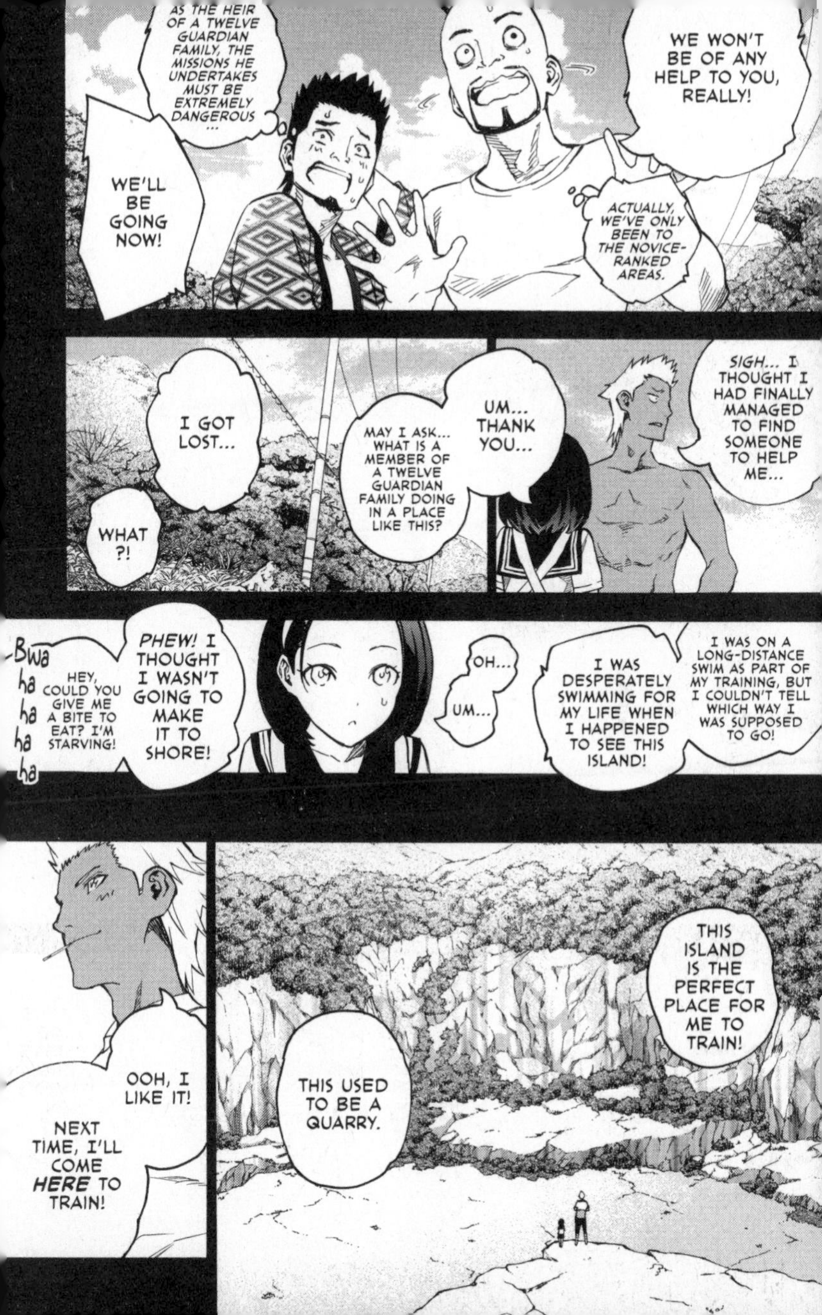
WE WON'T BE OF ANY HELP TO YOU, REALLY!
ACTUALLY, WE'VE ONLY BEEN TO THE NOVICE-RANKED AREAS.
AS THE HEIR OF A TWELVE GUARDIAN FAMILY, THE MISSIONS HE UNDERTAKES MUST BE EXTREMELY DANGEROUS ...
WE'LL BE GOING NOW!
SIGH... I THOUGHT I HAD FINALLY MANAGED TO FIND SOMEONE TO HELP ME...
UM... THANK YOU...
MAY I ASK... WHAT IS A MEMBER OF A TWELVE GUARDIAN FAMILY DOING IN A PLACE LIKE THIS?
I GOT LOST...
WHAT?!
I WAS ON A LONG-DISTANCE SWIM AS PART OF MY TRAINING, BUT I COULDN'T TELL WHICH WAY I WAS SUPPOSED TO GO!
I WAS DESPERATELY SWIMMING FOR MY LIFE WHEN I HAPPENED TO SEE THIS ISLAND!
OH...
UM...
PHEW! I THOUGHT I WASN'T GOING TO MAKE IT TO SHORE!
HEY, COULD YOU GIVE ME A BITE TO EAT? I'M STARVING!
Bwa ha ha ha ha ha
THIS ISLAND IS THE PERFECT PLACE FOR ME TO TRAIN!
THIS USED TO BE A QUARRY.
OOH, I LIKE IT!
NEXT TIME, I'LL COME *HERE* TO TRAIN!

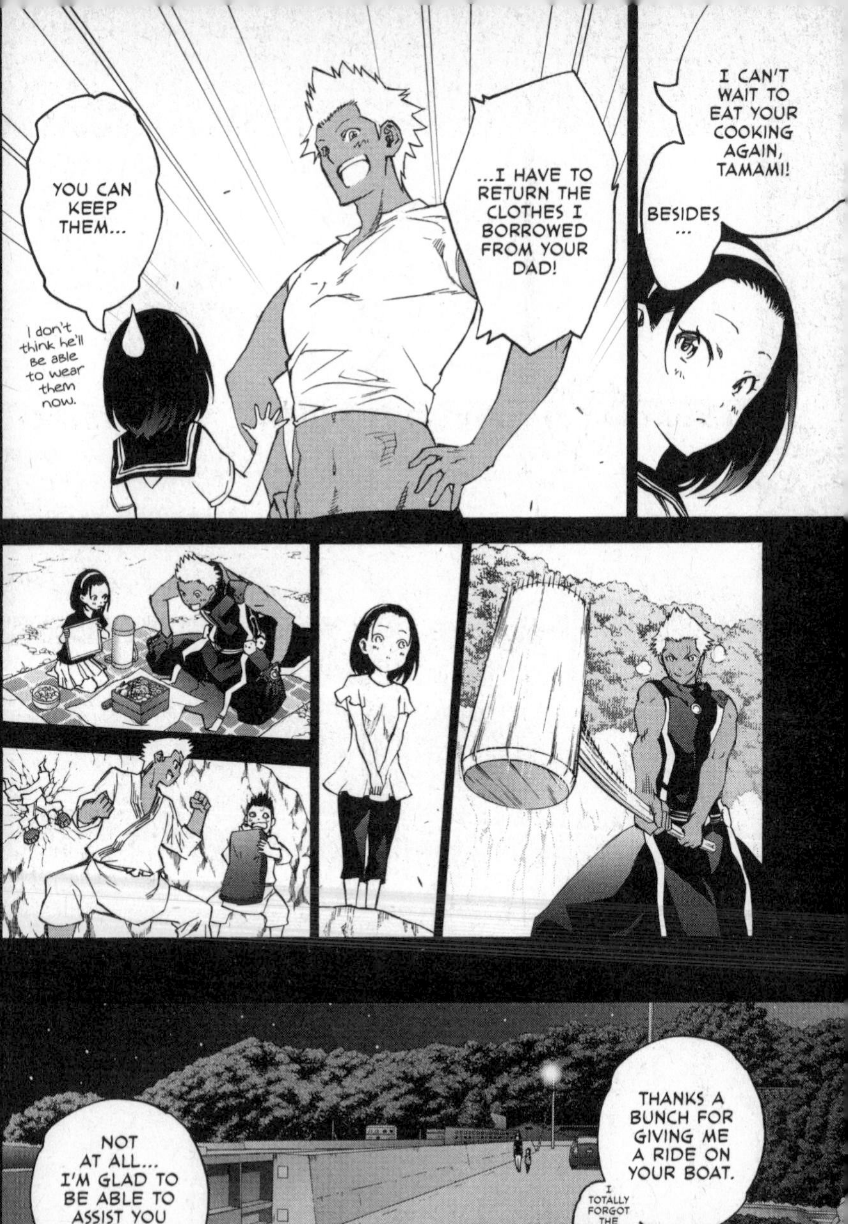
I CAN'T WAIT TO EAT YOUR COOKING AGAIN, TAMAMI!
BESIDES...
...I HAVE TO RETURN THE CLOTHES I BORROWED FROM YOUR DAD!
YOU CAN KEEP THEM...
I don't think he'll be able to wear them now.
THANKS A BUNCH FOR GIVING ME A RIDE ON YOUR BOAT.
I TOTALLY FORGOT THE TIMETABLE FOR THE FERRY.
NOT AT ALL... I'M GLAD TO BE ABLE TO ASSIST YOU WITH YOUR TRAINING.

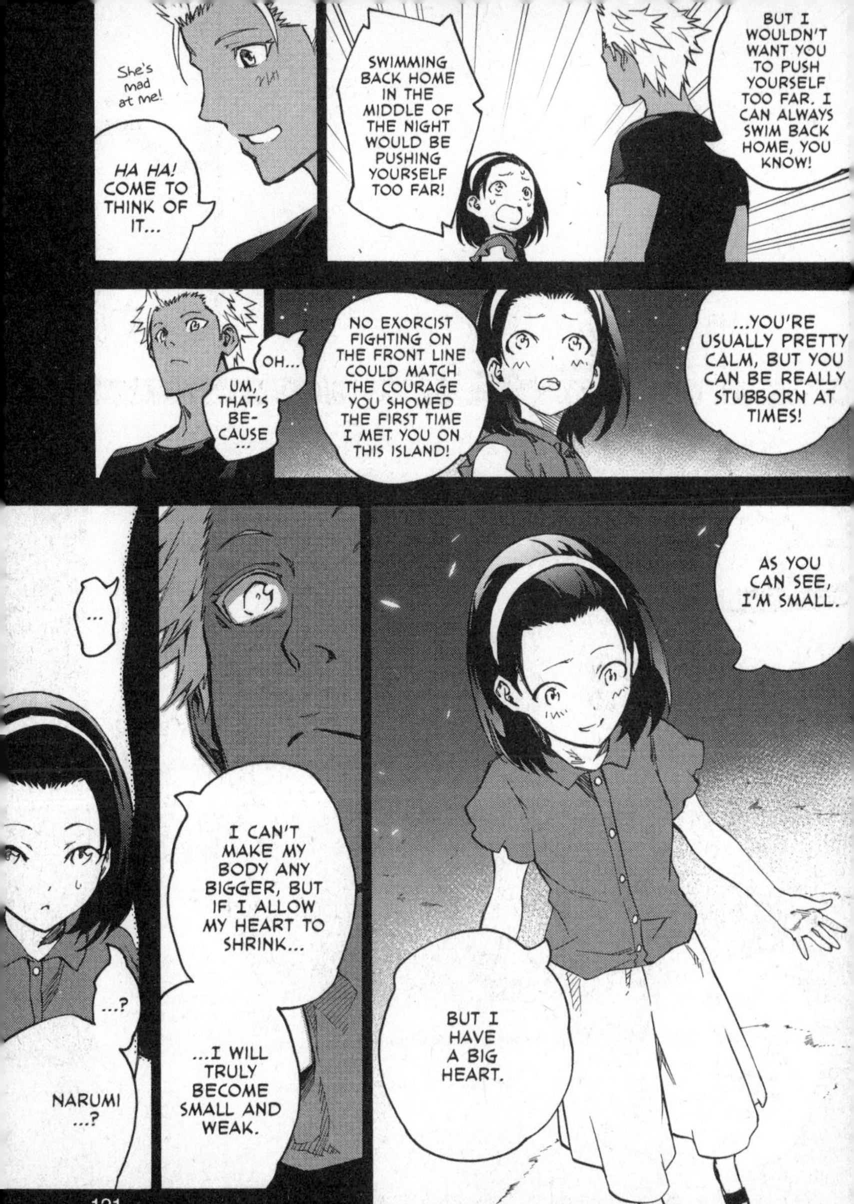
BUT I WOULDN'T WANT YOU TO PUSH YOURSELF TOO FAR. I CAN ALWAYS SWIM BACK HOME, YOU KNOW!
SWIMMING BACK HOME IN THE MIDDLE OF THE NIGHT WOULD BE PUSHING YOURSELF TOO FAR!
She's mad at me!
HA HA! COME TO THINK OF IT...
...YOU'RE USUALLY PRETTY CALM, BUT YOU CAN BE REALLY STUBBORN AT TIMES!
NO EXORCIST FIGHTING ON THE FRONT LINE COULD MATCH THE COURAGE YOU SHOWED THE FIRST TIME I MET YOU ON THIS ISLAND!
OH...
UM, THAT'S BE-CAUSE...
AS YOU CAN SEE, I'M SMALL.
BUT I HAVE A BIG HEART.
I CAN'T MAKE MY BODY ANY BIGGER, BUT IF I ALLOW MY HEART TO SHRINK...
...I WILL TRULY BECOME SMALL AND WEAK.
...
...?
NARUMI ...?

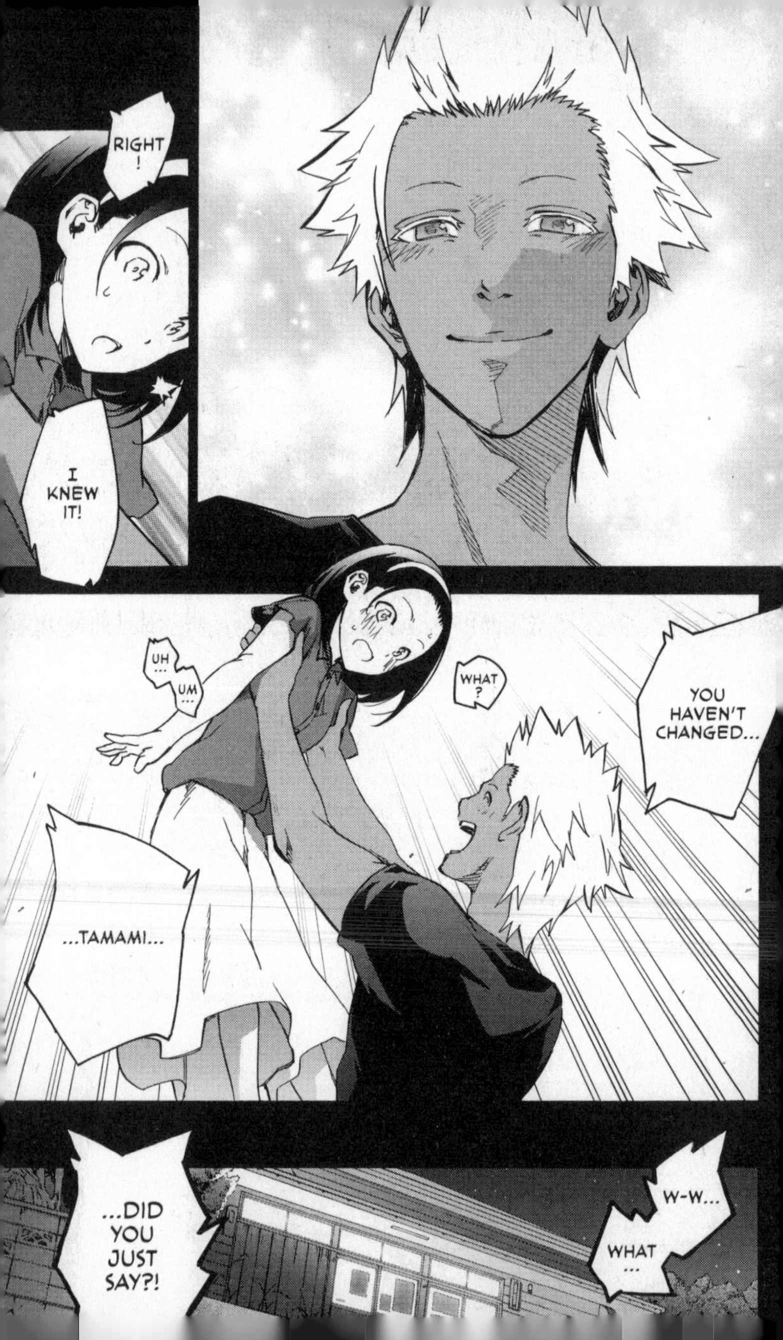
RIGHT!
I KNEW IT!
YOU HAVEN'T CHANGED...
WHAT?
UH... UM...
...TAMAMI...
W-W... WHAT...
...DID YOU JUST SAY?!

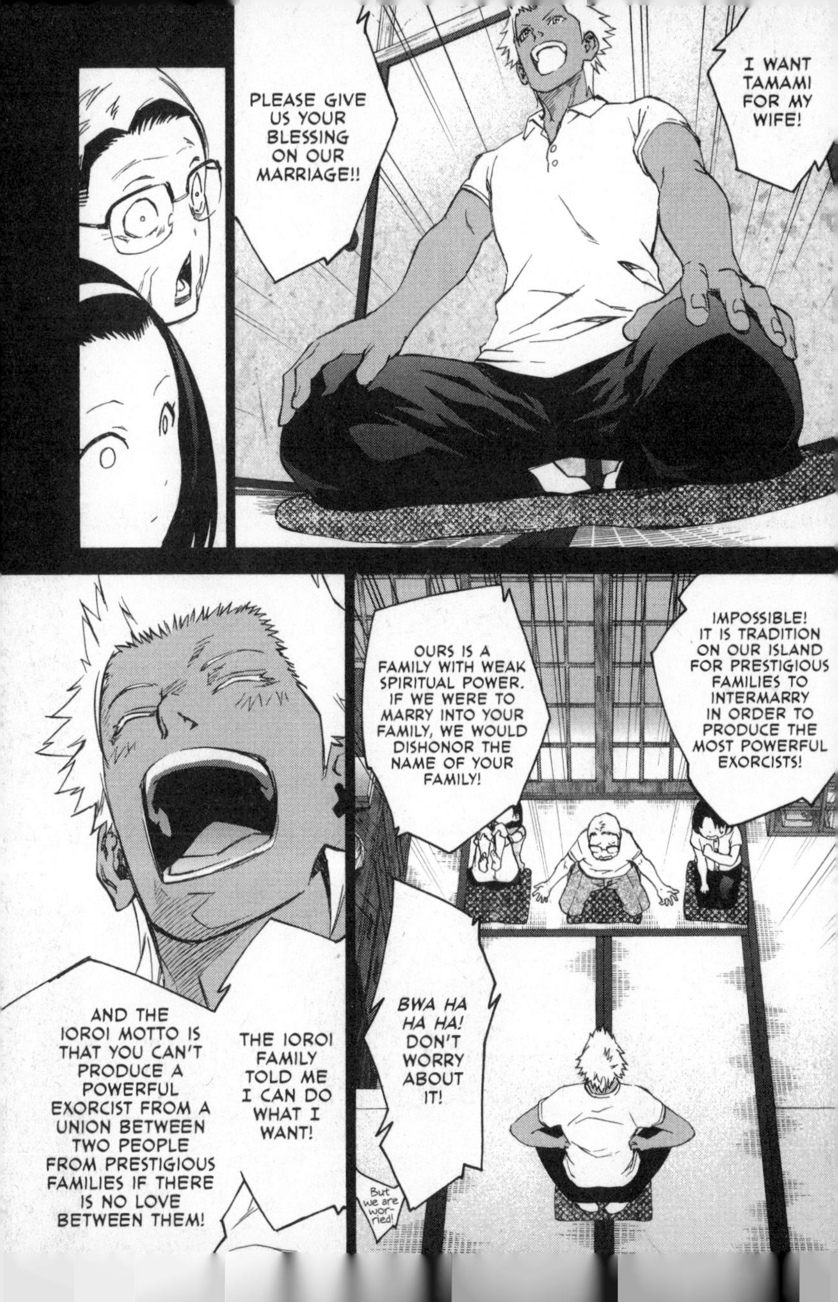
I WANT TAMAMI FOR MY WIFE!
PLEASE GIVE US YOUR BLESSING ON OUR MARRIAGE!!
IMPOSSIBLE! IT IS TRADITION ON OUR ISLAND FOR PRESTIGIOUS FAMILIES TO INTERMARRY IN ORDER TO PRODUCE THE MOST POWERFUL EXORCISTS!
OURS IS A FAMILY WITH WEAK SPIRITUAL POWER. IF WE WERE TO MARRY INTO YOUR FAMILY, WE WOULD DISHONOR THE NAME OF YOUR FAMILY!
BWA HA HA HA! DON'T WORRY ABOUT IT!
But we are wor-ried!
THE IOROI FAMILY TOLD ME I CAN DO WHAT I WANT!
AND THE IOROI MOTTO IS THAT YOU CAN'T PRODUCE A POWERFUL EXORCIST FROM A UNION BETWEEN TWO PEOPLE FROM PRESTIGIOUS FAMILIES IF THERE IS NO LOVE BETWEEN THEM!

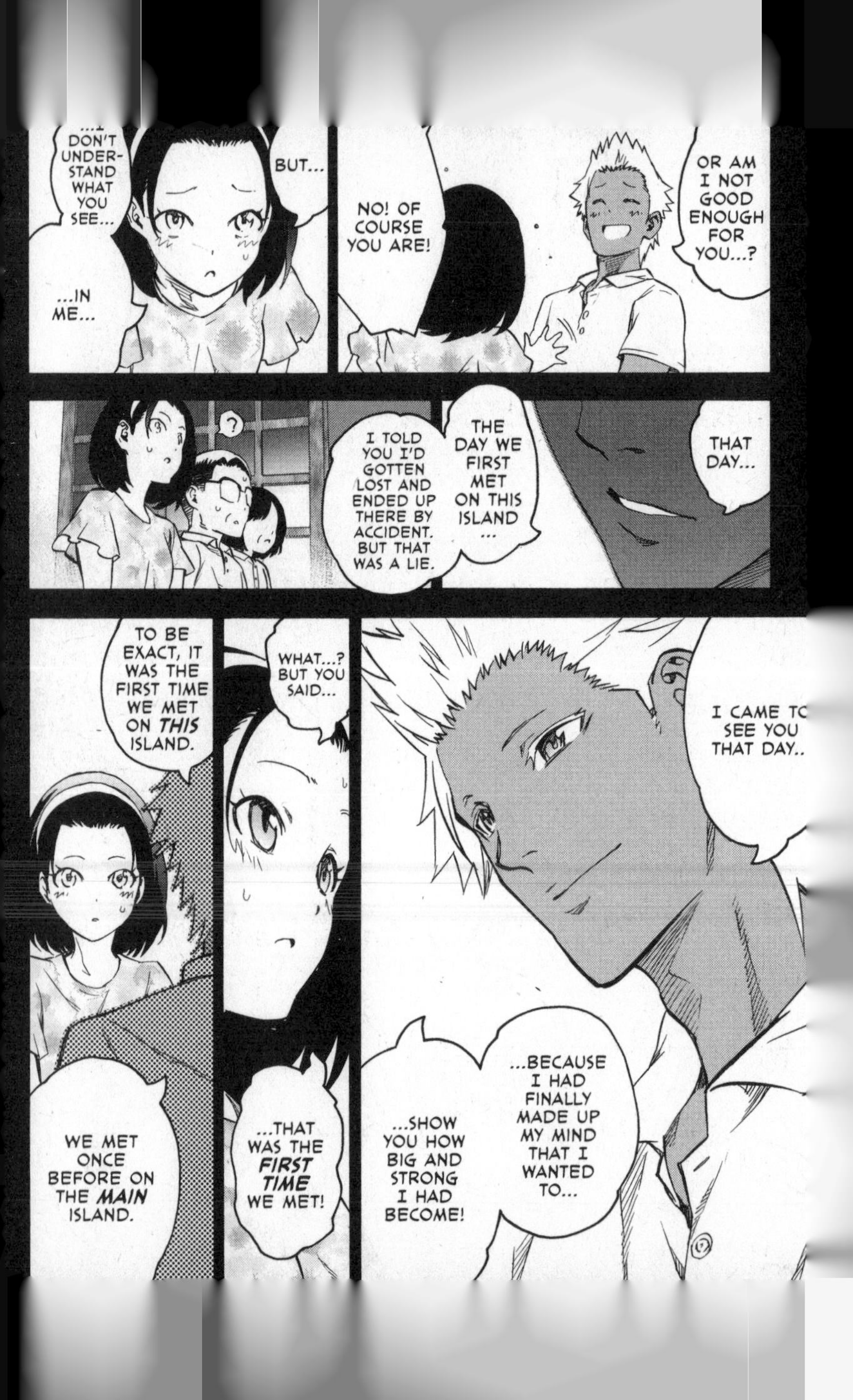
OR AM I NOT GOOD ENOUGH FOR YOU...?
NO! OF COURSE YOU ARE!
BUT...
...I DON'T UNDERSTAND WHAT YOU SEE...
...IN ME...
THAT DAY...
THE DAY WE FIRST MET ON THIS ISLAND...
I TOLD YOU I'D GOTTEN LOST AND ENDED UP THERE BY ACCIDENT. BUT THAT WAS A LIE.
?
I CAME TO SEE YOU THAT DAY..
...BECAUSE I HAD FINALLY MADE UP MY MIND THAT I WANTED TO...
...SHOW YOU HOW BIG AND STRONG I HAD BECOME!
WHAT...? BUT YOU SAID...
...THAT WAS THE *FIRST TIME* WE MET!
TO BE EXACT, IT WAS THE FIRST TIME WE MET ON *THIS* ISLAND.
WE MET ONCE BEFORE ON THE *MAIN* ISLAND.

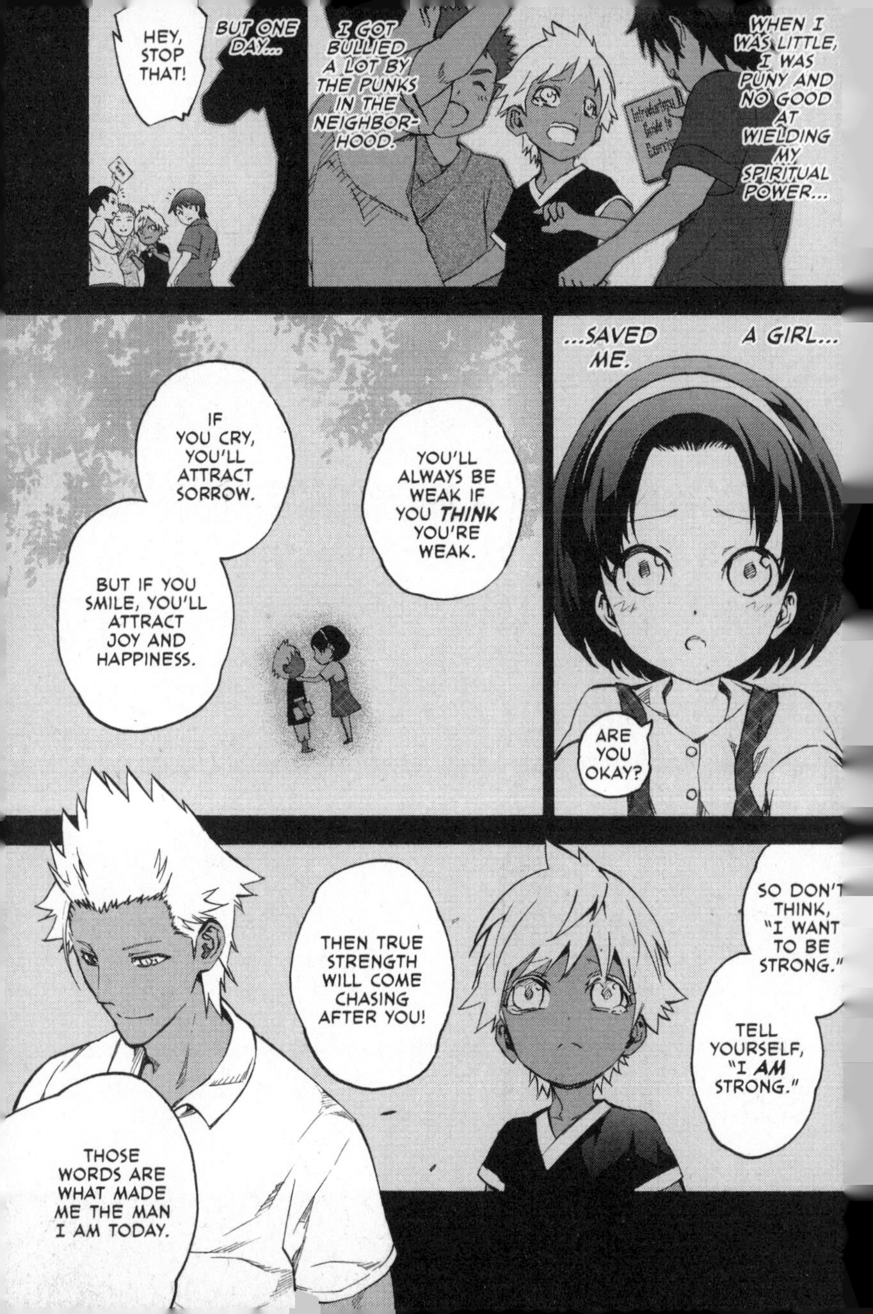
WHEN I WAS LITTLE, I WAS PUNY AND NO GOOD AT WIELDING MY SPIRITUAL POWER...
I GOT BULLIED A LOT BY THE PUNKS IN THE NEIGHBOR-HOOD.
BUT ONE DAY...
HEY, STOP THAT!
A GIRL...
...SAVED ME.
ARE YOU OKAY?
YOU'LL ALWAYS BE WEAK IF YOU *THINK* YOU'RE WEAK.
IF YOU CRY, YOU'LL ATTRACT SORROW.
BUT IF YOU SMILE, YOU'LL ATTRACT JOY AND HAPPINESS.
SO DON'T THINK, "I WANT TO BE STRONG."
TELL YOURSELF, "I *AM* STRONG."
THEN TRUE STRENGTH WILL COME CHASING AFTER YOU!
THOSE WORDS ARE WHAT MADE ME THE MAN I AM TODAY.

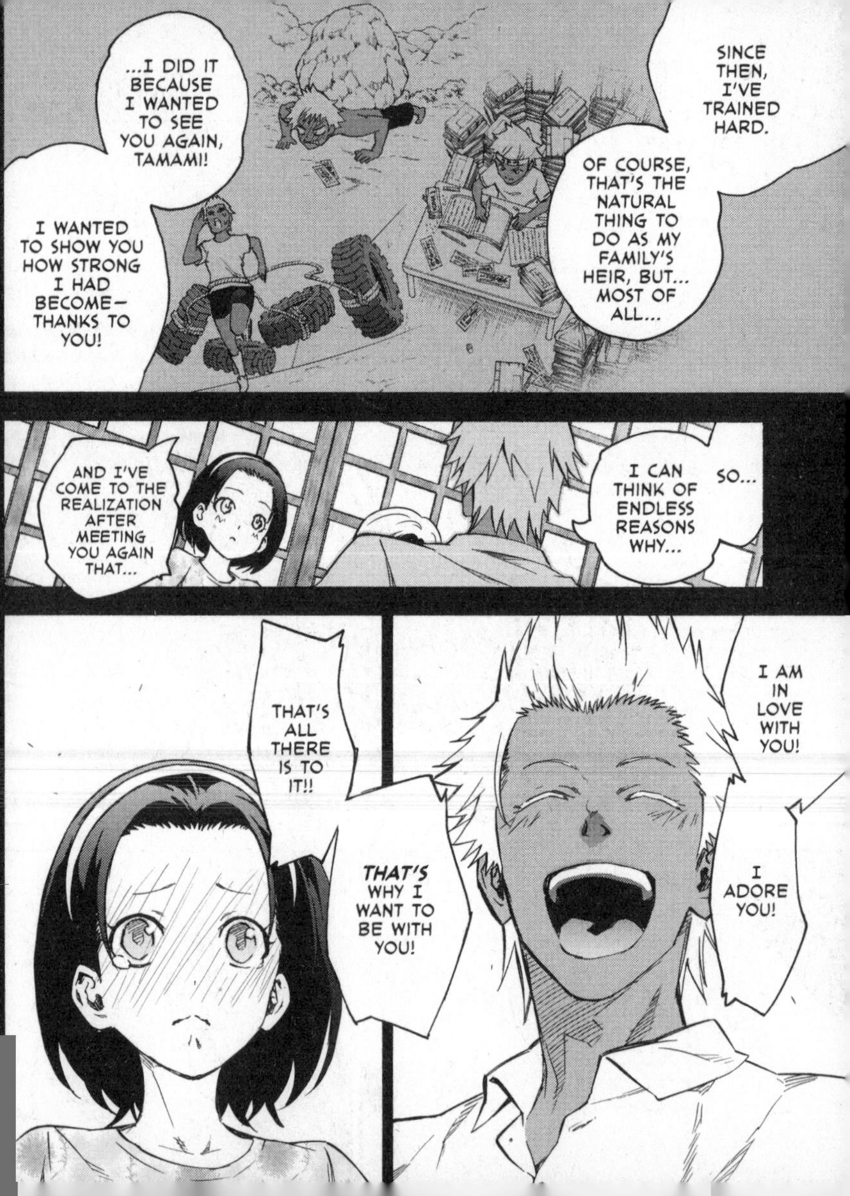
SINCE THEN, I'VE TRAINED HARD.
OF COURSE, THAT'S THE NATURAL THING TO DO AS MY FAMILY'S HEIR, BUT... MOST OF ALL...
...I DID IT BECAUSE I WANTED TO SEE YOU AGAIN, TAMAMI!
I WANTED TO SHOW YOU HOW STRONG I HAD BECOME—THANKS TO YOU!
SO...
I CAN THINK OF ENDLESS REASONS WHY...
AND I'VE COME TO THE REALIZATION AFTER MEETING YOU AGAIN THAT...
I AM IN LOVE WITH YOU!
I ADORE YOU!
THAT'S WHY I WANT TO BE WITH YOU!
THAT'S ALL THERE IS TO IT!!

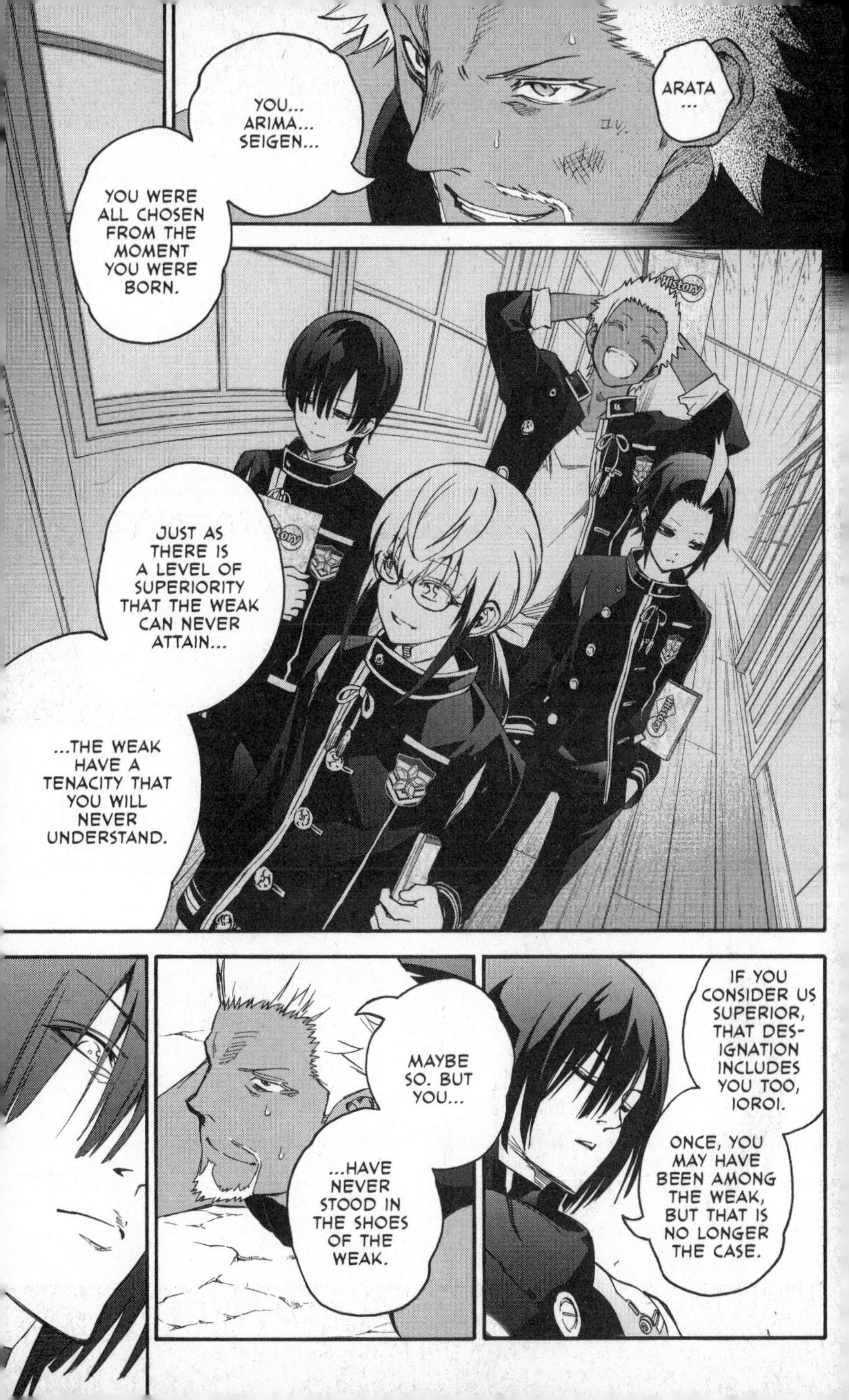
ARATA ...
YOU... ARIMA... SEIGEN...
YOU WERE ALL CHOSEN FROM THE MOMENT YOU WERE BORN.
JUST AS THERE IS A LEVEL OF SUPERIORITY THAT THE WEAK CAN NEVER ATTAIN...
...THE WEAK HAVE A TENACITY THAT YOU WILL NEVER UNDERSTAND.
IF YOU CONSIDER US SUPERIOR, THAT DES-IGNATION INCLUDES YOU TOO, IOROI.
ONCE, YOU MAY HAVE BEEN AMONG THE WEAK, BUT THAT IS NO LONGER THE CASE.
MAYBE SO. BUT YOU...
...HAVE NEVER STOOD IN THE SHOES OF THE WEAK.

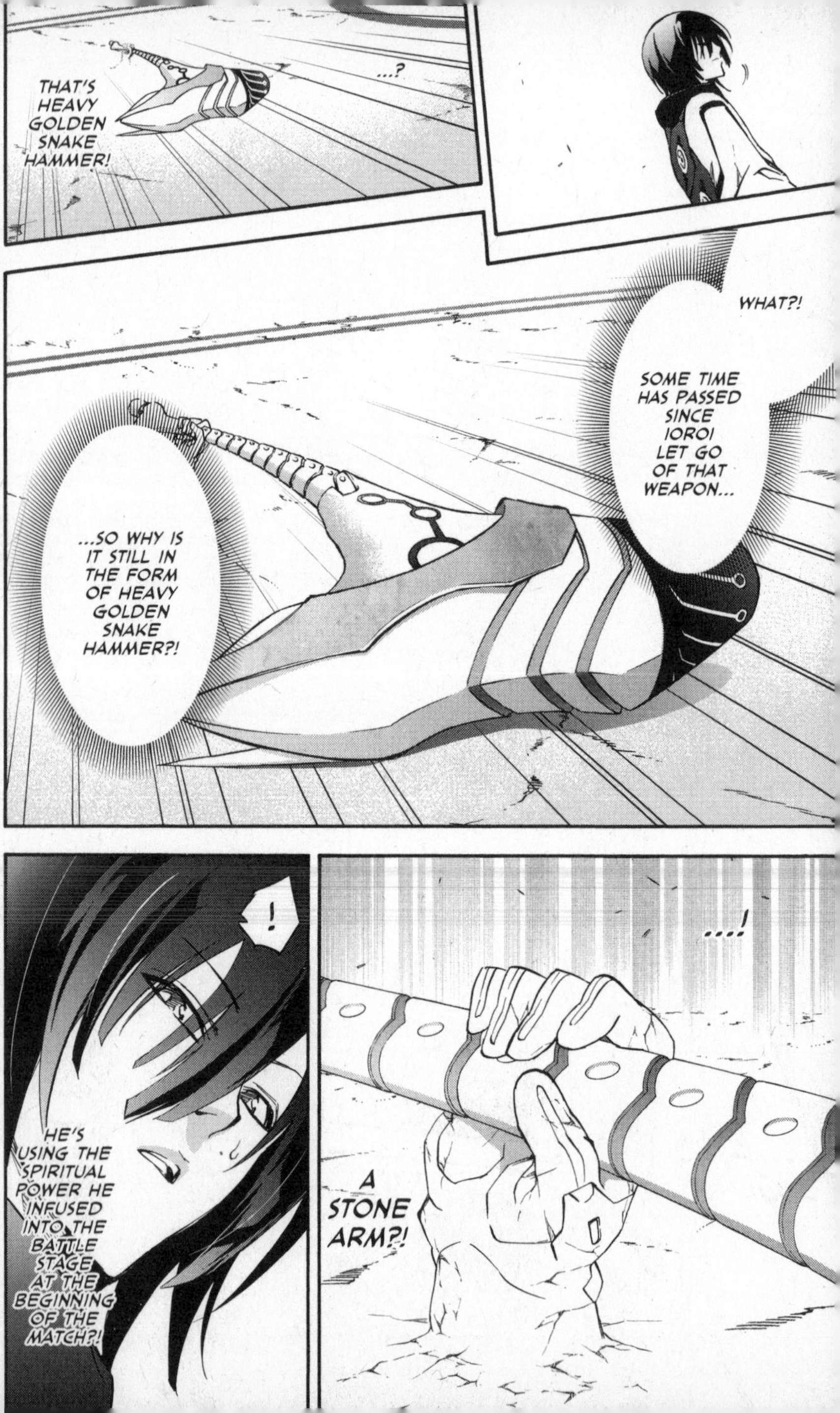
...?
THAT'S HEAVY GOLDEN SNAKE HAMMER!
WHAT?!
SOME TIME HAS PASSED SINCE IOROI LET GO OF THAT WEAPON...
...SO WHY IS IT STILL IN THE FORM OF HEAVY GOLDEN SNAKE HAMMER?!
...!
A STONE ARM?!
!
HE'S USING THE SPIRITUAL POWER HE INFUSED INTO THE BATTLE STAGE AT THE BEGINNING OF THE MATCH?!

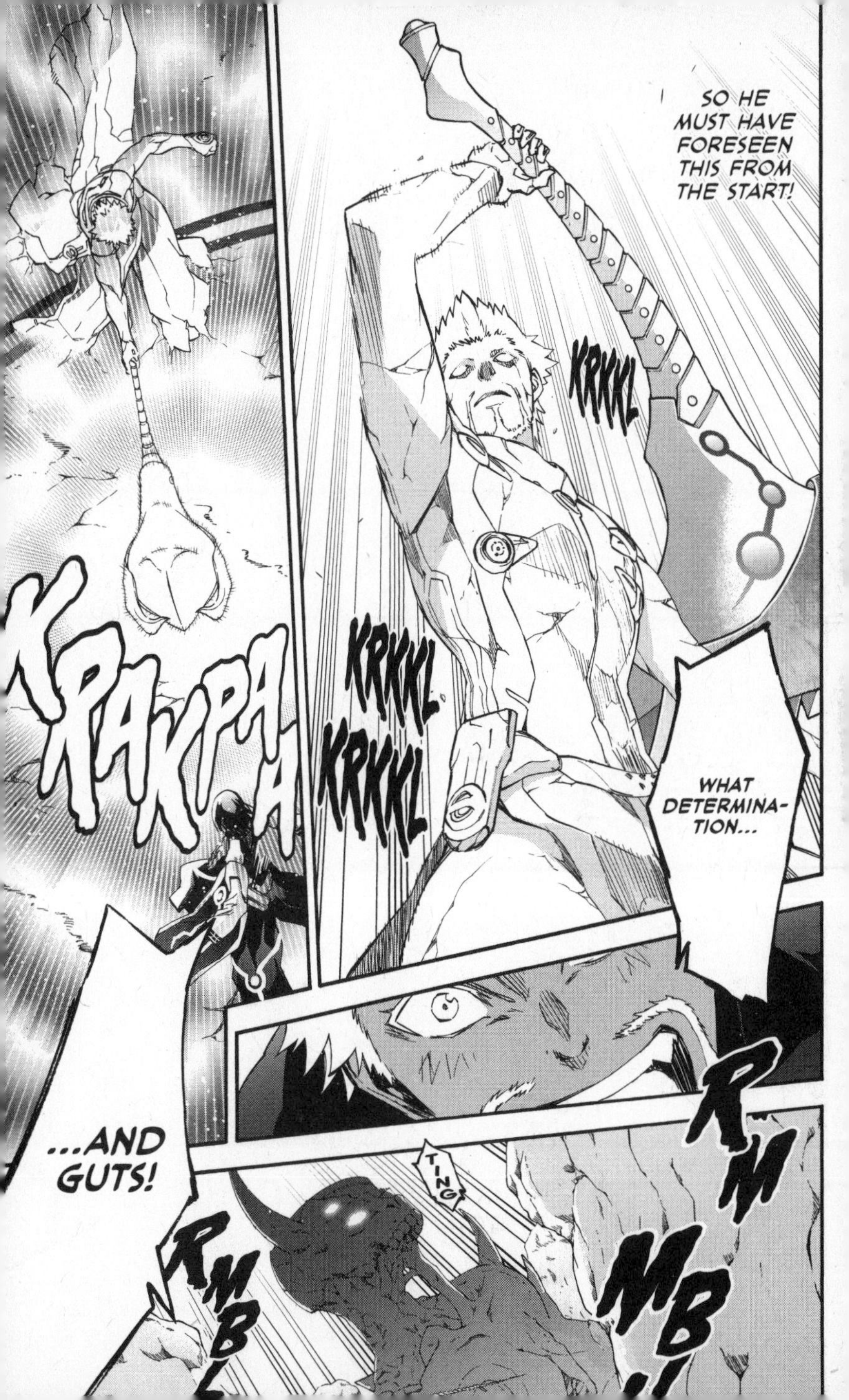
SO HE MUST HAVE FORESEEN THIS FROM THE START!
KRKKL
KRKKL
KRKKL
WHAT DETERMINA-TION...
...AND GUTS!
TING

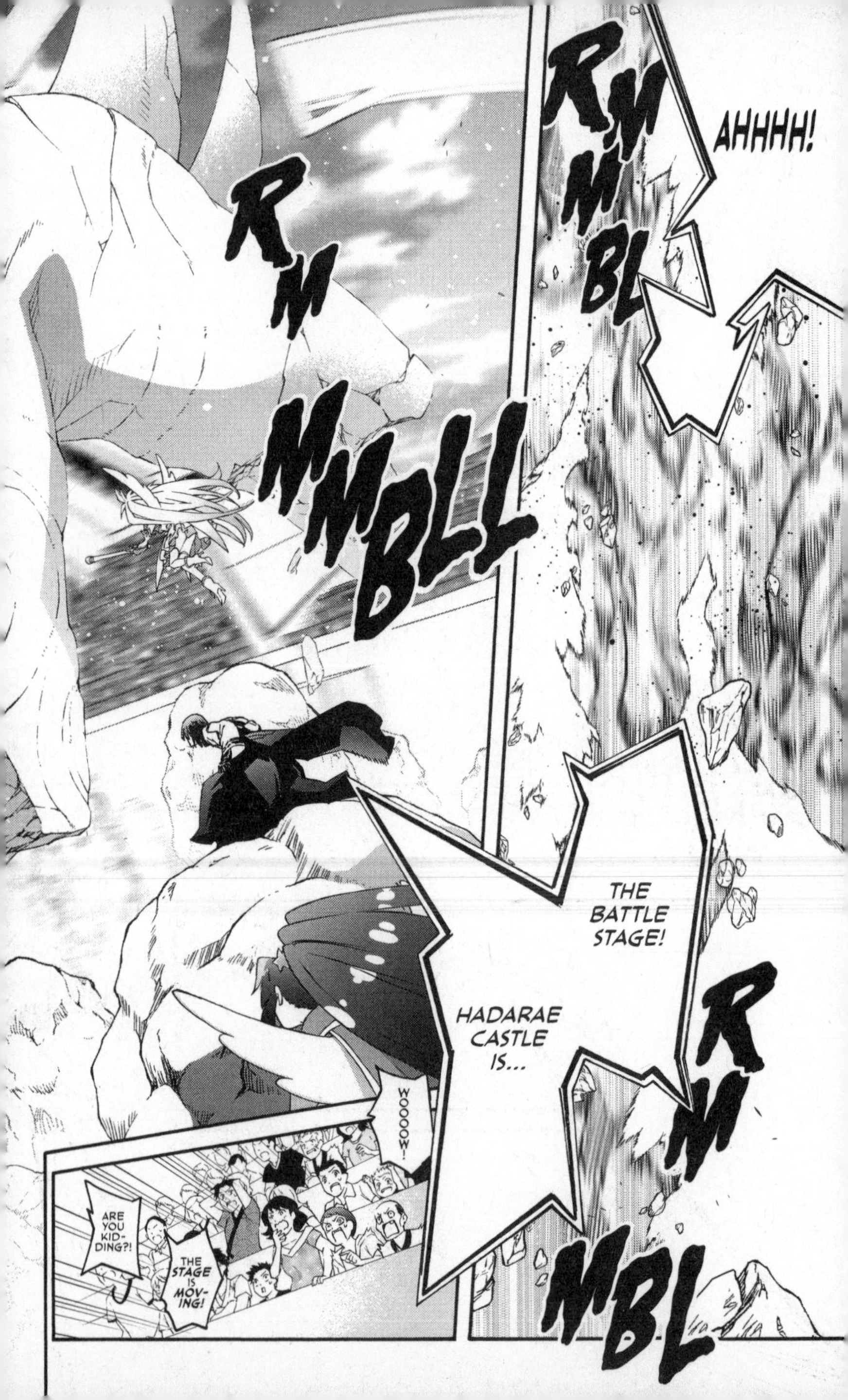
RMMBL
AHHHH!
RMMMBLL
THE BATTLE STAGE!
HADARAE CASTLE IS...
RMMBL
WOOOOW!
ARE YOU KIDDING?!
THE STAGE IS MOVING!

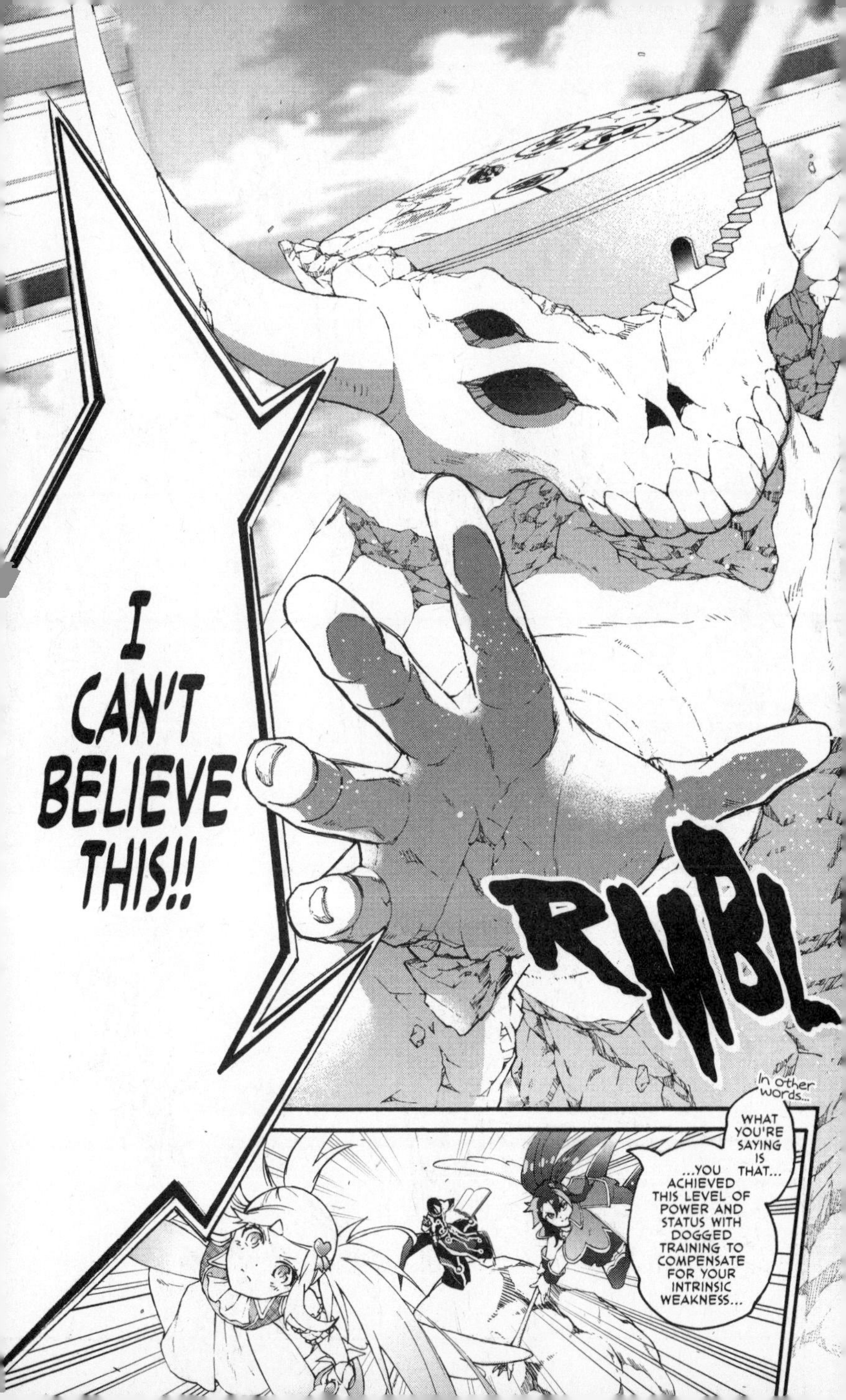
I CAN'T BELIEVE THIS!!
RMBL
In other words...
WHAT YOU'RE SAYING IS THAT...
...YOU ACHIEVED THIS LEVEL OF POWER AND STATUS WITH DOGGED TRAINING TO COMPENSATE FOR YOUR INTRINSIC WEAKNESS...

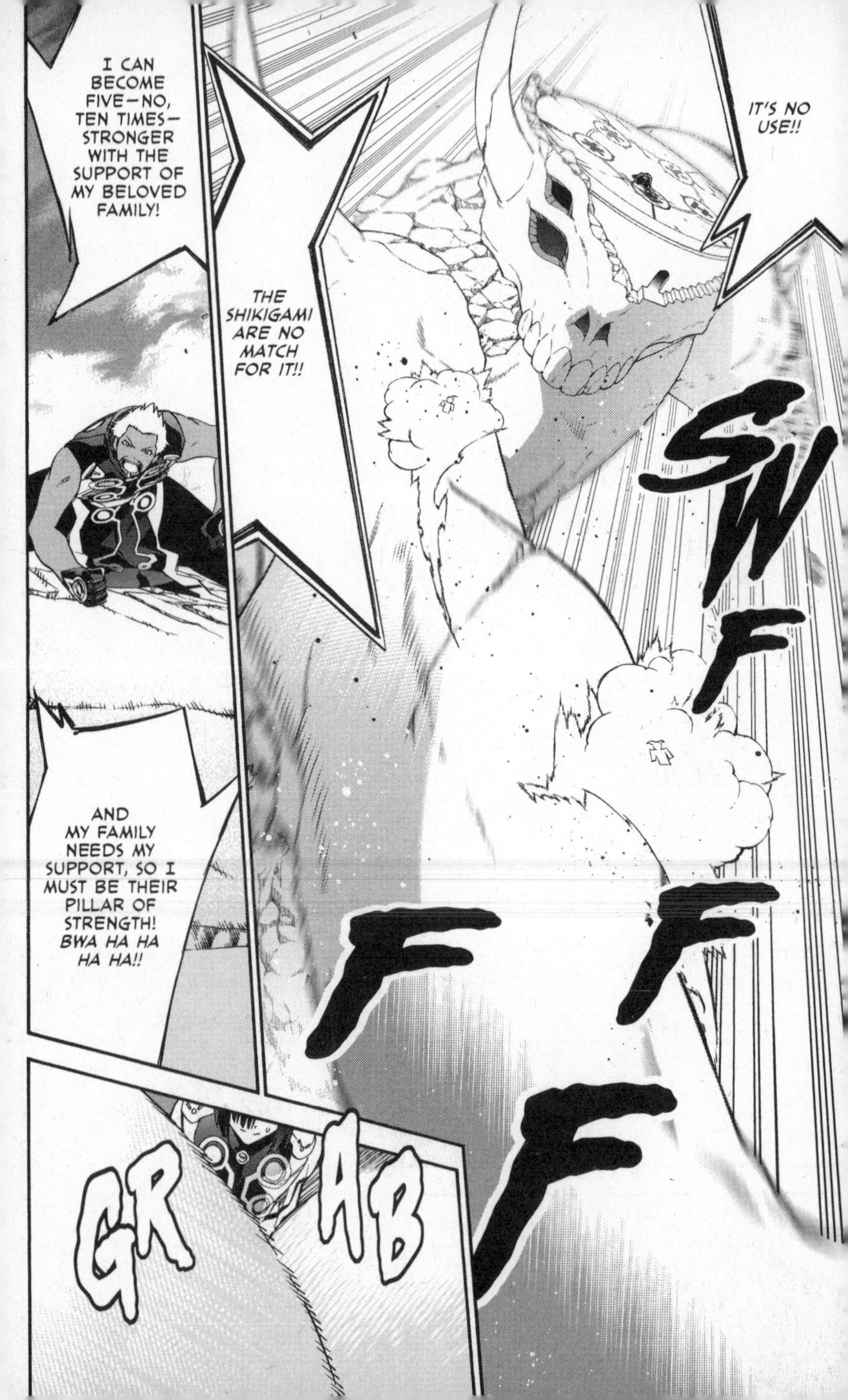
IT'S NO USE!!
THE SHIKIGAMI ARE NO MATCH FOR IT!!
SWFFFF
I CAN BECOME FIVE—NO, TEN TIMES—STRONGER WITH THE SUPPORT OF MY BELOVED FAMILY!
AND MY FAMILY NEEDS MY SUPPORT, SO I MUST BE THEIR PILLAR OF STRENGTH! *BWA HA HA HA HA!!*
GRAB

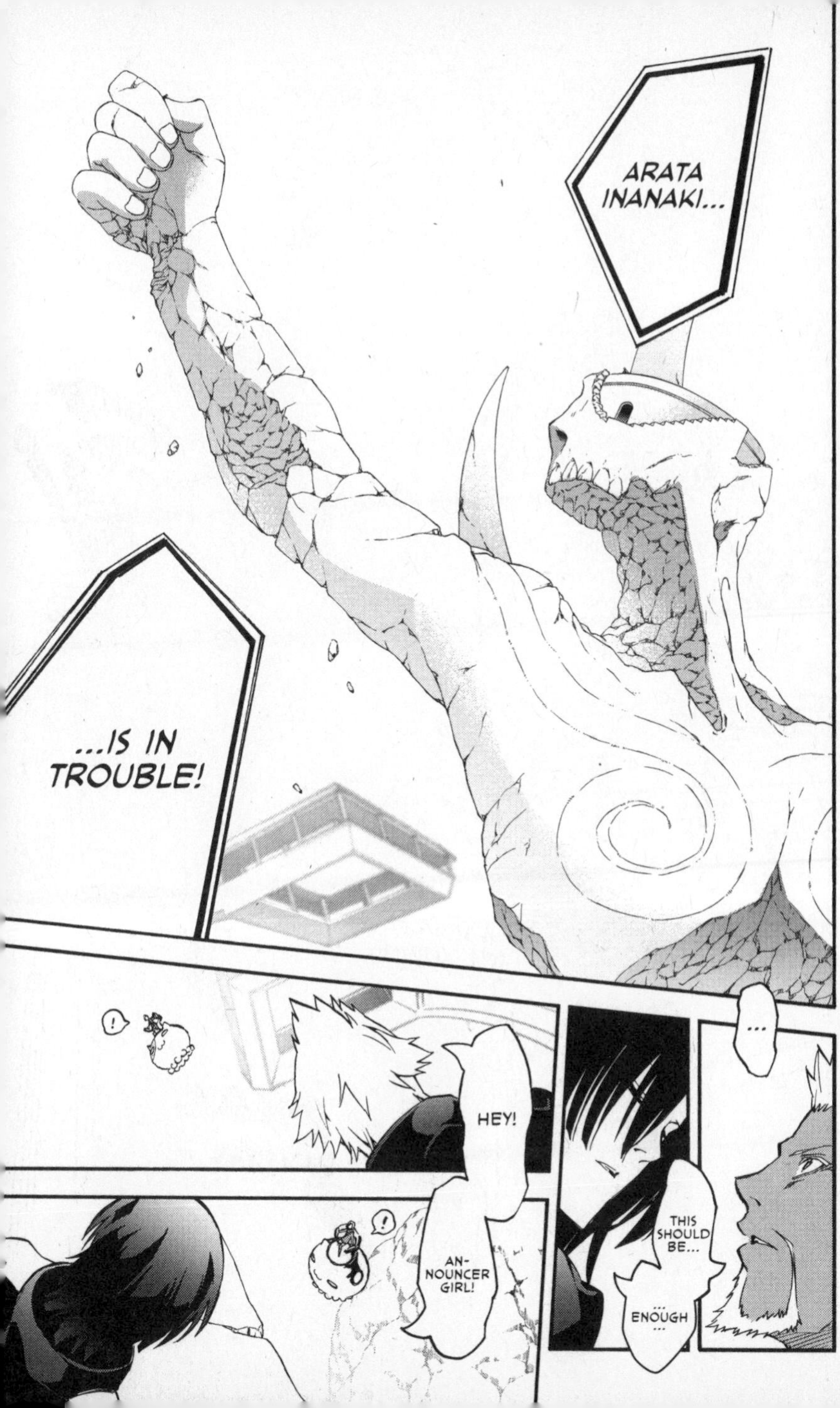
ARATA INANAKI...
...IS IN TROUBLE!
...
THIS SHOULD BE... ...ENOUGH...
!
HEY!
!
AN-NOUNCER GIRL!

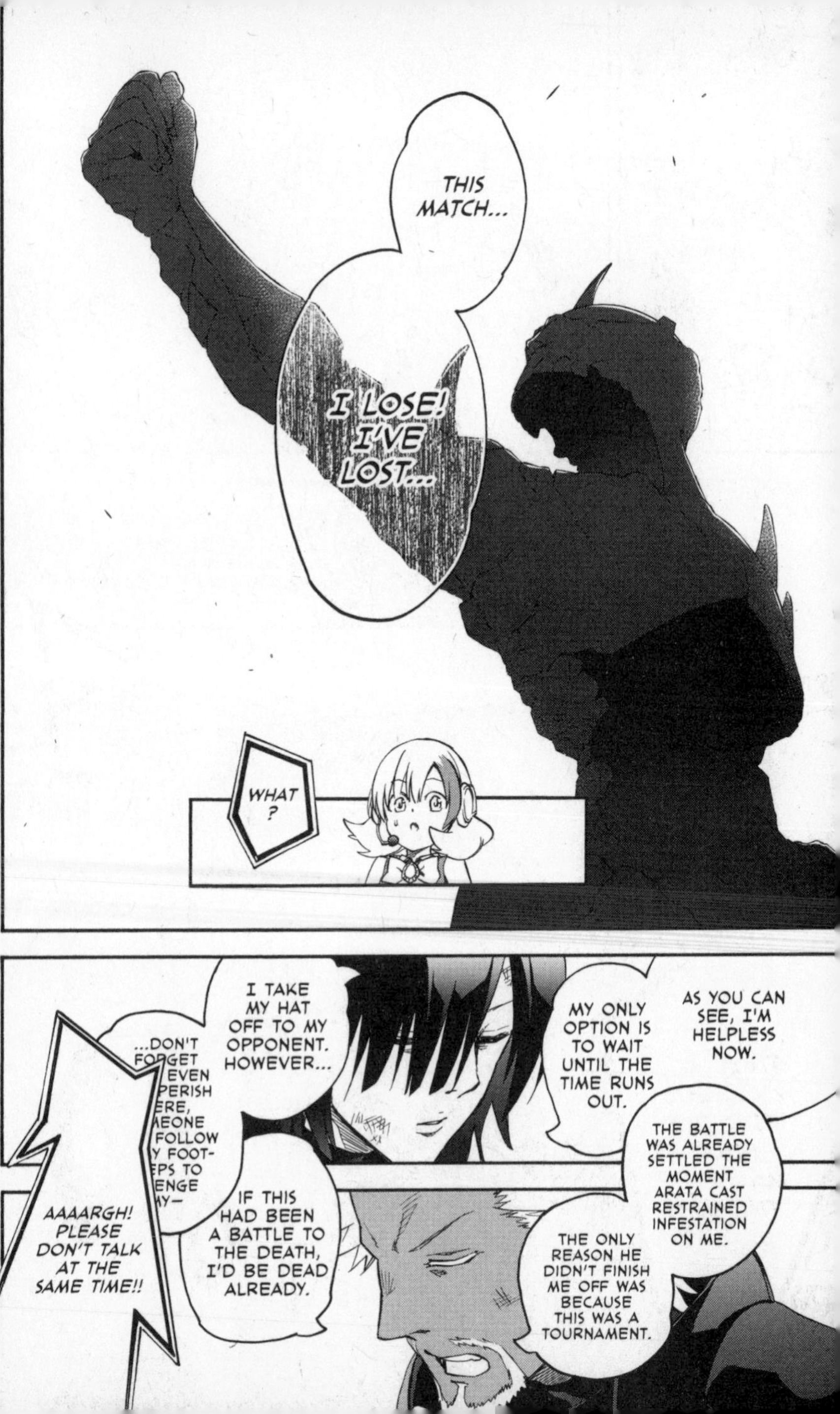
THIS MATCH...
I LOSE! I'VE LOST...
WHAT?
AS YOU CAN SEE, I'M HELPLESS NOW.
MY ONLY OPTION IS TO WAIT UNTIL THE TIME RUNS OUT.
I TAKE MY HAT OFF TO MY OPPONENT. HOWEVER...
THE BATTLE WAS ALREADY SETTLED THE MOMENT ARATA CAST RESTRAINED INFESTATION ON ME.
THE ONLY REASON HE DIDN'T FINISH ME OFF WAS BECAUSE THIS WAS A TOURNAMENT.
IF THIS HAD BEEN A BATTLE TO THE DEATH, I'D BE DEAD ALREADY.
AAAARGH! PLEASE DON'T TALK AT THE SAME TIME!!

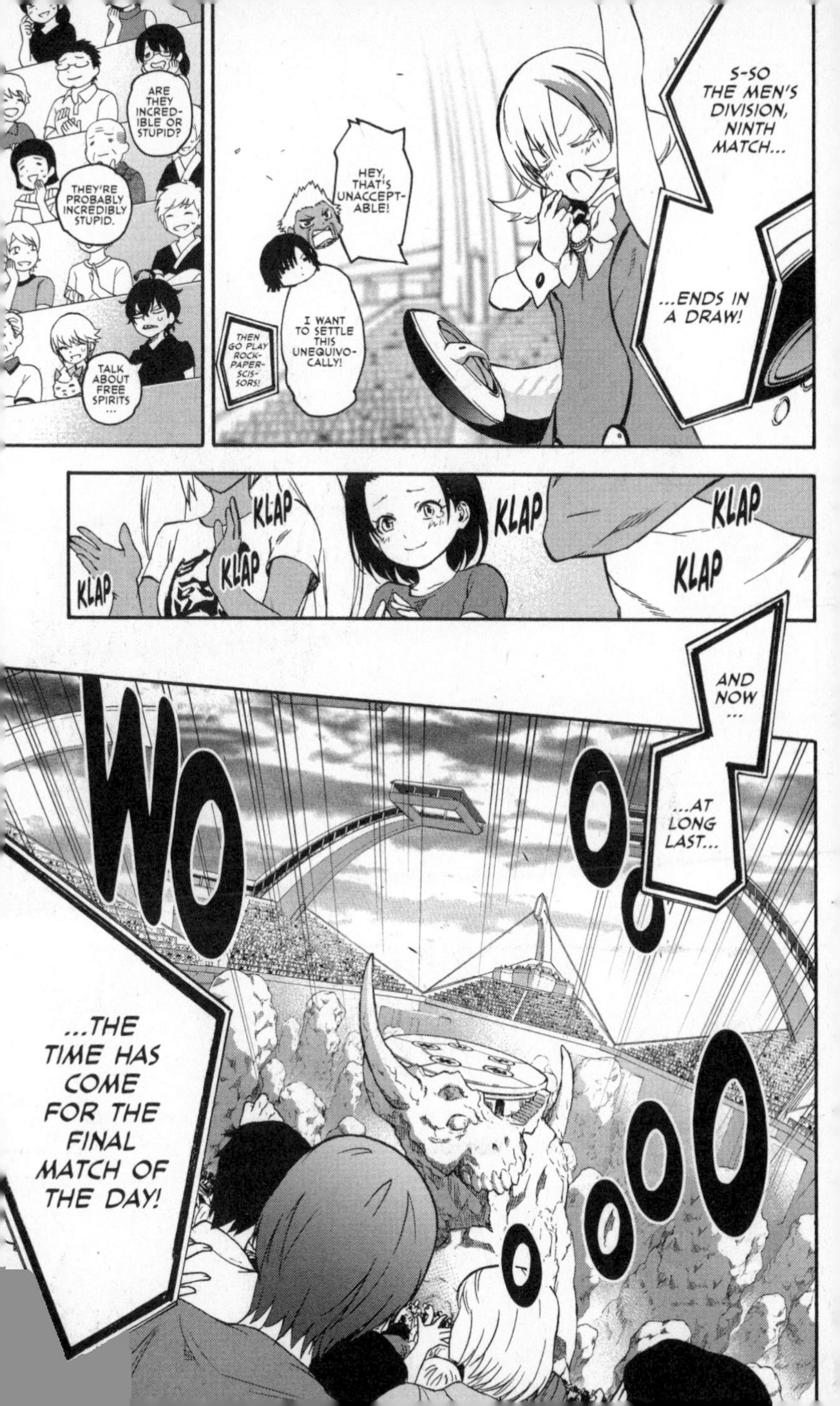
S-SO THE MEN'S DIVISION, NINTH MATCH...
...ENDS IN A DRAW!
HEY, THAT'S UNACCEPTABLE!
I WANT TO SETTLE THIS UNEQUIVOCALLY!
THEN GO PLAY ROCK-PAPER-SCISSORS!
ARE THEY INCREDIBLE OR STUPID?
THEY'RE PROBABLY INCREDIBLY STUPID.
TALK ABOUT FREE SPIRITS...
KLAP
KLAP
KLAP
KLAP
KLAP
AND NOW...
...AT LONG LAST...
...THE TIME HAS COME FOR THE FINAL MATCH OF THE DAY!
WOOOOOOOO

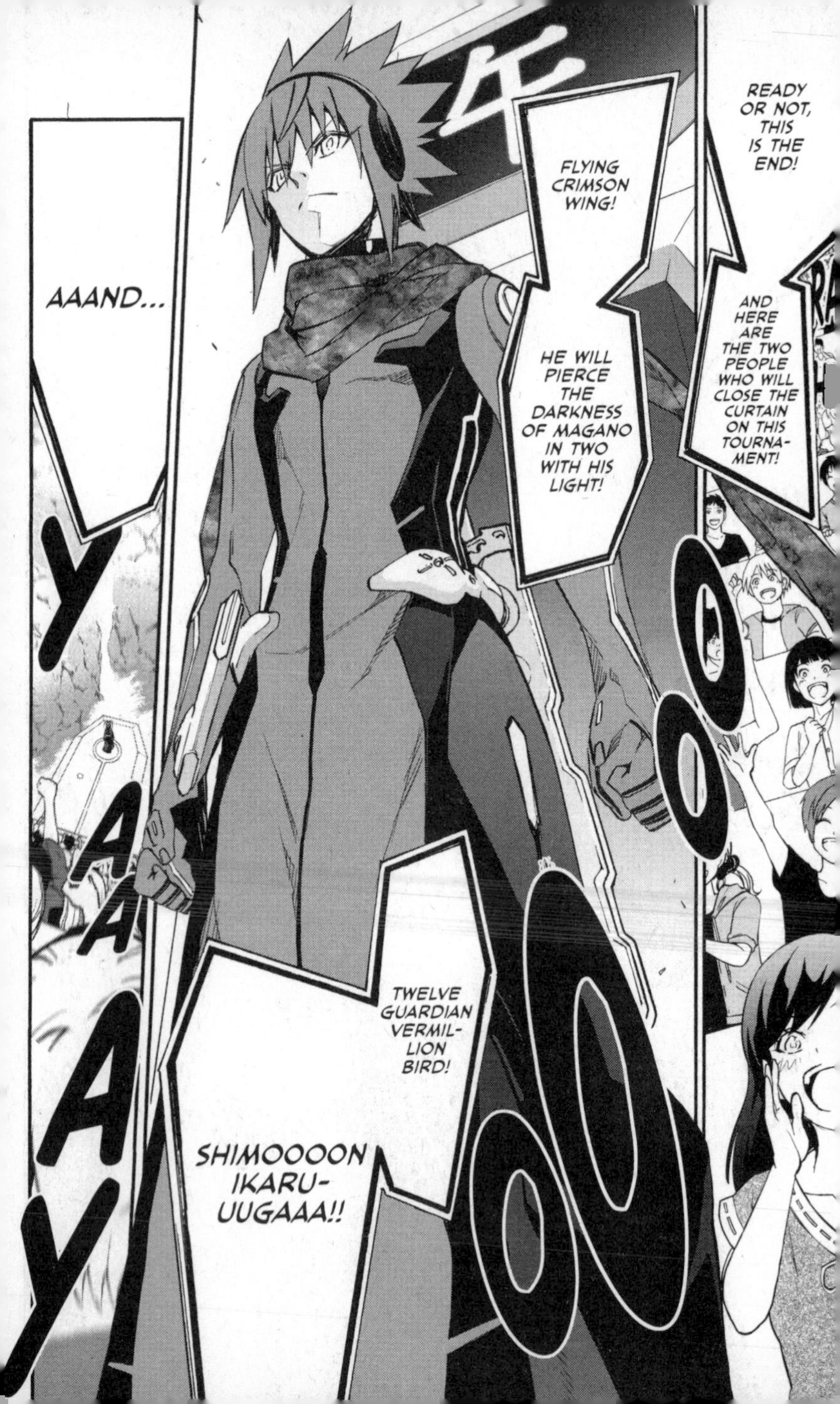
READY OR NOT, THIS IS THE END!
AND HERE ARE THE TWO PEOPLE WHO WILL CLOSE THE CURTAIN ON THIS TOURNAMENT!
FLYING CRIMSON WING!
HE WILL PIERCE THE DARKNESS OF MAGANO IN TWO WITH HIS LIGHT!
AAAND...
TWELVE GUARDIAN VERMIL-LION BIRD!
SHIMOOOON IKARU-UUGAAA!!
YAAAAY

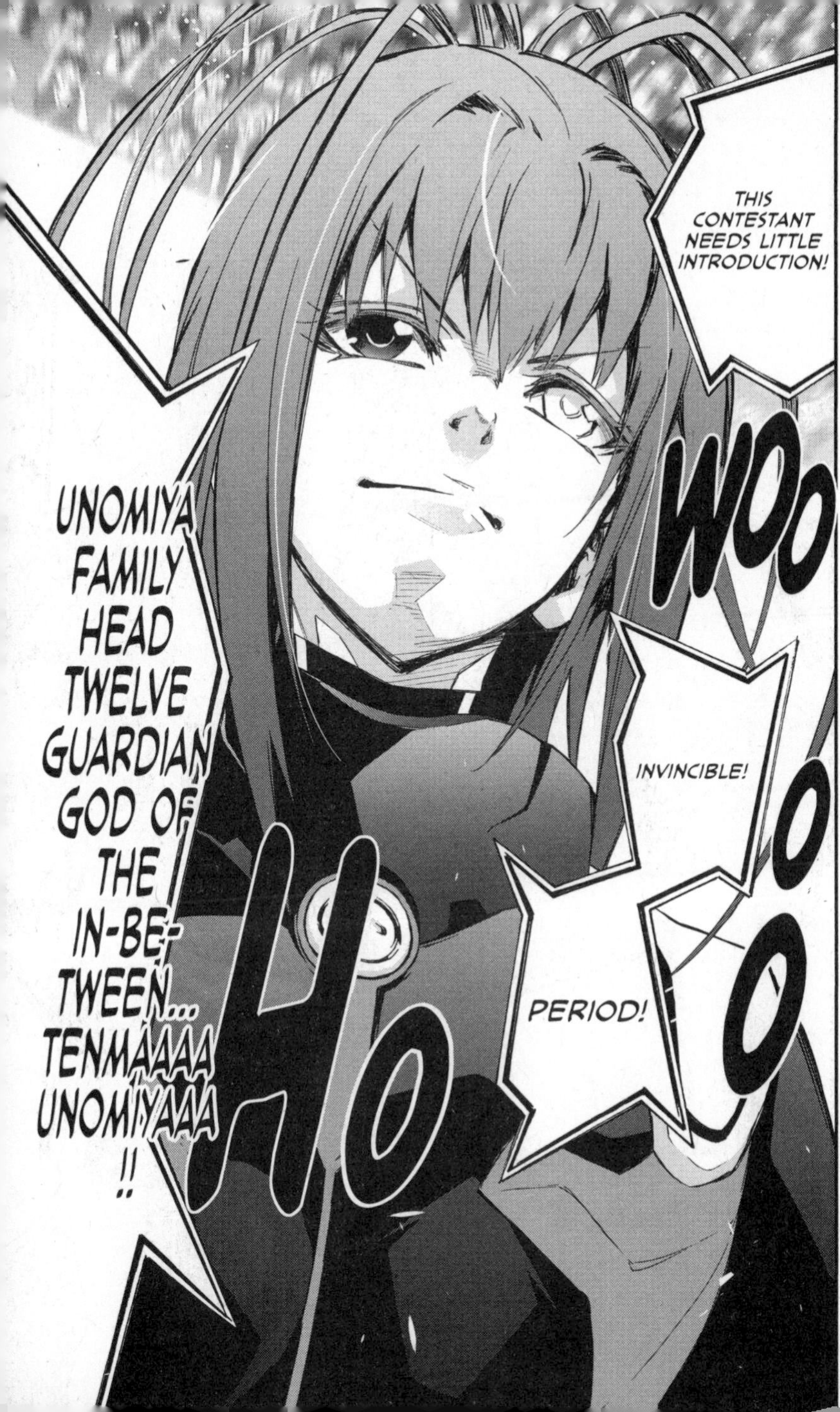
THIS CONTESTANT NEEDS LITTLE INTRODUCTION!
WOOOO
INVINCIBLE!
PERIOD!
HO
UNOMIYA FAMILY HEAD TWELVE GUARDIAN GOD OF THE IN-BE-TWEEN... TENMAAAA UNOMIYAAA!!

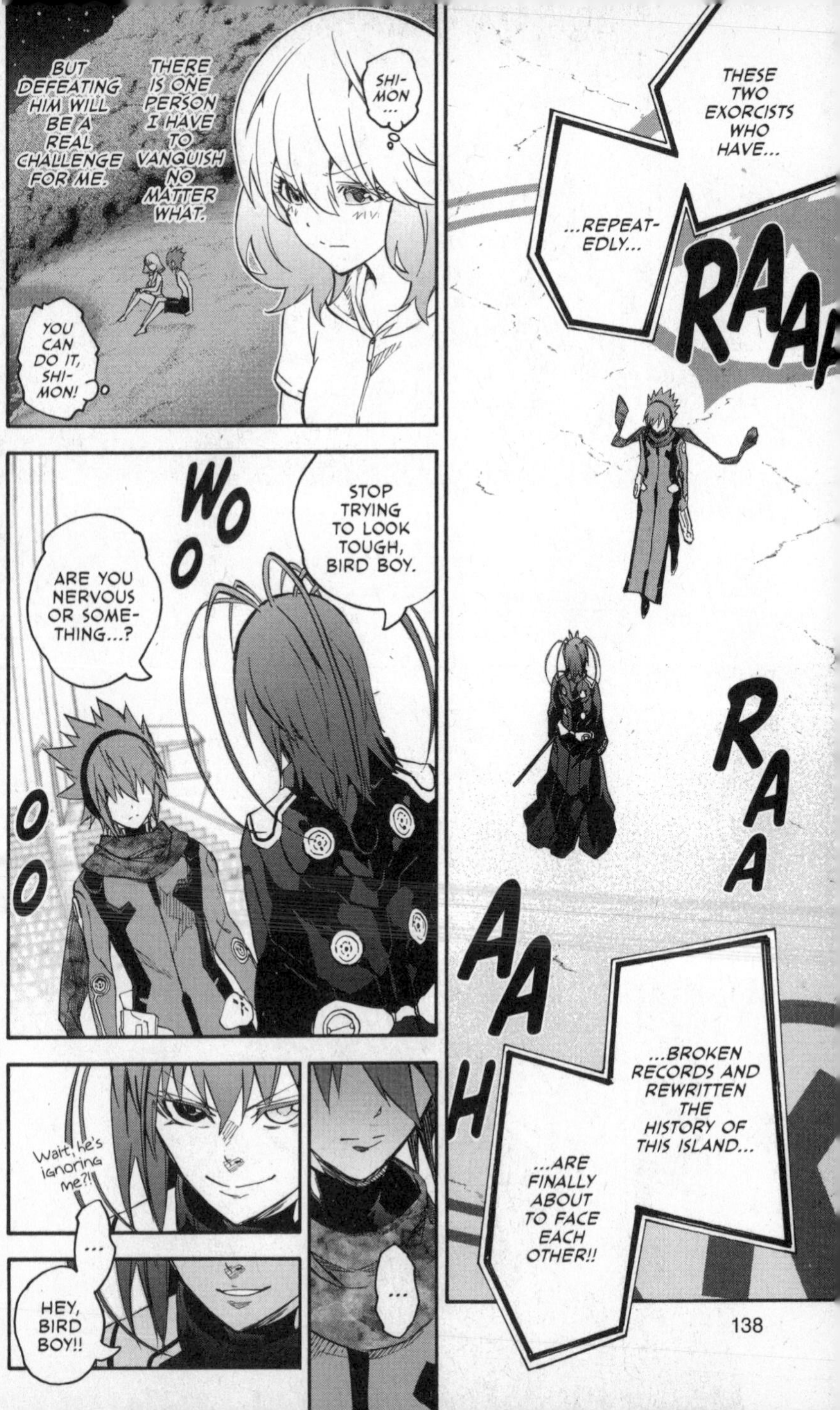
THESE TWO EXORCISTS WHO HAVE...
...REPEATEDLY...
RAAAH
RAAAAAH
...BROKEN RECORDS AND REWRITTEN THE HISTORY OF THIS ISLAND...
...ARE FINALLY ABOUT TO FACE EACH OTHER!!
SHIMON...
THERE IS ONE PERSON I HAVE TO VANQUISH NO MATTER WHAT.
BUT DEFEATING HIM WILL BE A REAL CHALLENGE FOR ME.
YOU CAN DO IT, SHIMON!
STOP TRYING TO LOOK TOUGH, BIRD BOY.
WOO
ARE YOU NERVOUS OR SOMETHING...?
OOO
...
Wait, he's ignoring me?!
...
HEY, BIRD BOY!!

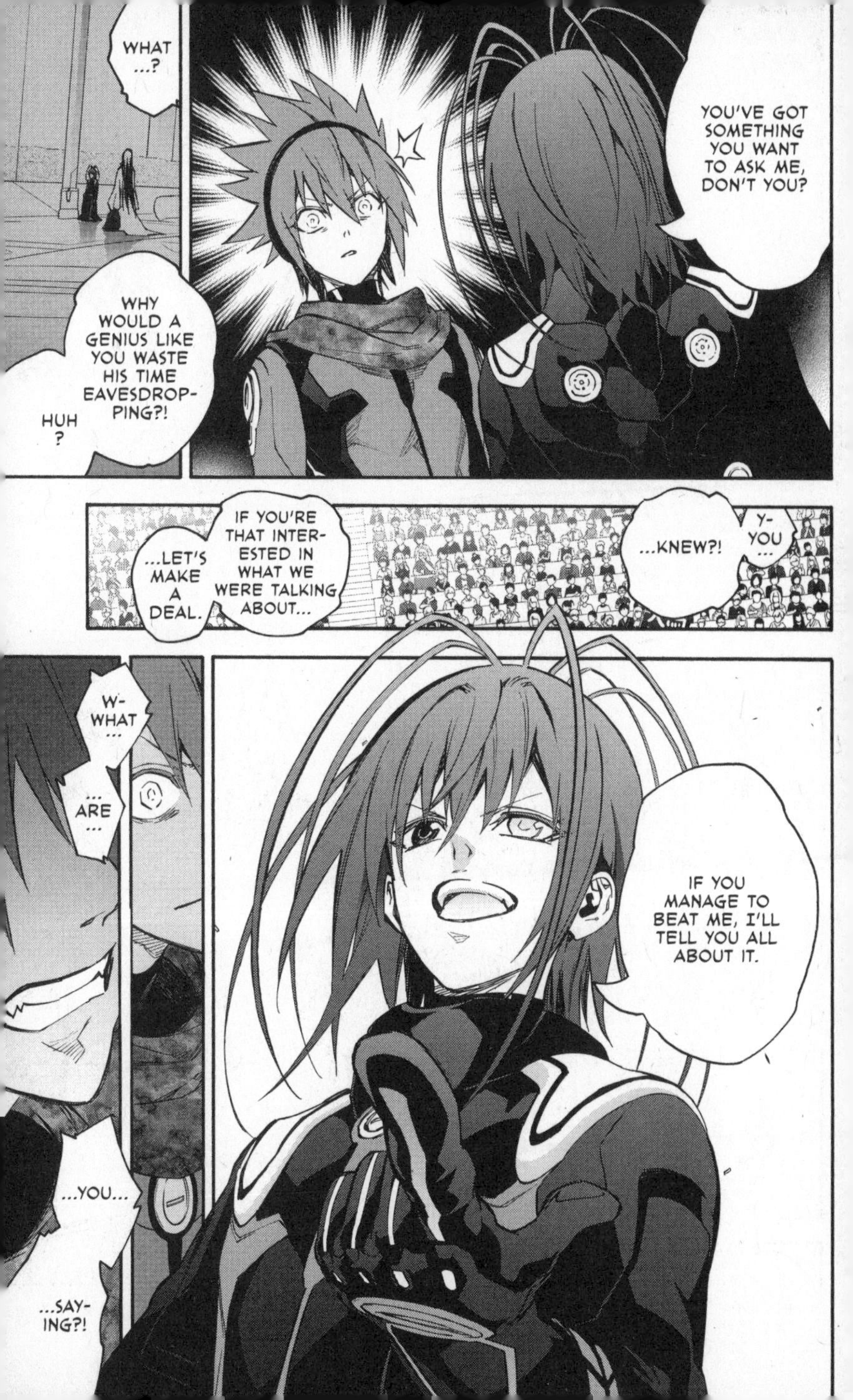
YOU'VE GOT SOMETHING YOU WANT TO ASK ME, DON'T YOU?
WHAT ...?
WHY WOULD A GENIUS LIKE YOU WASTE HIS TIME EAVESDROP-PING?!
HUH ?
Y-YOU ...
...KNEW?!
IF YOU'RE THAT INTER-ESTED IN WHAT WE WERE TALKING ABOUT...
...LET'S MAKE A DEAL.
IF YOU MANAGE TO BEAT ME, I'LL TELL YOU ALL ABOUT IT.
W-WHAT ...
... ARE ...
...YOU...
...SAY-ING?!

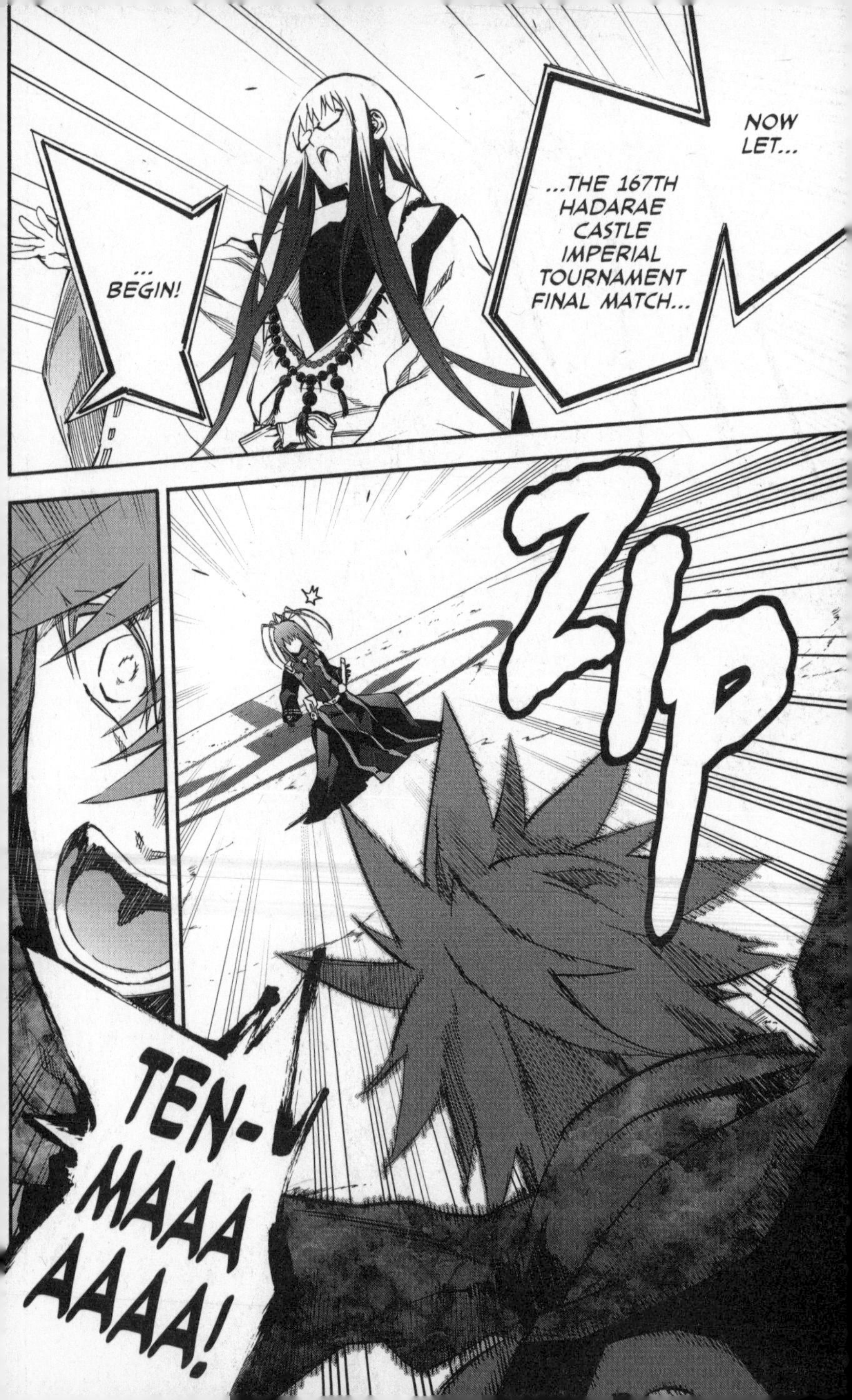
NOW LET...
...THE 167TH HADARAE CASTLE IMPERIAL TOURNAMENT FINAL MATCH...
...BEGIN!
ZIP
TEN-MAAAAAAA!

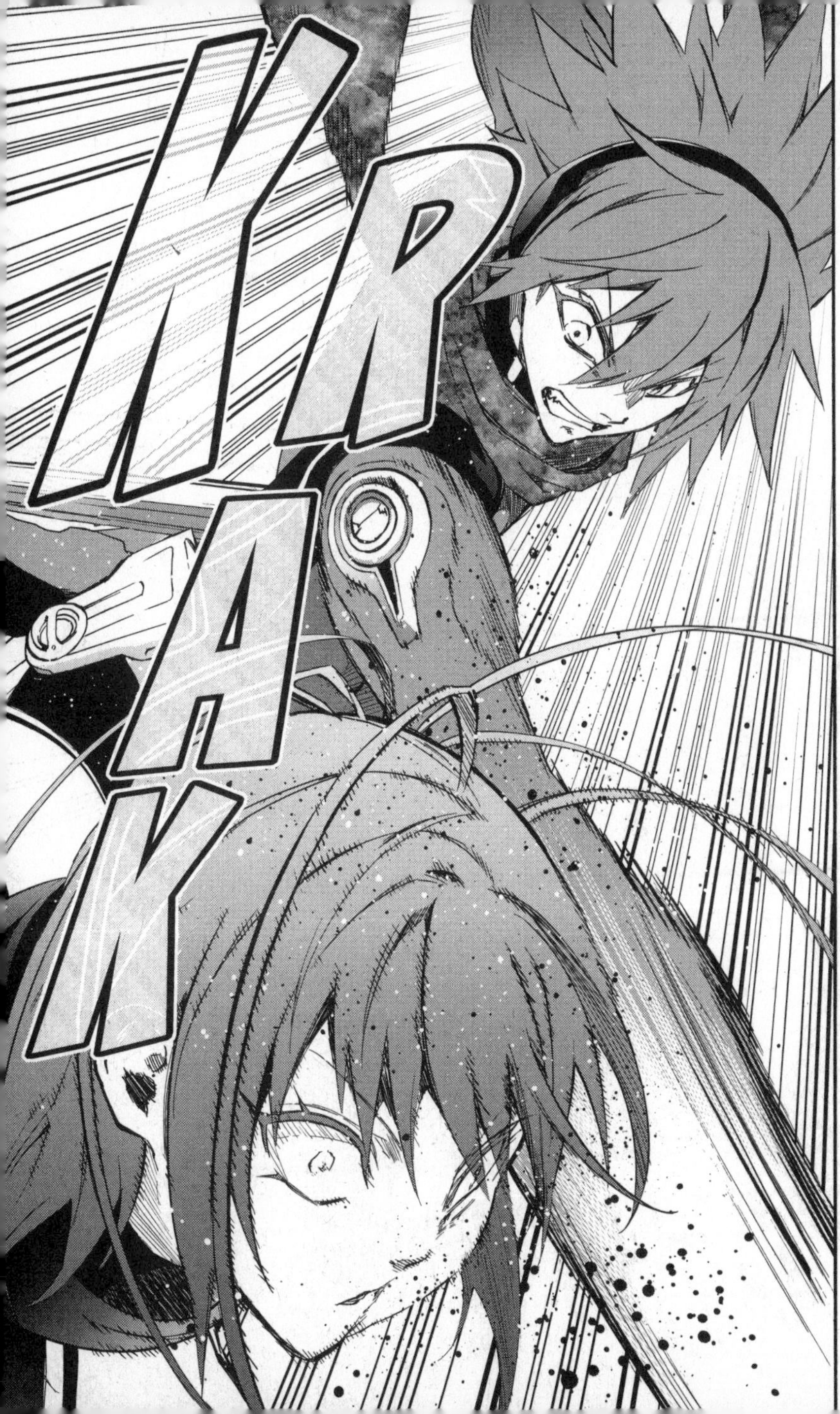
KRAK

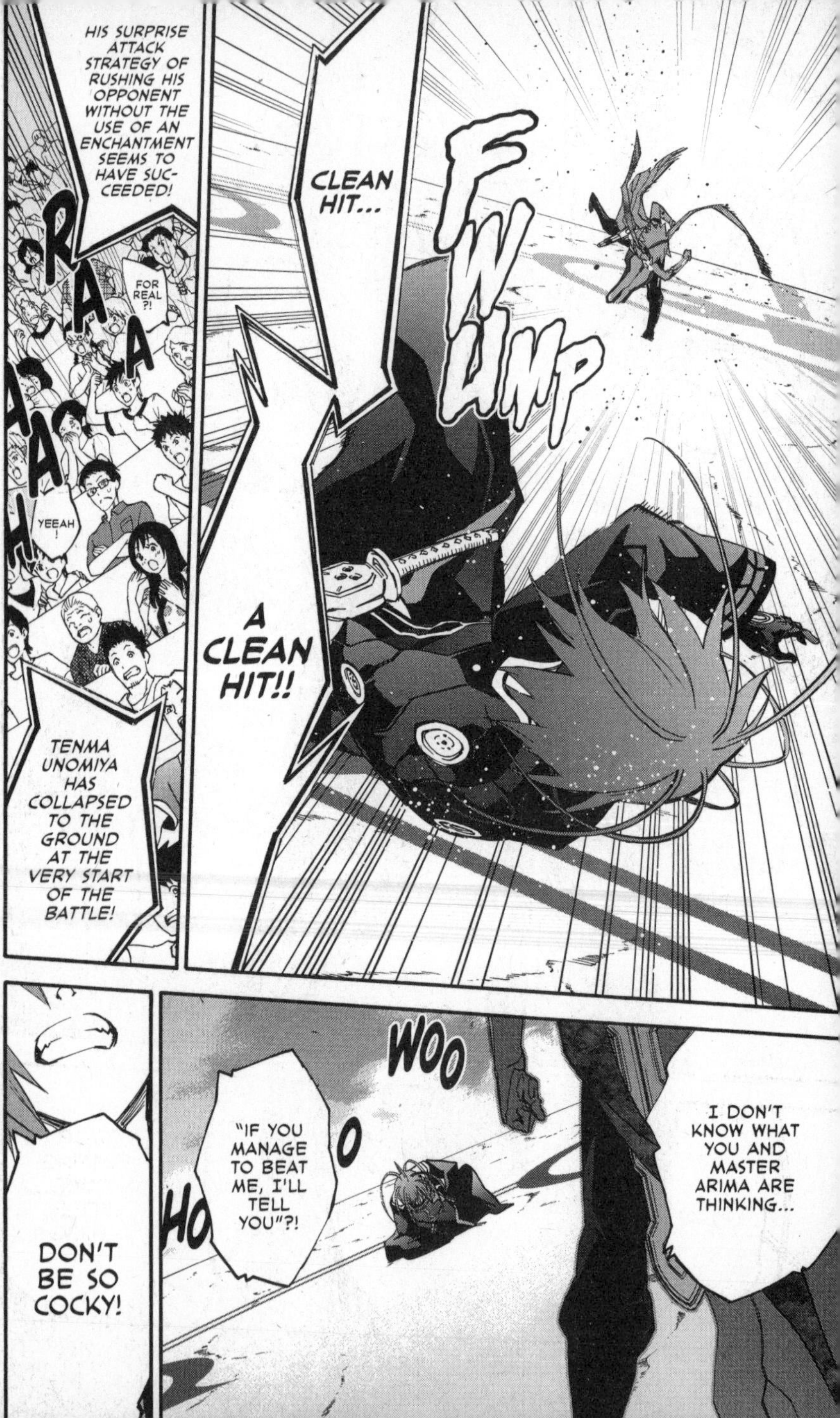

CLEAN HIT...
FWUMP
A CLEAN HIT!!
HIS SURPRISE ATTACK STRATEGY OF RUSHING HIS OPPONENT WITHOUT THE USE OF AN ENCHANTMENT SEEMS TO HAVE SUC-CEEDED!
RAAAAH
FOR REAL?!
YEEAH!
TENMA UNOMIYA HAS COLLAPSED TO THE GROUND AT THE VERY START OF THE BATTLE!
I DON'T KNOW WHAT YOU AND MASTER ARIMA ARE THINKING...
WOO
O
HO
"IF YOU MANAGE TO BEAT ME, I'LL TELL YOU"?!
DON'T BE SO COCKY!

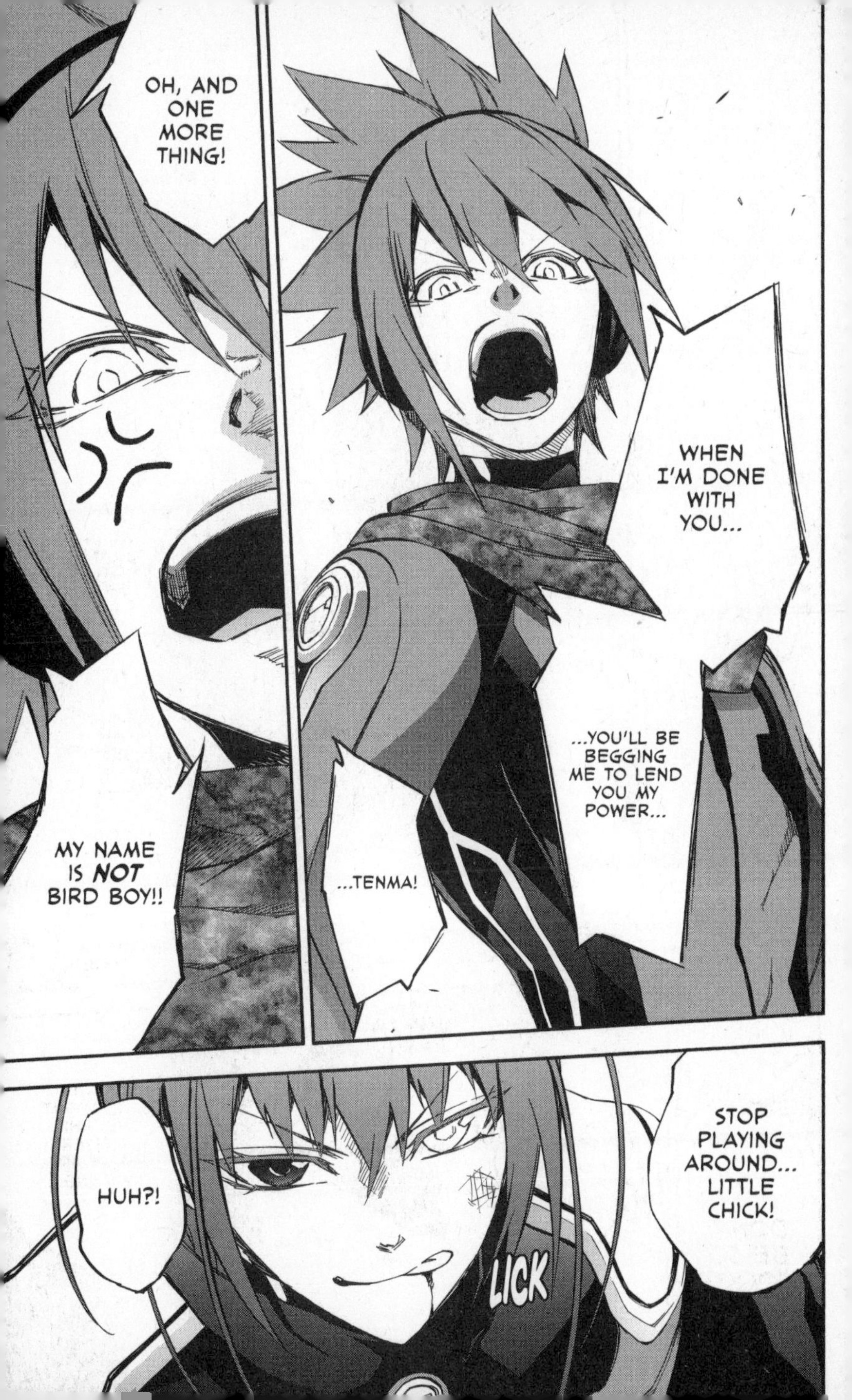
WHEN I'M DONE WITH YOU...
...YOU'LL BE BEGGING ME TO LEND YOU MY POWER...
...TENMA!
OH, AND ONE MORE THING!
MY NAME IS **NOT** BIRD BOY!!
STOP PLAYING AROUND... LITTLE CHICK!
LICK
HUH?!

Qnyoritsuryo!

Question Corner

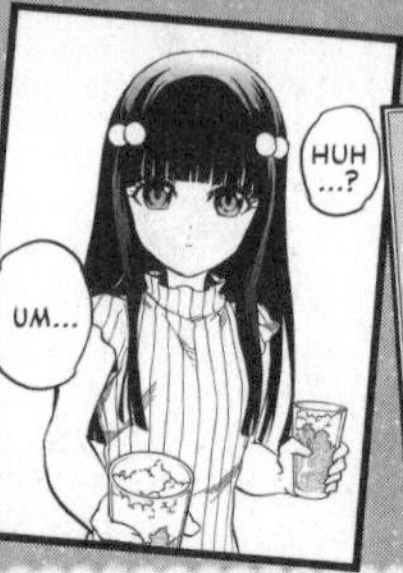
HUH ...?
UM...

Q Has Rokuro gotten used to drinking the Benio Special and Deluxe Benio Special? (From Kokorogi no Haru)

I'll never get used to it!

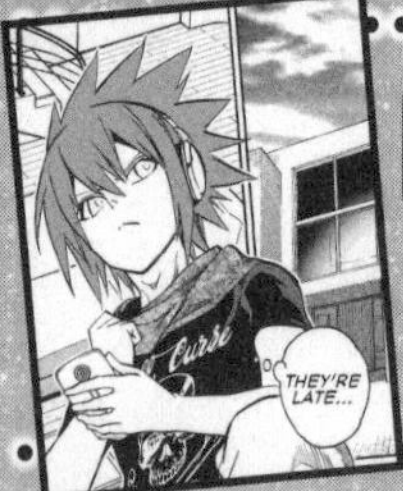
THEY'RE LATE...

Q What is Shimon always listening to? (From I LOVE Shimon)

I listen to prayers, Noh plays and sometimes *rakugo*.*

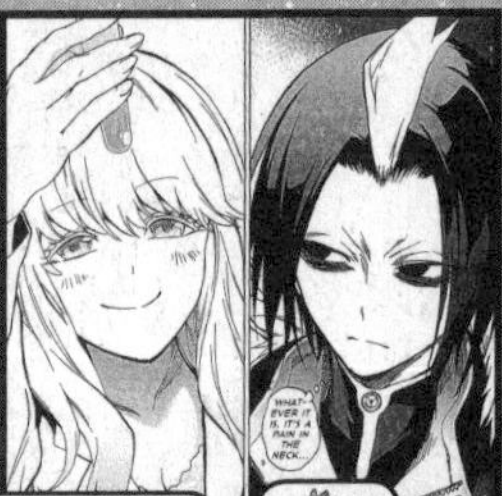

Request R I would like Seigen and Yukari's wedding anniversary to be June 12, Lovers' Day! Juno, the goddess of marriage (the origin of the tradition of the June bride)! The white rose of pure love! Romantic stuff like that (*laugh*). (From Ami Ouse)

A Sure. ☆ Henceforth that day will be their wedding anniversary.

Q Other than assassinations and training, what roles do the Twelve Guardian Families take on? (From Eringi)

A

- ★ Unomiya: Battle specialist (close combat)
- ★ Sada: Battle specialist (close combat)
- ★ Hagusa: Kegare and Magano research
- ★ Inanaki: Training facility management
- ★ Zeze: Management of families other than the Twelve Guardian families
- ★ Mitejima: Battle specialist (long-range combat)
- ★ Mitosaka: Medical and spell research
- ★ Ioroi: Magano geography management
- ★ Ikaruga: Battle specialist (long-range combat)
- ★ Amawaka: Scouting and Magano investigation
- ★ Kasukami: Weapon and armor development
- ★ Uji: Force field management

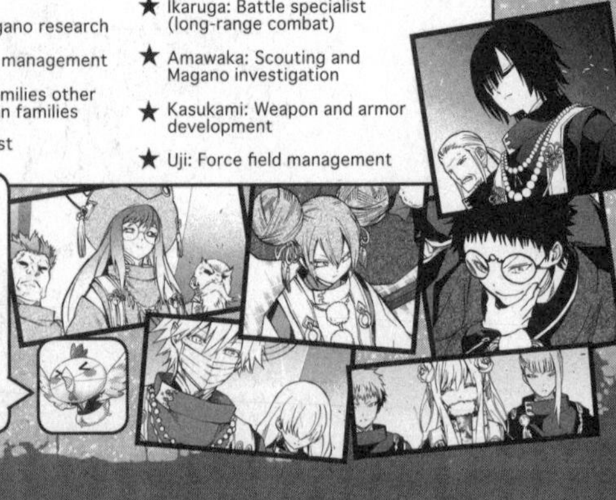

That should do it, I think. The families who specialize in battles usually spend time researching and developing spells and enchantments as well. The other families participate in battles too, of course, by making use of whatever they specialize in.

*Traditional Japanese storytelling including comedy, horror and melodrama genres

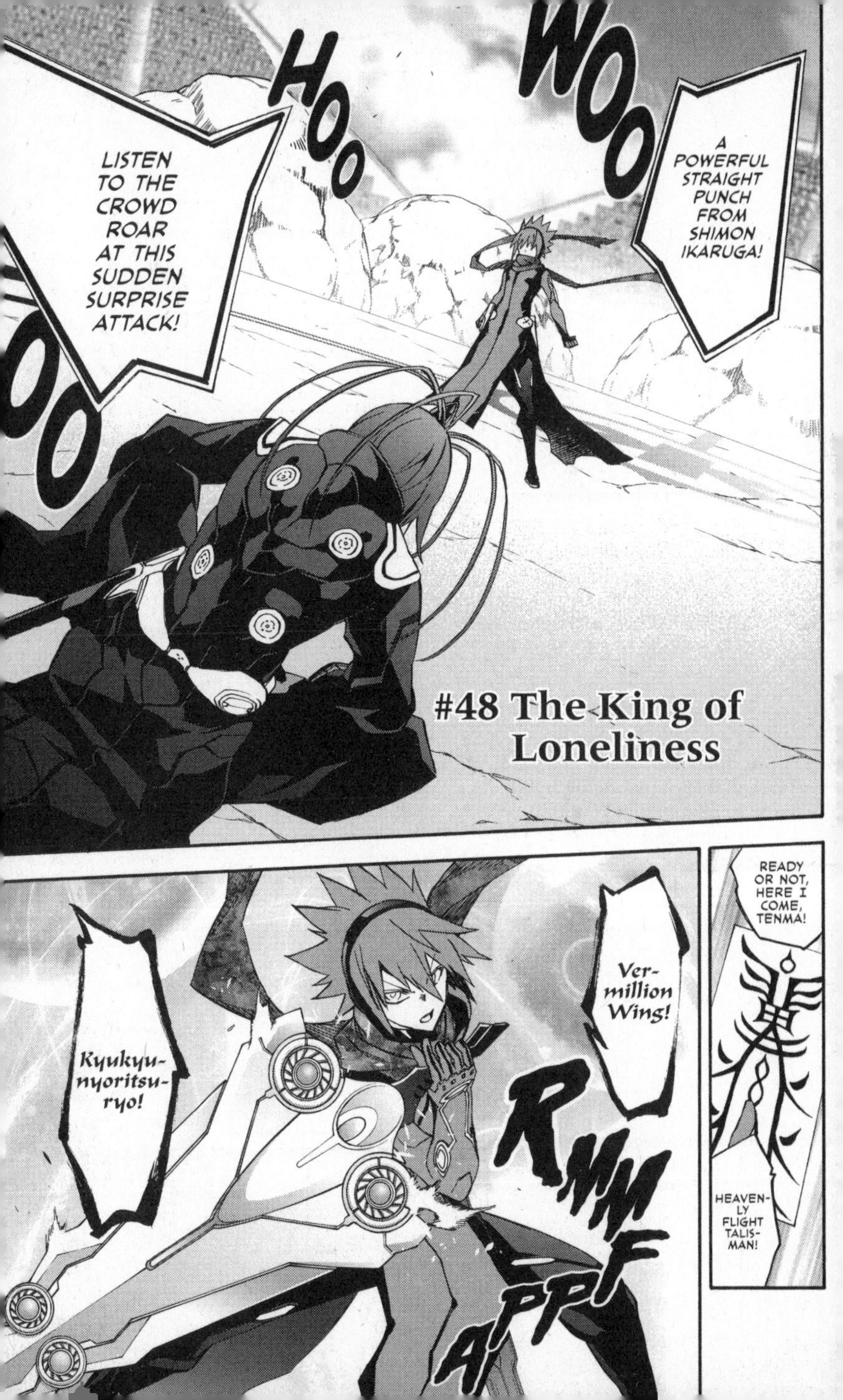
WOO
A POWERFUL STRAIGHT PUNCH FROM SHIMON IKARUGA!
HOO
LISTEN TO THE CROWD ROAR AT THIS SUDDEN SURPRISE ATTACK!
#48 The King of Loneliness
READY OR NOT, HERE I COME, TENMA!
HEAVEN-LY FLIGHT TALIS-MAN!
Ver-million Wing!
Kyukyu-nyoritsu-ryo!

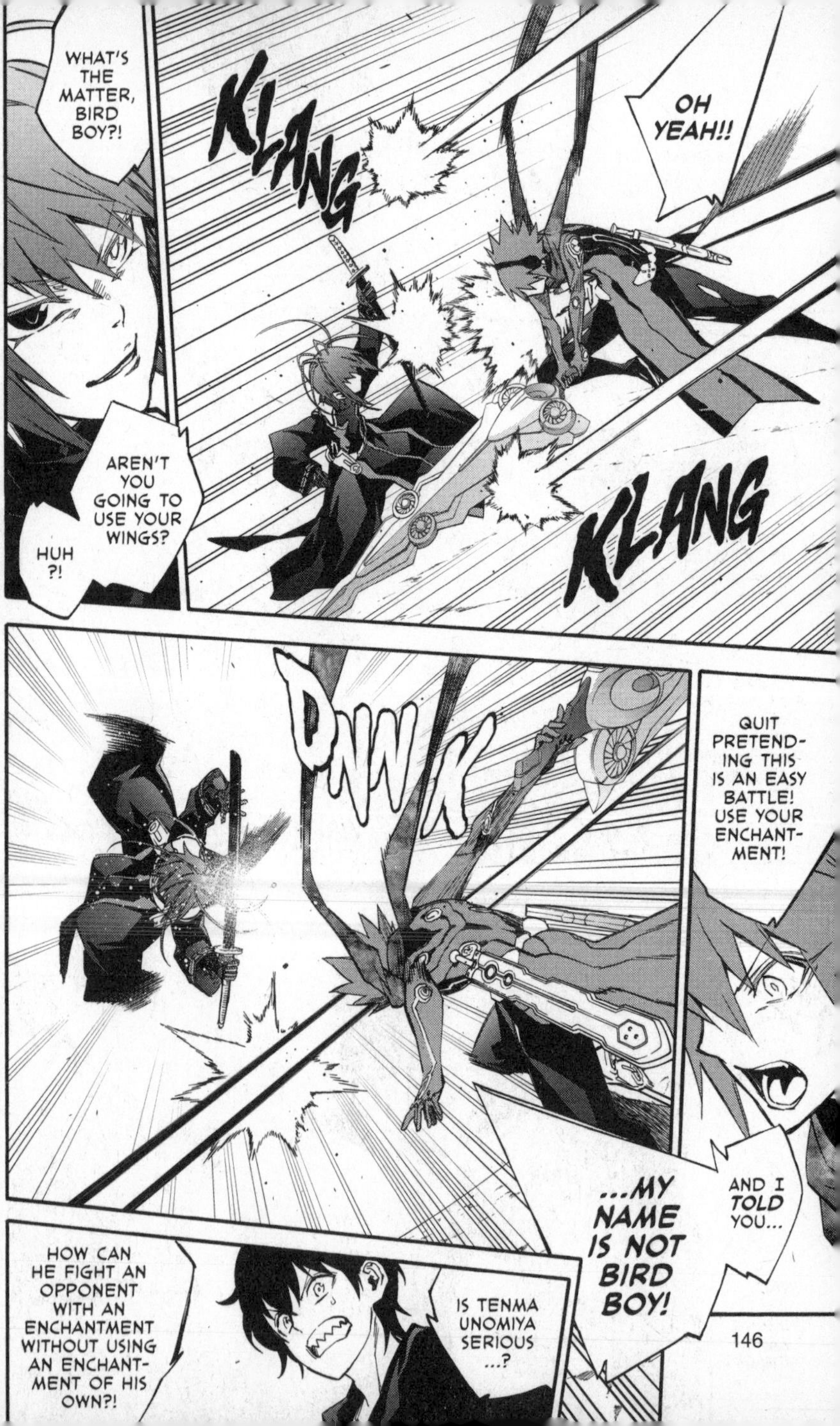

OH YEAH!!
KLANG
KLANG
WHAT'S THE MATTER, BIRD BOY?!
AREN'T YOU GOING TO USE YOUR WINGS?
HUH ?!
QUIT PRETENDING THIS IS AN EASY BATTLE! USE YOUR ENCHANTMENT!
AND I TOLD YOU...
...MY NAME IS NOT BIRD BOY!
DNNNK
IS TENMA UNOMIYA SERIOUS ...?
HOW CAN HE FIGHT AN OPPONENT WITH AN ENCHANTMENT WITHOUT USING AN ENCHANTMENT OF HIS OWN?!

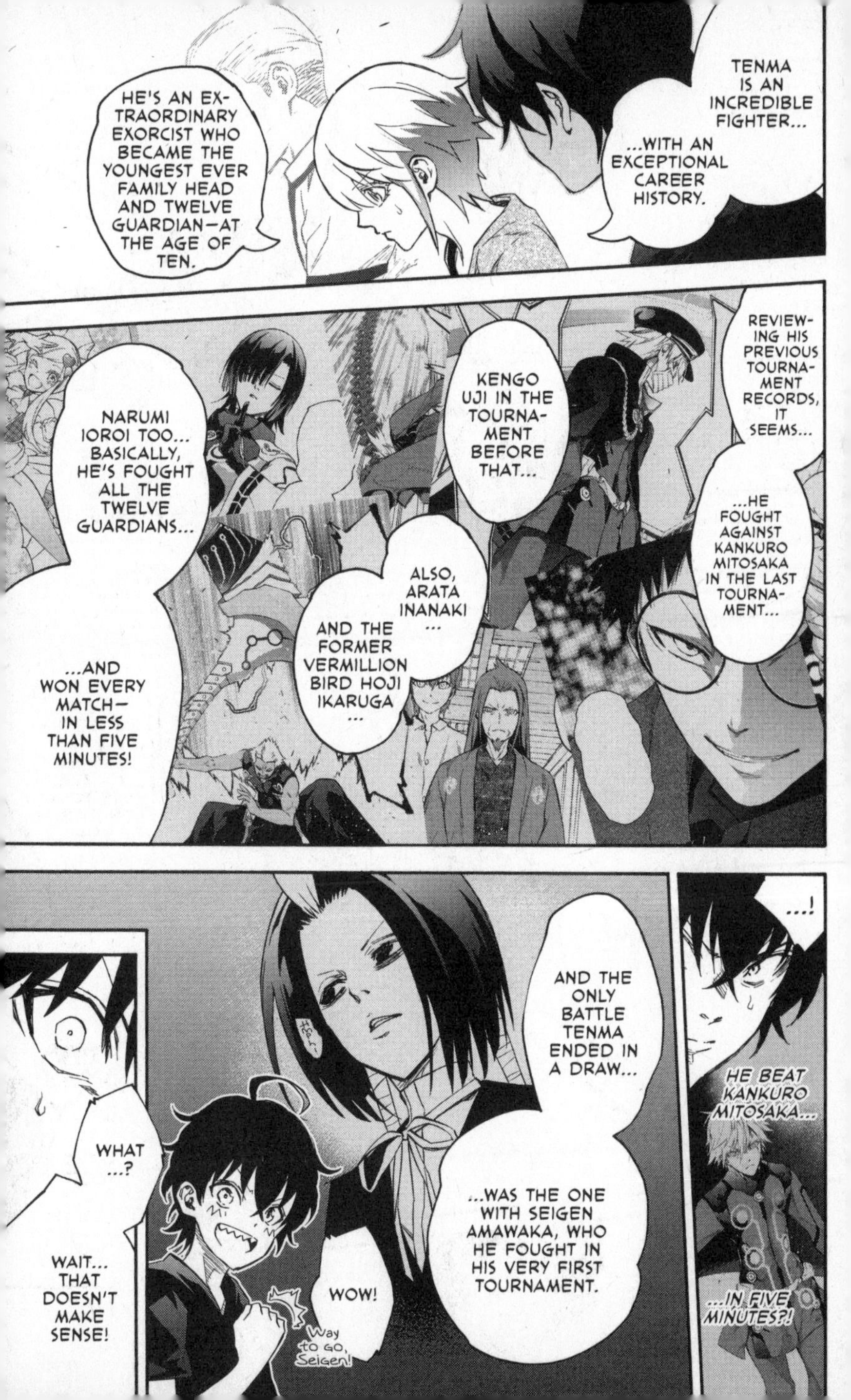
TENMA IS AN INCREDIBLE FIGHTER...
...WITH AN EXCEPTIONAL CAREER HISTORY.
HE'S AN EXTRAORDINARY EXORCIST WHO BECAME THE YOUNGEST EVER FAMILY HEAD AND TWELVE GUARDIAN—AT THE AGE OF TEN.
REVIEWING HIS PREVIOUS TOURNAMENT RECORDS, IT SEEMS...
...HE FOUGHT AGAINST KANKURO MITOSAKA IN THE LAST TOURNAMENT...
KENGO UJI IN THE TOURNAMENT BEFORE THAT...
ALSO, ARATA INANAKI...
AND THE FORMER VERMILLION BIRD HOJI IKARUGA...
NARUMI IOROI TOO... BASICALLY, HE'S FOUGHT ALL THE TWELVE GUARDIANS...
...AND WON EVERY MATCH—IN LESS THAN FIVE MINUTES!
...!
HE BEAT KANKURO MITOSAKA...
...IN FIVE MINUTES?!
AND THE ONLY BATTLE TENMA ENDED IN A DRAW...
...WAS THE ONE WITH SEIGEN AMAWAKA, WHO HE FOUGHT IN HIS VERY FIRST TOURNAMENT.
WOW!
Way to go, Seigen!
WHAT...?
WAIT... THAT DOESN'T MAKE SENSE!

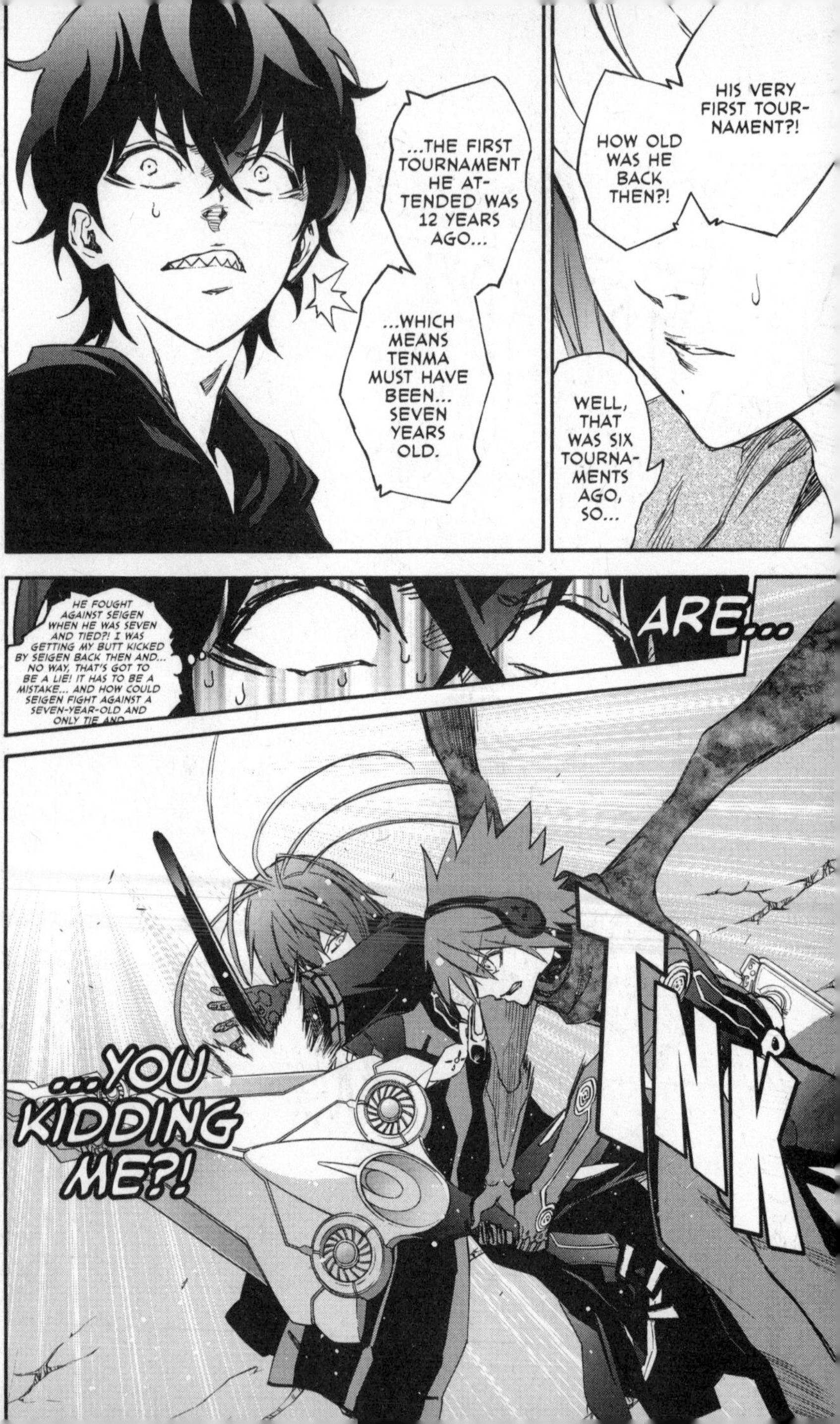
HIS VERY FIRST TOURNAMENT?!
HOW OLD WAS HE BACK THEN?!
WELL, THAT WAS SIX TOURNAMENTS AGO, SO...
...THE FIRST TOURNAMENT HE ATTENDED WAS 12 YEARS AGO...
...WHICH MEANS TENMA MUST HAVE BEEN... SEVEN YEARS OLD.
ARE...
HE FOUGHT AGAINST SEIGEN WHEN HE WAS SEVEN AND TIED?! I WAS GETTING MY BUTT KICKED BY SEIGEN BACK THEN AND... NO WAY, THAT'S GOT TO BE A LIE! IT HAS TO BE A MISTAKE... AND HOW COULD SEIGEN FIGHT AGAINST A SEVEN-YEAR-OLD AND ONLY TIE AND
TINK
...YOU KIDDING ME?!

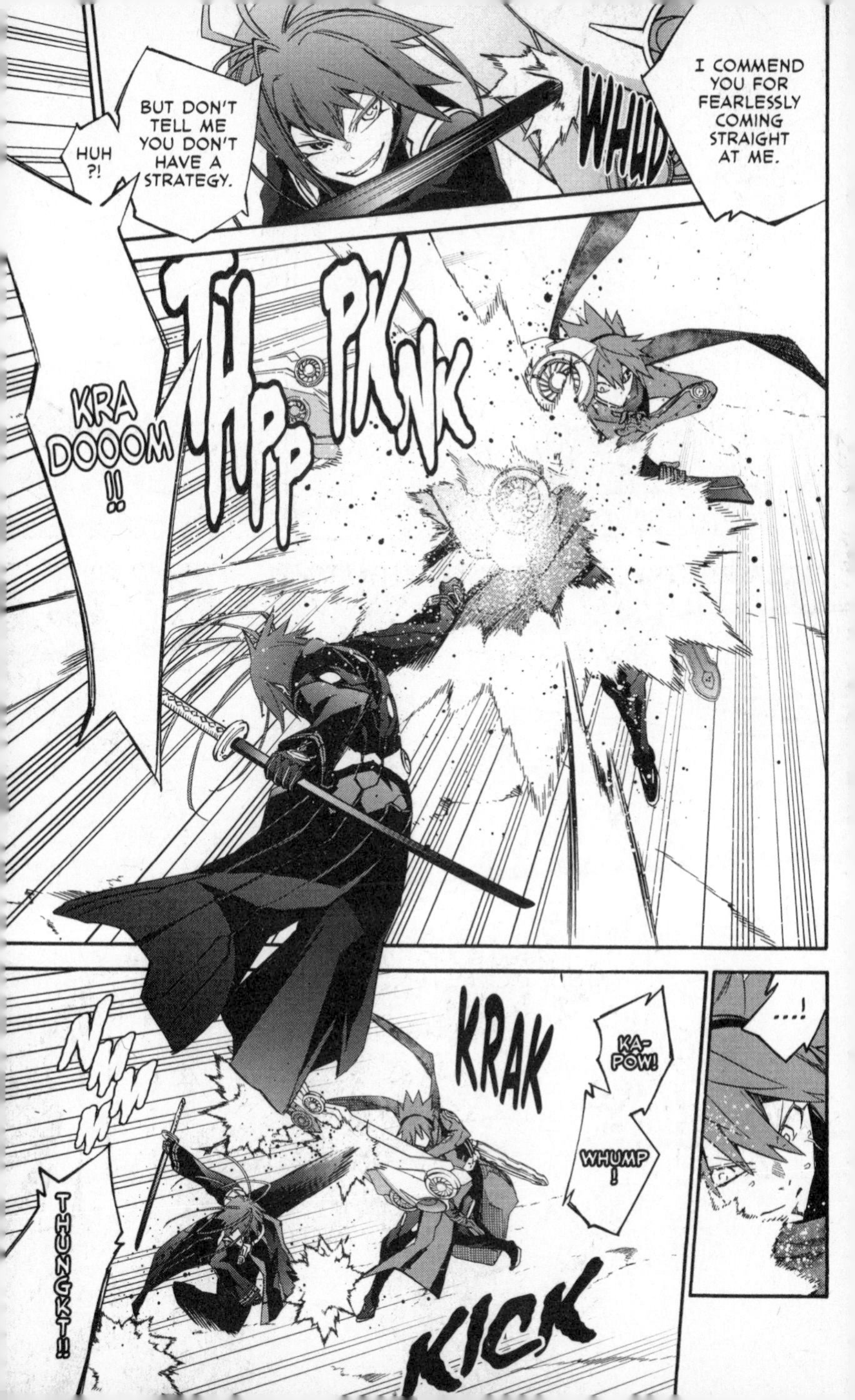
I COMMEND YOU FOR FEARLESSLY COMING STRAIGHT AT ME.
WHUD
BUT DON'T TELL ME YOU DON'T HAVE A STRATEGY.
HUH ?!
THPP
PKNK
KRA DOOOM !!
...!
KA-POW!
KRAK
WHUMP !
NMMMM
THUNGKT!!
KICK

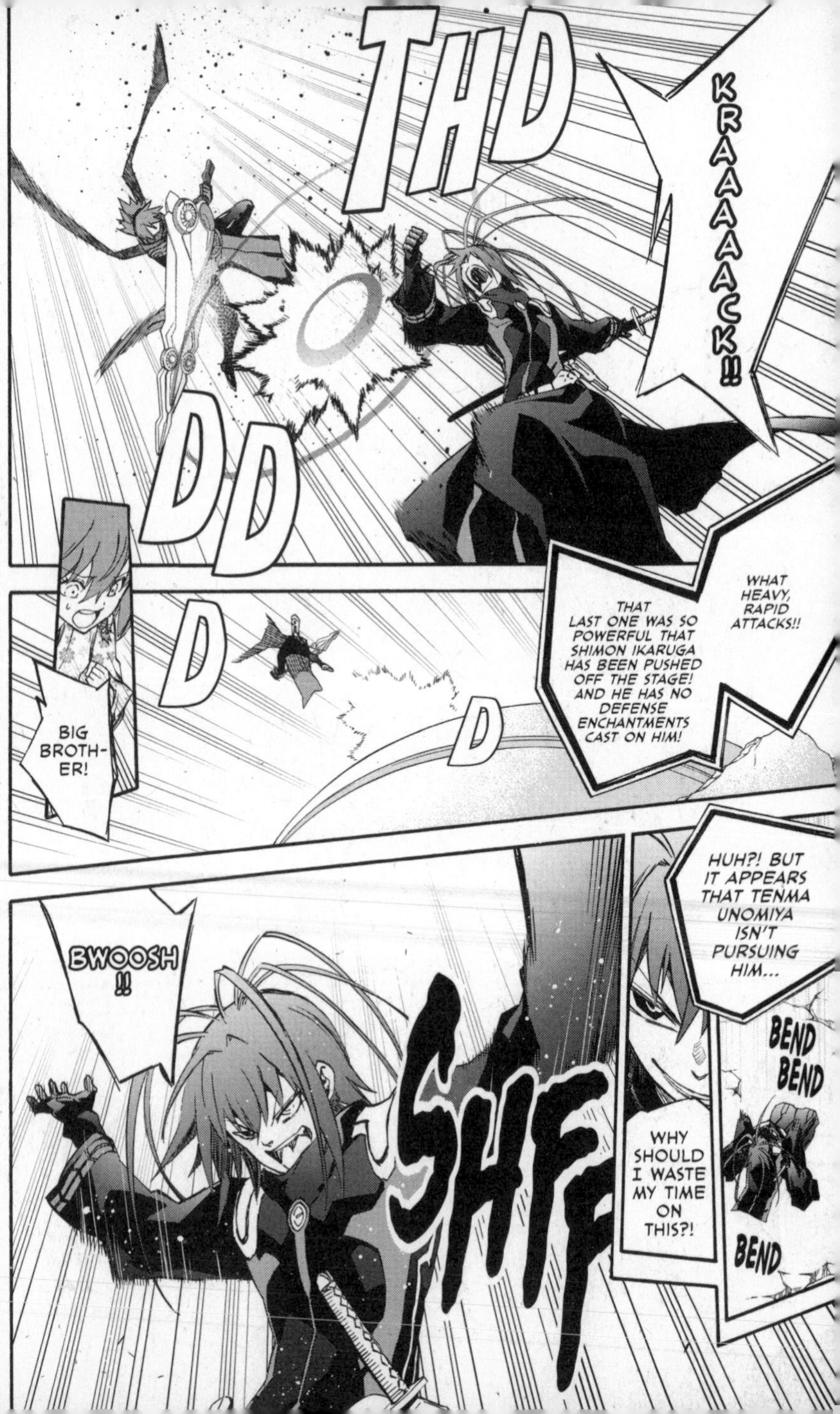
THD
KRAAAAACK!!
DDD
WHAT HEAVY, RAPID ATTACKS!!
THAT LAST ONE WAS SO POWERFUL THAT SHIMON IKARUGA HAS BEEN PUSHED OFF THE STAGE! AND HE HAS NO DEFENSE ENCHANTMENTS CAST ON HIM!
D
D
BIG BROTHER-ER!
HUH?! BUT IT APPEARS THAT TENMA UNOMIYA ISN'T PURSUING HIM...
BEND BEND
WHY SHOULD I WASTE MY TIME ON THIS?!
BEND
SHF
BWOOSH!!

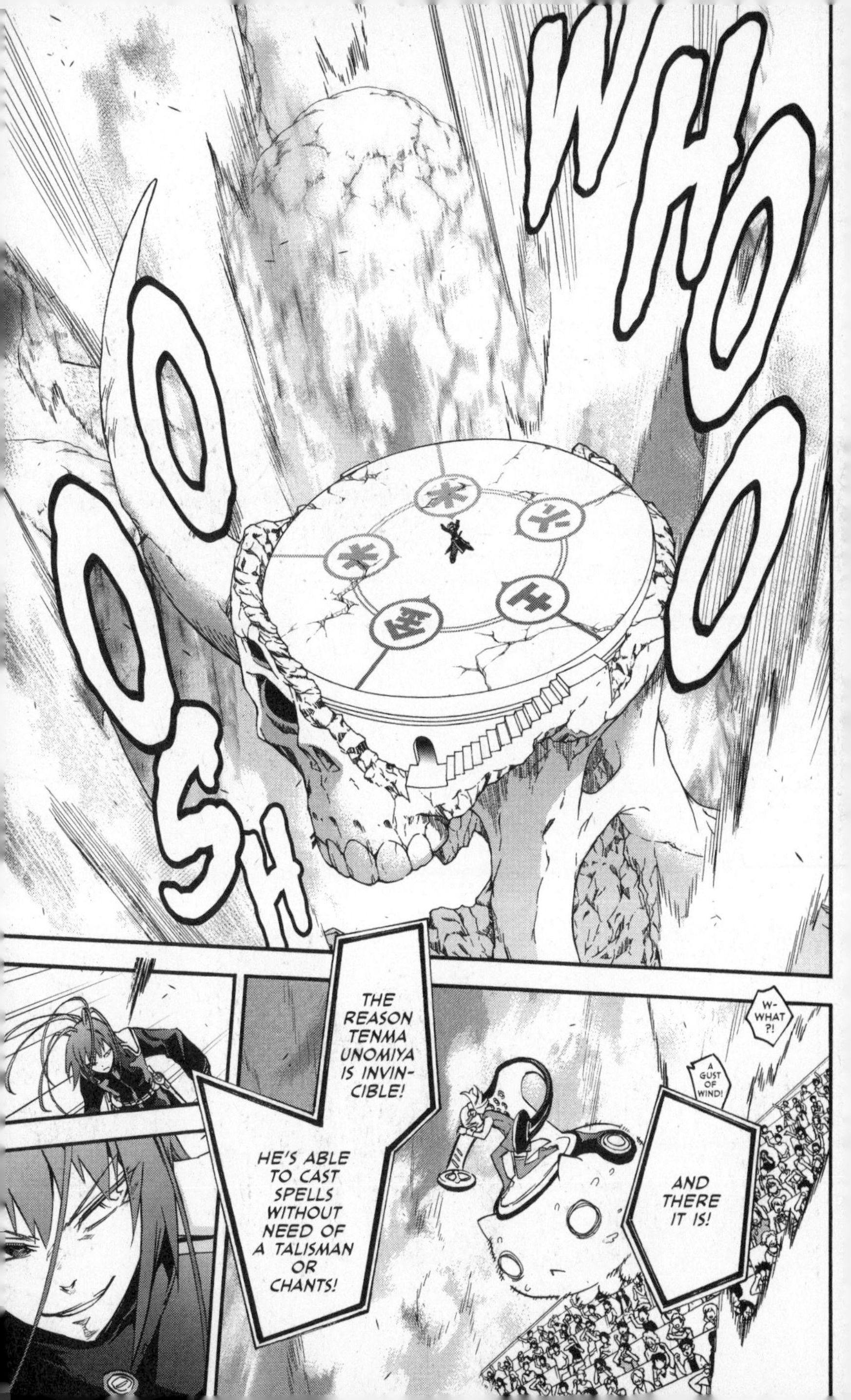
WHOOOOOOSH
W-WHAT?!
A GUST OF WIND!
AND THERE IT IS!
THE REASON TENMA UNOMIYA IS INVINCIBLE!
HE'S ABLE TO CAST SPELLS WITHOUT NEED OF A TALISMAN OR CHANTS!

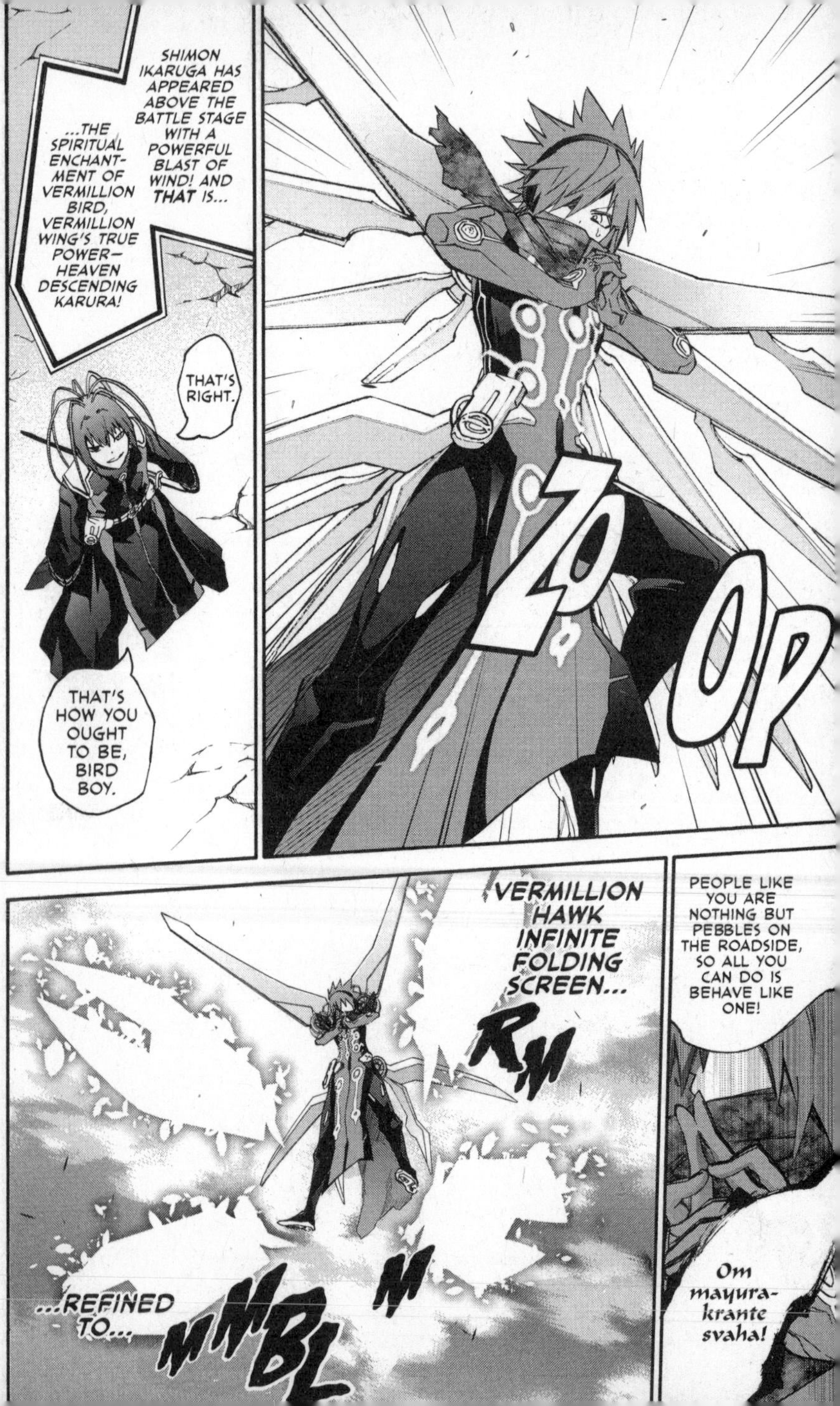
ZOOOP
SHIMON IKARUGA HAS APPEARED ABOVE THE BATTLE STAGE WITH A POWERFUL BLAST OF WIND! AND THAT IS...
...THE SPIRITUAL ENCHANTMENT OF VERMILLION BIRD, VERMILLION WING'S TRUE POWER— HEAVEN DESCENDING KARURA!
THAT'S RIGHT.
THAT'S HOW YOU OUGHT TO BE, BIRD BOY.
PEOPLE LIKE YOU ARE NOTHING BUT PEBBLES ON THE ROADSIDE, SO ALL YOU CAN DO IS BEHAVE LIKE ONE!
Om mayura-krante svaha!
VERMILLION HAWK INFINITE FOLDING SCREEN...
RM
...REFINED TO...
MMBLM

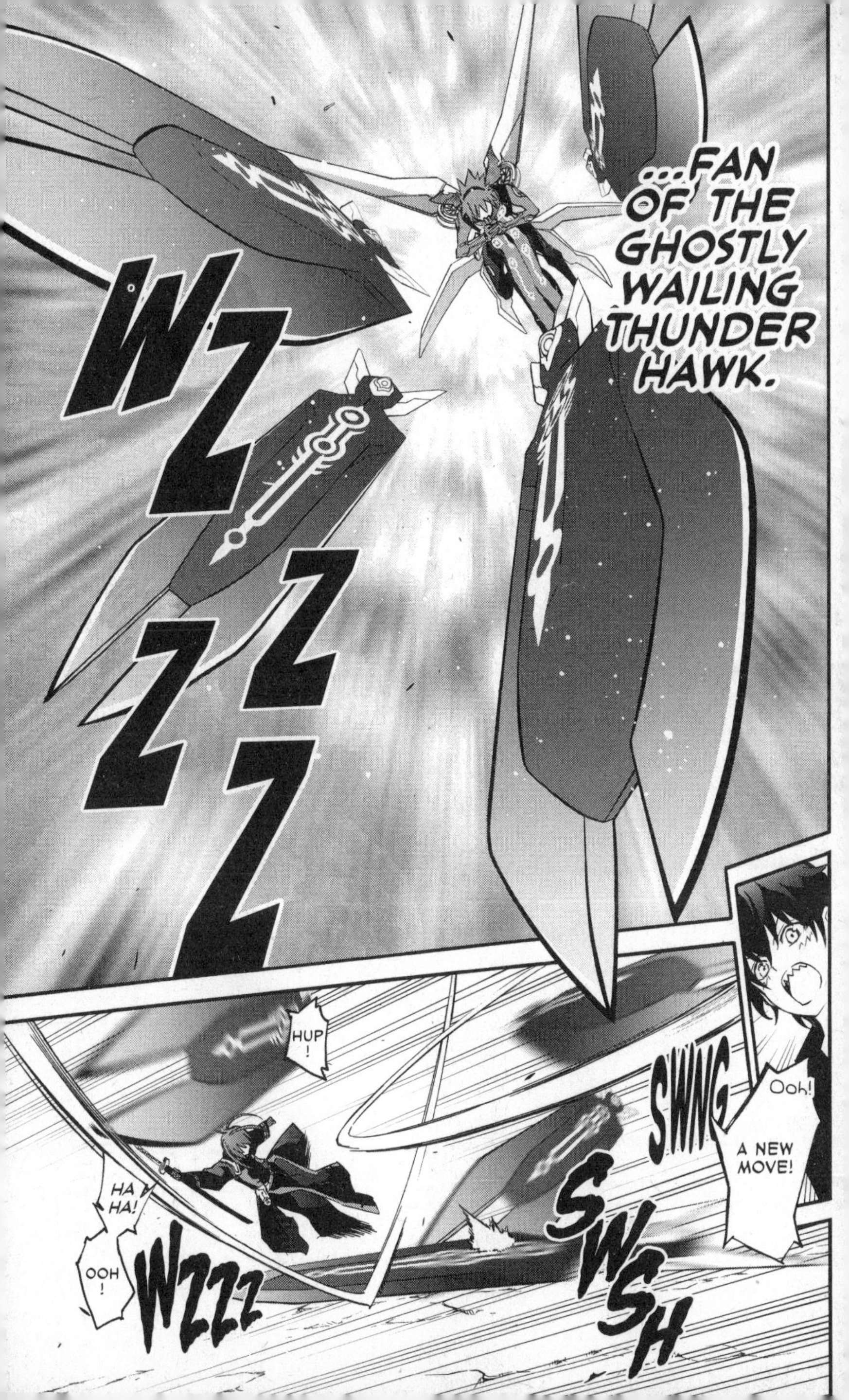
...FAN OF THE GHOSTLY WAILING THUNDER HAWK.
WZZZZ
Ooh!
A NEW MOVE!
SWNG
HUP!
SWSH
HA HA!
OOH!
WZZZ

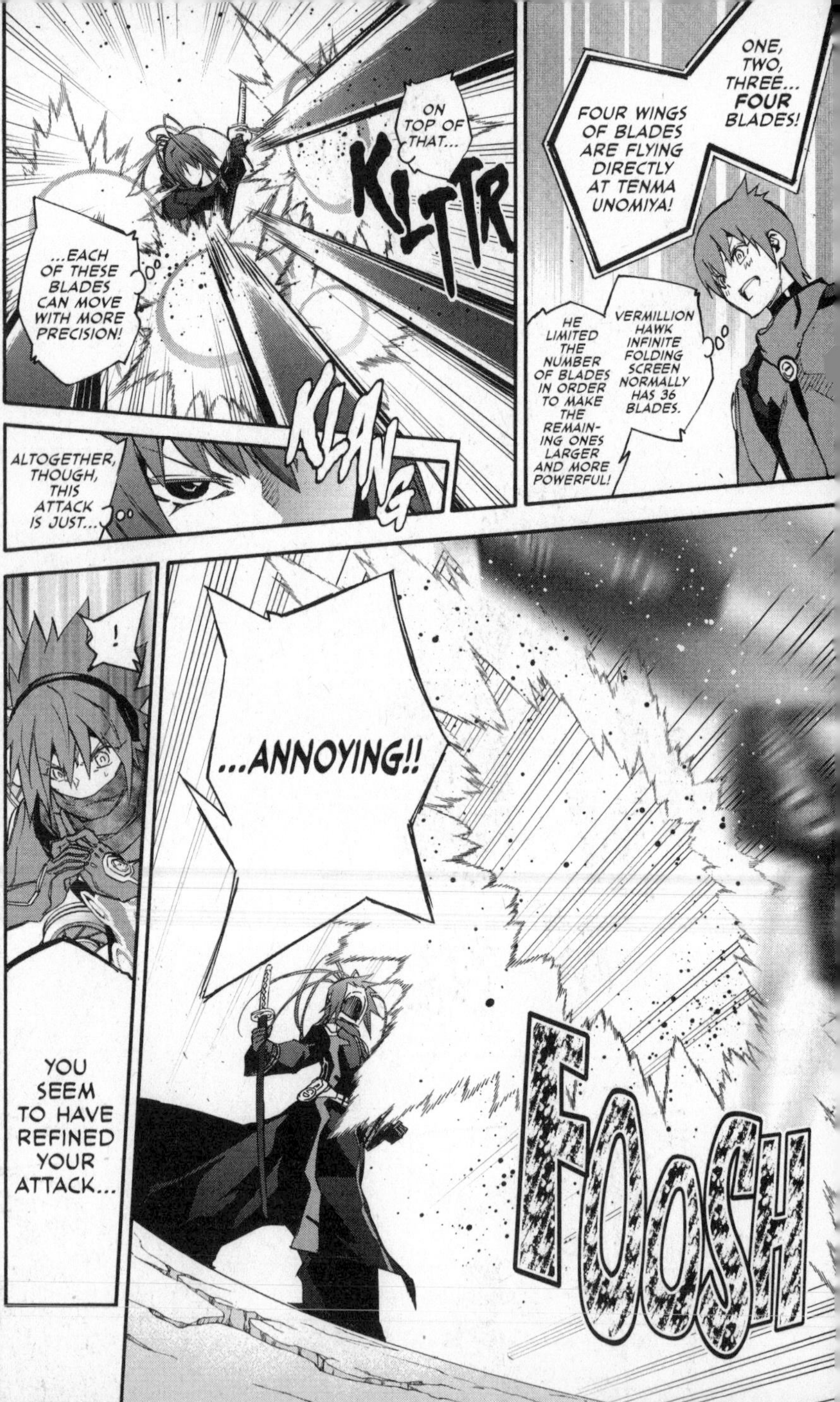
ONE, TWO, THREE... FOUR BLADES!
FOUR WINGS OF BLADES ARE FLYING DIRECTLY AT TENMA UNOMIYA!
VERMILLION HAWK INFINITE FOLDING SCREEN NORMALLY HAS 36 BLADES.
HE LIMITED THE NUMBER OF BLADES IN ORDER TO MAKE THE REMAIN-ING ONES LARGER AND MORE POWERFUL!
ON TOP OF THAT...
KLTTR
...EACH OF THESE BLADES CAN MOVE WITH MORE PRECISION!
KLANG
ALTOGETHER, THOUGH, THIS ATTACK IS JUST...
...ANNOYING!!
FOOSH
!
YOU SEEM TO HAVE REFINED YOUR ATTACK...

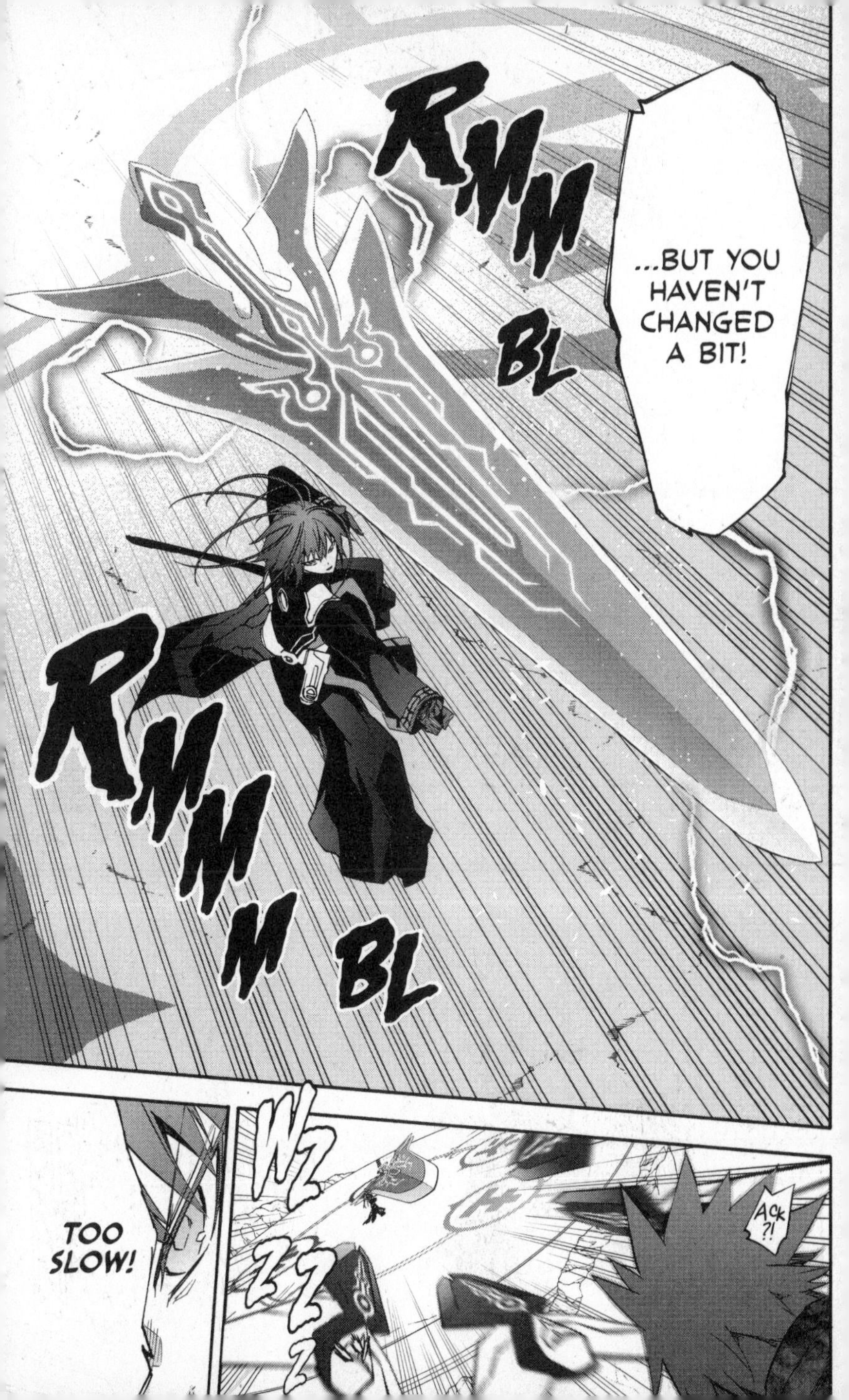
RMMBL
...BUT YOU HAVEN'T CHANGED A BIT!
RMMMMBL
ACK ?!
WZZZZZ
TOO SLOW!

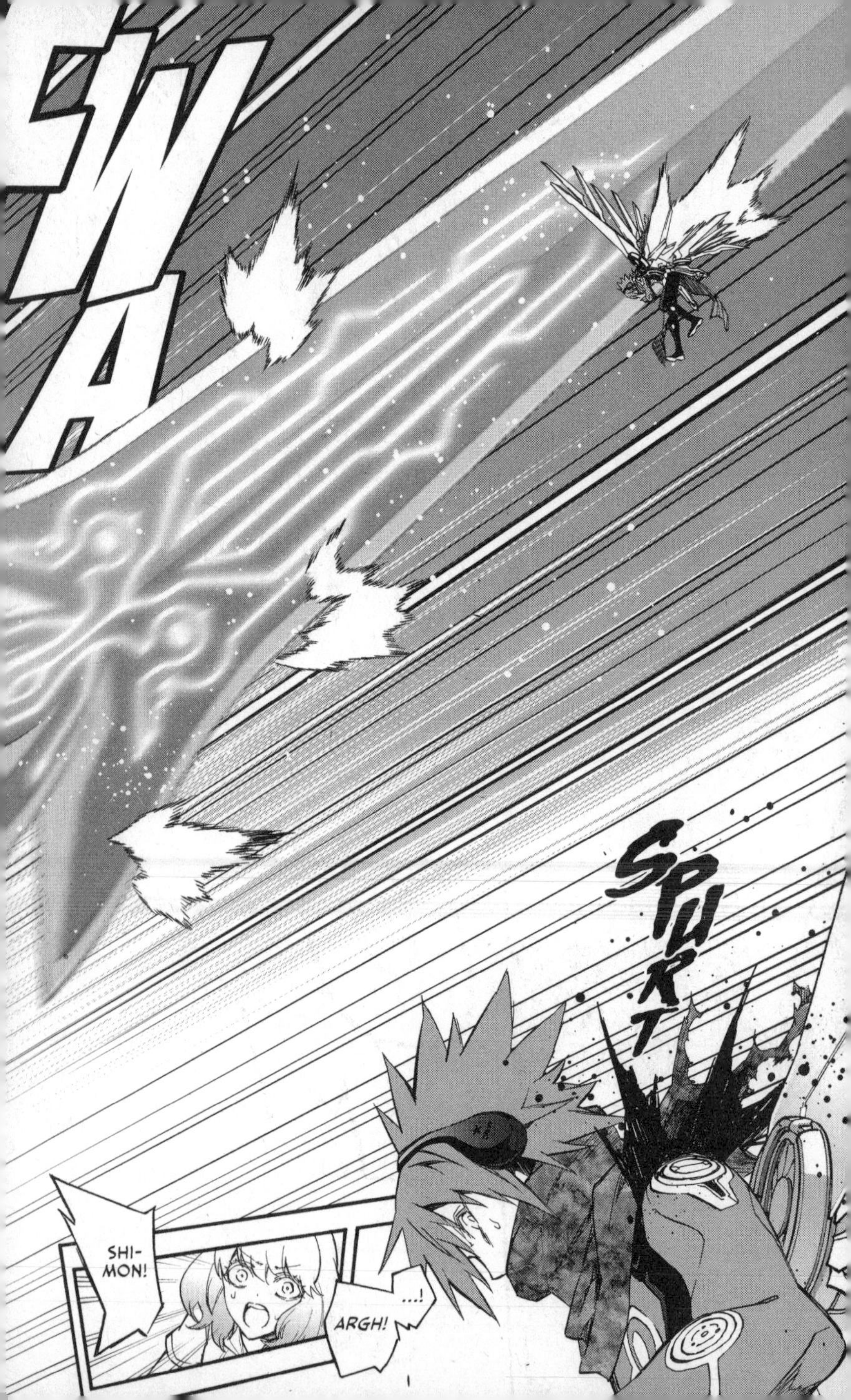
SPURT
...!
ARGH!
SHI-MON!

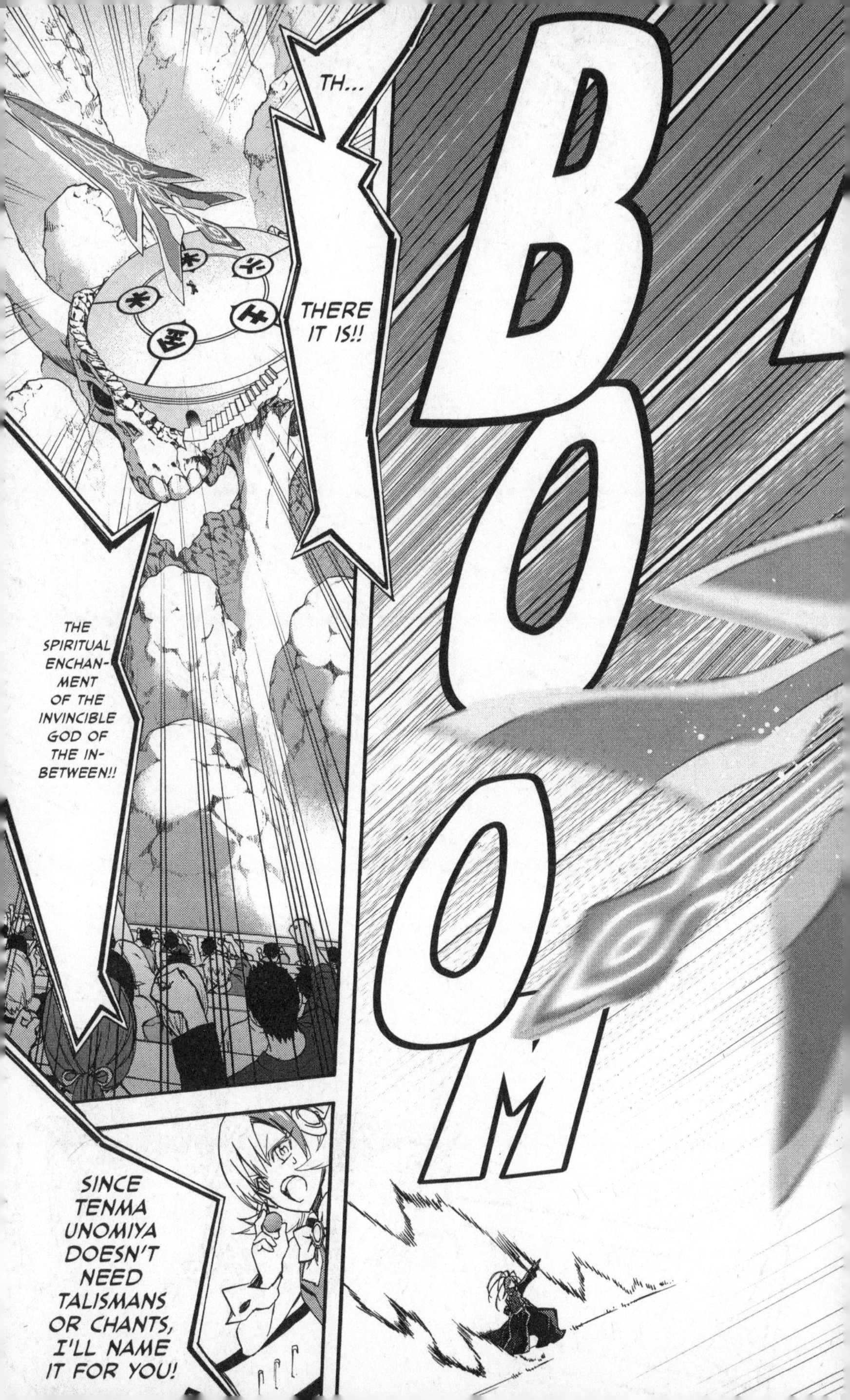
BOOM
TH...
THERE IT IS!!
THE SPIRITUAL ENCHAN-MENT OF THE INVINCIBLE GOD OF THE IN-BETWEEN!!
SINCE TENMA UNOMIYA DOESN'T NEED TALISMANS OR CHANTS, I'LL NAME IT FOR YOU!

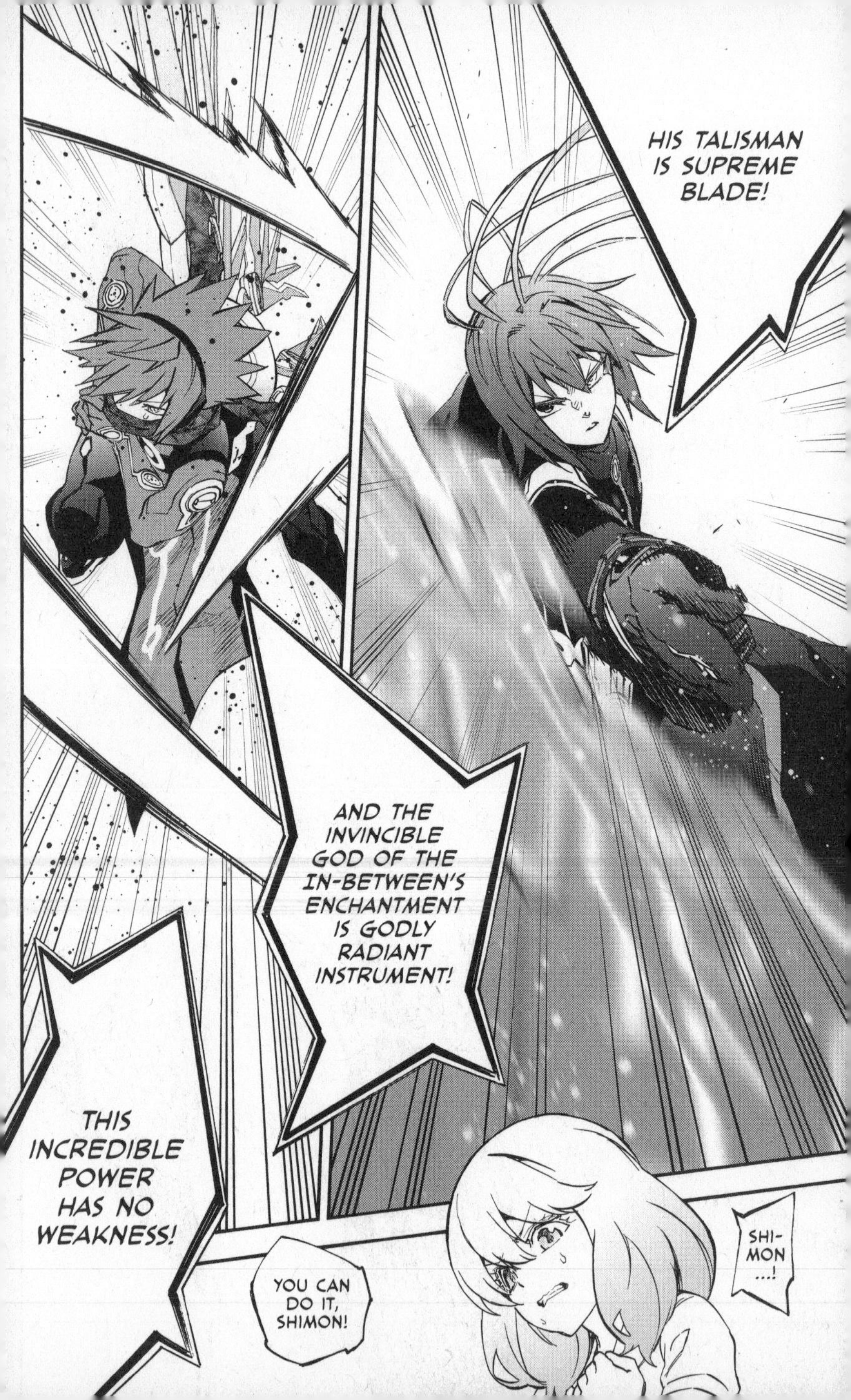
HIS TALISMAN IS SUPREME BLADE!
AND THE INVINCIBLE GOD OF THE IN-BETWEEN'S ENCHANTMENT IS GODLY RADIANT INSTRUMENT!
THIS INCREDIBLE POWER HAS NO WEAKNESS!
SHI-MON ...!
YOU CAN DO IT, SHIMON!

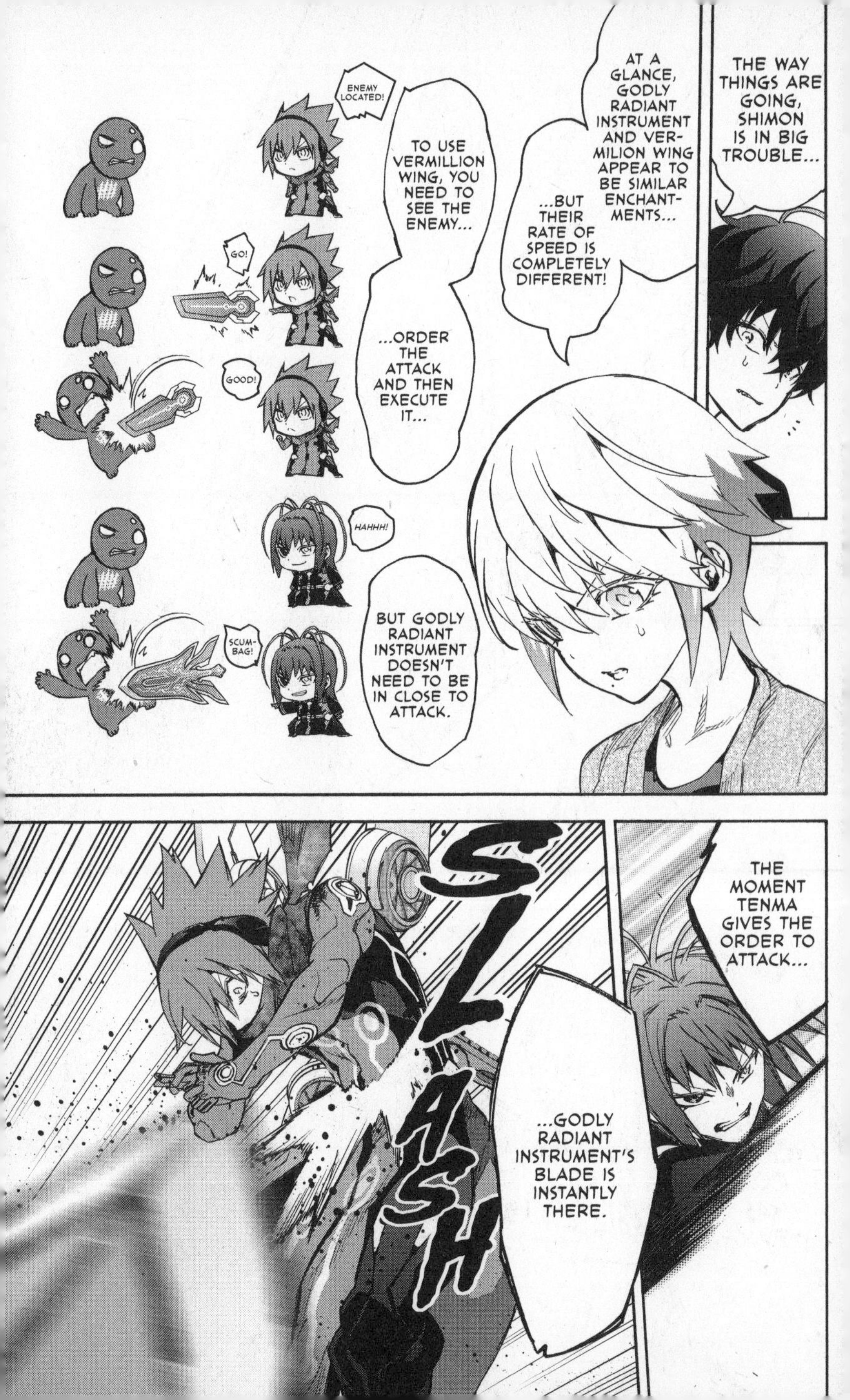
THE WAY THINGS ARE GOING, SHIMON IS IN BIG TROUBLE...
AT A GLANCE, GODLY RADIANT INSTRUMENT AND VER-MILION WING APPEAR TO BE SIMILAR ENCHANT-MENTS...
...BUT THEIR RATE OF SPEED IS COMPLETELY DIFFERENT!
TO USE VERMILLION WING, YOU NEED TO SEE THE ENEMY...
ENEMY LOCATED!
GO!
...ORDER THE ATTACK AND THEN EXECUTE IT...
GOOD!
HAHHH!
BUT GODLY RADIANT INSTRUMENT DOESN'T NEED TO BE IN CLOSE TO ATTACK.
SCUM-BAG!
THE MOMENT TENMA GIVES THE ORDER TO ATTACK...
...GODLY RADIANT INSTRUMENT'S BLADE IS INSTANTLY THERE.
SLASH

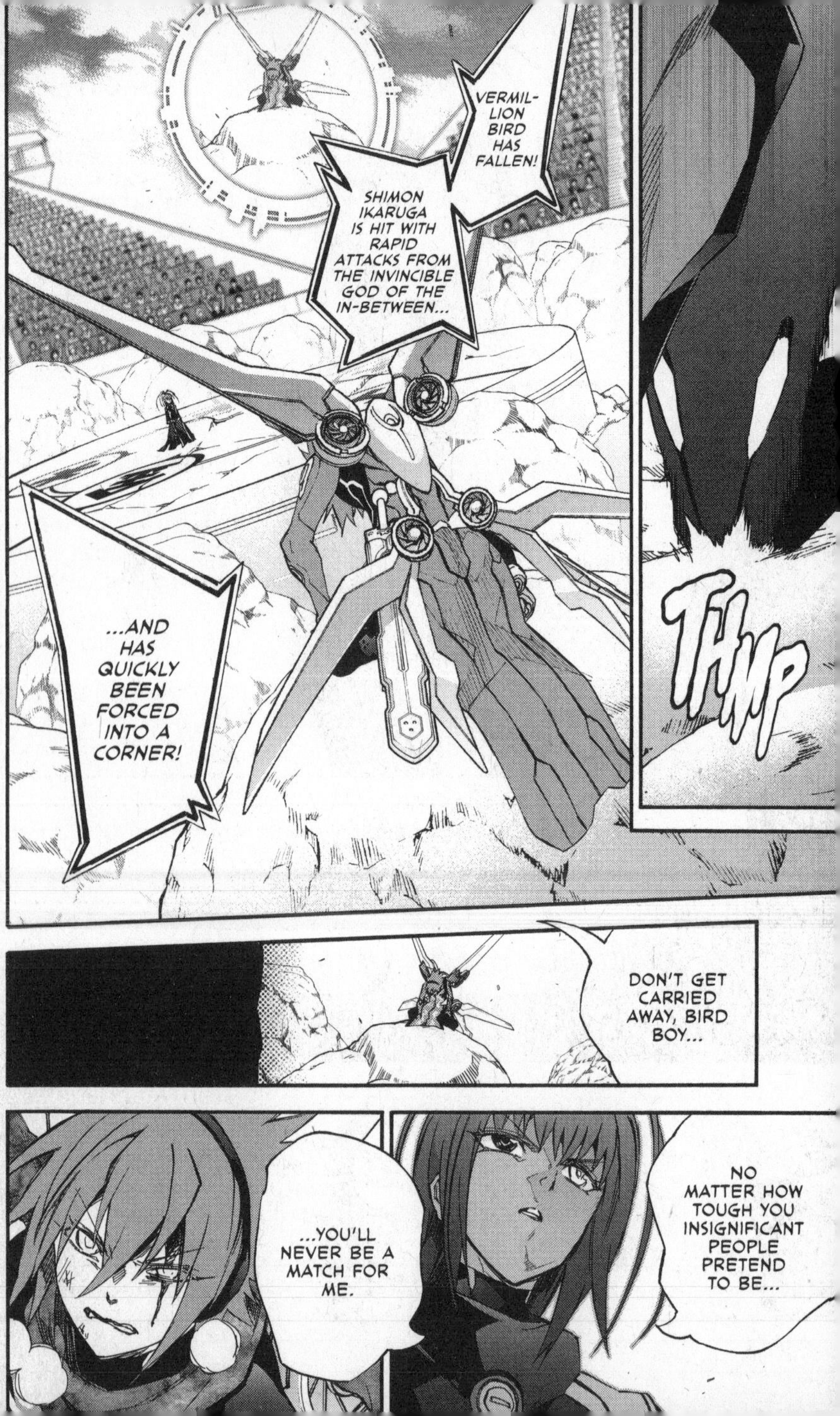
THMP
VERMIL-LION BIRD HAS FALLEN!
SHIMON IKARUGA IS HIT WITH RAPID ATTACKS FROM THE INVINCIBLE GOD OF THE IN-BETWEEN...
...AND HAS QUICKLY BEEN FORCED INTO A CORNER!
DON'T GET CARRIED AWAY, BIRD BOY...
NO MATTER HOW TOUGH YOU INSIGNIFICANT PEOPLE PRETEND TO BE...
...YOU'LL NEVER BE A MATCH FOR ME.

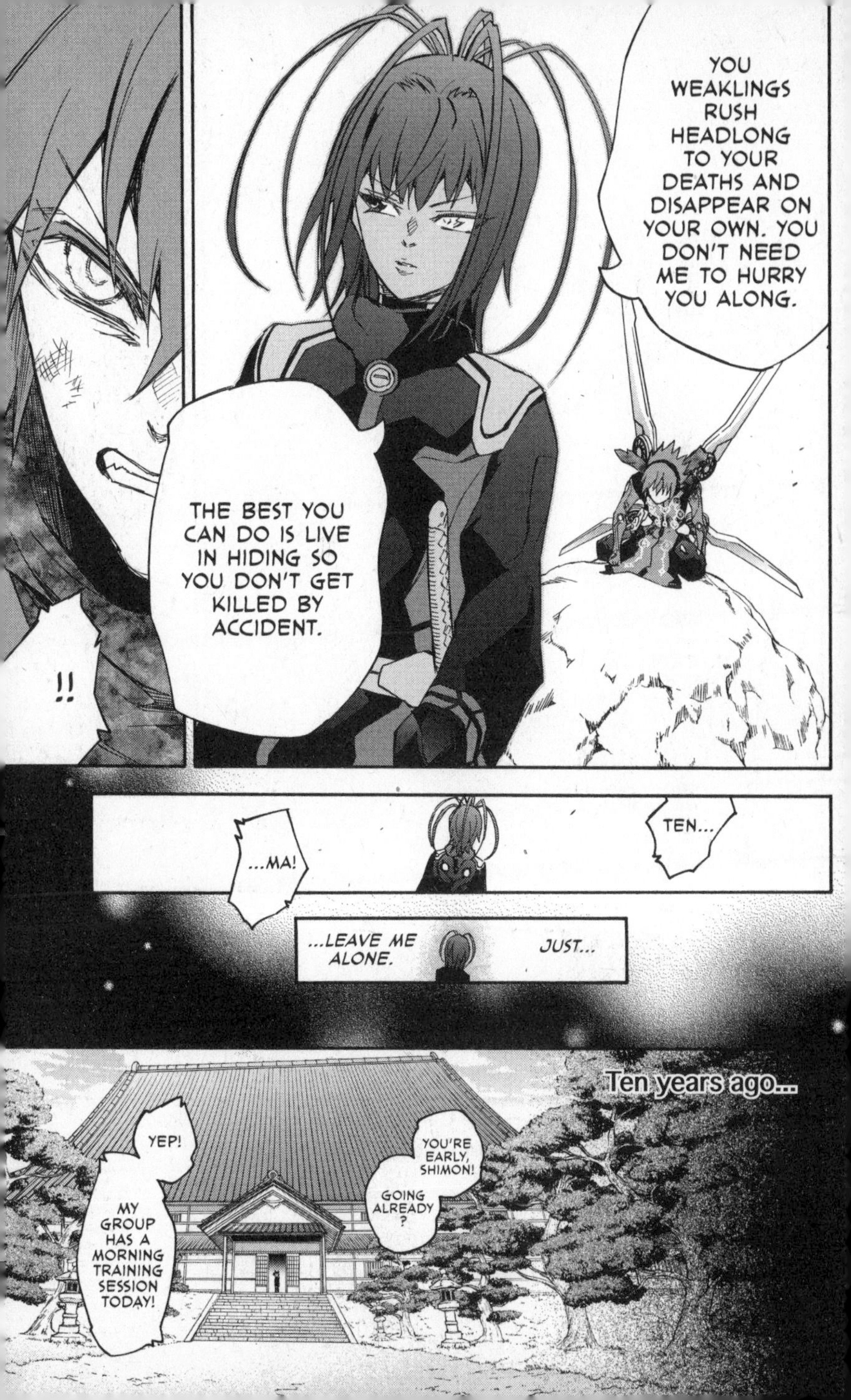
YOU WEAKLINGS RUSH HEADLONG TO YOUR DEATHS AND DISAPPEAR ON YOUR OWN. YOU DON'T NEED ME TO HURRY YOU ALONG.
THE BEST YOU CAN DO IS LIVE IN HIDING SO YOU DON'T GET KILLED BY ACCIDENT.
!!
TEN...
...MA!
JUST...
...LEAVE ME ALONE.
Ten years ago...
YOU'RE EARLY, SHIMON!
GOING ALREADY?
YEP!
MY GROUP HAS A MORNING TRAINING SESSION TODAY!

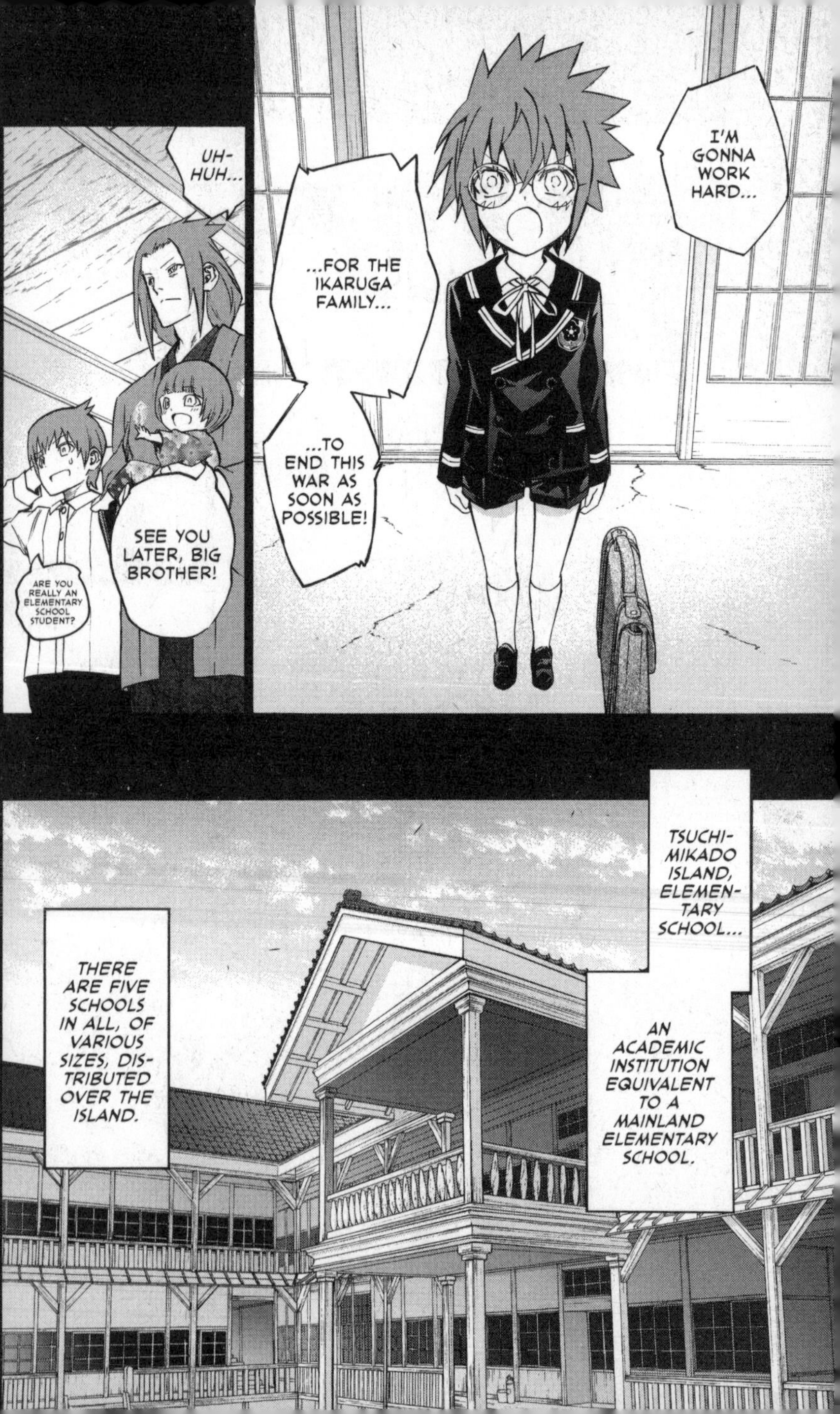
I'M GONNA WORK HARD...
...FOR THE IKARUGA FAMILY...
...TO END THIS WAR AS SOON AS POSSIBLE!
UH-HUH...
SEE YOU LATER, BIG BROTHER!
ARE YOU REALLY AN ELEMENTARY SCHOOL STUDENT?
TSUCHI-MIKADO ISLAND, ELEMENTARY SCHOOL...
AN ACADEMIC INSTITUTION EQUIVALENT TO A MAINLAND ELEMENTARY SCHOOL.
THERE ARE FIVE SCHOOLS IN ALL, OF VARIOUS SIZES, DISTRIBUTED OVER THE ISLAND.

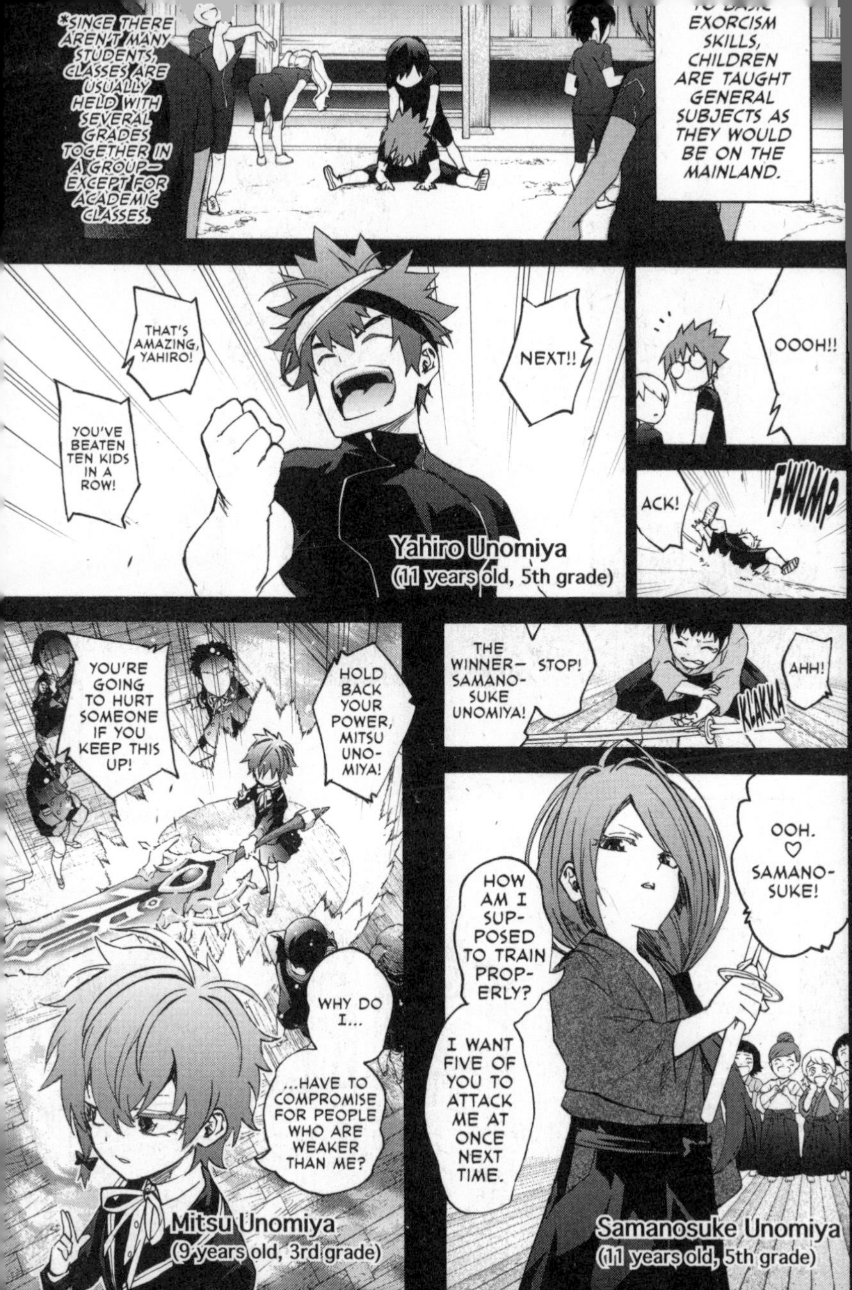
EXORCISM SKILLS, CHILDREN ARE TAUGHT GENERAL SUBJECTS AS THEY WOULD BE ON THE MAINLAND.
*SINCE THERE AREN'T MANY STUDENTS, CLASSES ARE USUALLY HELD WITH SEVERAL GRADES TOGETHER IN A GROUP—EXCEPT FOR ACADEMIC CLASSES.
OOOH!!
FWUMP
ACK!
NEXT!!
THAT'S AMAZING, YAHIRO!
YOU'VE BEATEN TEN KIDS IN A ROW!
Yahiro Unomiya
(11 years old, 5th grade)
AHH!
KLAKKA
STOP!
THE WINNER— SAMANOSUKE UNOMIYA!
OOH. ♡ SAMANOSUKE!
HOW AM I SUPPOSED TO TRAIN PROPERLY?
I WANT FIVE OF YOU TO ATTACK ME AT ONCE NEXT TIME.
Samanosuke Unomiya
(11 years old, 5th grade)
HOLD BACK YOUR POWER, MITSU UNOMIYA!
YOU'RE GOING TO HURT SOMEONE IF YOU KEEP THIS UP!
WHY DO I...
...HAVE TO COMPROMISE FOR PEOPLE WHO ARE WEAKER THAN ME?
Mitsu Unomiya
(9 years old, 3rd grade)

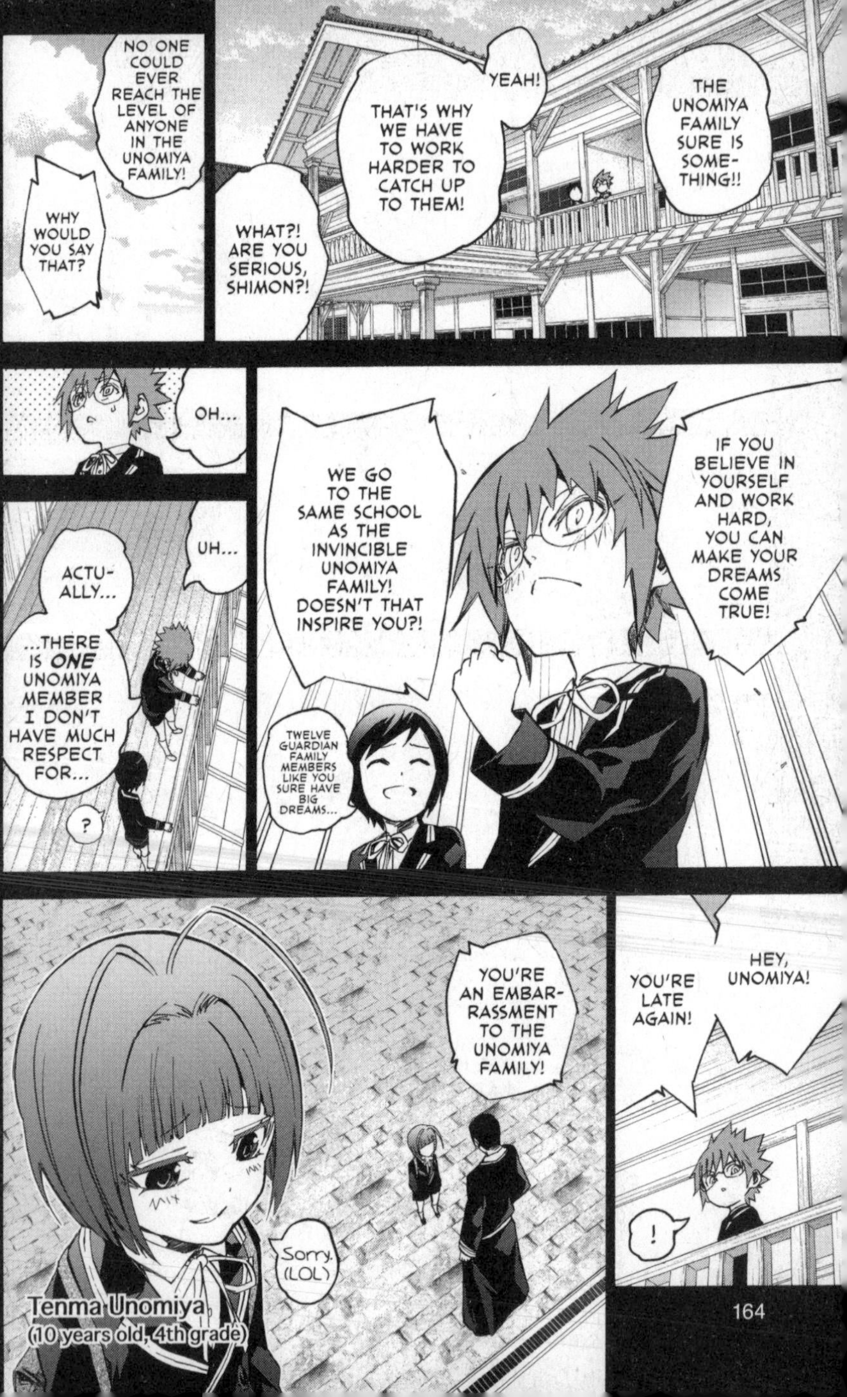
THE UNOMIYA FAMILY SURE IS SOME-THING!!
YEAH!
THAT'S WHY WE HAVE TO WORK HARDER TO CATCH UP TO THEM!
WHAT?! ARE YOU SERIOUS, SHIMON?!
NO ONE COULD EVER REACH THE LEVEL OF ANYONE IN THE UNOMIYA FAMILY!
WHY WOULD YOU SAY THAT?
IF YOU BELIEVE IN YOURSELF AND WORK HARD, YOU CAN MAKE YOUR DREAMS COME TRUE!
WE GO TO THE SAME SCHOOL AS THE INVINCIBLE UNOMIYA FAMILY! DOESN'T THAT INSPIRE YOU?!
TWELVE GUARDIAN FAMILY MEMBERS LIKE YOU SURE HAVE BIG DREAMS...
OH...
UH...
ACTU-ALLY...
...THERE IS *ONE* UNOMIYA MEMBER I DON'T HAVE MUCH RESPECT FOR...
?
HEY, UNOMIYA!
YOU'RE LATE AGAIN!
!
YOU'RE AN EMBAR-RASSMENT TO THE UNOMIYA FAMILY!
Sorry. (LOL)
Tenma Unomiya
(10 years old, 4th grade)

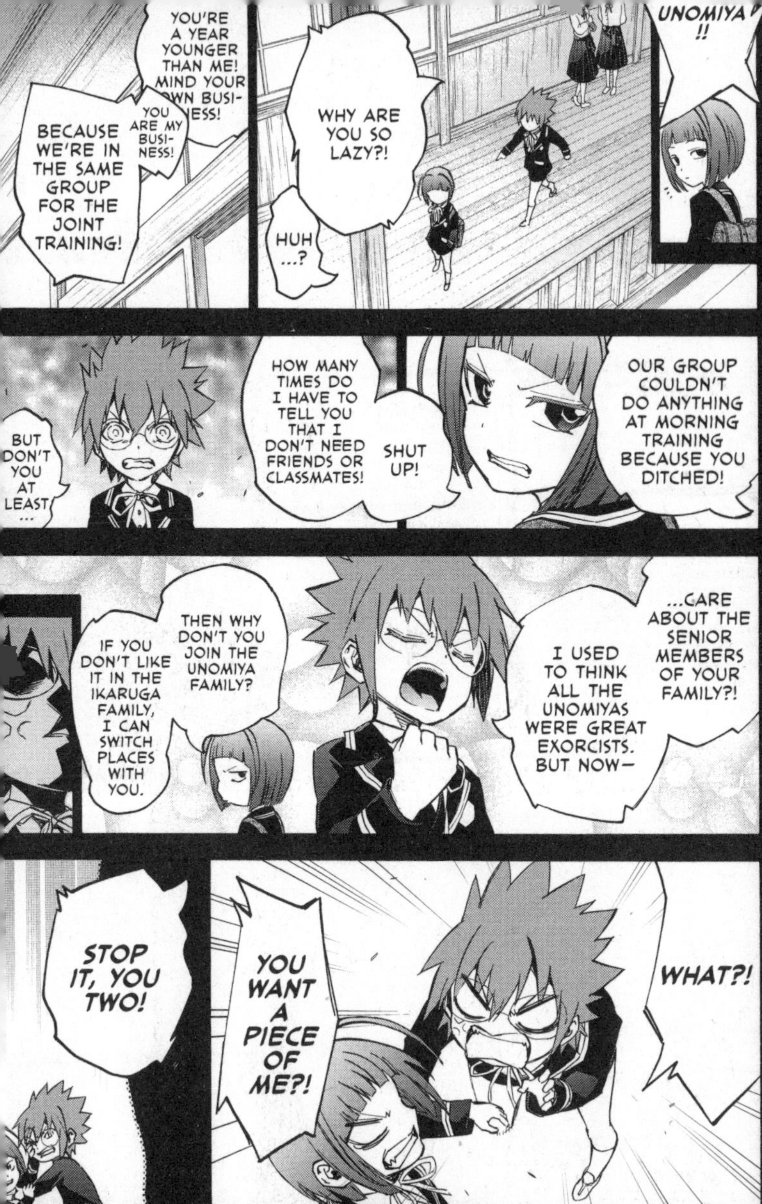
UNOMIYA!!
WHY ARE YOU SO LAZY?!
HUH...?
YOU'RE A YEAR YOUNGER THAN ME! MIND YOUR OWN BUSINESS!
YOU ARE MY BUSINESS!
BECAUSE WE'RE IN THE SAME GROUP FOR THE JOINT TRAINING!
OUR GROUP COULDN'T DO ANYTHING AT MORNING TRAINING BECAUSE YOU DITCHED!
SHUT UP!
HOW MANY TIMES DO I HAVE TO TELL YOU THAT I DON'T NEED FRIENDS OR CLASSMATES!
BUT DON'T YOU AT LEAST...
...CARE ABOUT THE SENIOR MEMBERS OF YOUR FAMILY?!
I USED TO THINK ALL THE UNOMIYAS WERE GREAT EXORCISTS. BUT NOW—
THEN WHY DON'T YOU JOIN THE UNOMIYA FAMILY?
IF YOU DON'T LIKE IT IN THE IKARUGA FAMILY, I CAN SWITCH PLACES WITH YOU.
WHAT?!
YOU WANT A PIECE OF ME?!
STOP IT, YOU TWO!

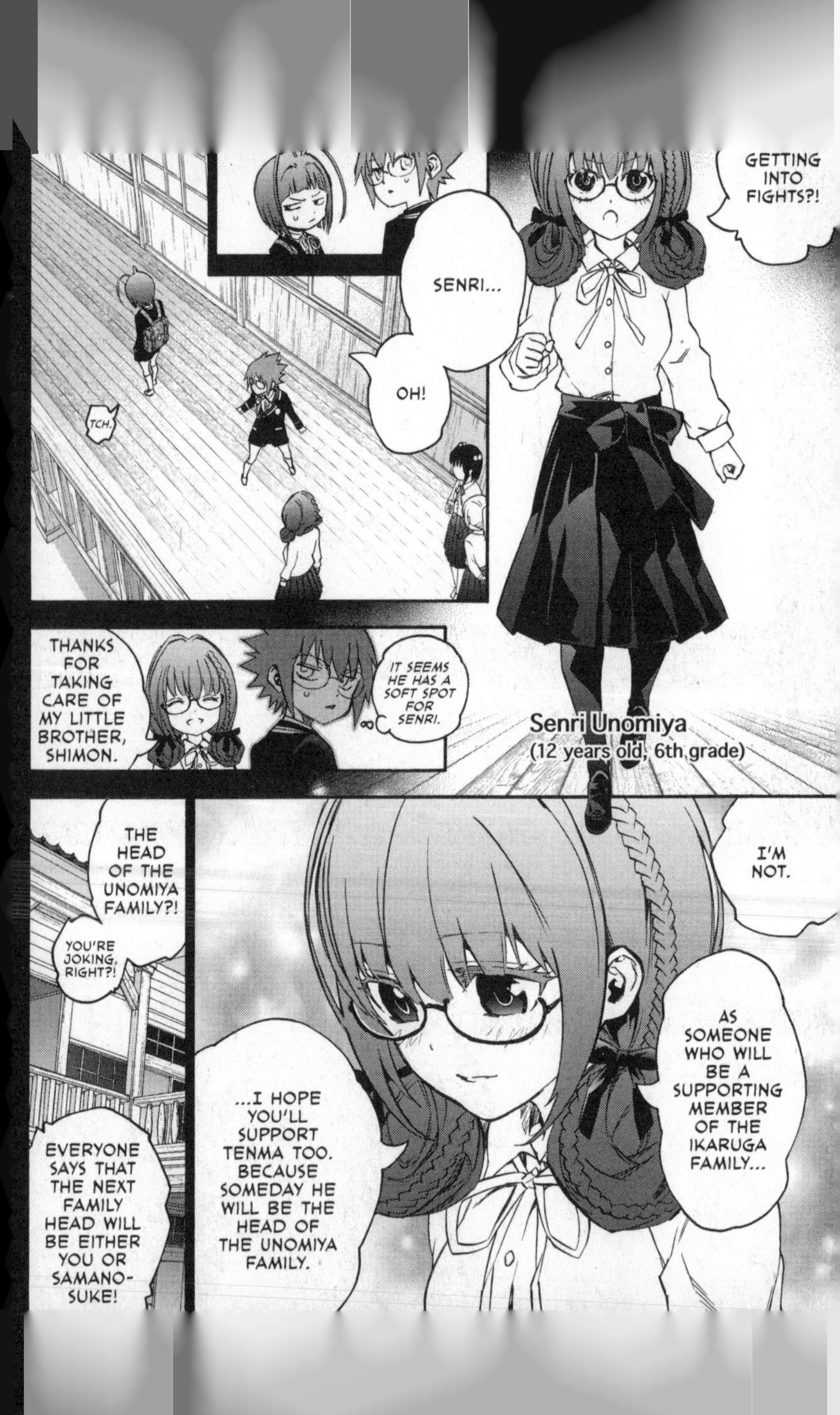
GETTING INTO FIGHTS?!
Senri Unomiya
(12 years old, 6th grade)
SENRI...
OH!
TCH.
THANKS FOR TAKING CARE OF MY LITTLE BROTHER, SHIMON.
IT SEEMS HE HAS A SOFT SPOT FOR SENRI.
I'M NOT.
AS SOMEONE WHO WILL BE A SUPPORTING MEMBER OF THE IKARUGA FAMILY...
...I HOPE YOU'LL SUPPORT TENMA TOO. BECAUSE SOMEDAY HE WILL BE THE HEAD OF THE UNOMIYA FAMILY.
THE HEAD OF THE UNOMIYA FAMILY?!
YOU'RE JOKING, RIGHT?!
EVERYONE SAYS THAT THE NEXT FAMILY HEAD WILL BE EITHER YOU OR SAMANO-SUKE!

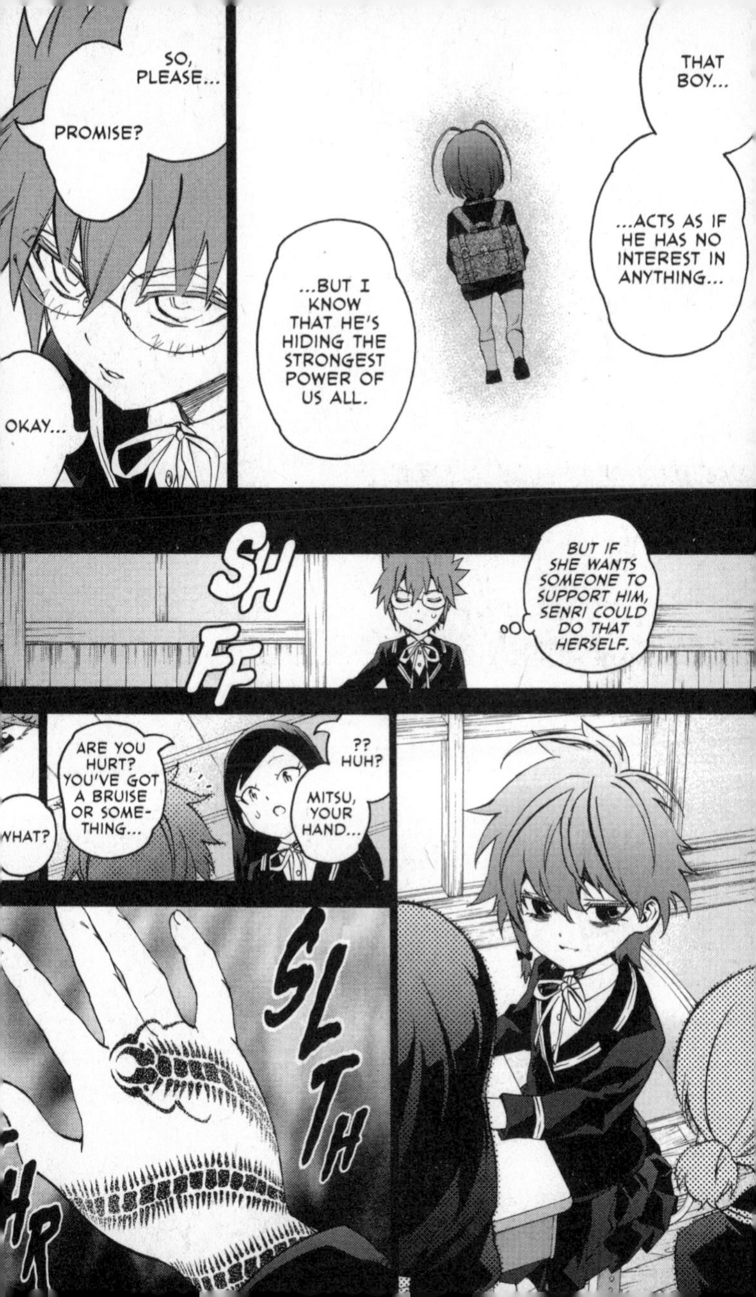
THAT BOY...
...ACTS AS IF HE HAS NO INTEREST IN ANYTHING...
...BUT I KNOW THAT HE'S HIDING THE STRONGEST POWER OF US ALL.
SO, PLEASE...
PROMISE?
OKAY...
BUT IF SHE WANTS SOMEONE TO SUPPORT HIM, SENRI COULD DO THAT HERSELF.
SHFF
?? HUH?
MITSU, YOUR HAND...
ARE YOU HURT? YOU'VE GOT A BRUISE OR SOME-THING...
WHAT?
SLTH
HR

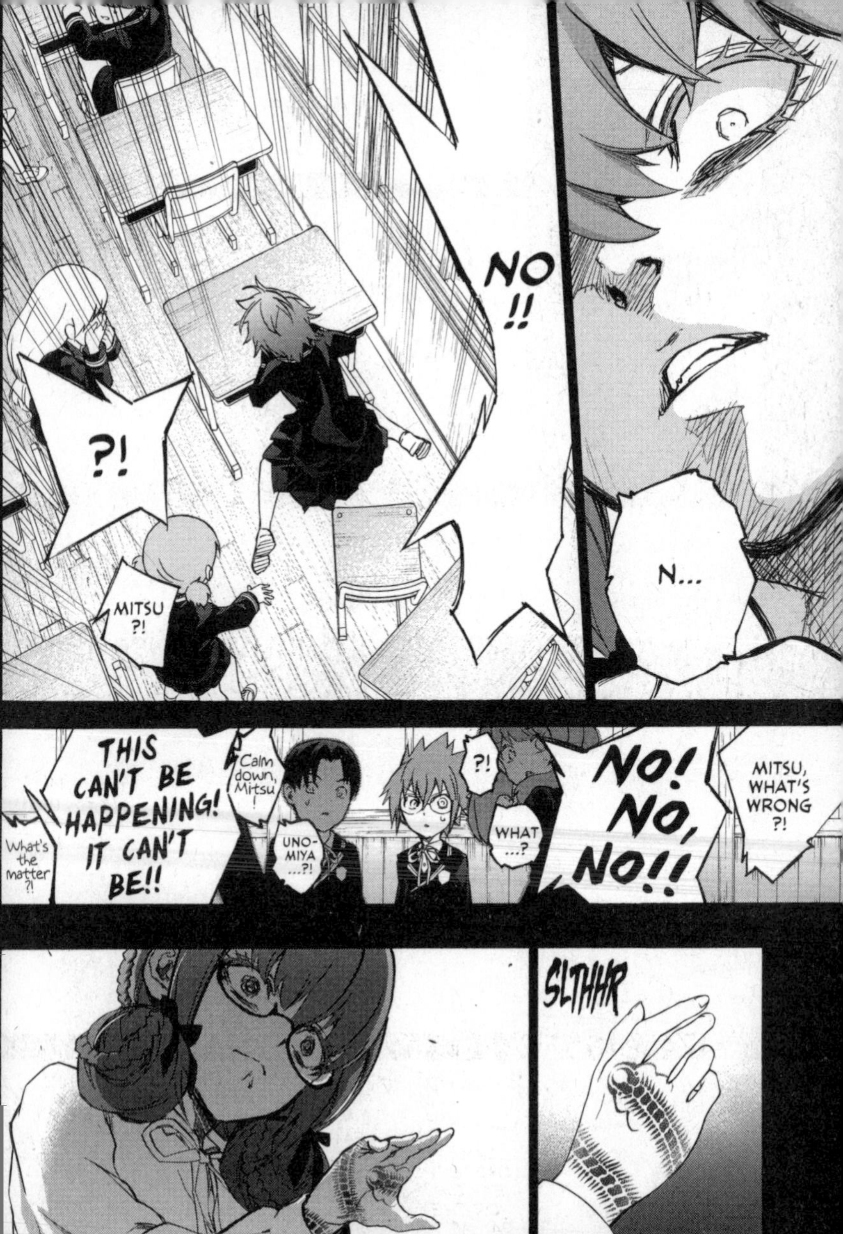
N...
NO!!
?!
MITSU ?!
MITSU, WHAT'S WRONG ?!
NO! NO, NO!!
?!
WHAT ...?
Calm down, Mitsu!
UNO-MIYA ...?!
THIS CAN'T BE HAPPENING! IT CAN'T BE!!
What's the matter ?!
SLTHHR

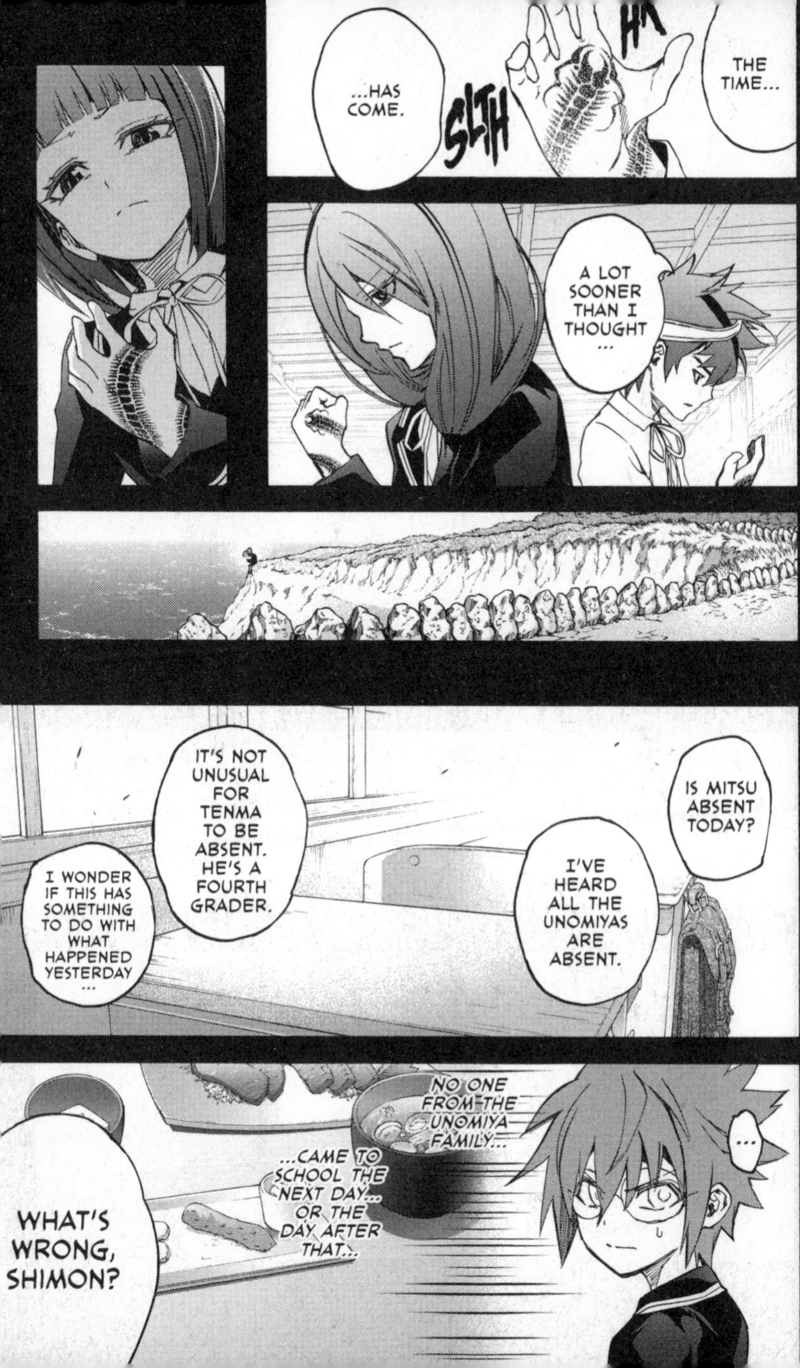
THE TIME...
HA
SLTH
...HAS COME.
A LOT SOONER THAN I THOUGHT ...
IS MITSU ABSENT TODAY?
I'VE HEARD ALL THE UNOMIYAS ARE ABSENT.
IT'S NOT UNUSUAL FOR TENMA TO BE ABSENT. HE'S A FOURTH GRADER.
I WONDER IF THIS HAS SOMETHING TO DO WITH WHAT HAPPENED YESTERDAY ...
...
NO ONE FROM THE UNOMIYA FAMILY...
...CAME TO SCHOOL THE NEXT DAY... OR THE DAY AFTER THAT...
WHAT'S WRONG, SHIMON?

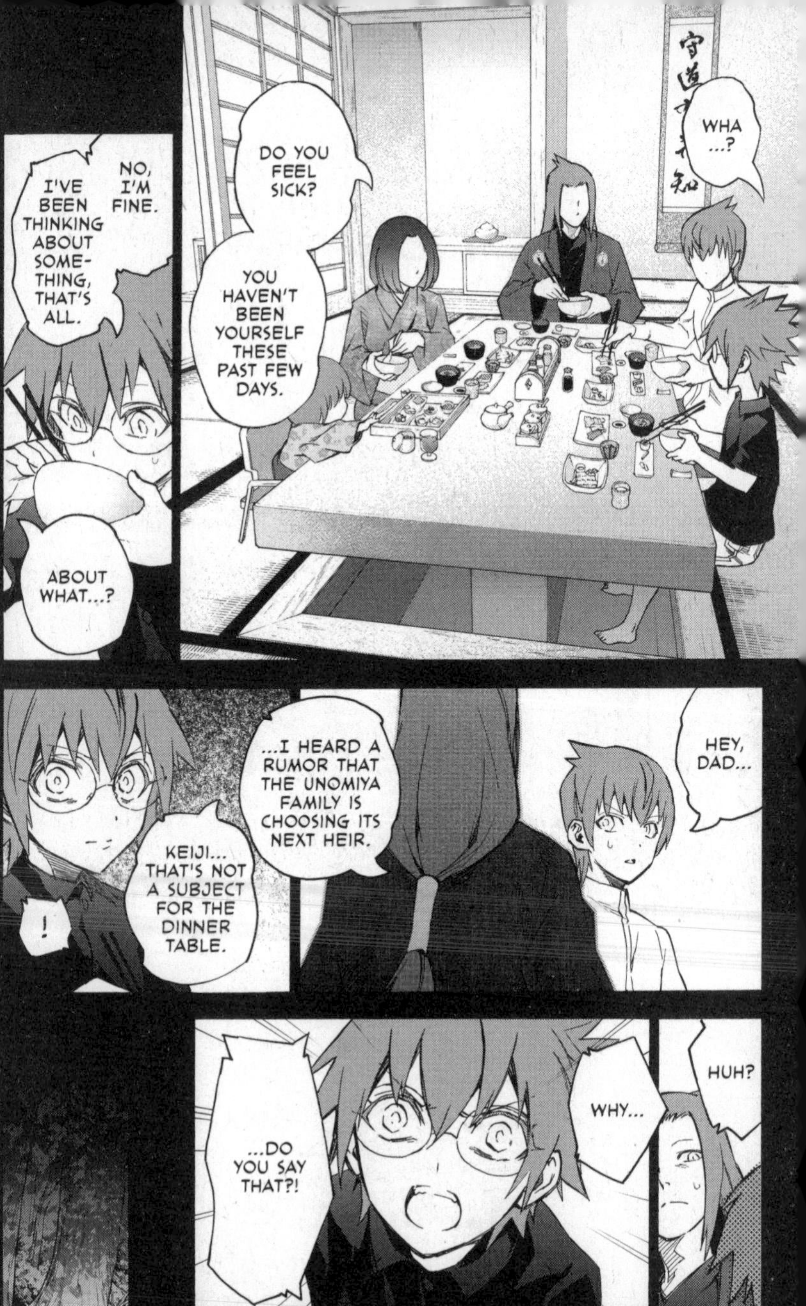
WHA ...?
DO YOU FEEL SICK?
YOU HAVEN'T BEEN YOURSELF THESE PAST FEW DAYS.
NO, I'M FINE.
I'VE BEEN THINKING ABOUT SOMETHING, THAT'S ALL.
ABOUT WHAT...?
HEY, DAD...
...I HEARD A RUMOR THAT THE UNOMIYA FAMILY IS CHOOSING ITS NEXT HEIR.
KEIJI... THAT'S NOT A SUBJECT FOR THE DINNER TABLE.
!
HUH?
WHY...
...DO YOU SAY THAT?!

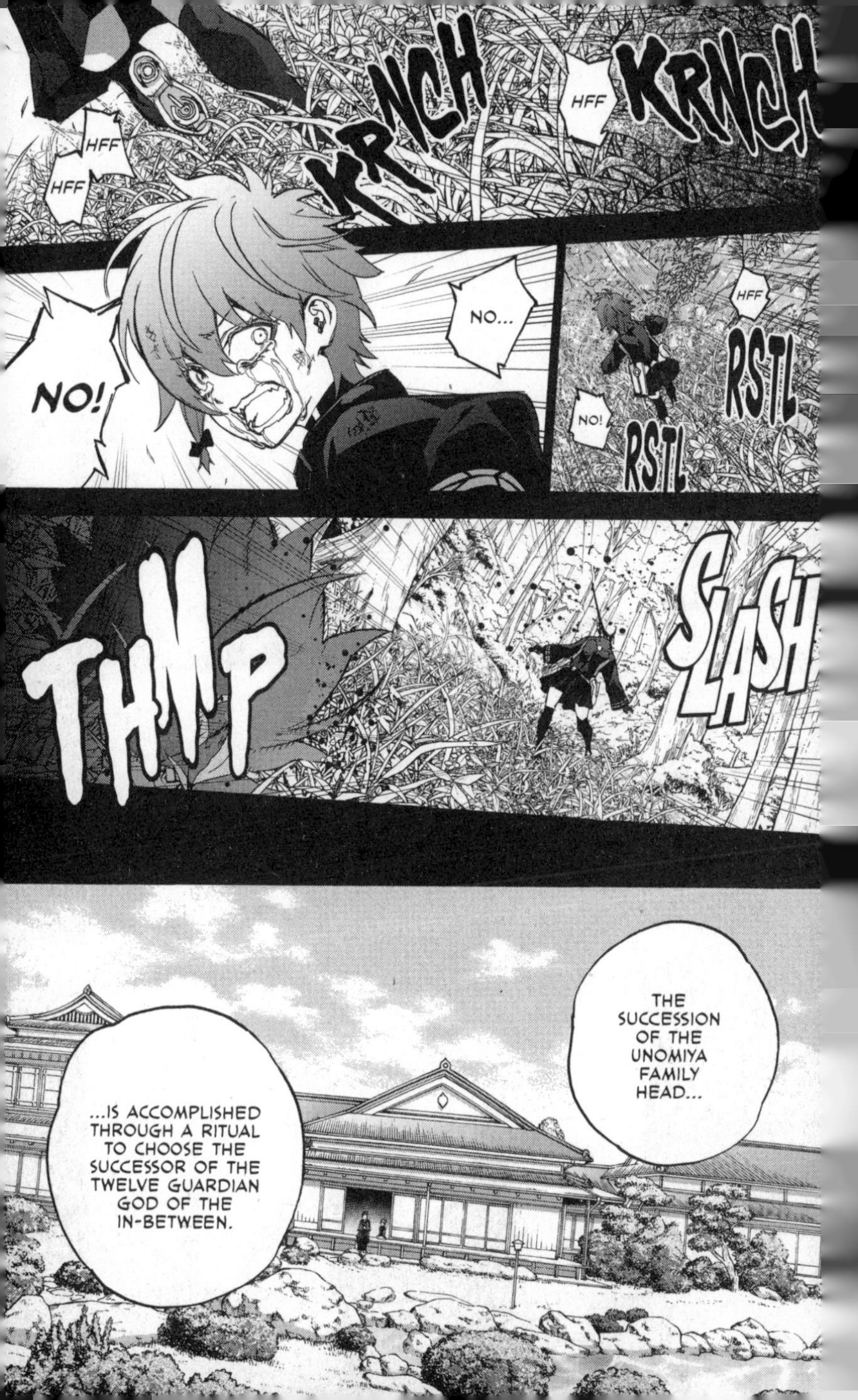
KRNCH
HFF
KRNCH
HFF
HFF
HFF
RSTL
NO!
RSTL
NO...
NO!
SLASH
THMP
THE SUCCESSION OF THE UNOMIYA FAMILY HEAD...
...IS ACCOMPLISHED THROUGH A RITUAL TO CHOOSE THE SUCCESSOR OF THE TWELVE GUARDIAN GOD OF THE IN-BETWEEN.

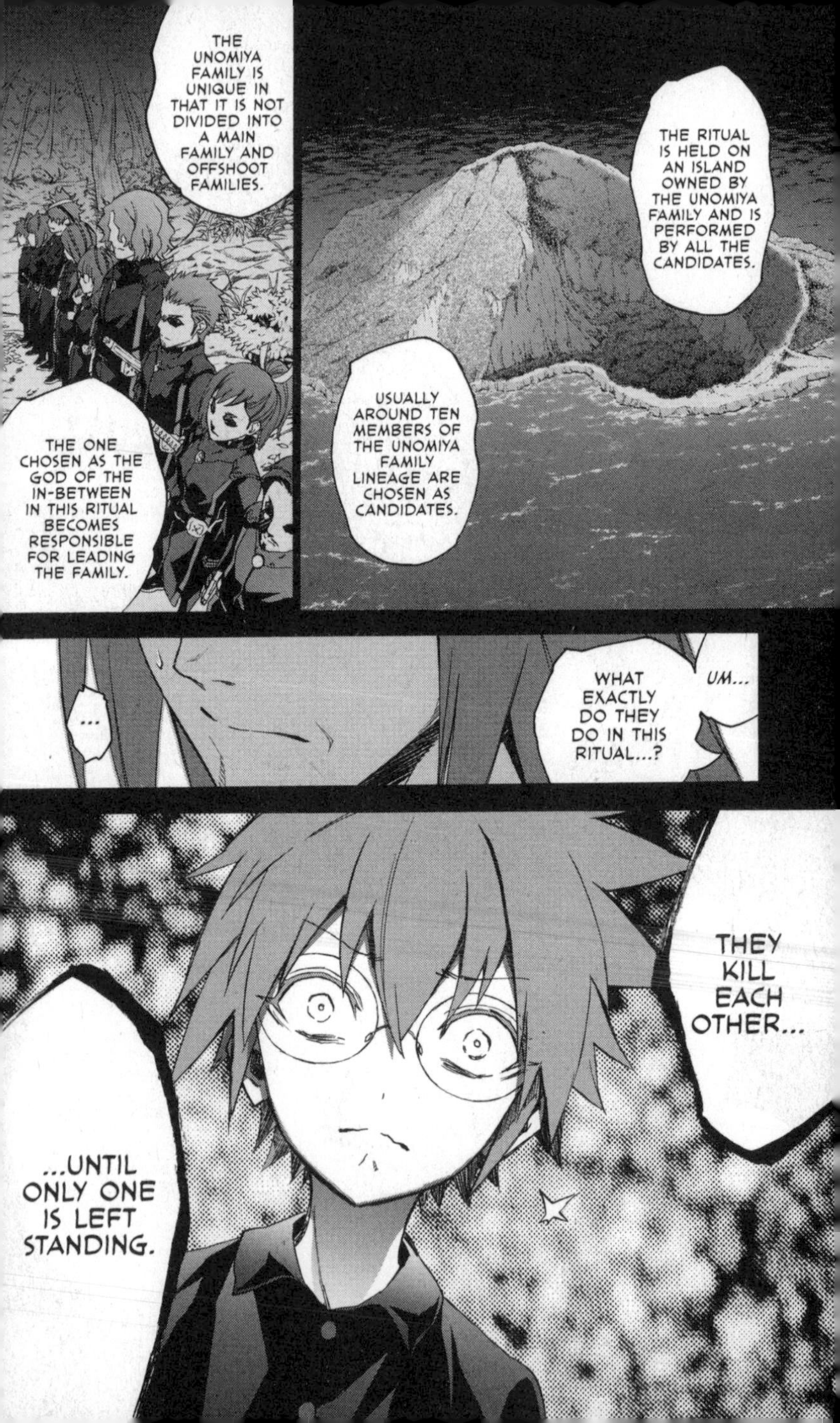
THE RITUAL IS HELD ON AN ISLAND OWNED BY THE UNOMIYA FAMILY AND IS PERFORMED BY ALL THE CANDIDATES.
USUALLY AROUND TEN MEMBERS OF THE UNOMIYA FAMILY LINEAGE ARE CHOSEN AS CANDIDATES.
THE UNOMIYA FAMILY IS UNIQUE IN THAT IT IS NOT DIVIDED INTO A MAIN FAMILY AND OFFSHOOT FAMILIES.
THE ONE CHOSEN AS THE GOD OF THE IN-BETWEEN IN THIS RITUAL BECOMES RESPONSIBLE FOR LEADING THE FAMILY.
UM...
WHAT EXACTLY DO THEY DO IN THIS RITUAL...?
...
THEY KILL EACH OTHER...
...UNTIL ONLY ONE IS LEFT STANDING.

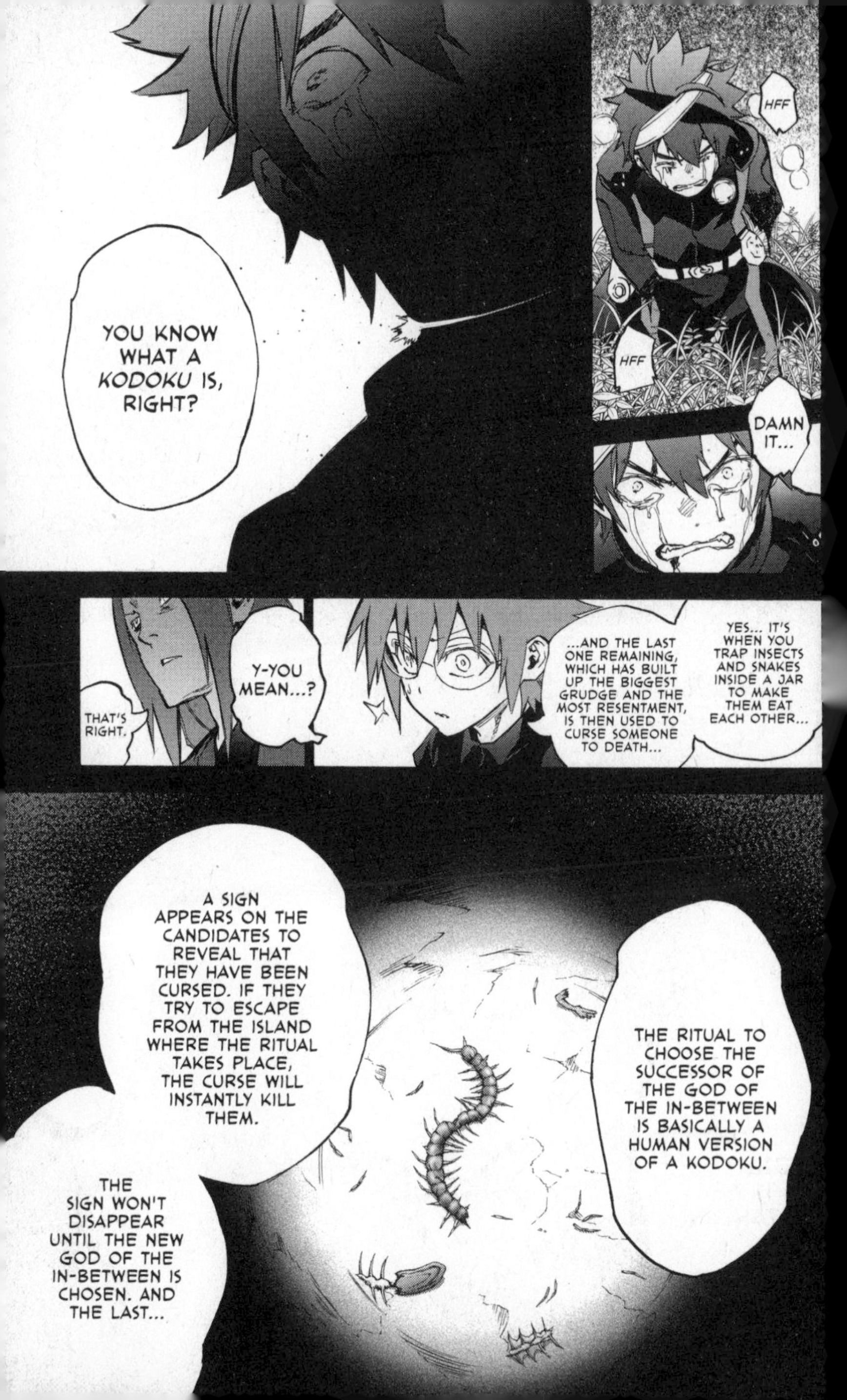
HFF
HFF
DAMN IT...
YOU KNOW WHAT A *KODOKU* IS, RIGHT?
YES... IT'S WHEN YOU TRAP INSECTS AND SNAKES INSIDE A JAR TO MAKE THEM EAT EACH OTHER...
...AND THE LAST ONE REMAINING, WHICH HAS BUILT UP THE BIGGEST GRUDGE AND THE MOST RESENTMENT, IS THEN USED TO CURSE SOMEONE TO DEATH...
Y-YOU MEAN...?
THAT'S RIGHT.
THE RITUAL TO CHOOSE THE SUCCESSOR OF THE GOD OF THE IN-BETWEEN IS BASICALLY A HUMAN VERSION OF A KODOKU.
A SIGN APPEARS ON THE CANDIDATES TO REVEAL THAT THEY HAVE BEEN CURSED. IF THEY TRY TO ESCAPE FROM THE ISLAND WHERE THE RITUAL TAKES PLACE, THE CURSE WILL INSTANTLY KILL THEM.
THE SIGN WON'T DISAPPEAR UNTIL THE NEW GOD OF THE IN-BETWEEN IS CHOSEN. AND THE LAST...

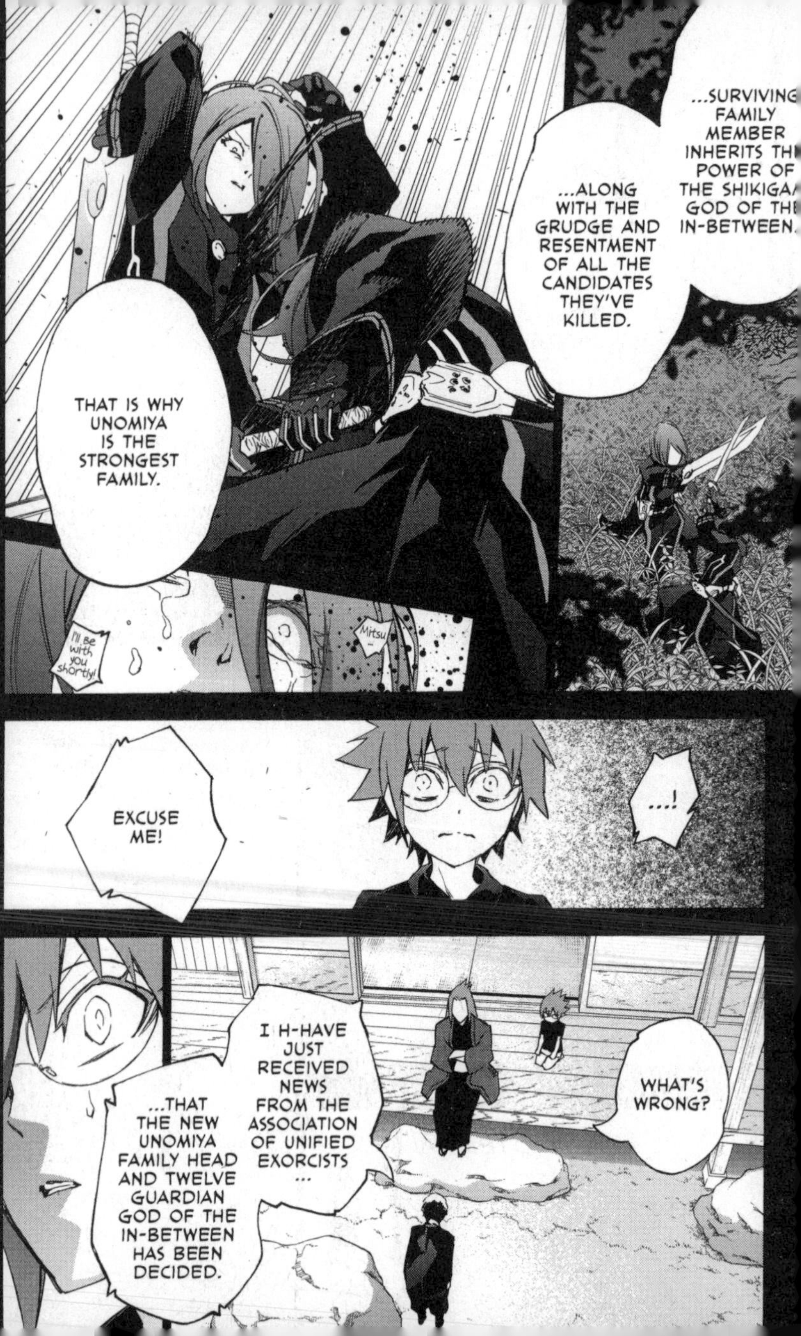
...SURVIVING FAMILY MEMBER INHERITS TH POWER OF THE SHIKIGA GOD OF THE IN-BETWEEN.
...ALONG WITH THE GRUDGE AND RESENTMENT OF ALL THE CANDIDATES THEY'VE KILLED.
THAT IS WHY UNOMIYA IS THE STRONGEST FAMILY.
Mitsu—
I'll be with you shortly!
...!
EXCUSE ME!
WHAT'S WRONG?
I H-HAVE JUST RECEIVED NEWS FROM THE ASSOCIATION OF UNIFIED EXORCISTS...
...THAT THE NEW UNOMIYA FAMILY HEAD AND TWELVE GUARDIAN GOD OF THE IN-BETWEEN HAS BEEN DECIDED.

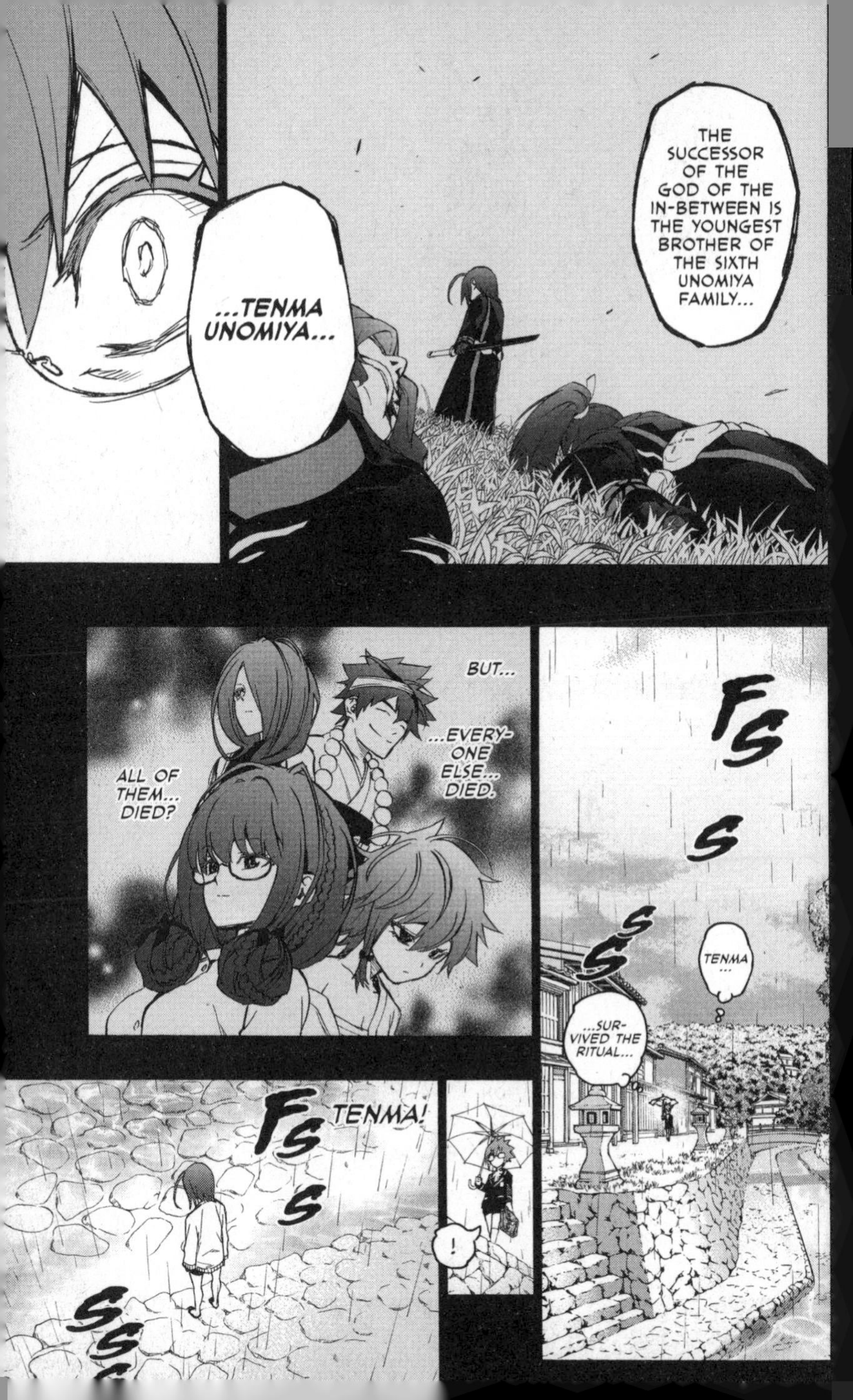
THE SUCCESSOR OF THE GOD OF THE IN-BETWEEN IS THE YOUNGEST BROTHER OF THE SIXTH UNOMIYA FAMILY...
...TENMA UNOMIYA...
FSSS
TENMA...
...SURVIVED THE RITUAL...
BUT...
...EVERYONE ELSE... DIED.
ALL OF THEM... DIED?
!
FSS
TENMA!
SSS

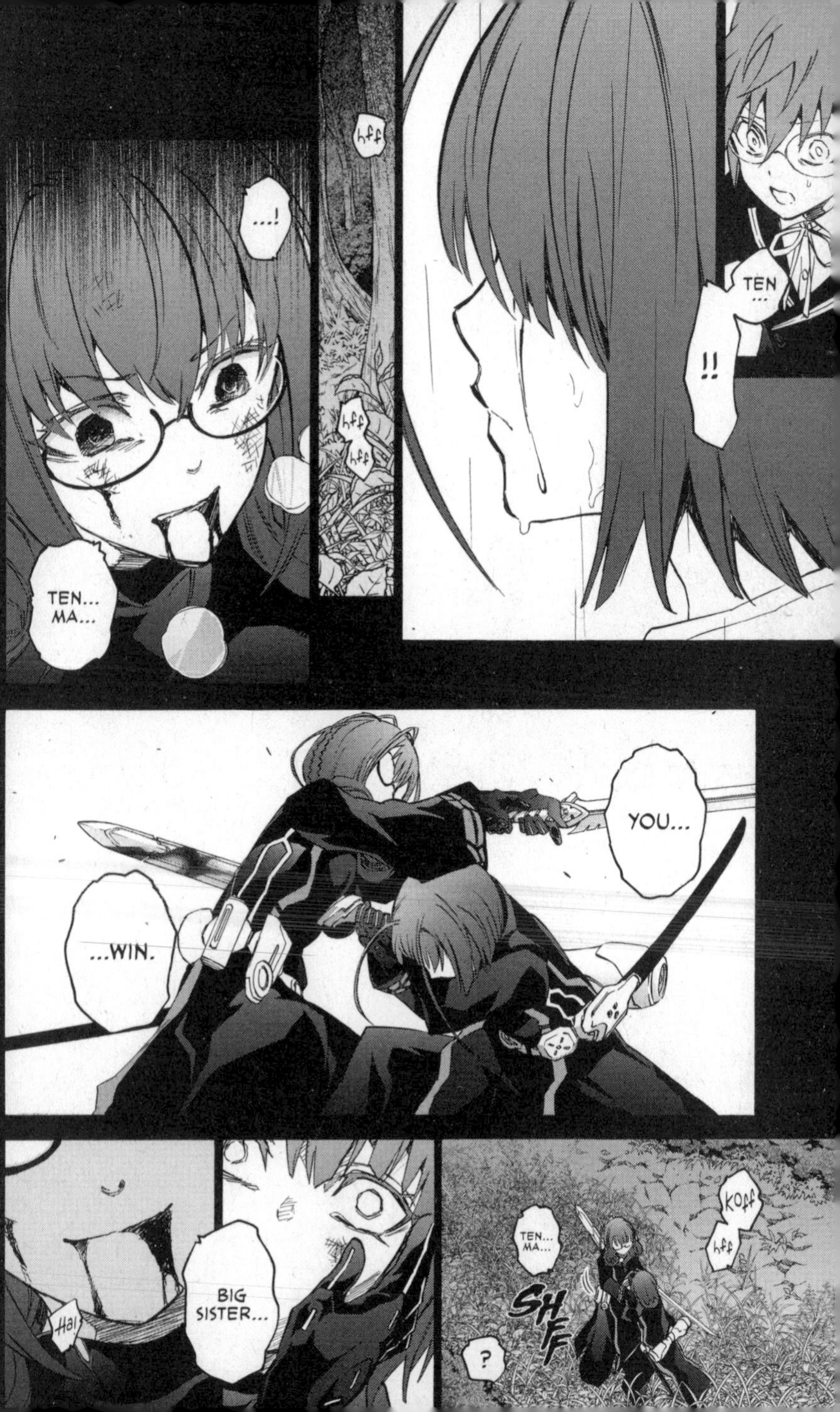
TEN ...
!!
hff
hff
hff
...!
TEN... MA...
YOU...
...WIN.
KOFF
hff
TEN... MA...
SHF
?
BIG SISTER...
Ha!

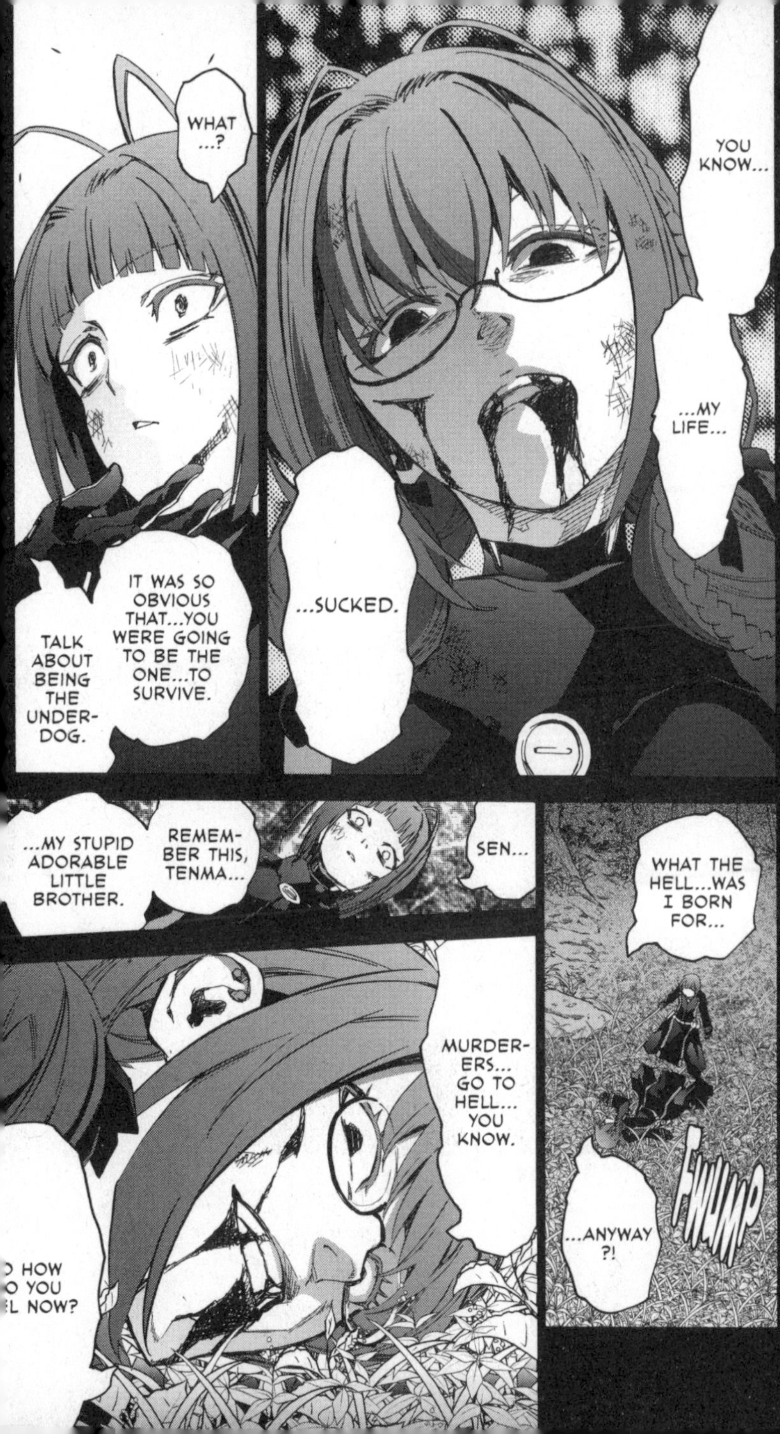
YOU KNOW...
...MY LIFE...
...SUCKED.
WHAT ...?
IT WAS SO OBVIOUS THAT...YOU WERE GOING TO BE THE ONE...TO SURVIVE.
TALK ABOUT BEING THE UNDER-DOG.
WHAT THE HELL...WAS I BORN FOR...
...ANYWAY ?!
FWUMP
SEN...
REMEM-BER THIS, TENMA...
...MY STUPID ADORABLE LITTLE BROTHER.
MURDER-ERS... GO TO HELL... YOU KNOW.
O HOW O YOU EL NOW?

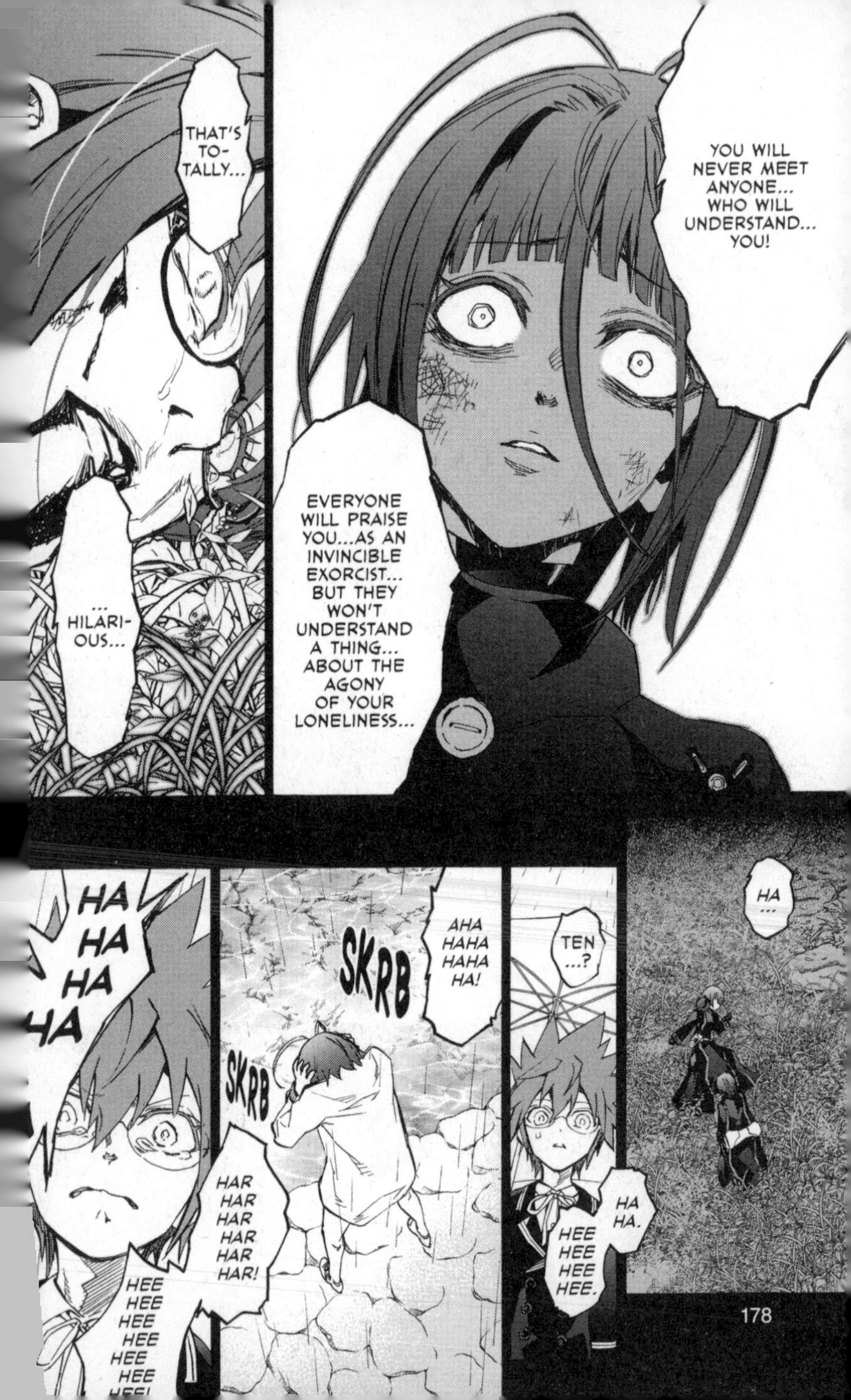
YOU WILL NEVER MEET ANYONE... WHO WILL UNDERSTAND... YOU!
EVERYONE WILL PRAISE YOU...AS AN INVINCIBLE EXORCIST... BUT THEY WON'T UNDERSTAND A THING... ABOUT THE AGONY OF YOUR LONELINESS...
THAT'S TO-TALLY...
...HILARI-OUS...
HA...
TEN...?
HA HA.
HEE HEE HEE HEE.
AHA HAHA HAHA HA!
SKRB
SKRB
HAR HAR HAR HAR HAR HAR!
HA HA HA HA
HEE HEE HEE HEE HEE HEE HEE

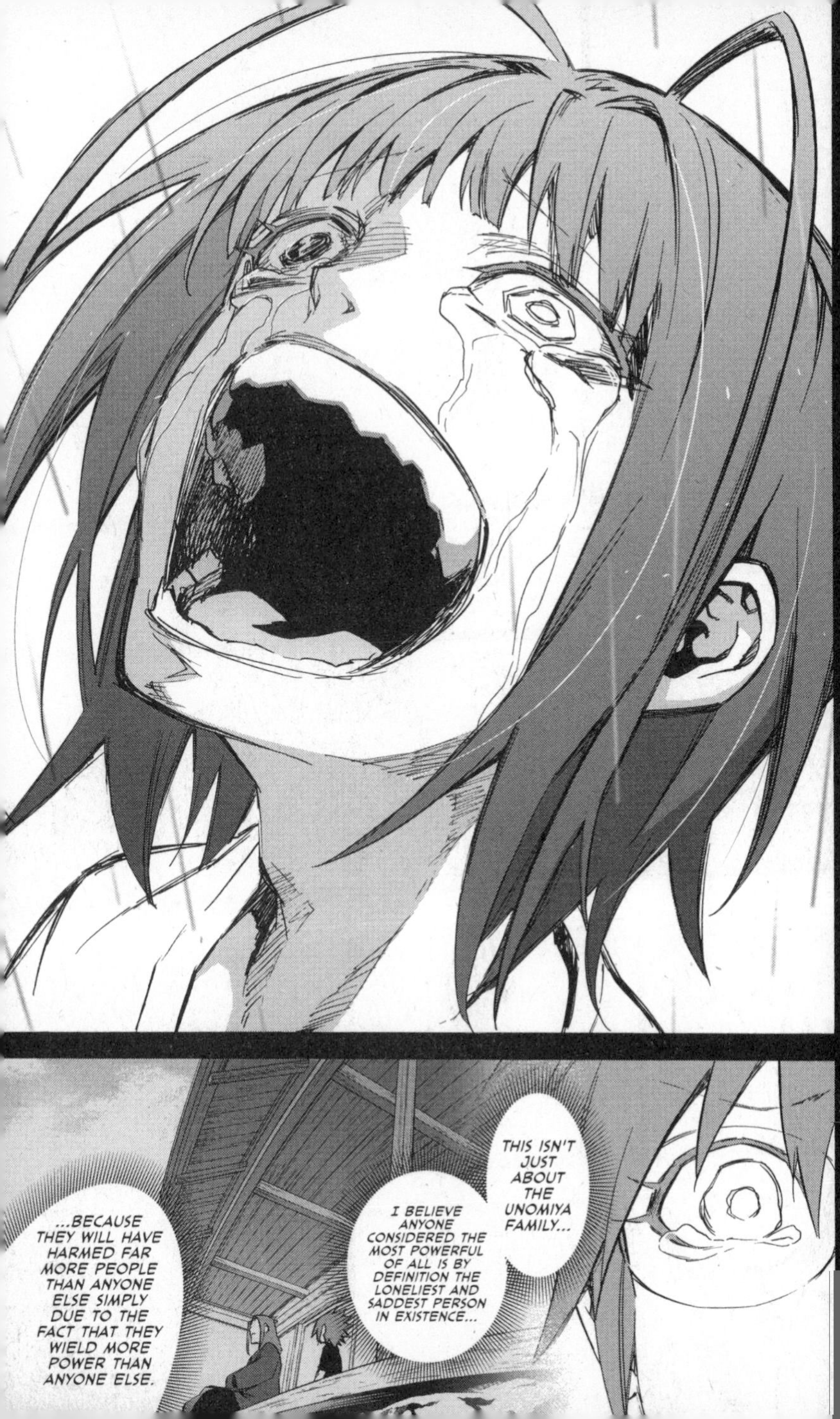
THIS ISN'T JUST ABOUT THE UNOMIYA FAMILY...
I BELIEVE ANYONE CONSIDERED THE MOST POWERFUL OF ALL IS BY DEFINITION THE LONELIEST AND SADDEST PERSON IN EXISTENCE...
...BECAUSE THEY WILL HAVE HARMED FAR MORE PEOPLE THAN ANYONE ELSE SIMPLY DUE TO THE FACT THAT THEY WIELD MORE POWER THAN ANYONE ELSE.

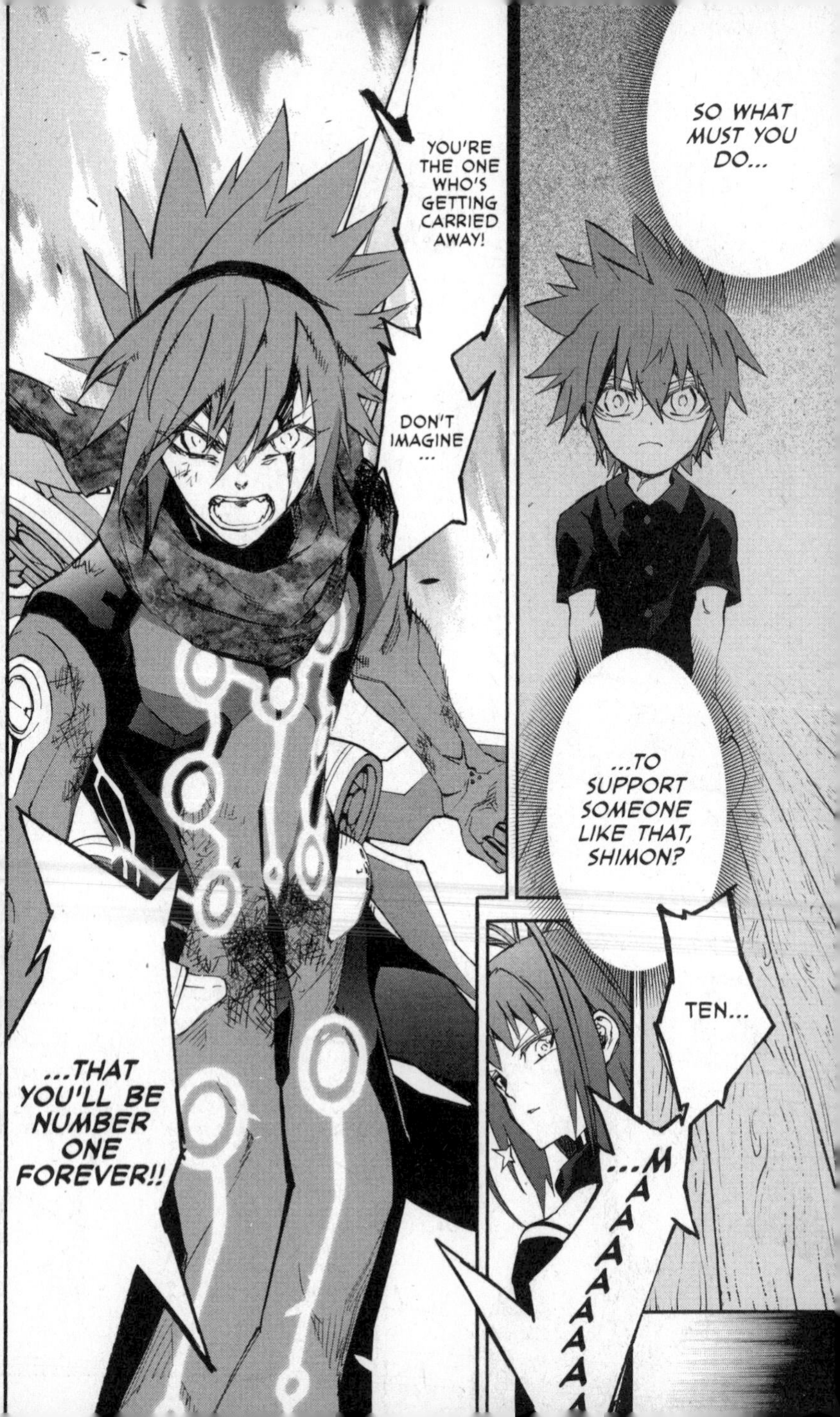
SO WHAT MUST YOU DO...
...TO SUPPORT SOMEONE LIKE THAT, SHIMON?
TEN...
...MAAAAAAAAA
YOU'RE THE ONE WHO'S GETTING CARRIED AWAY!
DON'T IMAGINE...
...THAT YOU'LL BE NUMBER ONE FOREVER!!

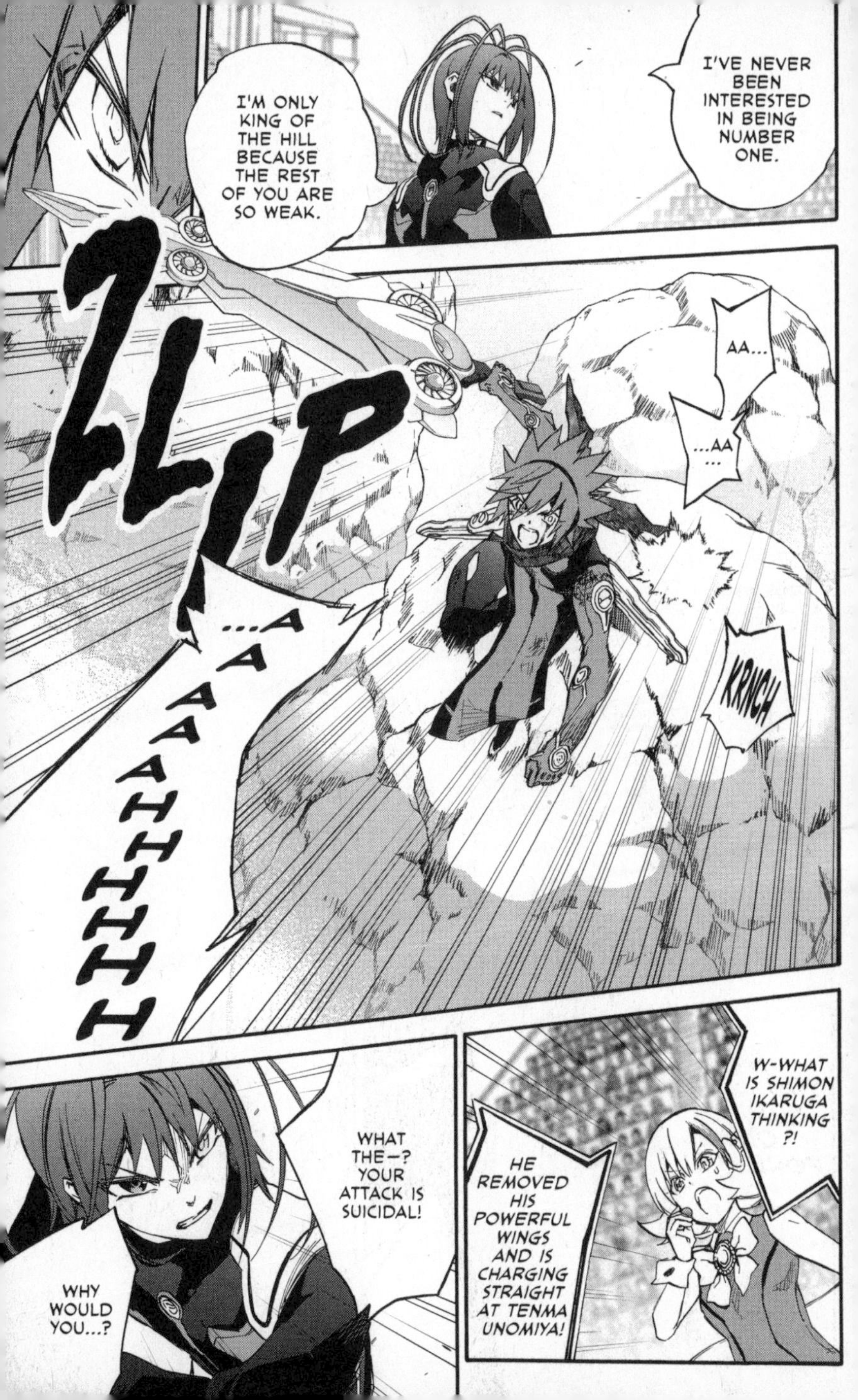
I'VE NEVER BEEN INTERESTED IN BEING NUMBER ONE.
I'M ONLY KING OF THE HILL BECAUSE THE REST OF YOU ARE SO WEAK.
AA...
...AA ...
ZZIP
KRNCH
...AAAAAHHHHHH
W-WHAT IS SHIMON IKARUGA THINKING ?!
HE REMOVED HIS POWERFUL WINGS AND IS CHARGING STRAIGHT AT TENMA UNOMIYA!
WHAT THE—? YOUR ATTACK IS SUICIDAL!
WHY WOULD YOU...?

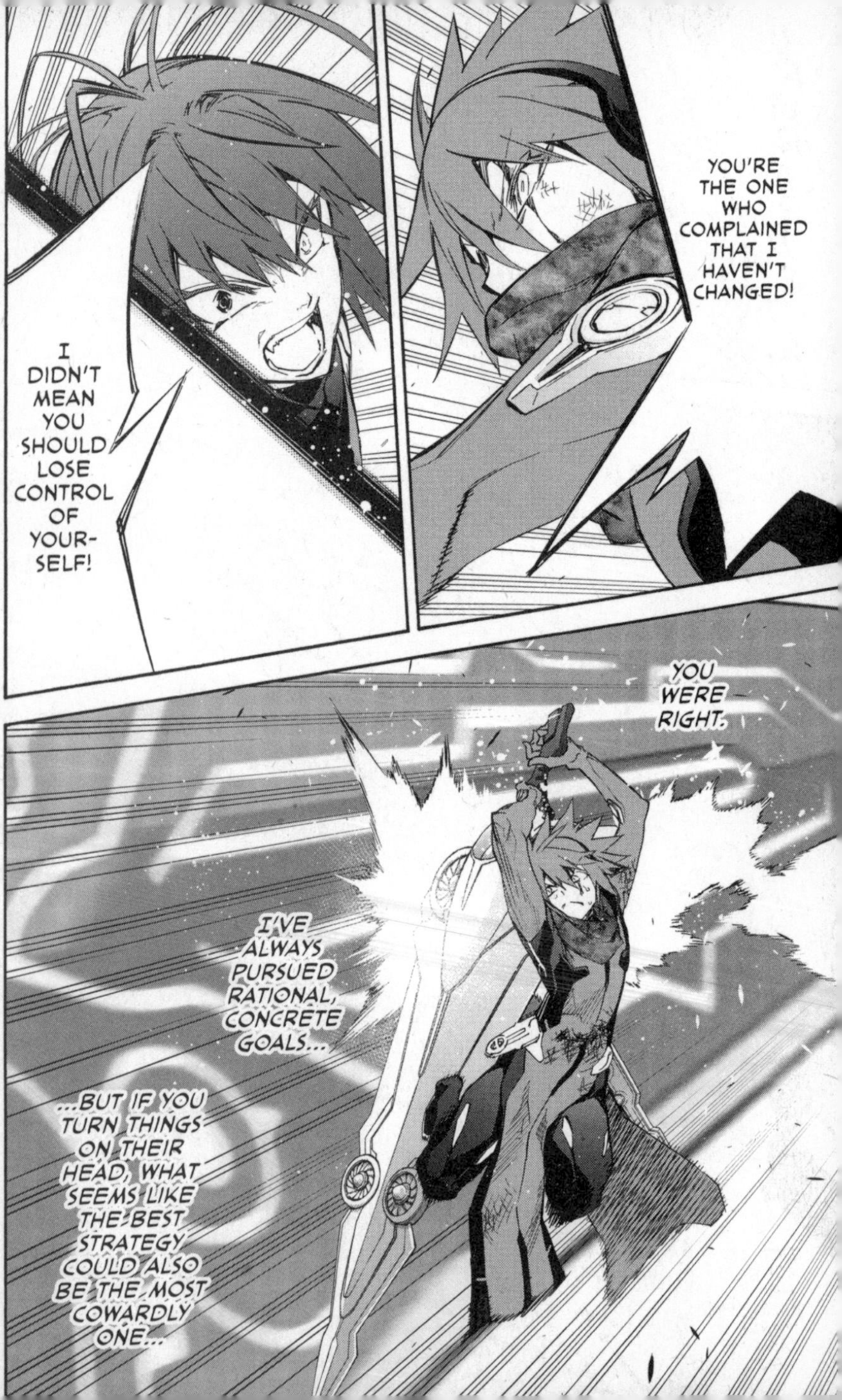
YOU'RE THE ONE WHO COMPLAINED THAT I HAVEN'T CHANGED!
I DIDN'T MEAN YOU SHOULD LOSE CONTROL OF YOUR-SELF!
YOU WERE RIGHT.
I'VE ALWAYS PURSUED RATIONAL, CONCRETE GOALS...
...BUT IF YOU TURN THINGS ON THEIR HEAD, WHAT SEEMS LIKE THE BEST STRATEGY COULD ALSO BE THE MOST COWARDLY ONE...

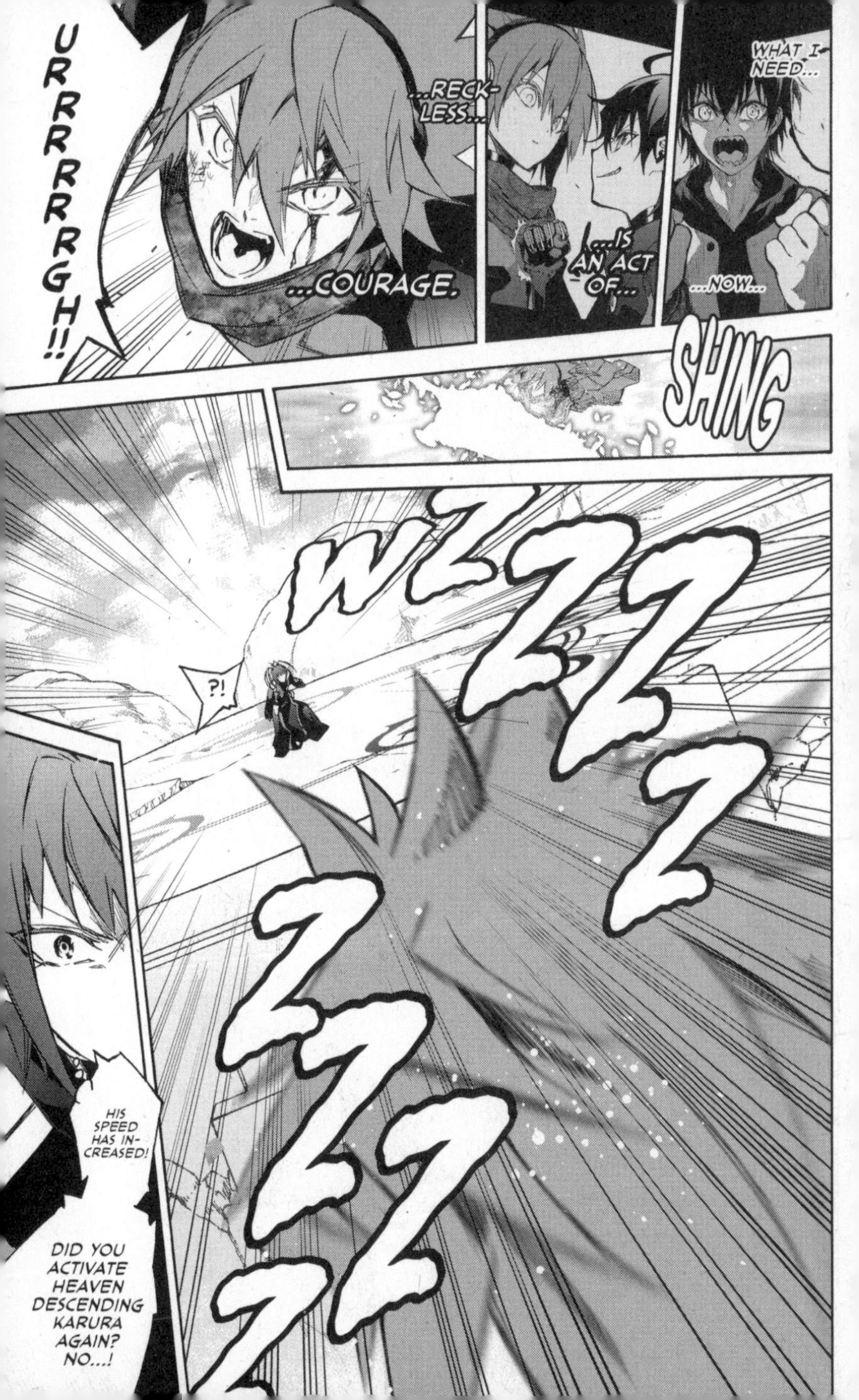
WHAT I NEED...
...NOW...
...RECK-LESS...
...IS AN ACT OF...
...COURAGE.
URRRRRGH!!
SHING
WZZZZZZZ
?!
HIS SPEED HAS IN-CREASED!
DID YOU ACTIVATE HEAVEN DESCENDING KARURA AGAIN? NO...!

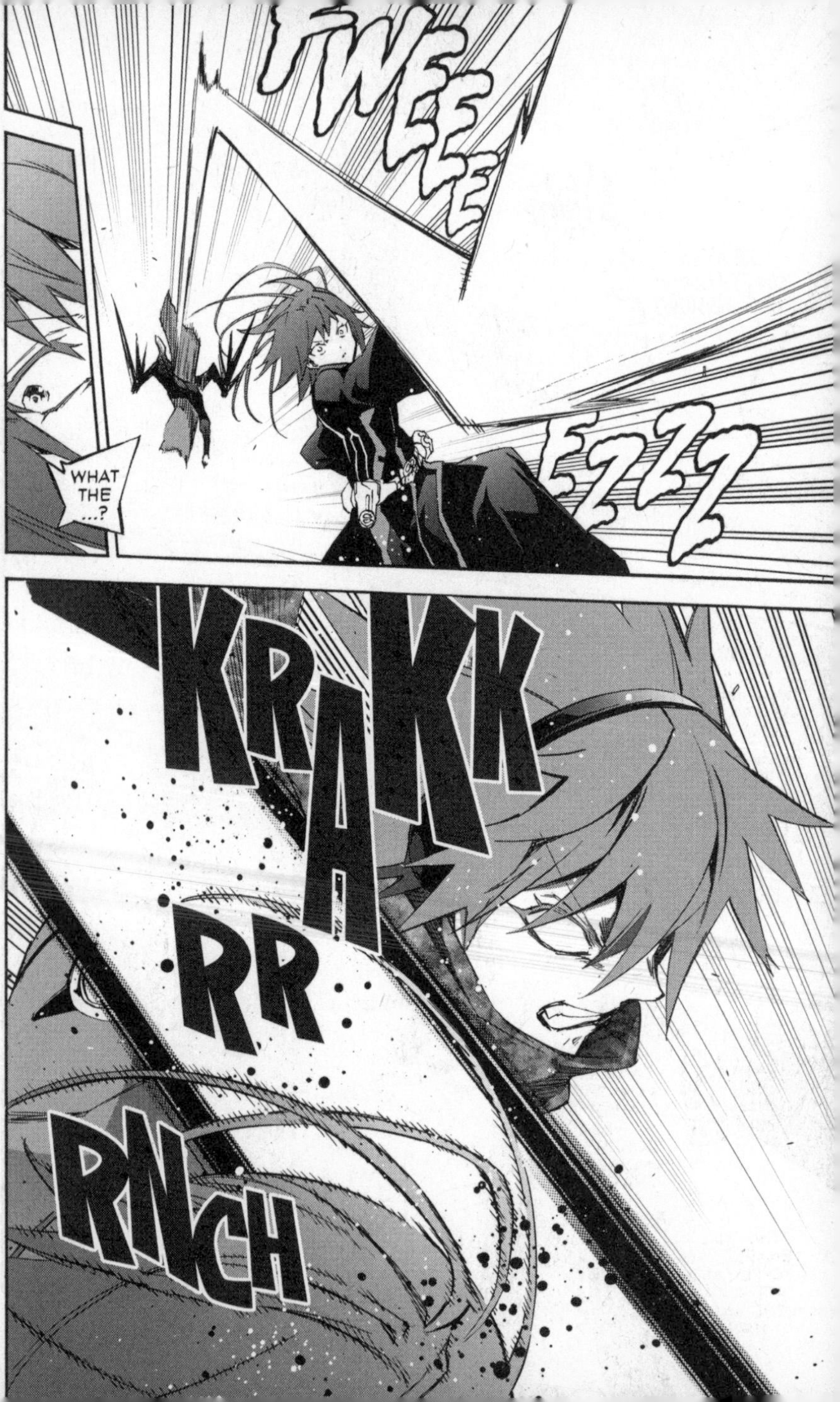
TWEEEE
EZZZ
WHAT THE ...?
KRAKK
A
RR
RNCH

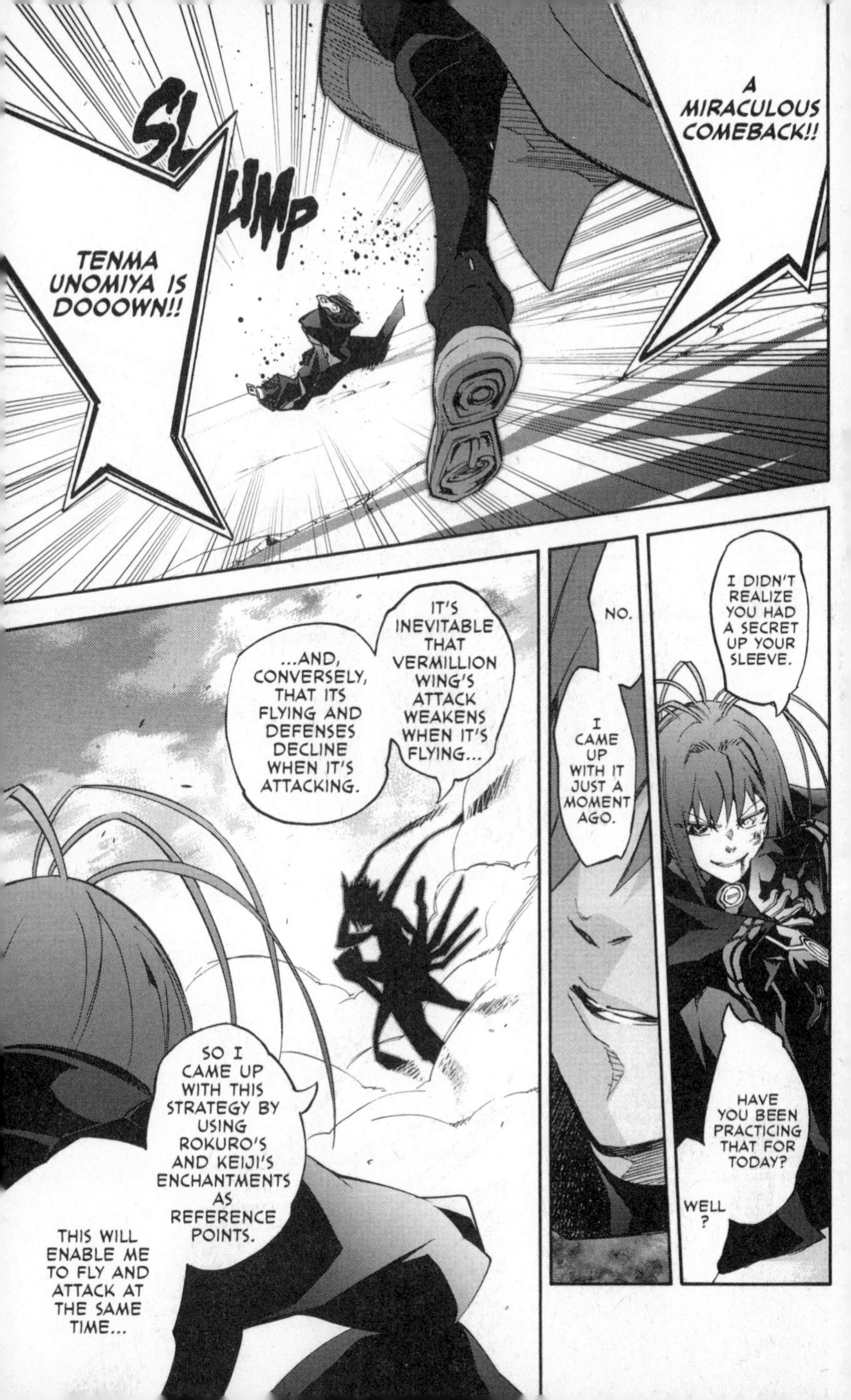
A MIRACULOUS COMEBACK!!
SLUMP
TENMA UNOMIYA IS DOOOWN!!
I DIDN'T REALIZE YOU HAD A SECRET UP YOUR SLEEVE.
HAVE YOU BEEN PRACTICING THAT FOR TODAY?
WELL?
NO.
I CAME UP WITH IT JUST A MOMENT AGO.
IT'S INEVITABLE THAT VERMILLION WING'S ATTACK WEAKENS WHEN IT'S FLYING...
...AND, CONVERSELY, THAT ITS FLYING AND DEFENSES DECLINE WHEN IT'S ATTACKING.
SO I CAME UP WITH THIS STRATEGY BY USING ROKURO'S AND KEIJI'S ENCHANTMENTS AS REFERENCE POINTS.
THIS WILL ENABLE ME TO FLY AND ATTACK AT THE SAME TIME...

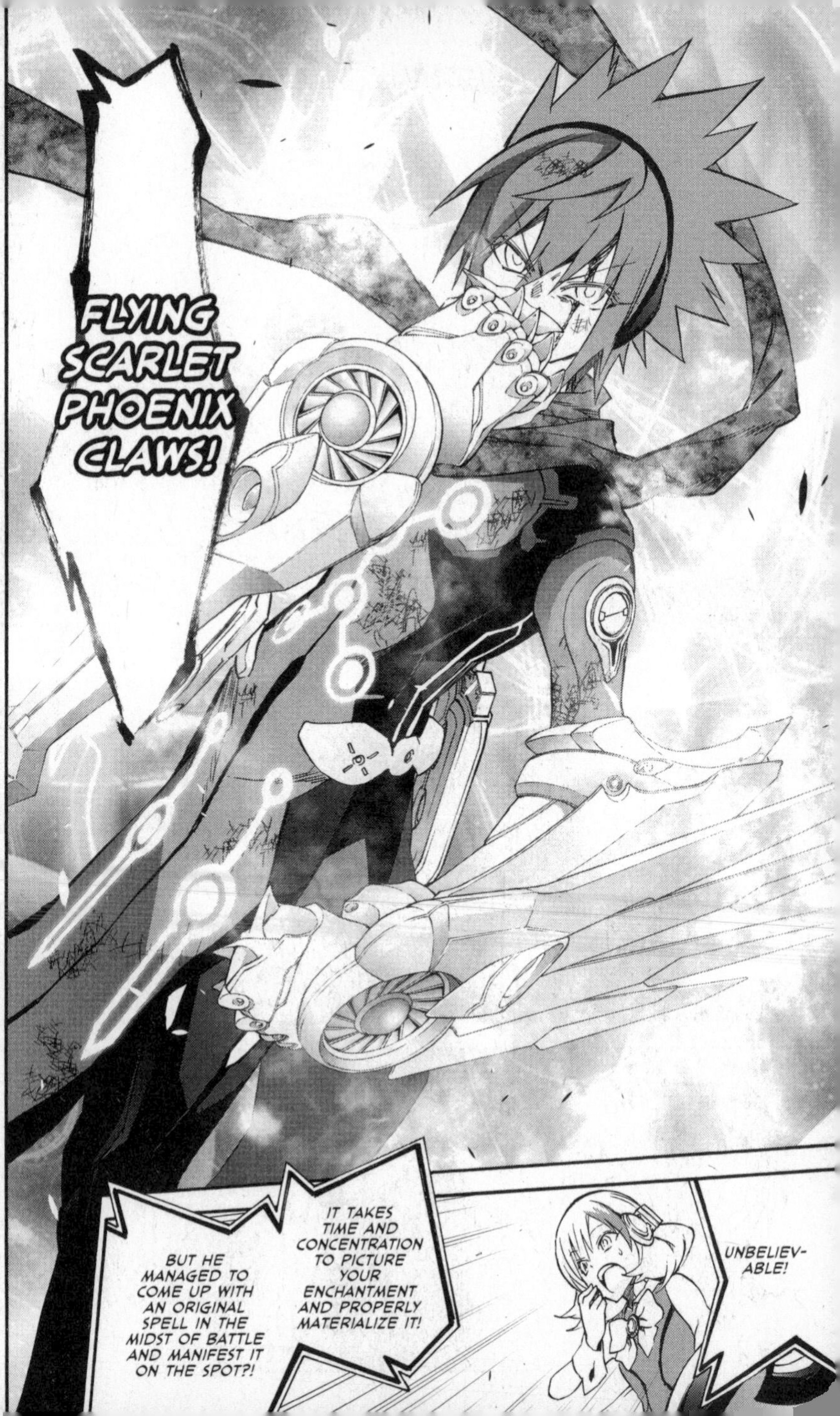
FLYING SCARLET PHOENIX CLAWS!
UNBELIEV-ABLE!
IT TAKES TIME AND CONCENTRATION TO PICTURE YOUR ENCHANTMENT AND PROPERLY MATERIALIZE IT!
BUT HE MANAGED TO COME UP WITH AN ORIGINAL SPELL IN THE MIDST OF BATTLE AND MANIFEST IT ON THE SPOT?!

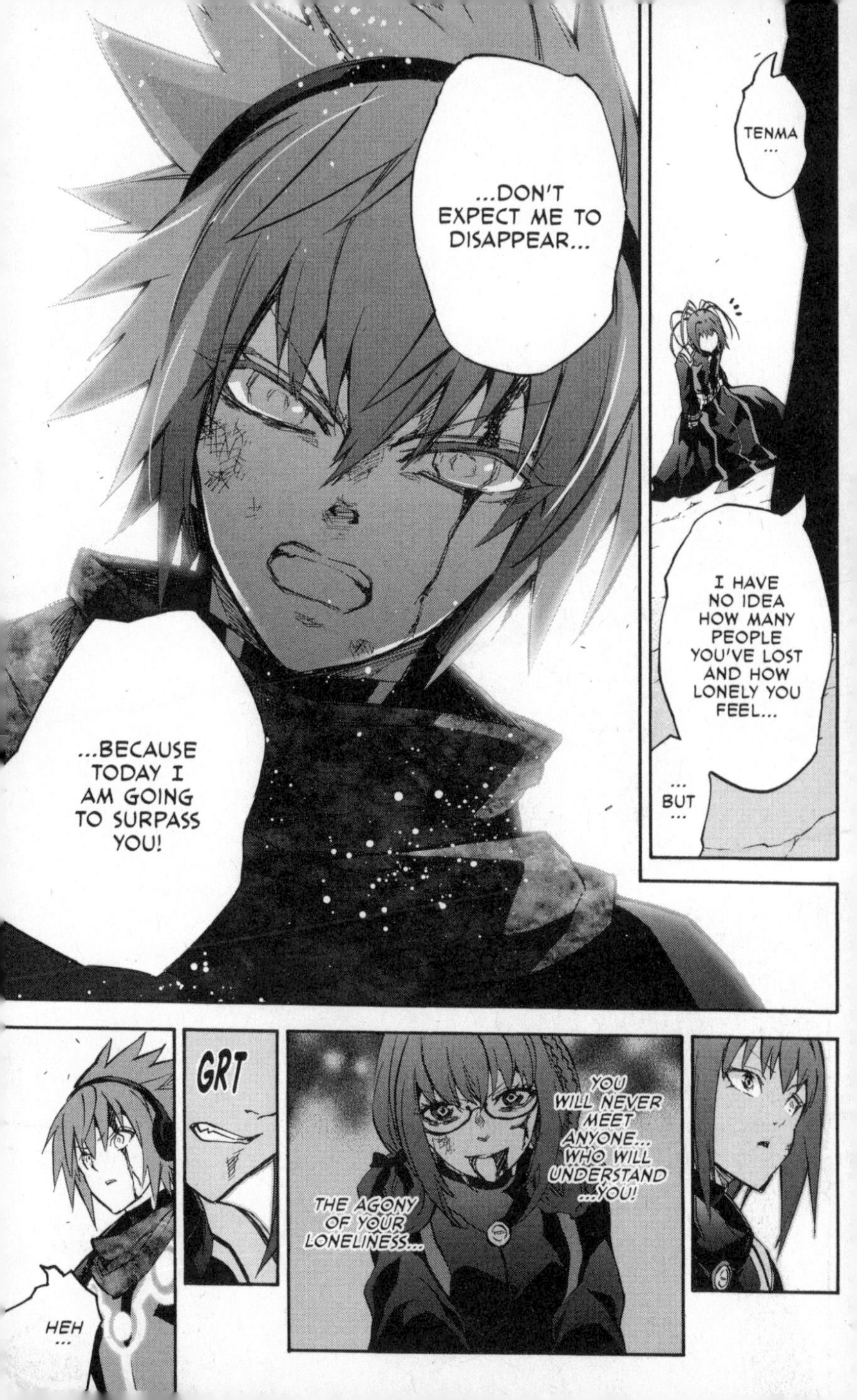
TENMA ...
I HAVE NO IDEA HOW MANY PEOPLE YOU'VE LOST AND HOW LONELY YOU FEEL...
... BUT ...
...DON'T EXPECT ME TO DISAPPEAR...
...BECAUSE TODAY I AM GOING TO SURPASS YOU!
YOU WILL NEVER MEET ANYONE... WHO WILL UNDERSTAND ...YOU!
THE AGONY OF YOUR LONELINESS...
GRT
HEH ...

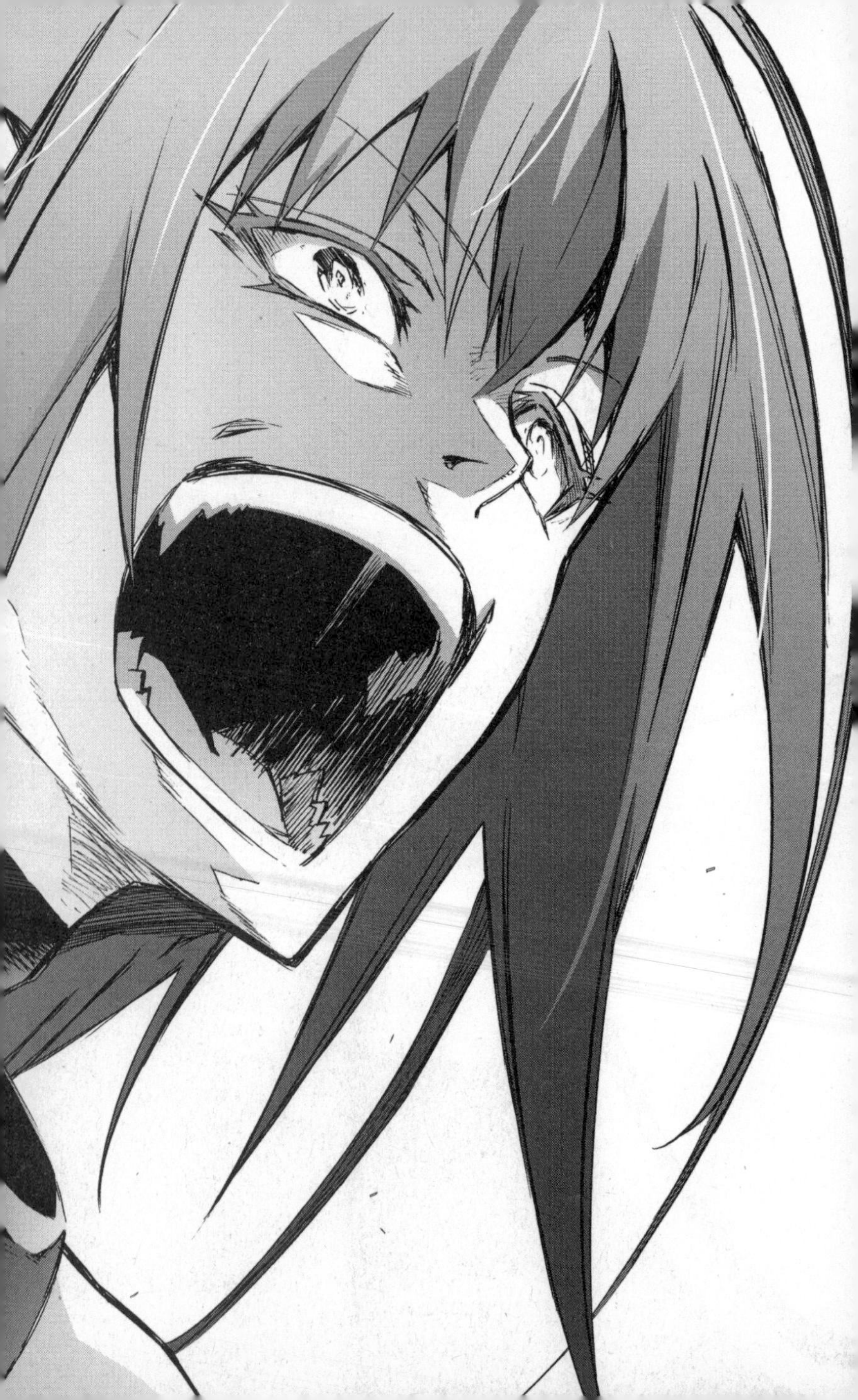

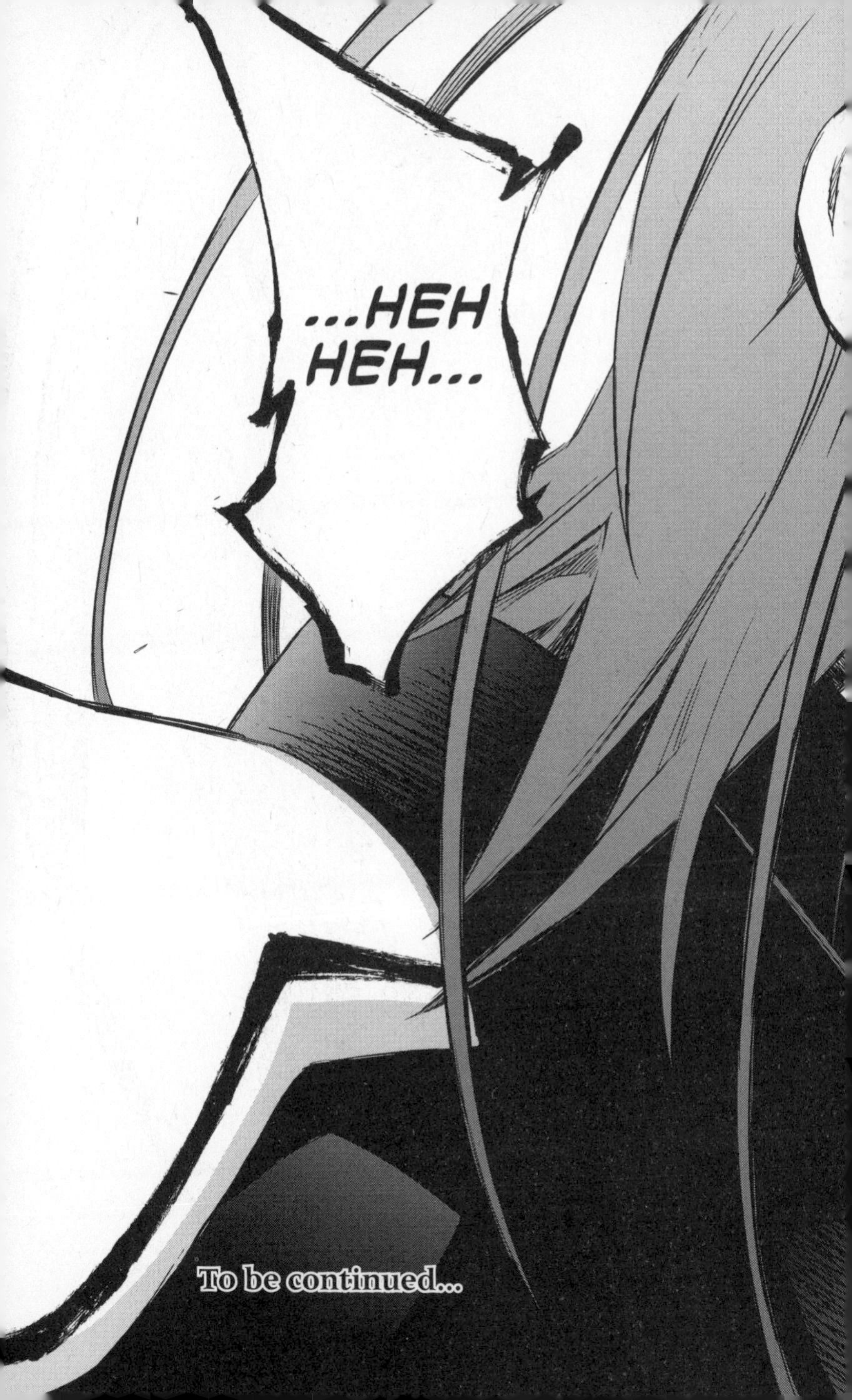
...HEH HEH...
To be continued...

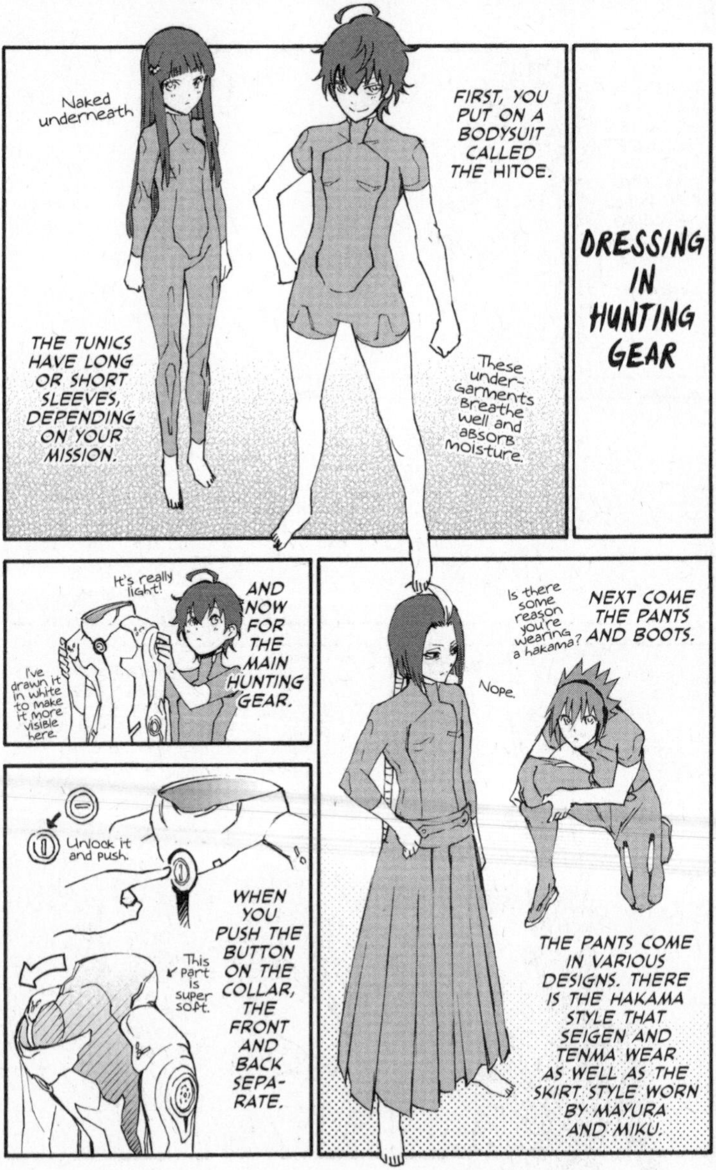
DRESSING IN HUNTING GEAR
FIRST, YOU PUT ON A BODYSUIT CALLED THE HITOE.
These under-Garments Breathe well and absorB moisture.
Naked underneath
THE TUNICS HAVE LONG OR SHORT SLEEVES, DEPENDING ON YOUR MISSION.
NEXT COME THE PANTS AND BOOTS.
Is there some reason you're wearing a hakama?
Nope.
THE PANTS COME IN VARIOUS DESIGNS. THERE IS THE HAKAMA STYLE THAT SEIGEN AND TENMA WEAR AS WELL AS THE SKIRT STYLE WORN BY MAYURA AND MIKU.
AND NOW FOR THE MAIN HUNTING GEAR.
It's really light!
I've drawn it in white to make it more visiBle here.
WHEN YOU PUSH THE BUTTON ON THE COLLAR, THE FRONT AND BACK SEPA-RATE.
Unlock it and push.
This part is super soft.

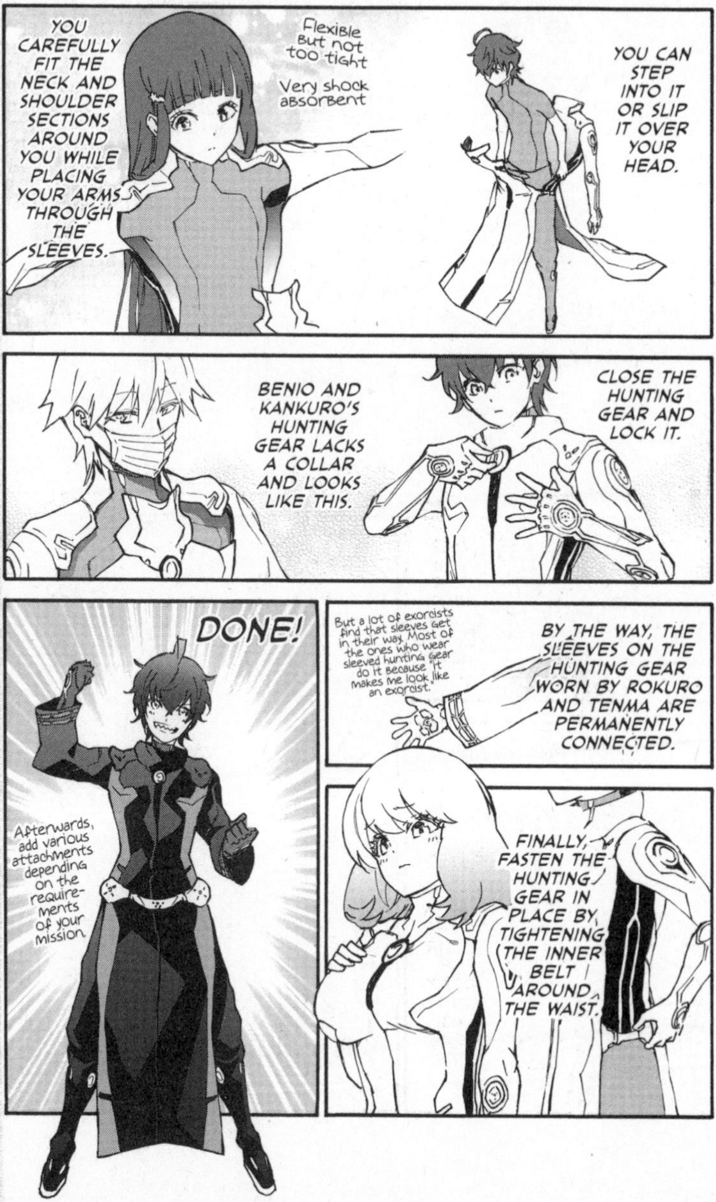
YOU CAN STEP INTO IT OR SLIP IT OVER YOUR HEAD.
Flexible but not too tight
Very shock absorbent
YOU CAREFULLY FIT THE NECK AND SHOULDER SECTIONS AROUND YOU WHILE PLACING YOUR ARMS THROUGH THE SLEEVES.
CLOSE THE HUNTING GEAR AND LOCK IT.
BENIO AND KANKURO'S HUNTING GEAR LACKS A COLLAR AND LOOKS LIKE THIS.
BY THE WAY, THE SLEEVES ON THE HUNTING GEAR WORN BY ROKURO AND TENMA ARE PERMANENTLY CONNECTED.
But a lot of exorcists find that sleeves get in their way. Most of the ones who wear sleeved hunting gear do it because "it makes me look like an exorcist."
FINALLY, FASTEN THE HUNTING GEAR IN PLACE BY TIGHTENING THE INNER BELT AROUND THE WAIST.
DONE!
Afterwards, add various attachments depending on the requirements of your mission.

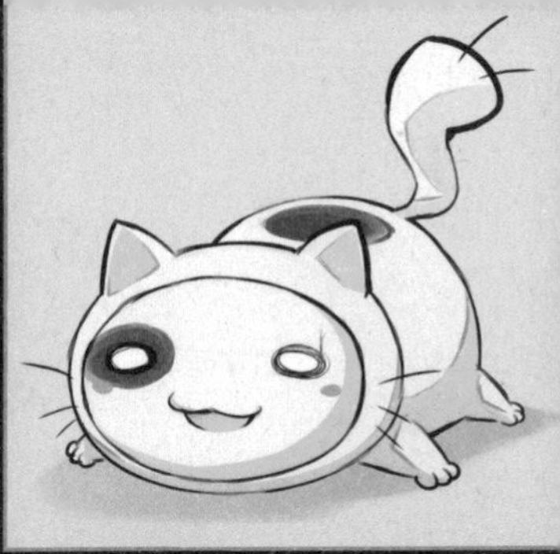

There aren't enough extra pages! I want more pages to show off all t fan art I get from readers and introd the character settings, as well as dr extra chapters and four-panel funni But there's a limit to how many pag I can have, and if I added any mor the price of the graphic novel wou go up! Darn it! What can I do-o-o-o Hrmm... (Sleep talking.)

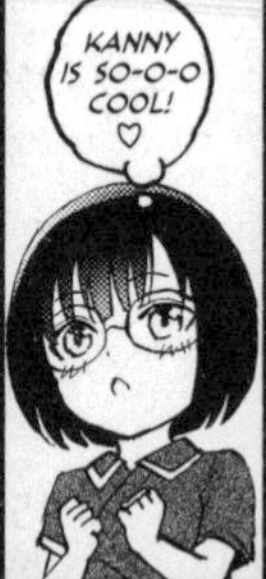
KANNY IS SO-O-O COOL! ♡

YOSHIAKI SUKENO was born July 23, 1981, in Wa He graduated from Kyoto Seika University, where he In 2006, he won the Tezuka Award for Best Newcomer Artist. In 2008, he began his previous work, the super *Binbougami ga!*, which was adapted into the anime *Good*

Juzo Nakiri's Lady Miku Memories

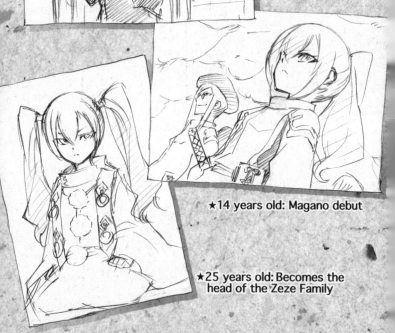

★6 years old: First day of elementary school

★14 years old: Magano debut

★25 years old: Becomes the head of the Zeze Family

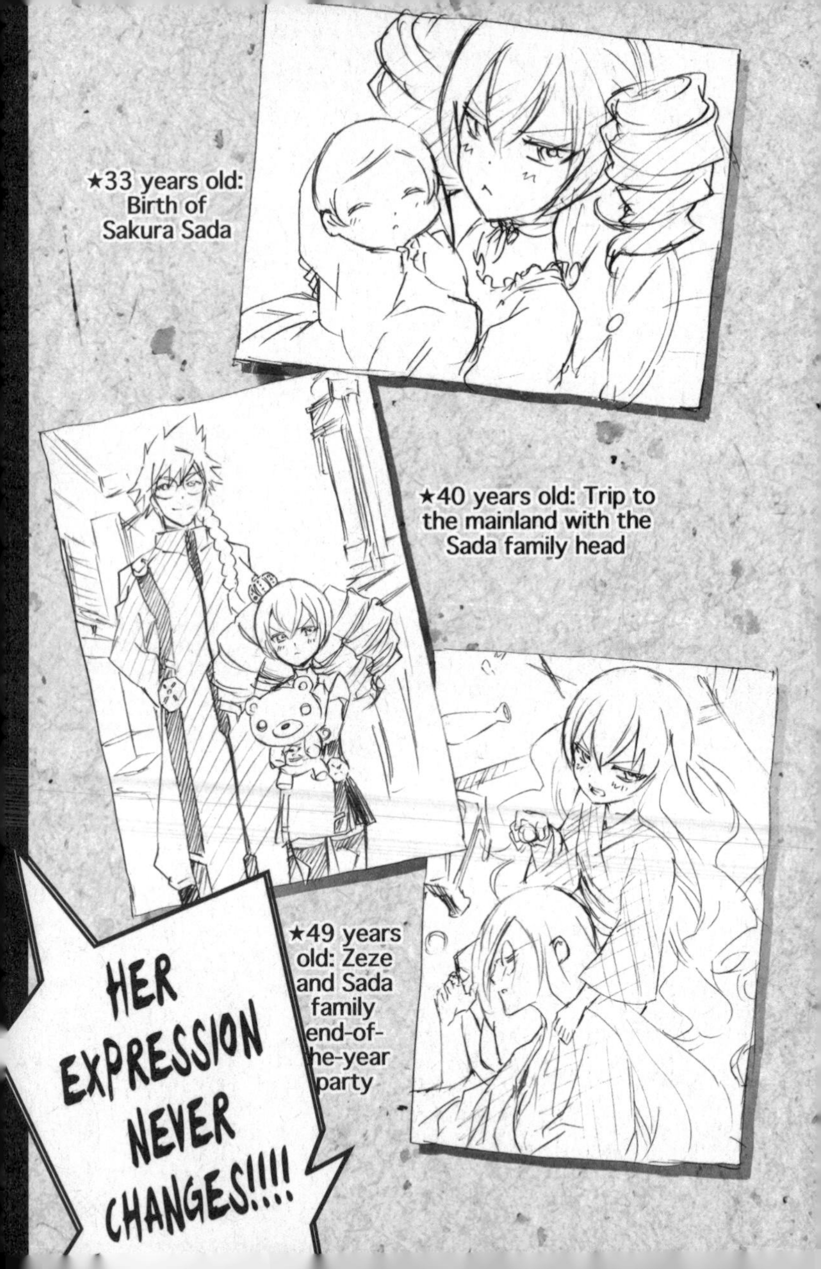

★33 years old: Birth of Sakura Sada
★40 years old: Trip to the mainland with the Sada family head
★49 years old: Zeze and Sada family end-of- he-year party
HER EXPRESSION NEVER CHANGES!!!!

TWIN STAR EXORCISTS
ONMYOJI

13

—SHONEN JUMP Manga Edition—

STORY & ART Yoshiaki Sukeno

TRANSLATION **Tetsuichiro Miyaki**
ENGLISH ADAPTATION **Bryant Turnage**
TOUCH-UP ART & LETTERING **Stephen Dutro**
DESIGN **Shawn Carrico**
EDITOR **Annette Roman**

SOUSEI NO ONMYOJI © 2013 by Yoshiaki Sukeno
All rights reserved.
First published in Japan in 2013 by SHUEISHA Inc., Tokyo.
English translation rights arranged by SHUEISHA Inc.

Printed in Canada

Published by VIZ Media, LLC
P.O. Box 77010
San Francisco, CA 94107

10 9 8 7 6 5 4 3 2 1
First printing, September 2018

shonenjump.com

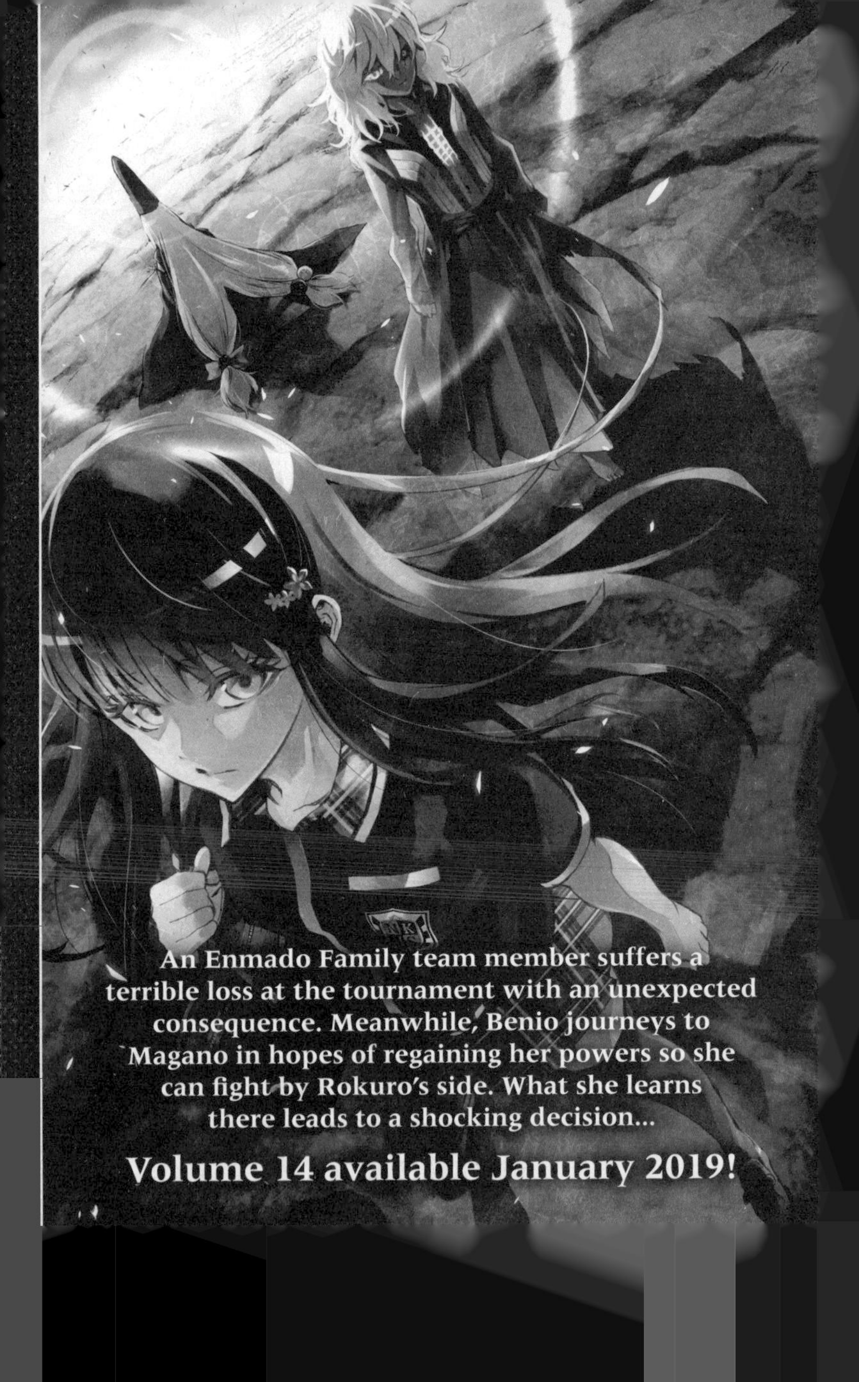

An Enmado Family team member suffers a terrible loss at the tournament with an unexpected consequence. Meanwhile, Benio journeys to Magano in hopes of regaining her powers so she can fight by Rokuro's side. What she learns there leads to a shocking decision...

Volume 14 available January 2019!

Black ✳ Clover

STORY & ART BY YŪKI TABATA

Asta is a young boy who dreams of becoming the greatest mage in the kingdom. Only one problem—he can't use any magic! Luckily for Asta, he receives the incredibly rare five-leaf clover grimoire that gives him the power of anti-magic. Can someone who can't use magic really become the Wizard King? One thing's for sure—Asta will never give up!

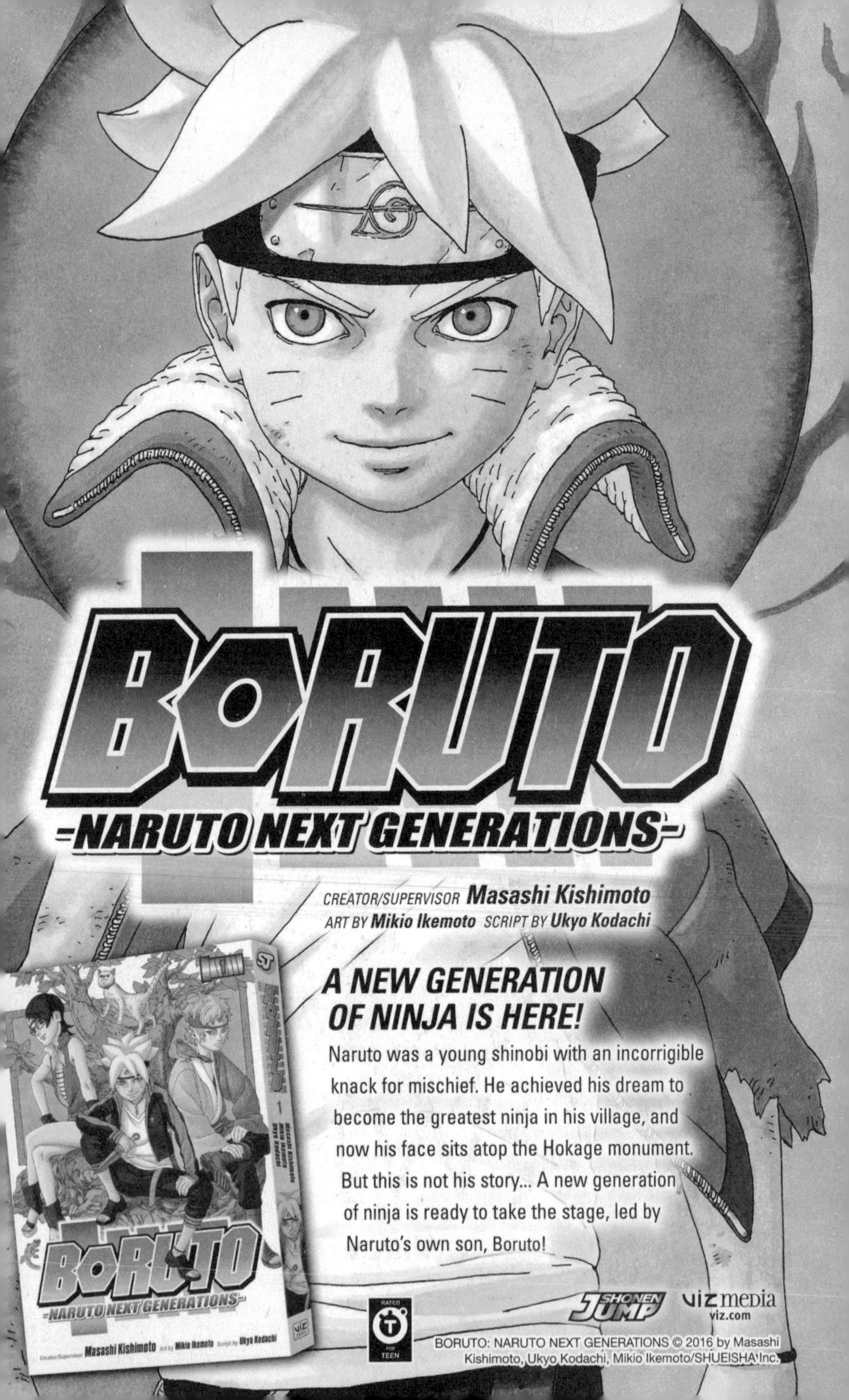

BORUTO
-NARUTO NEXT GENERATIONS-
CREATOR/SUPERVISOR Masashi Kishimoto
ART BY Mikio Ikemoto SCRIPT BY Ukyo Kodachi
A NEW GENERATION OF NINJA IS HERE!
Naruto was a young shinobi with an incorrigible knack for mischief. He achieved his dream to become the greatest ninja in his village, and now his face sits atop the Hokage monument. But this is not his story... A new generation of ninja is ready to take the stage, led by Naruto's own son, Boruto!
RATED T FOR TEEN
SHONEN JUMP
viz media
viz.com
BORUTO: NARUTO NEXT GENERATIONS © 2016 by Masashi Kishimoto, Ukyo Kodachi, Mikio Ikemoto/SHUEISHA Inc.

Ruby, Weiss, Blake and Yang are students at Beacon Academy, learning to protect the world of Remnant from the fearsome Grimm!

RWBY

MANGA BY **Shirow Miwa**

BASED ON THE ROOSTER TEETH SERIES
CREATED BY **Monty Oum**

YOU'RE READING THE **WRONG WAY!**

Twin Star Exorcists reads from right to left, starting in the upper-right corner. Japanese is read from right to left, meaning that action, sound effects and word-balloon order are completely reversed from English order.

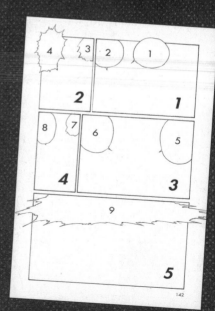